Capitalism's Future

Studies in Critical Social Sciences Book Series

Haymarket Books is proud to be working with Brill Academic Publishers (www.brill.nl) to republish the *Studies in Critical Social Sciences* book series in paperback editions. This peer-reviewed book series offers insights into our current reality by exploring the content and consequences of power relationships under capitalism, and by considering the spaces of opposition and resistance to these changes that have been defining our new age. Our full catalog of *SCSS* volumes can be viewed at https://www.haymarketbooks .org/series_collections/4-studies-in-critical-social-sciences.

CAPITALISM'S FUTURE

Alienation, Emancipation and Critique

EDITED BY
DANIEL KRIER
MARK P. WORRELL

Haymarket
Books
Chicago, IL

First published in 2016 by Brill Academic Publishers, The Netherlands.
© 2016 Koninklijke Brill NV, Leiden, The Netherlands

Published in paperback in 2017 by
Haymarket Books
P.O. Box 180165
Chicago, IL 60618
773-583-7884
www.haymarketbooks.org

ISBN: 978-1-60846-805-8

Trade distribution:
In the U.S. through Consortium Book Sales, www.cbsd.com
In the UK, Turnaround Publisher Services, www.turnaround-uk.com
In Canada, Publishers Group Canada, www.pgcbooks.ca
All other countries, Ingram Publisher Services International, ips_intlsales@
ingramcontent.com

Cover design by Jamie Kerry of Belle Étoile Studios and Ragina Johnson.

This book was published with the generous support of Lannan Foundation
and the Wallace Action Fund.

Printed in Canada by union labor.

10 9 8 7 6 5 4 3 2 1

Library of Congress Cataloging-in-Publication Data is available.

Contents

Acknowledgements   VII
Notes on Contributors   VIII

Introduction   1
Daniel Krier and Mark P. Worrell

PART 1
Towards a New Understanding of Critical Theory

1   Capitalism's Future: Self-Alienation, Self-Emancipation and the
    Remaking of Critical Theory   11
    David Norman Smith

PART 2
Capitalism's Future and the Critique of Political Economy

2   Beyond Left Liberalism: A Critical Look at Proposals to Reform the
    Capital/Wage Labor Relation   65
    Tony Smith

3   Left Thatcherism: Recent Critical Theory and Post-Marxism(s) in the
    Light of Marxian Social Ontology   93
    Christian Lotz

4   Capital's Reach: How Capital Shapes and Subsumes   113
    Patrick Murray

5   Easing the Encumbered Subject: Security, Speculation, and Capitalist
    Subjectivity   136
    Kevin S. Amidon and Daniel Krier

PART 3
Capitalism's Future and the Critique of Political Psychology

6   The Idolatry of Mind: Durkheim's Critique of Idealism   157
    Mark P. Worrell

7 Social Character in Western Pre-Modernity: Lacanian Psychosis in Wladyslaw Reymont's *The Peasants* 175
Daniel Krier and Tony Allen Feldmann

8 Critical Pragmatism's Status Wage and the Standpoint of the Stranger 217
Graham Cassano

9 Dark Spectacle: Authoritarianism and the Economic Enclosure of American Motorcycling 240
William J. Swart and Daniel Krier

Index 277

Acknowledgements

The editors thank David Fasenfest, Series Editor of *Studies in Critical Social Sciences* for his ongoing support and guidance in the preparation of this book. We thank Paul Lasley, Chair of the Department of Sociology at Iowa State University, as well as ISU's College of Liberal Arts & Sciences, Department of Philosophy and Religious Studies, and Department of World Languages and Culture for their support of the 2014 Symposium for New Directions in Critical Social Theory. We also wish to acknowledge ISU Department of Sociology staff and students who assisted with the symposium or with this manuscript: Darcy Besch, Rachel Burlingame, Brennan Goodman, Deb McKay, Amanda Runyan, and Nick Van Berkum.

Notes on Contributors

Kevin S. Amidon

(PhD Princeton) is associate professor of World Languages and Cultures at Iowa State University. A specialist in German language and history, his scholarship has focused upon the historical co-development of the social and biological sciences. He has published articles on critical theory, gender history and theory, eugenics, race theory, evolutionary thought, the Frankfurt School, German and American history, opera, and theater.

Graham Cassano

(PhD Brandeis) is an associate professor of sociology at Oakland University, outside Detroit, Michigan and serves as Culture and Media editor for the journal *Critical Sociology* (Sage). His most recent book is *A New Kind of Public: Community, Solidarity, and Political Economy in New Deal Cinema, 1935–1948* (Brill 2014). Currently, he is collaborating with Rima Lunin Schultz and Jessica Payette on the volume *Eleanor Smith's Hull House Songs: The Music of Protest and Hope in Jane Addams' Chicago* (Brill forthcoming).

Tony Allen Feldmann

(PhD Candidate University of Kansas) is a doctoral candidate specializing in political psychology, critical theory and political economy. His research focuses upon understanding aspects of authoritarianism, especially the reasons why some people hold self-defeating political attitudes while others do not and how social relationships impact political attitudes.

Daniel Krier

(PhD University of Kansas) is associate professor of Sociology at Iowa State University. Krier is author of *Speculative Management: Stock Market Power and Corporate Change* with SUNY Press and has published academic articles in the *American Journal of Economics and Sociology, Current Perspectives in Social Theory, Critical Sociology, Fast Capitalism* and a number of edited volumes in critical theory.

Christian Lotz

(PhD University of Marburg) is a professor of philosophy at Michigan State University. His main research area is post-Kantian European philosophy. Recent book publications include *The Art of Gerhard Richter: Hermeneutics, Images, Meaning* (Bloomsbury Press, 2015) and *The Capitalist Schema: Time, Money, and the Culture of Abstraction* (Lexington, 2014). His current research interests are in Marx, aesthetical realism, as well as contemporary European political philosophy.

Patrick Murray
(PhD St. Louis University) is professor of philosophy at Creighton University. He writes widely on political economy and Marxist thought. His books include *Reflections on Commercial Life: An Anthology of Classic Texts from Plato to the Present* (1997).

David Norman Smith
(PhD University of Wisconsin) specializes in sociological theory and the social psychology of inequality. He has published widely on classical and critical social theory, anti-Semitism, authority, authoritarianism, charisma, genocide, the Rwandan genocide, capitalism, and labor.

Tony Smith
(PhD State University of New York, Stony Brook) is professor of philosophy at Iowa State University. He has published widely in Marxist philosophy and political economy. His books include *The Logic of Marx's Capital: Replies to Hegelian Criticisms* (1990), *Technology and Capital in the Age of Lean Production* (2000), *Globalisation: A Systematic Marxian Account* (2005), and *Beyond Liberal Egalitarianism: Marxism and Normative Social Theory in the Twenty-First Century,* Brill (forthcoming).

William J. Swart
(PhD University of Kansas) is professor of Sociology and Director of the Honors Program at Augustana University. He specializations in theory, globalization and identities. His recent research (with Dan Krier) examined commodification and alienation within the culture of large-displacement motorcycling, soon to appear in a forthcoming book *NASCAR, Sturgis and the New Economy of Spectacle* (Brill).

Mark P. Worrell
(PhD University of Kansas) is Associate Professor of sociology at SUNY Cortland and an Associate Editor at the journal *Critical Sociology.* He has published widely in critical theory, with recent articles appearing in *Telos, Current Perspectives in Social Theory, Fast Capitalism* and *Logos.* His books include *Dialectic of Solidarity: Labor, Anti-Semitism and the Frankfurt School* (Brill and Haymarket), *Why Nations Go to War* (Routledge), and *Terror: Social, Political, and Economic Perspectives* (Routledge).

Introduction

Daniel Krier and Mark P. Worrell

This volume developed from the 2014 Symposium for New Directions in Critical Social Theory at Iowa State University, June 24–6. The Symposium began as an informal, biennial gathering of a handful of sociologists, Germanists, and philosophers in Ames, Iowa in 2007 with the goal of surveying the state of critical social theory in hopes of establishing vectors for future interdisciplinary research. As of May 2015, the Symposium has grown into a larger and more formally structured annual meeting incorporating several days of sessions devoted to the reinvention of critical social theory and critical sociology. Incidentally, a collection of papers from the 2015 meeting are scheduled to appear as *The Social Ontology of Capital*, edited by Krier and Worrell, as a part Professor Michael J. Thompson's Political Philosophy and Public Purpose series.

One of the central theoretical planks in the Symposium's constellation is the time-honored problem of alienation, most famously elaborated by Marx in his youthful 'Paris manuscripts' where alienation was probed along four main lines: products of labor, labor process, species being, and self-estrangement. Of course, a mountain of books on alienation have already been printed and another mountain looms on the distant horizon but the present collection offers, we think, a unique set of perspectives from which to tackle, arguably, the central and recurring problem of modern life.

Part 1: Towards a New Understanding of Critical Theory

In his keynote presentation, a version of which opens this volume, "Capitalism's Future: Self Alienation, Self-Emancipation and the Remaking of Critical Theory," David N. Smith proposes the unification of two kinds of critical theory: Marx's *critique of political economy*, which analyzes capitalism, and a second, intersecting *critique of political psychology*, which derives from work of the Frankfurt School and explores authoritarianism. Marx examined the commodity world and found that what was historically contingent appeared to consciousness as naturally inevitable and that, whereas people could, if they wanted, simply share with one another rather than exchange them on the basis of a profit motive. If value is a swamp of self-defeat it is a quagmire created by our own actions. Solving the value problem means approaching it from the angle of political psychology. Like commodities, leaders are imagined by followers to possess innate qualities that border on magic. This fetishism of authority, which confuses the personal with the impersonal, is a problem familiar to those who have pondered the nature of charisma, fascism, or the figure of "The Jew" within anti-Semitic propaganda.

In his presentation, Smith traces the entwined arcs of these twin critiques of commodity fetishism and authoritarianism by calling attention not only to intellectual history but also to the way in which this history intersects with key moments of crisis. In periods of crisis, when people think that capitalism is faltering, they often fear that charismatic dictatorship will succeed it – because crisis brings personal authoritarianism to the fore and disposes them to bow before dictators. Hence the link between capitalism and authoritarianism is not arbitrary. If capitalism fails, people fear that a toxic alternative – charismatic and authoritarian – will replace it. Engels once said that our future holds either socialism or barbarism. Charismatic movements, especially in the past century, have given us a very bitter taste of barbarism. Many people, as a consequence, believe that the only real choice is between capitalism and barbarism. Smith argues that Engels was closer to the truth, and that the prospect of a humane alternative to barbarism can be advanced most effectively via "defetishizing" critical insight into the socially constructed and hence contingent sway of fetishized people and products.

Part 2: Capitalism's Future and the Critique of Political Economy

Explaining society by making recourse to something non-social, or somehow outside of society, is a heritage industry at this point and both French post-structuralist thought, as well as lines developed in the wake of the Frankfurt School, represent currents of thought that take the political and the ethical as the proper grounds for social analysis. Tony Smith, in his chapter, "Beyond Left Liberalism: A Critical Look at Proposals to Reform the Capital/Wage Labor Relation," provides a fundamental Marxist critique of the predominant left liberal standpoint in contemporary political philosophy, John Rawls' *Theory of Justice*. Smith demonstrates that left liberalism, without a Marxist category of capital, is inadequate. While Marx viewed the capital/wage labor relationship as inherently coercive, dominating and exploitative, Rawls' liberalism posits that proper political background conditions could restrain these tendencies while preserving capitalism. The normative positions of left liberalism are shared by most Marxists, but as Smith demonstrates, these positions can not be achieved without a fundamental transcendence of the capital/wage labor relationship. The limitations of left liberalism are particularly pronounced under neoliberal capitalism. Smith argues that while liberal egalitarian reforms might constrain particularly irrational varieties of contemporary capitalism, Marxist critical theory is necessary to critique capitalist 'rationality' in general.

Weaknesses of non-Marxist criticism of capitalist societies are not limited to Rawlsian left egalitarianism. Christian Lotz, in his chapter "Left Thatcherism: Recent Critical Theory and Post-Marxism(s) in the Light of Marxian Social Ontology," explains that the results of this alienated academic gaze are lacking in dialectical nuance, falling into abstractions and what he refers to as a "left Thatcherism" that fails to include anything like society within their ontologies. A return to Marx's dialectical materialist critique of political economy and critical engagement with the value form is required if we desire a way forward from the antinomies of post structuralism and 'critical theory' that lacks a true, critical social edge, and cannot find the social in what Marx thought of as "purely social."

If post structuralism and post-Adornian critical theory seem like troubled perspectives we need to situate their failures within the larger failures of academic discourses that dominate the contemporary intellectual landscape. Striding forward from the standpoint of Marx's critique of political economy, Patrick Murray's chapter, "Capital's Reach: How Capital Shapes and Subsumes," examines what he calls the "catastrophe" that has befallen social philosophy and the social sciences as a whole at the hands of "economics imperialism" and challenges us to return to the missed "scientific revolution" that Marx initiated when he placed capitalism and its specific social forms within historical context. Economics fails, in its reductionism, to take into account actual social forms of production and accumulation – what is needed is a return to capital and its specific social formations, as well as a reassessment of foundational critical concepts, and a reconfiguration of academic boundaries that keep economics, sociology, and moral philosophy apart for the benefit of surplus value.

Kevin Amidon and Daniel Krier, in their chapter, "Easing the encumbered subject: Security, speculation and capitalist subjectivity," examine the history of capital development and its attendant social dynamics of alienation through a close reading of a canonical sociological text: Max Weber's *The Protestant Ethic and the Spirit of Capitalism* (1920). Amidon and Krier mine Weber's work to uncover an often overlooked internal dialectic unfolding over the history of capitalism: the complex, mutually-constitutive relationship between *speculation* and *securitization*. This chapter deploys the dialectic of speculation-securitization to analyze risk-pooling as a social form doubly-legitimated in the securitization-logic of Quaker-Pietist theology and in the speculative-logic of Calvinism. Like other capitalist social forms, risk-pools generate widely divergent subjectivities among various actors across cultural space and historical time. In our neoliberal moment, resistance to risk pooling (such as Obamacare) has emerged as a central modality of alienation. Fantasizing that they are autonomous subjects of speculative capitalism, estranged neoliberal subjects reject the security provided by pooled-risk. Weber's sociologically-grounded political economy provides the foundation for a nuanced critical theory of alienated neoliberal subjectivity.

Part 3: Capitalism's Future and the Critique of Political Psychology

For centuries, under various banners and a tangle of changing terminologies, the struggle over the mind-matter question dominated philosophy from the time of the subjective turn (Socrates) to the end of the 18th century, when a legitimate 'third way' was glimpsed by the German absolute idealists, dissatisfied as they were, with Kant's attempt to rescue the active mind from the reductionism of the British empiricists at the cost of transcendentalizing the categories of thought and morality. Though he was not the sole (or maybe even the chief) inventor of this third way that sublated idealism and materialism, Hegel was nonetheless the popularizer of this current of thought that, ultimately, found its fullest and 'inverted' expression in Marx's "historical materialism" from 1859 onward. Relatively ignorant of Hegel's writings and being a harsh critic of Marxism, Durkheim, in France at the turn of the 20th Century, accomplished his own variation on this 'third way' that his critics labeled a "social realism" but what Durkheim simply thought of as "sociology." Nowhere is this new paradigm better expressed than in the introduction to his magnum opus, *Elementary Forms of Religious Life*, where rationalism and empiricism are sublated, preserving their insights, negating their errors, and raising the whole thing up whereby reason and the processes of representation are placed on the solid ground of society. Despite the roughly century-long historical opening that saw the birth of Hegelian social philosophy, Marx's critique of political economy, and Durkheim's sociology, those achievements are perennially lost or misinterpreted resulting in the regression of social thought back into crude forms of materialism, realism, idealism, empiricism, etc. Nowhere is this regression seen more clearly, and catastrophically, than in the contemporary movement known as 'speculative realism.' Drawing upon a theoretical constellation constructed from materials found in Durkheim's classic work on suicide, Mark Worrell, in his chapter, "The idolatry of mind: Durkheim's critique of idealism," puts the sociological nail through the heart of idealism. Durkheim reveals that continental idealism in its various forms is a symptom of modern egoistic decadence. If critical sociology is to contribute to the making-transparent the social nature of the absolute and weird 'substances' like value, it must extricate itself from the twin dead ends of rationalism and empiricism, return to a *closer* reading of *Capital* and with an eye toward integrating Durkheim's sociology, especially his ideas on self-destructiveness and human sacrifice.

Daniel Krier and Tony Feldmann, in their chapter, "Social character in Western premodernity: Lacanian psychosis in Wladyslaw Reymont's *The Peasants*," update classical critical theory's formative concern with Western social character and its relation to capital. Studies of pre-modern social character were widespread in critical theory through the late 20th century but declined as Western pre-capitalist, preindustrial villages vanished into the historical distance and as Freudian psychoanalysis lost academic cache. Krier and Feldmann resurrect critical theories of social character by analyzing a rich narration of premodern Western subjectivity contained in *The Peasants*, a nearly forgotten, four volume Nobel Prize winning novel written by the Polish author Wladyslaw Reymont in the first decade of the 20th century. Combining critical theory's Freudian analytics with Jacques Lacan's theories of psychic structure, critical theory's *homo normalis* – the modern character – corresponds to Lacan's neurotic structure while the peasant villagers in Reymont's novels exhibit symptoms of Lacan's psychotic structure. After delineating these symptoms and analyzing Reymont's novel in terms of them, similarities are noted between contemporary anti-democratic characters (authoritarians, destructive personalities) and the psychotic model of peasant subjectivity developed here. Krier and Feldmann's Lacanian model of character presents several challenges to critical theories of alienation, opening new avenues for empirical and theoretical investigation.

Graham Cassano, in his chapter, "Critical Pragmatism's Status Wage and the Standpoint of the Stranger," explores the origins of an early American pragmatist theory of desire that prefigures David Roediger's influential "wages of whiteness." Cassano argues that Roediger's phrase contains the concentrated residue of the pragmatic theories of social desire found in the work of Charles Horton Cooley, Thorstein Veblen, and W.E.B. Du Bois. Cooley, Veblen and Du Bois are united by a social phenomenology of the subject in which the self is born through the gaze of the other. This phenomenology produces a pragmatic sociology of desire in which self desires the prestigious other's recognition or respect. Cooley uses the concept of the "looking glass self" in the service of a functionalist explanation of the manner in which subjectivity in search of recognition helps maintain social order and sustain dominant norms. Both Veblen and Du Bois also examine the problem of identification with systems of status and domination. But both reject Cooley's simple functionalist assumptions that consent and identification are immediate and automatic results of normative domination. Veblen turns his critique upon forms of hegemonic desire that potentially infect subjectivity and reinforce domination and working class division. And he situates these symbolic status systems in the context of economic and ideological tensions that potentially disrupt their easy operation. Du Bois adds to the Veblenian analysis of normative domination an examination of the counter-reaction of those excluded from status recognition. The "double-consciousness" produced by exclusion from the normative racial system allows for the development of a critical, sociological imagination based on the standpoint of the stranger.

William Swart and Daniel Krier, in their chapter, "Dark spectacle: Authoritarian performance and the commodity form," explore the role of authoritarianism in the economic enclosure of twentieth century motorcycling. Pre-War motorcycling exhibited orthodox authoritarian tendencies that stressed submission and conventionality, while the rebel authoritarianism of post-War motorcycle culture promoted aggressive and anti-establishment behaviors. Both forms of authoritarianism were crucial to the economic enclosure of American motorcycling. National organizations and the motorcycle industry exploited orthodox authoritarianism to build early motorcycle markets and promote a positive public image of motorcycling. When these markets were challenged by post-War motorcycle "outlaws," the media, film and motorcycle industries enclosed rebel authoritarianism into an outlaw biker diegesis that became central to its marketing and promotion. The resulting dark spectacle, in which spectators immerse themselves in a commodified environment themed with the outlaw biker diegesis, has become central to contemporary economy of American motorcycling. These are workers buying signs of their own self-debasement, trophies of alienation as a symbol of prestige.

The Future of Capitalism and Critical Social Theory

Well into the 21st Century, critical social theory has come to terms with the fact that the revolutionary proletariat always was, and remains, a fiction; anticapitalist revolution was not, and is not, inevitable; and we suspect that capitalism will not destroy itself and, even if it did, it would, in terms of pure probabilities, represent a vanishing mediator for something as bad or worse. Capitalism, ostensibly a system of production for the accumulation of surplus value (it all sounds so economistic) is just as much, if not more so, a spiritual system – indeed, one could argue that capitalism is the one true planetary religion, if, with Caillois, we see religion as the "administration of the sacred." Value is the absolute sacred substance of modernity and, even if Marx's goal of lifting humanity from the spell of value were achieved, the problem of social ebullience (Durkheim distinguished between the "collective effervescence" of life in a positive hell and "morbid effervescence" that plagued the negative heaven of capitalist society) remains. We should remember that 'value' as it appears in the lexicon of political economy is a one-sided appearance of a larger phenomenon; there is not one value but myriad values, including political value, religious value, cultural value, etc. Value is the spiritual sweat of human activity, broadly conceived, and not merely *ergon*. Human assemblage produces a surplus that, for 50,000 years, has eluded even the slightest comprehension from all but a tiny number of intellects. Capitalism is new, there is no doubt about it, however, from the standpoint of 'speculative' sociology, capitalism is but one more form that the movement of spirit and energy has assumed along its odyssey.

Never has Marx been more relevant but never before has Marxism and every academic discipline that draws sustenance from that current been more unprepared to deal with the prevailing situation. Sociology reached its zenith in the 70s, yet, what nobody noticed was that the discipline was already a living corpse reduced to wandering the night in search of money and administrative usefulness; 'Critical Theory' died in the early 70s soon after the "Frankfurt School" was turned into an object of fascination; *Telos* went bad in the 1980s; political economy is exhausted; a tiresome list of complaints would be easy to compile but the future of capitalism, and it has a future, is apparently, the twilight years for those few left with the abstract capacity to wrap their minds around capitalism. Theory cannot go into another 'hibernation' and hope for better times. This is another benefit of hindsight: there is no time like the present and we are the ones we have been waiting for.

Early neo-Marxists turned to Freud and the incorporation of Weberian sociology was an important development. We should not jettison or neglect the work of Reich, Fromm, Korsch, Lukács, Adorno, etc., but the days of mining those works for hidden treasures that have hitherto eluded generations of scholars have long since passed. We need a grasp on society not more academic cult industries. Irony insists, and that is the appropriate method of speculative sociology, that a reconstruction of Marx is due. Like Braverman's clean sweep that paved the way for the 'labor process' school of thought, historical materialism is due for a friendly deconstruction and rebuilt with an eye toward finding hidden interiors within the overall process of commodity production and exchange from which to direct theoretical work.

Perhaps it is time we face another hard truth: contemporary "critique of political economy" in the manner of Marx is made difficult by the lack of an adequate political economy to critique. The political economists that Marx studied symbolically comprehended much of capitalism's logical order, albeit in fetishized form. Material to theorize capital was there, potentially coherent, inside the work of political economists awaiting Marx's negating hand. The monstrous growth of speculative finance has overwhelmed political economists, who scarcely comprehend emerging financial technologies and speculative architectures. Speculative finance capital remains both fetishized and symbolically misrecognized: an adequate model of capital is no longer there, inside contemporary political economy, awaiting our Marx-like negation. Perhaps critical social theorists must now engage in basic political economy prior to its critique, but not to improve political economy but to better grasp reality. Marx critiqued political economy by negating and lifting it up to a sociological theory of the commodity. In capitalism's future, value will increasingly be accumulated and extracted outside of traditional labor processes in the realm of society itself (working consumers, immaterial co-production, etc.). Contemporary critical theory might better grasp capital by reaching down from society rather than stretching up from political economy.

Further, under-utilized streams of thought need to be mobilized: we suggest taking a look at what Lacan can do for critical sociology, and, while Zizek's stock has fallen precipitously in recent years, buffoonery aside, we think there is a goldmine of insights that can be salvaged and reworked. And where Weber's interpretive sociology was useful in expanding the resources of critical theory, we think that, along with the rebuilding of Marx's critique of the commodity, Durkheim's corpus (along with his disciples) needs to be reconsidered with an eye toward revisioning the modern sacred in its various facets. Hegel elucidates the manner in which people can be wronged and feel unjustly treated yet still cling tenaciously to terrible social conditions all the same because, even though wrong, they are still the facts of existence and, as such, sacred at least in part. The dregs of society can blame the system, blame their own debauched qualities, or they can hunt down a scapegoat and the latter is always more exciting and emotionally rewarding than decoding reality. The sacred always produces a leftover that is part of but simultaneously outside the domain of virtue and it is the virtue of the remainder to know its place and receive, by way of recompense, a share of moral indignation. The social circle, the absolute, is held together by the very thing that prevents its totalization. Without its impurities, society cannot even exist without devolving into a disorganized field of uncoordinated atoms. It is along this axis that we can, oddly enough, pull together Durkheim, Lacan, and Zizek, among many others.

PART 1

Towards a New Understanding of Critical Theory

∵

Capitalism's Future: Self-Alienation, Self-Emancipation and the Remaking of Critical Theory*

David Norman Smith

Usually, when people discuss the future of capitalism, they focus on economics. But today, I will discuss the future of capitalism and authoritarianism in the same breath. That isn't as random as it might sound. When capitalism prospers, threats to democracy tend to remain subliminal, in the background. But when crisis enters the picture, people of good will begin to worry about fascism.

Right now, crisis in the eurozone is acute, especially in Greece and Spain, where joblessness is soaring. In Greece, one effect of the crisis has been growing polarization, with the emergence of radical forces on the left (above all Syriza) and on the right. The most prominent radical-right party, Golden Dawn, won a disturbing number of votes in the most recent elections to the European parliament – and Golden Dawn is an overtly neo-Nazi party.

Many people worry reflexively about parties like Golden Dawn: If capitalism wobbles, will people respond by turning fascist? I will address that question today in connection with the theme of authoritarianism, which allows us to talk about economic and political crisis at the same time. But first, personally, I want to point out that today's talk is unusual for me. Last month I was at a conference in Tennessee with several people who are here today, including Dan Krier. We previewed today's session, and I said, "You know, I've given a great many 20-minute talks and 30-minute talks, which I always enjoy. But those talks are so short that I can only share a slice of my thinking. In Ames, if you agree, I'd like to talk about the big picture." So that's what I'm doing today.

Of course, this could be the worst of both worlds – a very long talk, giving short shrift to a great many subjects. But we'll see. I'll start by circulating a one-page handout, to give you an outline of what I'm going to say. Since it's a dense page, I'll begin with an overview.

---

* This is a lightly revised transcript of the keynote address, presented at Iowa State University on June 25, 2014, to the 3rd Biennial Symposium on New Directions in Critical Social Theory. Articles and books mentioned or tacitly cited in the text appear, in full bibliographic form, at the end of the lecture.

I'm proposing the unification of two kinds of critical theory, one of which analyzes capitalism – Marx's critique of political economy – and a second, intersecting theory that explores authoritarianism. That second theory I call the critique of political psychology.

Structurally, today's talk is like a PowerPoint presentation. My handout is a matrix, in which, in an actual PowerPoint presentation, each box would be a slide. But I want the unusual breadth of the presentation to be immediately clear, and that's what the matrix as a whole shows. You will see that the structure is two-fold, twice over. My core argument is that the critiques of political economy and political psychology should be in dialogue.

Under the heading *"critique of political economy,"* I'm talking about what Marx called "the world of commodities," *die Waarenwelt.* Marx's argument is that capitalism is the system based on the generalization of commodity relations, so the word "commodity" deserves our closest scrutiny. Beside the empirical reality of commodity relations there is also "the fetishism of the commodity world," which is the phrase Marx uses to introduce this concept in Chapter 1 of *Capital.* Fetishism is basically how people *see* the world of commodities. Marx argues that critique is needed because people seldom see the *essential* relations and contingencies in this realm. I'll come back to that.

TABLE 1.1   *Dimensions of Critical Theory*

Critique of Political Psychology	Critique of Political Economy
AUTHORITIES / AUTHORITY FETISHISM	COMMODITIES / COMMODITY FETISHISM

TABLE 1.2   *Commodities / Commodity Fetishism*

Waarenwelt	Capital fetishism and antibank politics
"Because the King is King."	Capital fetishism and anti-Semitism
treating and regarding	Communards, *pétroleuses*
fetish, fetishism	Capitalist crisis and conspiracism
Alfred Binet, Sigmund Freud	Unpopularity contest
Marx (*commodities fetishism*)	Capitalist crisis, anti-Semitism
Marx (*money fetishism*)	Great Recession
Marx (*capital fetishism*)	Crisis: *falling production, declining consumption*

TABLE 1.3   *Authorities / Authority Fetishism*

Enquête ouvrière, anti-Chinese riots in San Francisco (1880)	Arthur Maurice Hocart (*traditional authority*)
Adolf Levenstein, Eugen Leviné, Erich Fromm	Otto von Gierke (*legal authority*)
Anti-Semitism Projects, 1941–45	Moisei Ostrogorski (*charismatic authority*)
Authoritarian Personality, 1950	Max Weber
Henry Victor Dicks	Émile Durkheim
Bruno Bettelheim, Morris Janowitz	Theodor Adorno
Solomon Asch, Stanley Milgram	Hannah Arendt (*"totalitarianism"*)
Bob Altemeyer, Jim Sidanius & Felicia Pratto, ANES (2013)	authoritarianism, authority fetishism

The other side of the matrix is headed *"the critique of political psychology."* The column headed "authorities" parallels the commodities column across the page and the column headed "authority fetishism" parallels the "commodity fetishism" column. (I like rhymes and wordplay...so you will just have to bear with me here.) Authority fetishism is my term for what is usually called authoritarianism, which has been the subject of a long stream of research and which I am extending to the attitudes that lead people to follow so-called "charismatic leaders."

Those of you with a background in the critique of political economy might look askance at the very idea of a critique of political psychology. Can this really be more than an echoing couplet? Do the two critiques share intellectual substance? My answer is *Yes,* and I will illustrate that answer by reviewing the first column, which, you see, is headed:

Authority Fetishism

If you look at a standard history of empirical social research – a good one, for example, like the book by Oberschall – you will discover that Marx himself published a questionnaire for workers, the *Enquête ouvrière,* in a French socialist newspaper in 1880. At first hearing that might sound promising. But the questionnaire itself is actually fairly banal. Marx asks very mundane questions – "how much do your meals cost?", "how much are you paid?" – without delving into feelings or attitudes. But here is a relevant point:

Two years after Marx wrote the *Enquête ouvrière,* he explored the anti-Chinese riots which had scarred San Francisco in 1877 in a manuscript that is still available only in Marx's archive in Amsterdam. In 1877, San Francisco was fully one-third Chinese, thanks to the import of cheap Chinese labor, and a nativist party had arisen to drive the Chinese out – a group calling itself the Workingman's Party. Marx was keenly interested in this kind of ethnocentrism. Although he never formally theorized the ethnic fault lines that divide workers of different nationalities, Marx was acutely aware of the animosities that divided Black and White laborers in the United States and Irish and English workers in Great Britain. Marx and Engels warmly sympathized with Irish Republicanism and they found the enmity of Irish and British workers disturbing. In their correspondence they analyzed this division in depth, with sensitivity and nuance. Yet Marx never theorized ethnic division *per se.* The consequence is that, despite some powerful lines in *Capital* (most notably, his remark that "Labor in the white skin can never free itself as long as labor in the black skin is branded"), he otherwise only alludes to ethnic division in *Capital.*

Class Consciousness and Authority Fetishism

Still, the fact that Marx wrote his *Enquête ouvrière* at a point when he was keenly concerned about ethnic prejudices among workers is telling in itself. The working class is arguably the central category of Marx's critique of political economy, so his interest in the anti-Chinese impetus of the Workingman's Party in San Francisco gives us a hint, I think, of the direction Marx's own critique of political psychology might have taken.

Consider in this connection a survey in Germany by Adolf Levenstein in 1905. Levenstein was a radical who had begun to doubt the class consciousness of his fellow workers. Some of them, he wrote in his naïve preface to the survey results, appeared to be "spiritually dead." Worried by the implications of this finding, Levenstein made the interesting decision to consult the sociologist Max Weber for a second opinion. Weber had pioneered survey research a decade earlier and was steeped in industrial sociology. Weber was impressed. When the dismayed Levenstein was slow to publish his results, Weber lectured him sternly: "Publish – this is important, this needs to be addressed."

Weber, a generation after Marx, was also drawn to issues of class consciousness. In what was then regarded as "orthodox" Marxism, class consciousness was supposed to emanate automatically from class status. Weber knew this wasn't true for his own class. He was, he once wrote, a "class-conscious bourgeois," and he knew from direct experience as well as scholarly study that the "capitalist spirit" – that is, the spirit of self-denying and unremitting exertion in service to the enterprise – was now rare among major capitalists. For workers, too, the premise of automatic class consciousness was now beginning to be called into question. Levenstein's amateur effort was soon complemented by the work of the socialist radical Eugen Leviné, who wrote a doctoral thesis, supervised by Max Weber's brother Alfred, that reported on working-class consciousness in the factory town of Mannheim, near Heidelberg, shortly before World War I. Last year I visited Heidelberg, searching in vain for that thesis, which I have tried to track down for an embarrassingly long time now. So my knowledge of Leviné's thesis is still second-hand. But he remains an interesting and characteristic figure on several levels. As a Marxist, Leviné's goal was not only to study working-class consciousness but to cultivate it. This led him, ultimately, to become one of the martyred leaders of the working-class revolt in Munich at the end of World War I, where a "People's Republic" briefly held power. The carnage of the world war had struck a deep existential chord in many sectors of the Left, which, disturbed by the spectacle of workers fighting rather than uniting, began to doubt the socialist destiny and inevitable solidarity of the workers. Leviné's close associate, the socialist leader Rosa Luxemburg, wrote, in a bitter paraphrase of the *Communist Manifesto*, "Workers of the world, slit each other's throats!"

The fact that working-class consciousness is anything but inevitable seemed to be an obvious lesson of the Great War. That point leads us to the next figure named in the matrix, Erich Fromm. Fromm was once ultra-famous. In fact, you can still buy his book *Escape from Freedom* in airport bookstores, which is my index of mass-market fame. *Escape* was published over 70 years ago, and it's still selling in airports! In the 1950s alone, Fromm's books sold over 30 million copies. But few people know that Fromm's first big study was a survey of German workers in the years 1929–31. In that period, Fromm was an associate of the Frankfurt School, the Institute for Social Research, which introduced the concept of critical theory. That concept was directly relevant to Fromm's work because critical theory was intended as an authentic Marxist critique of the shallow pseudo-Marxism of the German and Russian ruling parties of the 1920s. What was wrong with traditional Marxism? According to Fromm, Max Horkheimer, and Herbert Marcuse, traditional Marxism assumed that workers would inevitably pursue socialism and that socialists could therefore rest content with building the party – "build it, and they will come." Critical theory called that assumption into question. Fromm's research, which he pursued with Horkheimer and Paul Lazarsfeld, among others, was central to that critique.

Fromm's team surveyed German workers, most of whom, at that point, supported the ruling Socialist party (SPD) while others backed the upstart Communist party (KPD). Above all, at that fraught moment in history, Fromm hoped to find that the working class was immune to the blandishments of authoritarianism. His results showed the contrary. A small but appreciable minority of KPD supporters would evidently have welcomed a left-wing dictator, even though they resisted Hitler, and many SPD supporters were unprepared to actually fight fascism, if push came to shove. In other words, the old assumption that workers would support democracy and extend democracy to the economy seemed to be simply false. History soon spoke as well. When Hitler came to power and the vaunted SPD and its army of trade unions and officials proved incapable of effective resistance, critical concerns about working-class consciousness – and democratic consciousness – were amplified.

Labor and Anti-Semitism

This brings us to the anti-Semitism studies of 1941–1944. Fromm had exited the Frankfurt School a few years earlier, but many other Institute members, most of whom had emigrated to the United States, continued the research. They remained interested in the working class and consciousness, but they added something new that harkens back to Marx's late-blooming concern about ethnicity, namely, an interest in anti-Semitism as a form of ethnocentrism. Labor attitudes towards ethnicity as well as authority were now subjects of inquiry.

Mark Worrell, who is with us, wrote his doctoral dissertation (published in 2008 under the title *Dialectic of Solidarity*) on a major and still unpublished four-volume study conducted by the Frankfurt School in the United States. Mark can give you the details. But for now it suffices to say that this study, *Anti-Semitism Among American Labor*, was truly remarkable; and it was, again, disturbing, since it found that a fair number of workers in the United States were at least susceptible to pre-fascistic and, often, anti-Semitic ideas, including exterminatory views. That was chilling. In 1935 the Congress of Industrial Organizations had been founded and labor was surging ahead. Many progressives expected labor and progressivism to march steadily forward. And yet, at that very moment, a genuine susceptibility to anti-democratic and anti-Semitic politics was becoming clear among some American workers.

Last year, at the postwar offices of the Institute for Social Research in Frankfurt, I discovered that the Frankfurt School in exile had completed an additional 1,000-page study of anti-Semitism in the early 1940s. This massive volume appears to be almost entirely unknown, even though it was produced by a team of eminent scholars and includes subtle inquiries into the appeal of neo-fascist agitators like George Allison Phelps and Joe McWilliams. Thus far, I've been able to find only one cryptic reference to this study anywhere. But that's a story for another day.

Soon afterwards, an overlapping group of Frankfurt School scholars, working with American psychologists, conducted the research that they reported in *The Authoritarian Personality* in 1950. The key Frankfurt School figure in this group was the renowned and enormously gifted Theodor Adorno, who was joined by another émigré, the exceptionally astute Else Frenkel-Brunswik. What they accomplished in *The Authoritarian Personality*, with Nevitt Sanford and Daniel Levinson, was to install the concept of authoritarianism in the psychological firmament. Adorno and the others had inherited this concept from Fromm, but they made it their own, theoretically as well as empirically. The book exploded onto the intellectual scene, becoming perhaps the most famous social-psychological study of the 20th century.

Authoritarianism and Authority Fetishism

In essence, *The Authoritarian Personality* was an attempt to study ethnocentrism through the prism of authoritarianism. Adorno and the others wanted a reliable index of anti-Semitism which did not directly discuss Jews. They also wanted a survey scale which could reliably tap the whole spectrum of out-group antipathies and in-group sympathies. When Fromm first deployed the concept of authoritarianism in 1936, he had aspired to link the critique of authoritarianism to the critique of patriarchy. That double critique remained present in the Frankfurt School's later work but it became secondary. In 1950 they wanted to probe ethnocentrism, in general, and anti-Semitism in particular. This led them to look beyond the working class. They decided to look at what Orwell called the big public, asking, "How does the public feel about democracy and equality? How does the public feel about fascism and ethnic division?" Their results were sobering and spurred a decade of research by countless sociologists and psychologists. So many researchers joined in the hunt that, by 1958, Richard Christie and Peggy Cook were able to publish a 29-page bibliography that simply listed the articles and research projects that had amplified *The Authoritarian Personality* through 1956.

A major British researcher in this period, whose work has been largely neglected, deserves to be much better known: Henry Victor Dicks. Dicks was a psychopathologist with the Tavistock Institute, which resembled the Frankfurt School. During World War II, many German prisoners of war were housed on British soil and Dicks was enlisted to interview them, in the hope of shedding light on German public opinion. Dicks interviewed 2,000 POWs at length, producing a trove of psychiatric data. When Hitler's chief deputy, Rudolf Hess, made his peculiar solo flight to Scotland in 1941 – where he crashed and was captured – he was placed under round-the-clock psychiatric observation. Henry Dicks conducted this observation. Twenty years later, in the 1960s, when SS leaders were being prosecuted and jailed, Dicks went to Germany to interview them in prison. He reported these interviews in his book, *Licensed Mass Murder*.

Earlier, in 1950, Dicks had written an article on his POW research in which he said, "I'm surprised. A group of Americans has just published a book called *The Authoritarian Personality*, which, to my amazement and pleasure, offers an analysis very much like my own, although, I have to say, somewhat better." This was accurate but unduly modest, since, in my view, what Dicks offered was in some ways superior to *The Authoritarian Personality*.

While Dicks continued his research into the 1960s, the attention of academia wandered and authoritarianism ceased to be a fashionable theme. The net result was a huge missed opportunity. Anti-Semitism, which had remained strong in the U.S. until the early 1950s, fell sharply by the 1960s. This was established by Bruno Bettelheim and Morris Janowitz, whose book *The Dynamics of Prejudice* (1950) had been published as part of the "Studies in Prejudice" series with *The Authoritarian Personality*. When Bettelheim and Janowitz looked back a decade later, they found that anti-Semitism, which in 1950 had been widespread in the U.S., had significantly dissipated. That is remarkable. I would argue, in fact, that the rise of anti-hate movements – and the cultural migration of many millions of people away from racism– is one of the least appreciated phenomena of our time. Future historians of the 20th century will see the world wars and genocides, but they will also see the emergence of humane and democratic currents of unprecedented power.

The Obedience Paradigm

Sadly, inquiry into authoritarianism fell out of favor just as mass resistance to prejudice sprang to life. As a result we know much less than we could about the subtle chemistry of tolerance in the decades when anti-Semitism and other forms of prejudice began to diminish. Currently, anti-Jewish attitudes are less common in the U.S. than in most other countries, and the overall decline since 1940 has been steep. But what caused that remarkable reversal? Just asking the question, it seems to me, is a significant step. If we hope to resist ethnocentrism, we need to understand why it waxes and wanes.

Adorno's team set a good example. They pursued authoritarianism from many angles, relying on multiple methods: survey research, which led them to elaborate the famous F scale ("F" for fascism); interview research, especially by Frenkel-Brunswik; and projective research, which revolved around Rorschach and Thematic Apperception tests. This many-sidedness was rarely fully appreciated, however, and few ensuing efforts were equally multi-faceted – and some of the best contributions were simply misunderstood. Consider, for example, the important but misconstrued work of the mid-century psychologists Solomon Asch and Stanley Milgram.

Asch and Milgram are transcendentally famous. Asch's studies of conformity are iconic, and Milgram himself is an icon, known everywhere for his obedience experiments. But the odds are good that you have not previously heard their names associated with the study of authoritarianism. That remains a well-kept secret. Both men, in fact, were key figures who studied authoritarianism by experimental means, with exemplary success.

In 1952, in an early report on his experiment, Asch noted that his findings seemed compatible with what had been reported two years before in *The Authoritarian Personality*. But academia heard him differently. When he began to receive wide attention later in the 1950s, Asch found that he was routinely misinterpreted and he wrote a paper to voice his puzzlement. (Milgram, at that stage, was his graduate research assistant). Asch wrote, in effect: "I'm a lifelong opponent of the idea that individual differences are irrelevant, that everyone is the same" – and yet that was precisely how his fellow psychologists construed his findings. Asch objected that, in everything he had written about his experiment, he had meticulously shown that, while many test subjects did indeed conform under group pressure, many others dissented. Yet curiously, his colleagues appeared sensitive only to the evidence of conformity; they disregarded his findings concerning dissent.

For Asch this was more than an academic concern. He was keenly aware that, if we deny that people differ individually, we thereby deny that some people are genuinely democratic while others are antidemocratic. Asch believed firmly that authoritarian and anti-authoritarian dispositions differ, and that, in fact, they spur *opposite* forms of behavior. Milgram too, when he first reported his experiments in the early '60s, noted that he had found significant individual differences. While many of his test subjects obeyed compliantly, many others refused to obey, at times defiantly. Even in his famous film about the experiment, which many people construe as proof of the proposition that obedience is universal, four of the five subjects who appear on screen ultimately refuse to obey.

In a little-noticed article, and in an appendix to his book *Obedience*, Milgram reported that, with his assistant Alan Elms, he had administered the F scale from *The Authoritarian Personality* to 40 of his experimental subjects. Half of these subjects had been compliant and the others had been defiant. What Elms and Milgram found was that F scale scores – *that is, authoritarianism scores* – are strong predictors of whether people obey or disobey. Those test subjects who complied in the experimental situation scored significantly higher on the F scale than those who resisted.

In other words, Milgram's obedience experiment was also *an authoritarianism experiment*. It is, in my opinion, a major contribution to the study of authoritarianism. Yet that eye-opening fact is almost never noticed. It almost seems as if the world *wants* to believe that Milgram proved the universality of obedience. In that spirit, from the very beginning, Milgram's research was featured in the press under headlines warning, darkly yet complacently, "You would have been a Nazi, too," if you had lived in Hitler's Germany. The fact that Milgram's experiment showed nothing of the kind – and the historical fact that countless Germans fought and were persecuted by Nazism – went unheeded.

Social Dominance and Authority Fetishism

Interest in authoritarianism began to revive during the storm and stress of the late 1960s. A lone psychologist in Canada, Bob Altemeyer, deserves much of the credit for this revival. For two decades he was effectively the only researcher to attempt to rethink and measure what he called "right-wing authoritarianism" (RWA). The result was that, by 1990, as he reported with cheerful modesty, "a flood" of five other researchers had followed his lead. In the ensuing decade, though the floodgates of RWA research actually did open wide. While the academic subfield of "political psychology" is still modest in size and influence, RWA research is now central to that field. (The scale's name, I should say in passing, is a tad ironic, since Fromm in 1929–31 found left-wing as well as right-wing authoritarianism. But Altemeyer said he simply couldn't find enough left-wing authoritarians in Winnipeg to justify ongoing attention to that end of the spectrum.)

So, what have we learned? Once again, a wide distribution of attitudes has been revealed. Many people reflexively support domineering authorities, but only fairly small minorities are either radically democratic or undemocratic. Most people have mixed feelings. I can illustrate this point with respect to the aftermath of 9/11 in the U.S. At that point, there was a big discussion: Should we abridge civil liberties, if that would enhance national security? If so, how far should we go? Are there liberties we should refuse to limit?

In the trauma of the moment, many people after 9/11 were in a state of acute ambivalence. People very understandably wanted more security. At the same time, most people did not want to water down too many civil liberties too permanently. So, to briefly summarize: Altemeyer has essentially rediscovered what Adorno's team found, namely, that most people, most of the time, are ambivalent. Unfortunately, this finding has never been properly theorized. Adorno's team focused almost exclusively on the top and bottom quartiles of the attitude distribution, and subsequent F-Scale and RWA researchers have done the same. But even so, the fact remains: The majority is in the middle, feeling torn. And it also appears that the middle is mutable. Under pressure, people in the middle often move left or right.

The question, then, is what moves us? What moves us away from tolerance or towards democracy? Another key stream of 1990s research casts light on this question. This is the study of "Social Dominance Orientation" (SDO), which was pioneered by the American psychologists Jim Sidanius and Felicia Pratto. Their SDO scale focuses mainly on attitudes towards equality and, like RWA, correlates strongly with ethnocentrism. For students of authoritarianism that is a defining fact, since the very concept of authoritarianism emerged from the effort to indirectly measure ethnocentrism – to tap ethnocentric pride and prejudice without referring directly to ethnic minorities or majorities. Both RWA and SDO achieve that aim. And research has consistently shown that RWA and SDO are weakly associated with each other, so that, in many respects, SDO is quite different from RWA. The gist of the difference is this: People who score high on RWA tend to be self-righteous and moralistic. But people who score high on SDO, when they are guaranteed anonymity, do not talk self-righteously; they do not portray themselves in a morally positive light.

High RWA scorers say, "Bad people should be punished and suppressed, not because we enjoy punishing or suppressing them – that would be cruel – but because that's what they deserve. We're the good people and that is simply our duty." That mentality differs markedly from the SDO worldview. High SDO scorers say that morality is for simpletons – that the world is divided *not* between good and evil, but between strength and weakness. Unlike high RWA scorers, they care only about the difference between winners and losers. They see themselves as winners, and most other people – *including high RWA scorers* – as losers.

The discovery of SDO was a critical breakthrough. We now know that authoritarian traits are not unique to a single personality type. Instead of facing a monolithic "authoritarian personality," we confront a spectrum of personal dispositions. And SDO and RWA also divide into subgroups. High SDOs tend to cluster around either (1) opposition to equality or (2) support for in-group dominance, while high RWAs include what Altemeyer calls "wild cards" – authoritarians who *rebel* against authorities they regard as too soft. All these tendencies are instances of what I call authority fetishism. Authority is fetishized by many people, in many ways – and the better we understand this fetishism, the better our chance of undoing it.

There is still much to learn. In 2011, with my associates Eric Hanley and Mick McWilliams, I submitted nine questions drawn from the RWA and SDO scales to the American National Election Study, which has surveyed public attitudes since 1948. Last fall we learned that all nine of these questions were included in the 2013 ANES survey. This means that we now have extensive new data from the recent past – and, since the RWA and SDO scales had never before been included in a major national survey, we have the chance to learn something new. Preliminary data analysis suggests that our "RWA_5" and "SDO_4" scales both outperform traditional ANES measures with respect to predicting racial prejudice.

Authority *Sans Phrase*

Oddly, authority and authoritarianism are almost never studied simultaneously. Authority, as most famously defined by Max Weber, is domination that is "legitimate" in the sense that it depends on the consent of the governed. In other words, authority is enjoyed by people whom the public "authorizes" to rule. Since people with authoritarian tendencies are likelier than average to regard domination in general as legitimate, and to "authorize" dictatorship in particular, it might seem natural to study authority, in part, by exploring the psychological dispositions that impel support for antidemocratic rule. But alas, a disciplinary divide is found here. Sociologists study authority, psychologists study authoritarianism and never, it seems, shall the twain meet.

Nonetheless: I would argue that authority fetishism is the secret truth of many forms of authority. So-called "traditional authority," for example, rises on the foundation of mass support for ruling castes that are regarded, and treated, as pre-eminent by virtue of their magical or divine endowment. So-called "charismatic authority" springs from mass support for aspiring rulers who say their personal magic or right cancels, and replaces, the waning authority of traditional rulers. The point is that authority is conferred by the public, and that authority is strongest when the public is psychologically *invested* in treating and regarding its rulers as innately supreme.

In what follows, I will use Max Weber's typology of authority as the framework for our discussion. This typology is imperfect in some ways, but it is also conceptually rich. For our purposes, Weber's categories offer structure and nuance to the issues under consideration.

Traditional authority. This is what Weber calls the authority of "the eternal yesterday." The ways we inherit from the past are sacred to us, and therefore become traditional. Did you know that the word "traditional" has the same root as "trade" and "traitor"? The Latin "trad-" refers to something handed from one person or generation to another. Tradition thus denotes something handed down from the past, just as trade denotes something handed from one person to another; and the word "traitor" derives from the word *"traditor,"* which refers to someone who hands secrets to an enemy.

Many traditions are held to be sacred, and it is that quality which gives them authority in our eyes. Consider lines of royal authority. To this day, many people can recite the history of the kings and occasional queens of England. The underlying idea is that royal status is passed down from one generation to the next. Elizabeth, at present, has been queen so long that it is now almost traditional to ask whether Prince Charles will ever become King. This family drama is a faint survival of traditional authority, although, now, it more closely resembles a soap opera than an actual form of authority, since the British royal family obviously doesn't rule.

Few scholars can rival the British anthropologist Arthur Maurice Hocart as an analyst of kingship. Since Hocart was never famous, I can't call him forgotten – but he deserves to be discovered. Beginning in the early 1900s, Hocart spent decades in the field (in the Fiji islands, Sri Lanka, Egypt and elsewhere) and he commanded vast stores of classical, cross-cultural, and linguistic insight. Two of his books subject kingship to searching comparative scrutiny; both are remarkable works of the imagination, comparable to the best works of Jane Ellen Harrison, Hendrik Wagenvoort, and Ernst Kantorowicz.

Today, tradition retains only the lingering shadow of the eternal yesterday. Hence, Weber's other categories (charismatic and "legal-rational" authority) are now more immediately relevant. Here, too, obscure figures command our attention – not least, Otto von Gierke, who influenced Weber and deserves our attention as well.

Legal-rational authority. Gierke, who was Weber's older contemporary, wrote a multi-volume study of the Roman origin and subsequent evolution of the concept of legal authority. He showed that Roman lawyers distinguished two basic ways of transferring power from the people to a ruler. The first is *delegation;* the second, *alienation,* consists of surrendering your power permanently.

Power, once alienated, can never be reclaimed, because it now belongs, quite literally, to the ruler. That logic is also reflected in the word *"domination,"* which derives from the Latin word for ownership, *dominium.* Domination is the *ownership of power,* the *legal title to rule.* Acts of alienation confer domination in this strong sense. Delegation is more democratic. Delegation (for example, in the form of an election) transfers rulership to an authority, but only temporarily. The elected ruler is invested with power *conditionally,* for a specified period; the public, which delegates this power, can reclaim it at will.

The rational side of legal-rational authority is the inverse of what we see in traditional and charismatic authority. Rather than supporting candidates who claim magical or divine gifts, rational voters seek evidence of competence and dedication. They support the rule of law for rational reasons, seeing it as a safeguard against self-serving or delusional autocrats. Electoral legal principles of the kind Gierke explained offer rational ways to attain rational ends. For that reason, and fearing charismatic leaders, Weber regarded legal-rational authority as the only form of authority compatible with ethical responsibility.

Much more can be said about legal-rational authority. But rational respect for enacted law is not authority fetishism. Of course, in principle, anything can be fetishized. That includes laws. An example would be the "strict constructionism" of fundamentalist jurists who regard the Constitution as quite literally sacred, beyond change or challenge. Ceding the authority of all future generations to the will of the "founding fathers" is alienation to the *Nth* degree. The irony is that, in this doctrine, rationally constituted law acquires a new kind of traditional authority, and hence becomes an object of fetishism. But consideration of that irony takes us beyond the legal-rational, to Weber's most famous category, charismatic authority. Here, too, an overlooked figure gives us a good point of entry: Moisei Ostrogorski.

Charismatic authority. Ostrogorski, like Gierke, wrote a brilliant, massive opus that deeply influenced Max Weber. This was a two-volume study of party politics in England and the United States. The 135-page closing chapter, in itself, is a stellar contribution to the critique of authority fetishism. Ostrogorski argues that modern society gives rise to what he calls "party fetishism." He says that parties have increasingly become fetish objects, venerated in the way that royal dynasties and priestly castes were venerated in the past. He pairs this point with a sharp criticism of Rousseau's concept of the General Will, which he treats (convincingly, in my opinion) as an authoritarian excuse for rule by ideologues who claim to know the public's "true" wishes better than the public itself.

A century later, a similar critique would apply equally well to the vanguard fetish of Bolshevism, which Trotsky, early in the 20th century, stingingly rebuked as "substitutionism" – that is, the substitution of Proletarian Dictatorship, embodied in the vanguard party, for the will of the actual proletariat. This metaphysic reached a lyrical zenith in the work of Gyorgy Lukács, but it was no less fetishistic in Lenin's writings.

The Rise of Charisma, the Fall of Capitalism?

Charismatic authority is often associated with the potential failure of capitalism. Charismatic parties and leaders, claiming a monopoly of legitimacy, command people to follow them. The chance that this command will be obeyed is clearly a function, in part, of the degree to which people *respond positively* to charismatic claims. Such responses are most likely when people have relatively greater authoritarian tendencies. So charismatic authority is feared, when capitalism wobbles, for much the same reason that authoritarianism is feared at such moments. In my opinion, Weber's critique of charisma helps us understand thi. But this is hard to fully appreciate, since Weber's concept of "charisma" has proven very difficult for people to keep clearly in mind.

What interests Weber is *authority,* which he affirms as a *social* phenomenon. His interest does not revolve around "charisma" in some individual or sub-social sense. "Charismatic authority," like authority *per se,* is not a personal trait but a social right and power that is transferred to leaders by followers. Only people with followers are leaders – and following is a *choice.* That choice transfers power and transforms it into rightful rule. Specifically "charismatic" authorities are those individuals who are chosen to rule because they are thought to have super-normal qualifications, which consist, typically, of divine or magical power.

Aspiring charismatic rulers tell their prospective followers, "We must break from the past, utterly and forever. Neither tradition nor law can save us in this desperate hour. Follow me, for I alone know the path and the truth." In the 20th century, several volcanic movements led by figures of this kind engraved themselves in our memory, and most of them culminated in dictatorships, whether "left-wing" or "right-wing." When we recall Mao or Ho, Hitler or Mussolini, we recall figures who were "charismatic" in the precise Weberian sense that they were entrusted by their followers with personal authority to remake society. "Follow me, follow my party, and we will renew the world."

This "renewed world" is not capitalism as usual. So we return to my starting point. When people think that capitalism is grinding to a halt, they often fear that charismatic dictatorship will take its place – and it is authoritarianism that disposes people to follow dictators. Hence the link between capitalism and authoritarianism is not arbitrary. If capitalism fails, people fear that what will replace it will be toxic. And "toxic" in this context is practically a synonym for "charismatic." People fear that capitalism will fail because the only alternative they can imagine – charismatic authoritarianism – seems worse. Engels once said that our future holds either socialism or barbarism. Charismatic movements, especially in the past century, have given us a very bitter taste of barbarism. Authoritarianism, which is the firewood of that barbarism, requires deeper analysis.

Adorno, Weber, and Beyond

Critical inquiry into charismatic authority and authoritarianism is still in its infancy, despite the chilling fascination exerted, above all, by Hitler and his followers. Few of the best insights to date have been widely appreciated. Even Weber's canonical work on charisma has been studied only fitfully, and only a few of the best "Weberians" have carefully studied Weber's massive volumes on charisma, religion, and the capitalist spirit in India and China. The same applies even more to works by scholars who are not widely acclaimed as experts on charisma. Here I would single out Weber's contemporary Émile Durkheim, whose masterpiece, *The Elementary Forms of the Religious Life* (1912), offers an unrivalled account of the Melanesian concept of *mana* (which Weber equates with charisma) and introduces the indispensable notion of collective effervescence. It is the "effervescence" of mass assembly that gives people the feeling that they are subjected to and participate in a power greater than themselves.

Earlier in the conference, we discussed collective effervescence and Durkheim's notion of piacular ritual quite a bit. But Durkheim is seldom studied in connection with authority, just as Henry Dicks is seldom studied in connection with authoritarianism. Even Adorno, despite his celebrity as a philosopher, has been given only modest attention with respect to authoritarianism. Very few scholars have probed Adorno's main contributions to *The Authoritarian Personality* (the notions of "pseudoconservatism," "the usurpation complex," "personalization") and fewer still have explored his invaluable small book on the ultra-right agitator Martin Luther Thomas or his book-length study of authoritarianism in postwar Germany in the collective work *Gruppenexperiment* (1955). Charismatic authority and psychological authoritarianism are dimly appreciated, in other words, partly because Weber and Adorno have not yet been adequately studied. Even scholars who know their work – the example I will give today is Hannah Arendt – do not always build on this work.

Arendt is a major figure, and a creative source of fresh thinking about authority and authoritarianism. Her magnum opus, *The Origins of Totalitarianism* (1951), is a razor-sharp exposition of the concept of totalitarianism. In the hands of grim Cold War liberals like Carl Joachim Friedrich and Zbigniew Brzezinski, this theme could devolve into mere rhetoric. But Arendt's work is seminal. The lengthy final third of her book is scintillating. Coasting on the rapids of a cascading argument, Arendt portrays Nazism as an extremist movement with a spiraling dynamic of nihilistic violence and negativity that prevented it from becoming a "state" or even a normal dictatorship. Stalinism was similar, a whirlpool that drew even its leaders into the vortex. Traditional categories could not pin down the specificity of this perpetual motion and negation.

Emphasizing dynamics enabled Arendt to open a new frontier in the study of charismatic authority and authoritarianism. While she clothed her ideas in different language, it is not artificial to link Arendt to Weber and Adorno, since she was in direct dialogue with each of them. This is not well known, because Arendt did not underscore this point. In the revised edition of *Origins* she deleted key references to Weber, and she offered her most relevant remarks on *The Authoritarian Personality* in an obscure article. But in these texts she made it plain that she was, in fact, contending with the concepts of authoritarianism and charisma.

Authoritarians fetishize authority – but not every kind of authority. Wildcard RWAs idealize iron-fisted rulers but they hate authorities who seem too gentle. Of Weber's ideal-typical forms of authority, two are conventionally fetishized, traditional and charismatic; and in a sense, both are "charismatic," since both are esteemed as divine or magical.

Is it true that charismatic authority is supported, above all, by authoritarianism? Let's consider this carefully. What motives lead people to support potential dictators, or to see them as "charismatic" saviors or miracle workers? We should not simply assume that these motives are always or mainly authoritarian. When a demagogue advocates dictatorship, who finds that promise appealing? People who want dictatorship. When demagogues claim miracle-working powers that qualify them to lead the masses to salvation, who is attracted by that claim? Someone who wants a savior and believes in miracles.

I would be very surprised if ardent support for charismatic dictators could be dissociated from the wish to submit to leaders who reward the "good" while punishing morally deviant outsiders. By the same token it would be remarkable if we did not find *both* RWA and SDO among the psychic forces that inspire people to follow charismatic dictators. If this is true, then authoritarianism and charismatic authority qualify as two aspects of authority fetishism and the traditions associated with Adorno and Weber are enduringly important for inquiry in this fetishism. Arendt saw the relevance of these traditions, even when she opposed them.

Question: I'd like to raise a question about Arendt. What I derive from her work, which is crucial in my teaching, is that the internal processes of totalitarianism generate complicity with the system. That system is a recursive structure which enables those who might be in the middle to enter a gradient toward complicity with the totalitarian system.

Smith: Right, very definitely. Arendt says at one point that, once you're entangled in the policies of the regime, once you're assigned some degree of responsibility, even if you haven't volunteered for that responsibility, you become an accomplice – and it's easy to rationalize that fact. It's easy to internalize the sense that your complicity wasn't just required, it was right.

Question: And the system requires very high-stakes participation in which one's own boundaries of behavior are breached.

Smith: Right. As you make the choices that are demanded by the system, your identity is forged anew. Arendt is particularly good when she explains that Nazism was neither a state or even a party. She says that, of course, Nazism dominated the German state; of course, it took the form of a party. But it was above all a movement, which, like a surging river, carried people along and changed them – not in the sense that they turned into their opposites, but rather that, if they had some susceptibility towards Nazism, the attractive dynamism of the movement brought that susceptibility to the surface.

Question: And she is very good at showing that there is no hypostasized Nazi ideology, that the construction of the processes of what we can expose as ideology are part of the system and the generation of complicity and that as soon as well call it ideology, we're hypostasizing something that falsifies the nature of the system.

Right, that's true as well. If you study the development of Nazi doctrine in the 1930s and after, you will find that there were different power centers in the ideological world: the Amt Rosenberg, and quite a few others. And the Nazis had fixed doctrines on only a few points – the supreme position of the Leader, hatred for the Jews, opposition to finance. They had core principles, but they were also remarkably willing to let competing views jostle for influence.

Question: Can I ask why C. Wright Mills's book *The New Men of Power* isn't listed in your bibliography? Doesn't that book fit in with Arendt, especially when Mills looks at the labor movement and really turns an eye on the authoritarians?
Smith: I know what you mean. But in *The Sociological Imagination,* Mills wrote a line to which I'm profoundly allergic. He calls the public "cheerful robots," which reflects a level of condescension that I find almost incomprehensible.

Question: But can't you find very similar lines in *The Dialectic of Enlightenment?*
Smith: That's true. I'm not contending that any of these figures are entirely consistent. Even Fromm made the shallow claim, which contradicts his own emphasis on personal differences, that "automaton conformity" permeates society. That closely resembles what Mills said. The thinkers I have praised today should not be fetishized; most of them have feet or at least toes of clay. I cite them, not to call attention to them personally, but to anchor some of the substantive points I'm making in history, including intellectual history.

Commodity Fetishism

Now that we have sailed around the island of authoritarianism, we're returning to the mainland of capitalism. As Marx explained, capitalism is the form of society in which wealth takes the form of commodities – mountains and mountains of commodities. The question that Marx poses under the rubric of fetishism, which will be our starting point here, is how people see this world of commodities.

Here's something I've enjoyed doing for a long time. Typically, when I discuss capitalism, I ask people to look around the room to see if they can find anything in sight – anything – that was not bought or sold for money. Anything.

In all the many years I have posed this challenge, I have never yet received an answer besides this: *Everything in sight was produced for exchange.*

That, briefly, is Marx's definition of the commodity. Any labor product that is produced for sale is a commodity. Conversely, anything that is *not* sold, that is simply used, is not a commodity. But the capital fact, so to speak, is that in our society, nearly everything *is* produced for sale – everything, in nearly every room you have ever entered, was produced for exchange, except, say, incidentals like twigs carried in from the yard.

We live in what Marx called the *Waarenwelt* – which means, *commodity world.* When Marx first uses the phrase fetishism, he refers to "the fetishism of the world of the commodities," the *Waarenwelt.* For me, that phrase conjures up images of Disney World. But Commodity World is not fanciful, not a theme park – it's our reality.

The Making and Unmaking of Commodity World

The word "fetishism" derives from the Latin for *making.* It was used by Portuguese voyagers to describe African religion. The idea is that a fetish, or *feitiço,* is an object *made by people* which they think contains supernatural powers. "Fetishism," then, is the system of beliefs that people hold about the fetishes they make. The critical point is that, even though they make these fetishes themselves, people in the grip of fetishism believe that these objects have power *intrinsically.*

Marx, in the opening chapter of *Capital,* criticizes an error that he regards as fundamental to capitalist society. He says, in a note, that people think they are subjects because the king is king. In other words, the king has divine right; the king is inherently royal. This inverts the truth. People think they are subjects because the king is king, but, in reality, the king is only king because the people *think* they are subjects. The authority the king enjoys is *conferred upon him – delegated or alienated to him – by the public itself.* If the public did not obey his commands, he would *have* no power of command. And yet people imagine that the power of command belongs to the king as a fact of nature. It was that kind of illusion to which Marx applied the phrase fetishism.

This might sound like authority fetishism – and it is. Marx's larger point here is that people view authorities and commodities in ways that are structurally isomorphic. He says that commodity producers think they are commodity producers because labor products are commodities by nature. But products, in reality, only become commodities when people exchange them, when they are "treated and regarded" as things with prices. That simple phrase, "treated and regarded," appears in *Capital* more than once; Marx says that, until we treat and regard products as commodities, they remain just labor products.

What's the difference? Well, there is a difference, and it makes a difference. A commodity, Marx says, is an object not only with utility, or usefulness, but with value. Usefulness is easy to understand, and, at first glance, value seems straightforward, too. How much is something worth? Hegel had a phrase that's directly relevant. A labor product, he said, has two dimensions: *first,* what it is, and *second,* what it's worth. Those are the two dimensions of the commodity. Marx says that fetishism is the belief that labor products are *intrinsically* valuable in some definite proportion in relation to other labor products. In his most famous example, he discusses a coat that is equal in value to 20 yards of linen. Not 21 yards, not 19 yards: 20. Fetishism is the belief that the coat and 20 yards of linen are *inherently* equivalent, that they are valuable (and *equally* valuable) by nature. The fetishistic illusion is that commodities have value *within* them, just as fetishes are held to house supernatural powers. In fact, Marx says, products have value only because we treat and regard them as exchangeable. We make them, and, if we share them rather than selling them, they *never* acquire "value" in the market sense. They have uses, but not prices.

Let me be as clear about this as possible. Marx says no two objects are ever materially identical. No two coats are the same, no two 20-yard rolls of linen are the same. Marx insists on the irreducible *particularity* of the world. He says that, in order to regard two distinct things as equal in the dimension of value, we have to *disregard their concrete differences.* We can look at anything that anyone has ever made under a microscope, or under a magnifying glass – and we will never find "equivalence." We can see product's *body* but not its ghostly soul: "value."

Commodities, of course, actually do have values. But that is true only because we exchange them. A coat, once we equate it to 20 yards of linen, is *therefore* worth 20 yards of linen. Marx says that, to become equal as values, things which are materially different must be "forcibly equated." Without a price tag, the product is not a fetish. It is just a useful thing.

Consider, again, the parallel between the king's authority and the commodity's value. If you want to say that the king actually has authority, I won't contradict you. If you want to say that the commodity actually has value, Marx would agree. Authority and value are statuses that people *confer,* respectively, on people and products. The authority is not *in* the person, nor is value *in* the thing. These statuses exist only in society; neither can be found nature. They arise only when people collectively treat and regard *others* as authorities and *products* as commodities.

Let's look at this from another angle. In the matrix, you will see the name of Charles de Brosses, whose book *Du culte des dieux fétiches* called wide attention to the subject of fetishism in 1760. Also influential in this respect was Brodie Cruickshank, who wrote about west African peoples, particularly the Ashanti. Max Weber, who knew quite a lot about fetishism, learned about it largely from Cruickshank. Hegel, characteristically, wrote brilliantly about fetishism (but not very extensively); and I mention Alfred Binet and Sigmund Freud here as a kind of precaution. Nowadays, in the post-Freud era, most listeners hear an echo of Freud in the word *fetishism;* and Freud was extending the work of his predecessor Binet. I would be the last person to cast aspersions on either Binet or Freud. But to grasp Marx, to grasp fetishism in connection with the critique of political economy, we need to set aside Binet and Freud. They used the same word that Marx used and their ideas (especially Binet's) occasionally parallel Marx. But Marx had unique concerns when he spoke about commodity fetishism. He was thinking, above all else, about capitalism's future – which, for people under the spell of fetishism, appears eternal.

Marx says that value takes three fundamental forms: commodities, money, and capital. The commodity is the starting point because, according to Marx, money is also a commodity – the commodity "universally equivalent" to all others in exchange – and capital, in turn, is money invested in production.

Commodities are contradictory unities of usefulness and value. On the one hand they are concrete things that can be used to satisfy human needs; on the other hand, they are bearers of value. If you don't have a value equivalent for the commodity you want, you can't obtain its uses. I sometimes think of value as a force field around the usefulness of the commodity. You walk into a store, you see a sandwich, and you're hungry. But there's a social force field around the sandwich. You can't just take it off the shelf and walk out the door. If you do, a surveillance camera will establish your identity and prove that you took a sandwich without paying for it. The physical act of taking the sandwich has *social* consequences.

In other words: You can't simply appropriate usefulness; you have to pay for it. You must unlock the invisible cabinet to access the thing. You must have the equivalent in your hand, either money (in the typical instances familiar to us) or an ordinary equivalent commodity, in instances of barter.

So, what does it mean to "fetishize" commodities? It means accepting the force field around the product. It means regarding the product as inherently an "equivalent" to other products. Commodity fetishism is the conviction that this social reality is natural. "Products have value," the fetishist thinks. "How could it be otherwise?" Commodity fetishism is the belief that exchange is natural – and, therefore, eternal. We can't rewrite the laws of nature, so what we inherit from nature we must simply endure. Capitalism's destiny, for the commodity fetishist, is already known – to last forever.

Money Fetishism

Most people who discuss commodity fetishism stop with the first form of value, but in Marx's systematic theory there are two others as well. The second value-form is money, which Marx calls the commodity equivalent in some proportion to all others. If you have 20 dollars you can buy 20 yards of linen; if you have 40 dollars you can buy 40 yards of linen; and so on. There is basically nothing that you can't obtain with money. And again, according to Marx, money is itself a commodity. Money arose, Marx says, as one commodity among others.

Take gold. Gold, which is mined, is a labor product with unique properties. Because it is finely divisible, it can be minted in many different sizes and shapes. That permits gold to serve as an equivalent, in varying proportions, to all other commodities. Small amounts of gold, which require only small amounts of mining labor, are equivalent in value to other products of little value. Larger amounts of gold, which require larger quantities of labor, are equivalent in value to products of greater value.

So far, so good. But Marx's theory is not just about equivalence; he also posits commodity *fetishism*. To appreciate that point properly we have to consider the *people* who make commodities. When Marx first talks about fetishism, he says, consider not just the linen or the coat, but the weaver who makes the linen, the tailor who makes the coat. These are real people and they have a real connection. What on the surface appears to be a relationship of equivalence between two things is actually, beneath the surface, a social relationship between two people mediated by the things they make and exchange. This gives the world of commodities a topsy-turvy appearance. In technical terms, Marx says, this is a world in which *things* appear to have social relations and *people* appear to have material or thinglike relations (which, by the way, is what the term "reification" means, since "re" is Latin for "thing"). The producers are connected, but also separated, by the products that stand between them. Only the linen and the coat appear to have direct unmediated ties.

Let's suppose you are the weaver in Marx's example, and that you're asked: "What's the value of your 20 yards of linen?" If you answer, simply, "One coat," then Marx says you are manifesting commodity fetishism – because you think your own labor product finds its actual value, its identity, in the realm of value, in this physically distinct thing, the coat. Of course, there could be a very insightful weaver who thinks, "My 20 yards of linen actually has a relationship of equivalence with this one particular coat only because society renders my concrete labor, and the tailor's concrete labor, into matching quantities of abstract labor." What if Marx were a weaver? He clearly would not just think, "Oh, my bolt of linen is worth a coat." So it's certainly possible to see beyond surface appearances. But Marx says, let's look at what happens normally.

In most situations, when people are asked, "What's your coat worth?" they say "$29.95." You will seldom hear them ponder the metaphysics of value or the sociological status of products with prices. "What's the coat worth?" "It's worth $29.95." If you think the dollar value is actually *in* your product, Marx says you are fetishizing a thing that you actually made yourself – that the value you gave the product yourself (by working on it) appears to be a kind of fate, something that you simply discover in the market. You're at the mercy of whatever price it will bring. In our society, of course, that's true. But it isn't natural.

Marx says that seeing beyond this "naturalness" is easiest when we are still at the barter stage – when we simply trade one commodity for another. In that situation, if you think about the coat, it's hard to forget the tailor. She's standing right there, you can talk to her directly. If you wish, you can even agree to change the normal principles of exchange. You can ignore the average quantity of labor that goes into your products. If the tailor needs 30 yards of linen, and you have 30 yards, and you really want the coat – you can simply ignore the fact that, in normal cases, one coat is worth 20 yards of linen. The exchange can take place at whatever price you agree upon.

In cases like this one, the unfettered choices of the exchange partners can overrule considerations and calculations of "equivalence." You can agree, "Let's not worry about what 'the market' would tell us to do." When people relate to each other face-to-face, as fellow producers who are also fellow buyers, they can see beyond the surface, beyond the relations between their products. Even here there may be a tendency to fetishize the linen and the coat, to assume that the two products "really" have a natural relationship of equivalence, which the weaver and tailor are willfully violating; but this fetishistic tendency does not become the stable, *normal* way of seeing the world until money becomes the commodity equivalent to all others. Facing a buyer with cash in hand isn't the same as facing the tailor who made the coat. And facing a coat is far simpler than facing abstract, mysterious money.

Marx says that, when commodities routinely exchange for money, the chain of mystifications is doubled. Now, the weaver's counterpart in the exchange is not a fellow producer but a consumer. Instead of *making* the money, rather than minting or printing money, the buyer simply appears, money in hand – and that money seems automatically and obviously valuable by nature. In fact, value appears to *be* the nature of money, since it is used only in exchange. Even if, over time, the value of a dollar rises or falls, a "dollar" is always and only something valuable. Each dollar goes through exchange after exchange. It never ceases to have value, and it is never used for anything except exchange.

Money is also profoundly anonymous. It changes hands again and again, going from person to person. As money circulates in this way, people have an increasingly hard time visualizing the labor that produces money. Money just seems to *be* "value," pure and simple.

This appearance Marx calls money fetishism, which is, he says, commodity fetishism raised to the second power. And even harder to fathom, he says, is the third form of fetishism, which he calls "capital fetishism." This is an essential concept, which only a few people have expertly discussed. One of them is Moishe Postone who published a masterful essay, "Anti-Semitism and National Socialism," in 1980. Also notable in this respect is an excellent essay, "Hostile Brothers," which the economist Fred Moseley published in 2002.

Capital Fetishism

So, without further ado: What is capital fetishism? This is a major topic, which could detain us for a while. But very simply, to start with: According to Marx, capital is money invested in production. This investment takes a double form. On the one hand, capital purchases "means of production." That phrase refers to what we can elegantly call the "stuff" that goes into production: machinery, land, buildings, equipment, materials, etc. And, second, capital purchases labor-power – in other words, it hires workers. So capital buys stuff and hires workers. The result is "the capitalist production process," which is Marx's subtitle for Volume 1 of *Capital*. The aim is to accumulate capital by making and selling commodities. This is what is accurately and concisely called "the profit motive." Workers are hired by capitalists to make commodities with, and from, the means of production.

Obviously, I don't have time now to allude to more than the rudiments of Marx's core theory, but I need to say enough to make the concept of capital fetishism intelligible. The key is that capitalists accumulate capital by extracting surplus value from their employees. This is the process Marx calls exploitation. In other words, surplus comes from unpaid surplus labor by the workers, whose products are more valuable than their wages.

Surplus value in capitalist society takes the form of a *money* surplus. (In earlier societies, surplus often took the physical form of surplus products. But our society runs on money.) Part of that money surplus accrues to the capitalist in the form of profit. But since capitalists typically owe money to lenders and landlords, part of the surplus goes to bankers in the form of interest and another part goes to landlords in the form of rent. In short, surplus value sustains not only capitalists but bankers and landlords. But at the surface of experience, bankers and landlords seem very different from capitalists. While capitalists are closely identified with industry, bankers and landlords seem remote from production. The reality is that capitalist production *requires* lenders and landlords *as well as* industrialists. But that is difficult to discern. Marx says that, given this difficulty, we need not just political economy but a "critique of political economy," if we hope to see beneath the surface to the underlying unity of profit, rent, and interest. Capitalists, bankers, and landlords are co-participants in the capitalist production process. But that isn't what people ordinarily see, at first or even second glance.

Industrialists, who steer the production process, appear to earn their profits as a kind of wage for enterprise. Landlords may not contribute quite as directly, but developers, at least, play an obvious role in building factories and infrastructure. Bankers, on the other hand, seem wholly parasitic. They thrive in what Marx called the "occult" realm of money – they make money *from* money, by arcane financial sleight of hand, without ever putting their shoulders to the wheel of production. Or so it seems. This appearance, Marx says, is deceptive, another instance of fetishism. In reality, capitalists typically invest with money borrowed from lenders. Interest is hence as much a natural outcome of the extraction of surplus value as profit. But this is rarely what people see or say. Bankers, more often than not, are reviled, while capitalists, "captains of industry," may even be revered.

This is a key point for insight into Marx, who is very famous for a category that does not capture his thinking well: "false consciousness." It is assumed, in connection with this phrase, that people whose consciousness is false – cheerful robots? – simply accept capitalism lock, stock, and barrel. Rather than recognizing that capitalism is contrary to their best interests, they applaud it for advancing productivity and morality. That, in essence, is what people think Marx meant by "false consciousness." But in fact, in his major, substantive texts, that is not what Marx portrays. His critical theory focuses on capital fetishism, which, upon reflection, we recognize as a phenomenon of *ambivalence*. Most people, most of the time, have mixed feelings about capitalism. They are aware of the evils of capitalism, but they either regard them as unavoidable or blame them on bankers. And when only bankers are blamed, industrialists are exonerated.

In *Theories of Surplus Value,* which he wrote as an addendum to *Capital,* Marx explains this point very clearly, above all in the final chapter of Vol. 3, "Revenue and Its Sources." Here he argues that capital fetishism is not simply an extension of commodity fetishism – the belief, namely, that production is always by nature commodity production and that commodity production is therefore always ultimately capitalist – but that it is also a very specific failure to grasp the character of "capital." Investment doesn't happen in a vacuum. Investors need money, much of which they get from bankers and other lenders; and they need offices and factories, which they often rent from landlords. All three of these groups (investors, lenders, and landlords) are integral to capital accumulation. All three survive, and thrive, on surplus value extracted from workers, which they share, like booty divided by pirates. But people in thrall to capital fetishism *idealize* capital and capitalists. They have trouble countenancing the idea that capitalists resemble pirates. They think, instead, that capitalists, like workers, are gouged by bankers and landlords. So, rather than criticizing capitalism, they blame *finance* capital.

Bankers, who loom large in public discourse, can seem innately unproductive. Capitalists enjoy a kind of "virtue by association" with production, but what, people plaintively ask, do bankers produce? The capital fetishist error, Marx says, is to reply: "Nothing."

Where do investors get their money? Often, typically, from bankers. If investment makes the world go 'round – and that is, in essence, what capital fetishists think – then it is not irrelevant to note that productive investment is a team effort. Industrialists and bankers pool the financial resources that enable the industrialist to set the labor process in motion by purchasing labor power and means of production.

Capital fetishism has roots in ancient, "anti-chrematistic" hostility towards money-lenders. But the modern phenomenon, in which productive and unproductive capitalists are sharply contrasted as moral opposites, is truly modern. I want to call your attention now to a very fundamental transition that occurred in the latter half of the 19th century, namely, the emergence of anti-bank politics. Anti-bank politics grew very powerful for the first time in the 20th century. The young Adolf Hitler, in fact, was recruited to the group that became the Nazi party by a reactionary economist, Gottfried Feder, who was an ardent capital fetishist. Feder persuaded Hitler that Germany faced two fundamental enemies: the "Red International" of socialist workers and the "Golden International" of Jewish bankers. This remained core Nazi doctrine until the bitter end; and the fact that bankers were now equated with Jews was not incidental to that doctrine. How did that equation come to life?

Capital Fetishism and Anti-Semitism

One early manifestations of mass anti-bank sentiment arose during the panic of 1819 in the United States. In Germany, the "Hep Hep" riots in that same year prefigured the kind of radical anti-Semitism that would later be coupled with anti-bank antipathies. The two sentiments melded for the first time in central Europe in the 1840s, when anger over railroad construction took an anti-bank and anti-Jewish turn. But it wasn't until the 1880s, when the European depression that had begun in 1873 was compounded by a stock market crash, that anti-bank politics became merged with anti-Semitism. Until that point, anti-bank politics, in the U.S. especially, had been detached from ethnic prejudice.

But as the depression lingered, finger pointing became common. It was widely felt that someone was to blame. The question was, who? And how did people reach the conclusions they did?

When I first explored this question, I assumed that the Paris Commune of 1871 played a catalytic role in fusing capital fetishism with anti-Semitism. I knew that, in the 1870s, Marx was widely blamed by right-wingers for inspiring the socialism of the Commune, and Marx, of course, would soon become a hated symbol for anti-Semites everywhere. Since conspiracist animosity towards bankers, socialists, and Jews converged in roughly this period, I guessed that the Commune had contributed to precipitating this convergence. But that proved to be a poor guess.

In fact, when I tried to ascertain exactly when mass anti-Semitism fused with anti-bank feeling, I was surprised to find that this took place in the 1880s, and not earlier. Here's how I reached that conclusion. The Paris Commune was a quasi-revolution in what became the first heartland of mass anti-Semitism: France. This quasi-revolution, which was led by workers and pursued egalitarian ends, was soon crushed in blood. 30,000 leaders and activists were killed when the Commune was suppressed – a larger number, in fact, than died in the Reign of Terror after the French revolution of 1789. The Commune was a stunning and traumatic event, which precipitated a vast amount of reactionary paranoia. And yet, when I combed through trial records and other archival materials concerning the Commune, I was unable to find any real evidence of anti-Semitism.

The phrase "anti-Semitism" wasn't coined until 1879. But even the simple word "Jew" (*juif*) scarcely if ever appears in the voluminous provincial records that recount the trials of Communards. Jews, as Jews, were seldom accused of being arch-conspirators or subversives. France was effervescent with right-wing conspiracy theory, but the leading targets of this conspiracy theory were not Jews. Is anyone here familiar with the word *pétroleuses?* The *pétroleuses* were nightmare figures for the French bourgeoisie in the final days of the Commune. They were fantasy arsonists, plebeian women armed with incendiary devices which they hurled into cellars. Though historians can find no evidence of such *pétroleuses*, fevered rumors gave them imaginary life. So conspiracies were alleged, but not Jewish conspiracies. Even Marx, who was widely castigated, was castigated as a radical, not as a Jew.

A decade later, however, when France suffered a major crash, public opinion turned decisively against finance. At that point a kind of ideological arms race erupted, pitting anti-Semites against anti-Masons. The question was whether banking was dominated by Jews or freemasons. The reality, of course, was that most bankers were neither – but that didn't satisfy the restless, aggrieved public. Finger pointing devolved from realistic doubt about the soundness of the capitalist economy to capital fetishism infused with paranoia. Step 1 was to blame finance rather than capitalism. Step 2 was to personalize finance, so that bankers were blamed, not just banks. Step 3 was to demonize these bankers, who came to appear, in the lurid public imagination, as malign, shadowy figures.

Initially, freemasons were more often indicted for the sins of finance than Jews. But for every gutter publicist who scapegoated the masons, another singled out the Jews. Ultimately, Jews were the unhappy winners of this peculiar unpopularity contest. Though anti-masonic sentiment remained lively, Jews and banks became virtually synonymous. Capital fetishism and anti-Semitism cross-pollinated. The consequences, as we all know, were fateful.

This is not to suggest that modern anti-Semitism is *reducible* to capital fetishism. Paranoid hostility towards Jews can be found in many other places and periods, with many independent roots. The association of Jews with money dates back to medieval times, and flourished for centuries before capitalism arrived on the scene. But in modern discourse, Jews are equated not simply with money, but with finance capital. In the German tradition, a sharp distinction was made between *"schaffende"* and *"raffende"* capital – that is, between productive capital and rapacious capital. Rapacious *capital,* not just "money," is what modern anti-Semites associate with Jews. In my opinion, this association is colored by capital fetishism as well as by ethnocentrism. Interestingly, Marx's friend Engels wrote fascinating essays about the anti-Jewish agitation of the late 1840s in which he came to the brink of saying precisely this. His reflections on the poetry of Karl Isidor Beck deserve particular attention. Engels was concerned by the anti-Jewish bigotry that tainted the populist opposition to railroad construction in this period, and in discussing this bigotry he stopped just short of concluding that capital fetishism and anti-Semitism have the potential to merge and become very, very lethal.

While capital fetishism and anti-Semitism have an affinity, they remain distinct. Capital fetishism can be entirely free of anti-Semitism. Bankers can be opposed simply as bankers. Complaints about "vulture capital" or "Bankenstein's monster" are not automatically signs of anti-Semitism. It is also clear that anti-bank conspiracy theory can target figures besides Jews. We saw that, in France, Masons were also targets of paranoid abuse – and the same was true in the United States. Has anyone here heard of the New York politician Thurlow Weed? In the 1820s and 1830s, Weed led the Anti-Masonic Party, which ultimately merged into the Whig Party and then, when the Whigs split over the issue of slavery, became one of the tributary streams flowing into what became the Republican Party. Weed himself remained a leading Republican until his opposition to Radical Reconstruction sidelined him after the Civil War. In other words, anti-Masonry was a force to reckon with in the U.S., too – and here, too, it was associated with anti-bank sentiments.

What I find really striking here is that, *structurally,* anti-bank politics in this country closely resembled anti-bank politics in Europe. This was true even though in Europe, but not in the United States, anti-bank sentiment gave a powerful impetus to the anti-Semitism that cast such long shadows over the twentieth century. Capital fetishism has been a galvanizing force on both continents, but with different consequences; and it remains influential today, as we see in the fact that "financialization" has been the singular focus of so much attention since the start of the Great Recession in 2007–2008. Of course, much of what we have experienced *has been* specifically "financialized"; but, rather than betraying capitalism, that financialization *stems from* the inner nature of capitalism, which is *always* torn between production and speculation. Capitalists are in business to make money; and if production is decreasingly profitable, they invest speculatively in finance rather than productively in manufacturing. "Financialization" is thus a *symptom* of a deeper problem – namely, that investing in capitalist production now seems *less profitable* to investors than speculative investment in derivatives, collateralized debt, junk bonds, hedge funds, and so on.

Why does speculative finance appear to offer a better profit rate than production? One obvious possibility is that industrial profit rates actually *have* fallen, as Marx said we should expect. If that is true (which I have argued elsewhere is likely), then we can regard "financialization" not as a betrayal of capitalism but as its natural consequence.

Capitalist production is thus not the *antidote* to financial crisis, as capital fetishism would suggest. It is, rather, the *source* of crisis.

Investment, in a phrase, makes the world *go aground.* The question, then, is what happens when capitalism no longer has a future. Will we opt for authoritarianism? Or will we build a society that is post-authoritarian as well as post-capitalist?

Parting Thoughts

We remain in the midst of a major global crisis. The "Great Recession" that began in 2007 is still unspooling. Historical levels of unemployment are idling workers in South Africa, Spain, and many other countries. It is often said that, in the history of capitalism, only the Great Depression was worse. And seven years later, we remain mired in crisis.

In some respects, today's crisis may even exceed the Great Depression. Capitalism now encircles the globe in a way that was not true in 1929. China, India,

Russia and Brazil were not then pivots of capitalism. There were many corners of the world that capitalism had not reached. But now, nearly the whole planet is capitalist. The phrase *Waarenwelt,* in Marx's day, was a figure of speech, since much of the world was not yet engulfed in commerce. But today the world is a pulsing lattice of commodity chains, speeding products from one market to another across oceans and continents. Commodities now meet their equivalents very, very far from where they were produced. This might seem like strength; but it is also weakness, since commodity chains have chain *reactions.* A collapse of production or circulation in one place can shake the *Waarenwelt* as a whole. That seems to be what we are witnessing today, as industry continues to slow. In countless places, countless people have lost jobs, wages, and social benefits. Untold tens of millions of people are out of work and out of luck.

Many of the themes I have discussed are relevant to this crisis. But I want to conclude by focusing briefly on public sentiment. A recent survey found a high level of prejudice towards Jews in countries which, collectively, contain most of the world's population. If this study is credible, over a billion people are willing to say "probably" when they are asked to take a stand on the likely truth or falsity of nearly a dozen hostile stereotypes about Jews. Two of these stereotypes are especially popular: the notion that Jews have too much power over global finance, and the claim that Jews are the cause of many of the world's woes.

I cite this point to indicate the promise of a concept like capital fetishism. While we plainly need to grasp capital accumulation, we also need to grasp capital fetishism, if we hope to anticipate how people will respond when accumulation slows.

Often, when capitalism stumbles, people blame scapegoats. If Marx is right, the main tendency is to blame bankers; and when bankers are equated with Jews, anti-banking sentiment quickly becomes anti-Semitism, which Marx's colleague August Bebel called "the socialism of fools." Anger towards "Jewish bankers" substitutes for socialism; anti-Semitism takes the place of what otherwise might have become anti-capitalism.

Will capitalism stumble? At this moment capitalists are employing a shrinking percentage of the world's public. Even in China, the world's greatest engine of industry, trillions of dollars have been diverted from production. Many tens of millions of people who want jobs are now in limbo because no one will hire them. Why is capital leaving so many people jobless? Is the system slowing? Is there a long-term trend for capitalism to grind to a halt? That clashes with the way most economists frame the issue. For the economics profession, change is cyclical. Rates go up before they go down, and vice versa. Essentially, economists tend to assume that what goes up must come down – but also, that what goes down *will later go up again.*

Well, maybe. Marx's perspective, the premise of the critique of the political economy, is that capitalism is a system with historic tendencies, not simply a roller coaster. Marx says that capitalism does indeed have a tendency to slow down and, ultimately, stop, because at a certain point capitalists become increasingly reluctant to invest. When the profit per unit of investment falls so low that even a minor market failure can threaten the overall viability of profits, money-owners look for better bets – typically, in the sphere of speculation.

Here's a thought experiment. If you read *The Wall Street Journal* or *The Financial Times,* you encounter hedge funds, sovereign wealth funds, and the investment arms of major corporations, like GE Capital. You will learn that Investment Firm A "has $120 billion under management" while Investment Firm B "manages 2 trillion dollars." But have you ever heard of an investment firm building a factory or investing in production?

When I pose that question, people are usually surprised. An investment fund? Invest in production? What a strange thought! But why should we find that surprising? Yes, oceans of money now scurry around the globe, chasing "yield" in nearly every arena except production – in currency markets, bond markets, and so on. But if the goal is to make money, why don't they make products and sell them? Once, that was normal – making money the old fashioned way. But no longer. Today, money owners are eager to trade in equities, but reluctant, it seems, to produce commodities.

Have you followed the recent phase of so-called "quantitative easing"? Basically, the Federal Reserve Bank has been pumping new money into the banks at the rate of $85 billion every month for over two years. Lately, they have begun to "taper" this spending – they call this "The Taper" – by $10 billion per month. The market hates "The Taper" – but well over $2 trillion has already been spent in exchange for distressed bonds.

Remember "The Sequester"? That was a recent phase when many federal programs were cut because Washington was short of cash. Do you know how much money was saved by The Sequester? $85 billion – exactly what the Fed has been pouring into the banks *each month for over two years.* The Fed Board of Governors said they were pumping money into the banks in the hope that the banks would lend more freely to businesses, which would stimulate production, so that jobs would be created.

Well, it hasn't happened. And since I begin to hear myself giving the talk about economics that I promised not to give – I'll pause. (*laughter*) Thanks to everyone for being so patient.

Question: So now we have the famous "jobless recovery." The term you used earlier was "real expulsion."
Smith: Right, you're referring to an earlier conversation.

Question: I'm curious: Everything you said points towards something beyond capital that is even uglier – an authoritarian system with anti-Semitic, anti-bank anti-speculator fantasies. Is that right?

Smith: Well, I don't mean to imply that authoritarianism is the obvious sequel if capitalism falls. Engels famously said that, if capitalism fails, it will be replaced by either socialism or barbarism. By socialism he meant sharing wealth and power; by barbarism, he meant many things we can visualize.

The data we gathered last year is encouraging if you're pro-democracy. Until now, it has been thought that the median point on the spectrum would tilt slightly towards authoritarianism. But now we have national data, so we can test that assumption. It turns out that, on average – in the United States in 2013, relying on our short RWA and SDO measures – people tilt a bit *away* from authoritarianism. In Greece, Golden Dawn has been getting massive attention, even though they got just 10% of the vote while the leftwing party, Syriza, won three times as many votes. So I want to caution against undue alarmism. There are a great many people of good will and democratic intent, and it is absolutely unclear to me what would happen if the economy faltered on a grand scale: Perhaps socialism, perhaps barbarism, perhaps something else.

Meanwhile, since you raise the issue, I'll add a comment about "real expulsion." Capitalism couldn't have started in the first place without the expropriation of farmers. It's very simple. Just a few centuries ago nearly everyone on the planet lived on farms and grew food to subsist. But since the 16th century, farmers have been forced from the land in ever-growing numbers – and if you don't have a farm, you need a job. When you get that job, you become a "proletarian." That transition, from farm to job, happened on a vast scale well into the 20th century. But today, and this is an accelerating process, people are losing their jobs. I call this "the second expropriation."

When your great-grandparents lost their land, your grandparents typically found jobs and your parents also had jobs. But now, you've lost your job, with no clear prospect of being rehired. To my way of thinking, this is a second, and graver, expropriation. Farmers who lost their land had some chance of getting a job, but people who lose their jobs don't get land. So what happens then? A book called *Expulsions* by the sociologist Saskia Sassen just appeared. I haven't had a chance to read it yet, but a quick scan shows that Sassen is keenly aware that people are being expelled *en masse* from the labor process.

Here's a related point in connection with austerity politics. Orthodox postwar economics under the sign of Keynes held that in a downturn the economy should be stimulated. But we've been observing a curious phenomenon in the Great Recession. This downturn has yielded the opposite of stimulus – austerity – in many places. Now, when the economy throws people out of the work, the austerity state causes many more people to lose their jobs, which is an outright "second expropriation," or drives down wages, which I see as a partial expropriation.

Now, why is this happening? One factor might be authoritarianism, since research shows that many legislators are acutely authoritarian. In his new book, *Stress Test,* former Treasury Secretary Timothy Geithner calls austerity advocates "austerians" – and I consider it likely that austerian personality traits play a direct role in austerity politics Much of what austerity imposes has the ring of the punitive. But I'll suggest another answer as well, namely, that the state appears to have entered into a sharp fiscal crisis.

Take a glance at the final box in my Table. The problem, in a nutshell, is that states need money, and historically that revenue has come largely from taxes. But what happens when tax revenues run short? What happens when fewer workers have jobs and those workers have lower wages? Clearly, they become a declining revenue source. And what happens if corporations find tax loopholes? Just two days ago *The Wall Street Journal* highlighted "tax inversions," in which U.S. corporations purchase foreign firms which don't have U.S. tax obligations; the parent companies transfer capital abroad, and taxes are evaded.

So then: If states can no longer obtain the money they need by taxing capital or labor, where do they get it? They borrow it. Kevin Amidon said yesterday that a bond is essentially a promissory note to repay a loan. That's accurate; and governments today are increasingly borrowing from so-called bond markets. That means that governments are borrowing from wealthy lenders. Austerity policies, I contend, are largely driven by the need to retain favor with these lenders.

Assume that you run a state. To get money in the future, you will need new loans. But unless you repay today's loans, no one will lend to you tomorrow. And how can you repay your loans if tax revenues are down? By a scavenge operation called "austerity" – you cut wages, fire public workers, and squeeze money from the poor by raising sales taxes. That, at least, will get you some of the money you need to repay bond investors.

This is extraordinarily harsh; and it is also catastrophically short sighted. Government bonds, in my opinion, are increasingly and obviously sub-prime investments. Who is going to risk a trillion dollars on government bonds when states all over the world are slashing wages and displacing workers? You can never effectively raise revenue for long by scavenging falling wages, firing workers who still pay taxes, and squeezing the poor. And once the tax base is cut to the bone, even scavenging becomes impossible.

Question. I was glad to see you emphasize the capital fetish. I want to revisit how we understand commodity fetishism. Aren't there really two things going on in Marx that we could distinguish? One, let me suggest, has to do with what actually happens and the other concerns how people think about what happens. What actually happens is that, as bearers of value, commodities are fetishes. That is to say, they have power, purchasing power. When Marx says that your social clout is in your pocket, I think that is the primary meaning of the fetish character of the commodity. In this kind of society, since production is organized this way, it is inescapable that labor products, having that social form of labor, will be invested with this power. We might call it purchasing power.

Sometimes, when you talked about this, I was reminded of Max Stirner – if we just think about things differently, they would go away. No, I think Marx's point is that when you organize production along capitalist lines, it isn't a question of how you think about it. Commodity circulation is like a big electromagnet – generating a force. I think that's the primary meaning. With respect to how people think, classical Ricardian theory of value is fetishistic because Ricardians think that you put labor in and then things have value. That's a misunderstanding. So I think there are two things going on here.

Smith: I accept your premise that there are two things going on, but I'm going to argue that they are integrally connected in the following way.

First of all, does money have value in our society? The key phrase here is "in our society." The answer is absolutely yes. Does the king have authority in a genuine, robust monarchy? The answer is absolutely yes. But I contend that both value and authority are socially constructed. That doesn't make them any less real, but they are only real for this moment in history. Outside society, outside this historical phase, products often do not have "value" in Marx's sense. And the disappearance of monarchy from society is already nearly complete.

The issue here is the degree to which thought is *social,* that is, collective. If only two or three people think in fetishistic ways, that has no effect on the world. No one has to notice and, if they change their minds, the phenomenon vanishes. But when treating and regarding products as commodities becomes normal, they acquire a status that far transcends the ability of individuals to think differently. No individuals can just think differently and secede from commodity relations. So you're clearly right in this sense, that now, when everything we see is made and sold for money, if you choose not to believe that value is natural and eternal, you're like a bird beating its wings on the windows of a passing train – your choice has no power.

This takes us back to the sociological concept of "social construction." As individuals, we lack the power to delete the social status from a person or thing. That status is real in our society. Marx's premise is that fetishism is the thought process that confers the status of *value* on the product. This process is especially important when the *Waarenwelt* is first constituted, because, at first, products are only commodities when small groups of people treat and regard them as things for sale. But today, since the world of commodities already exists, it has an inertial force, a staying power, all its own. Commodities exist as values whether or not a few people think in fetishistic ways. That value status is now independent of the opinions of small groups. When we fetishize products, we persist in the belief that they are naturally and forever bearers of value; we thereby *reinforce* the system of commodity relations. But my opinion as a solo individual has only a vanishingly small effect.

Here's another thought experiment. What if we had a science fiction moment tomorrow and, when everyone woke up, they had forgotten that products have value? What if they had forgotten about money? It would be like waking up from a nightmare. For eons, there *were* no commodities; there simply was no money. Even today, if people did not treat and regard labor products as commodities, they wouldn't *be* commodities; they wouldn't have that social status.

It isn't either/or. It isn't that money *has* value, and that how we think about it doesn't matter. And it also isn't true that money would simply vanish if a few people stopped believing in it. Money has value because, for centuries, people treated and regarded labor products as commodities, and money emerged from that history.

Question: But it's not just how you think about it, it's how you treat it. When you organize a production process, you are precommensurated, you're saying, "How much am I going to spend?" In other words, it's not just thinking about it, it's the way everything is organized, too.

Smith: Absolutely. In simple terms, treating a product as a commodity means exchanging it for something regarded as an equivalent. *Treating* in this sense is *trading.* When you trade 20 yards of linen for a coat, that's an action – specifically, it's the action of handing your linen to the tailor, to the person who made the coat. Technically, Marx says that, when you exchange your product, you render the concrete labor that went into it qualityless, you transform your concrete labor into labor that is socially abstract.

I like to say that, in commodity society, *abstraction* is an *action.* And not just any action – specifically, the action is *exchange.* Exchange is the moment when you choose to disregard what is secondary for your purposes, namely the usefulness, the specificity of the product. You are not personally planning to use your linen as linen; you plan to sell it. So you concentrate on what is, for you, the most salient aspect of the product.

In Hegel's terms, you're interested in "what the product is *worth,*" not "what it *is.*" And your counterpart, the coat-maker, the tailor, thinks similarly – she wants linen, not another coat. Tailors make coats to *sell* them, not wear them.

Here's a seldom-noticed point. The first chapter of *Capital* in the first German edition is slightly different than Chapter 1 in the third edition, which is what most people read. That first edition is 100% compatible with the third edition and includes some phrases that are very important, including, for example, Marx's statement that value is "a thing of thought."

When Marx said that, he was not echoing Stirner. He was not implying that ideas are the motor of society, or that thought alone can change the world. But he did not think that labor products embody abstract labor naturally. No product has equivalence in nature. It's only because we treat them as commodities – by exchanging them – that they have equivalence. This is a quality found only in the market, not in nature.

In the book Marx wrote before *Capital,* which we know under the clumsy title *A Contribution to the Critique of Political Economy,* Marx says that exchange is an action that "forcibly equalizes" things which are not naturally equal. No two things will never be exactly alike in nature, they can only share an identity in society. We *force* them to share a common identity. Does that just happen? No, it also happens in part because we *make* it happen. When products are actively treated and regarded as commodities, they acquire that status. That entails both *action,* "treating," and *ideation,* "regarding." Society, today, is the crystallized result of past "treating and regarding."

In the sixteenth century, as Max Weber once said, people had to *exert* themselves to build capitalism, but now, centuries later, we have no choice – capitalism has become a "vast cosmos" that envelops us from birth to death. That formula is very Marx-like. For Marx, social statuses that seem natural and fixed result from of centuries of action and ideation. When labor products are treated and regarded as commodities by millions and ultimately billions of people, they become commodities *as a result.* That's where fetishism enters in. These things *seem* to trade for each other inherently, and that semblance grows stronger over time, for two reasons:

First, because the commodity status of the product *actually* becomes more fixed; and second, because people have an ever-harder time shaking the idea that something so fixed could be anything other than natural.

Question: I was struck by your mention of Fromm on the critique of patriarchy. Fetishism sounds very similar to essentialism in sex and gender relations. The idea is that gender relations are so natural that we have no alternatives. I try to get students to think about the possibility of something beyond capitalism and gendered society. It's difficult, and I'm curious about the relevance of this concept of fetishism. Is commodity fetishism similar to essentialism in the way we often think about race or gender?

Smith: Yes, very much so. When Fromm wrote the essay that introduced the concept of authoritarianism in 1936, he made that argument directly. Gender statuses, like statuses in general, are socially constructed. Biology is not destiny, and neither is capitalism. So yes, the critique of essentialism is very much on par with the critique of fetishism. Seeing the value of the commodity as natural could just as well be called "commodity essentialism" as fetishism.

Question: I want to ask about the climate crisis. The species *Homo sapiens* is 120,000 years old, and it took until the mid-nineteenth century to finally reach a billion people. At that exact time the world hit one trillion dollars in global GDP. Now, under 200 years later, there are 7.2 billion people and a global GDP of $80 trillion. Capitalism requires constant growth in GDP and depletion of resources. But the fate of the human species, and all other species, requires some containment: "Take a pill and chill." I'm thinking, maybe capitalism has had its run. And for the species to survive, the profit motive needs to disappear, in some fashion.

Smith: I'll echo my friend Bob Antonio, who has been digging deeply into the climate crisis. Bob likes the phrase popularized by Jameson that people can more easily imagine the apocalyptic end of the world than they can envision the end of capitalism. Think of all the popular dystopias – zombie apocalypses, *The Hunger Games,* scenarios of planetary annihilation. Where are the utopias? Why does it seem embarrassingly naïve to even hope for sharing and caring?

Here's another simple thought experiment. Forget about utopias and dystopias. What if people just came to this thought? That the pursuit of profit – of money – is leaving countless people jobless, hungry, and poor. Not long ago, 46 million people in the U.S. were living in households with incomes below the poverty line; over 20 million were living in households with annual incomes under *half* the poverty line. When I discussed this subject a few years ago, I could say that one in five children were raised in poverty in the U.S. But now the figure is closer to one in four – and this is a rich country.

If people are losing their land and jobs, if children are poor and malnourished, here's a simple thought: Money isn't working.

The wealthy are awash in money, but they don't know what to do with it. Once they invested in industry; then they tried mortgage-based securities; now they're buying government bonds. But none of that seems to be working very well. So people with lots of money don't know what to do with it, while the rest of us, the 99%, have endless uses for money but less and less to spend. And chasing wealth in the abstract form of money is also causing the desecration and destruction of the concrete world.

Is money a poison? Is striving for money folly? Why don't we just forget about money and decide to survive? Should we let ourselves starve if we're short on funds? Why not just grow food?

This returns us to fetishism. There is a kind of bewitchment here. We're in thrall to the idea that, without money, we can't eat. Why should that be true? Climate change hasn't yet destroyed the earth's capacity to feed us. Nature isn't the problem – society is. But people assume that depressions and economic misery are somehow natural, that we have to resign ourselves to the dire consequences of money troubles. That's fetishism.

Herbert Hoover, who was president when the Great Depression began in 1929, blamed the crisis on sunspots. He was wrong. But in 2008 we didn't even have sunspots. Everything in nature that permitted us to thrive in 2007 was still in place; but just months later, society was in a shambles. Was the planet suddenly unable to support us? Did we suddenly have less ability to support ourselves? Of course not. If we simply decided to survive and cooperate, what force could prevent us from doing that?

Question: I'm curious about whether the center of capitalism is shifting, maybe from the U.S. to Asia? Is this really a global crisis of capitalism or just a crisis of Western capitalism?
Smith: I think the current crisis *is* a global crisis of capitalism. If you wanted to pick a starting point, I would pick the late 1990s. What do I mean by worldwide crisis of capitalism? In large part, it's a failure of global consumer demand. Production is steadily falling because fewer and fewer people can afford to buy what is produced. That began to be apparent in the crisis at the end of the 20th century. People were briefly reassured when the credit bubble began to inflate in the early years of this century, but that was an illusory moment of growth. It was a conjuncture that can't be repeated.

In the first decade of this century, working people in Europe and the U.S. came to believe that their wages were secure, that they would be paid tomorrow as well as today. Culturally, that's what credit cards represent. People who use credit cards are spending tomorrow's wages today – and the working public became accustomed to the idea that they could safely do that. They would be paid tomorrow. At that exact moment, China emerged as the Manchester of the 21st century. The locus of productive capitalism *has* now shifted substantially away from the U.S. and Europe.

Has production been eclipsed by speculation and financialization? No. Globally, there is still a tremendous amount of commodity production – but the locus has shifted. During the bubble years, Chinese workers were paid pennies to produce for the export market, mainly in the United States and Western Europe. China was able to sell abroad because the demand crisis was deferred while people were still buying with credit cards. But the Great Recession made it clear that credit spending is unsustainable. So people decided to tighten their belts and save instead of spending. The credit bubble burst.

Look at China now. China is still the world's most dynamic productive economy but many troubles are brewing. China's rulers are worried that the global export market is nearing or even beyond the saturation point. If fewer people have jobs and farms and fewer people are paid living wages, there is less demand. It's that simple. Either people can consume or they can't. If they don't have money, they can't spend. China's strategy was furnace-like production for people with credit cards. Now, people have cut up their credit cards.

When we talk about "the bond market," what are we talking about? Investors, including states, who buy bonds in bulk. This category includes, not least, China's government, which has diverted trillions of dollars from production because they have shrinking markets. So the consumption deficit in Europe, the U.S., and elsewhere is exerting pressure on China to pull back on production.

Is anyone here familiar with the work of Stephen Roach? I see Tony Smith nodding. Roach was Morgan Stanley's chief economist and he ultimately chaired Morgan Stanley Asia. Roach is what Gramsci called an "organic intellectual" of the monied class. He writes punchy little articles about the status of the world economy based on research by an army of Morgan Stanley staffers – wonderfully sensible articles that I began to read in the late '90s. Roach focuses like a laser on the United States and China, showing that, in the global economy, when you say the U.S., you are also saying China, and when you say China, you are also saying the U.S. It's one very integral system. Roach published a great book in 2009, *The Next Asia,* which is an exceptionally data-rich treatment of the U.S.-China relationship. But curiously, Roach, who was for many years a skeptic about global growth, has become optimistic. He thinks that China will successfully develop a domestic market, freeing themselves from over-reliance on exports. I see few signs of that. It would make sense. The Chinese government could pay pennies to displaced farmers in the interior to make consumer goods for better-paid workers on the coast. But, as far as I can tell, the Chinese state is still addicted to exports and to reckless spending on construction.

Question: I'm fascinated by this discussion. We keep coming back to the differentiation of profit, rent, and interest. Who is the custodian of rent? The landlord. Who is the custodian of interest? The banker. Who is the custodian of the rate of return on productive capital represented by profit? I would venture to say that, in China, it's the party. I'm pretty sure that, in Germany, it's the banks. In the U.S., you can probably date this to the interventions of Louis D. Brandeis in his pre-Supreme Court days. He argued, for example, for reforms to put pricing barriers on railroad transportation as an assertion of the power of the state to oversee the rate of return on productive capital. He argued that the damned railroads are lousy custodians of their own rate of return. They can't manage their own damn capital. We need to do it; we're smarter, we're better.

The historical trajectory is that this consensus in the United States was entirely dismantled by the 1970s. The idea that the capitalist is always the best custodian of the rate of profit was re-naturalized. This is anomalous with respect to China, Germany, and elsewhere in Europe. In China the state keeps a tight grip on the reins. Germany, where meta-productive capital dominates, invests a very high portion of productive capital at a high rate of wages, uniquely among Western powers. I don't think that is an accident.

Smith: With respect to Germany: I think one reason Germany is so stern and complacent in its efforts to force austerity on the eurozone is that Germany produces capital goods, which China buys. So you're right, the wheel of global production and consumption turns around Germany as well as the U.S. and China. But as Chinese production slows, as the global purchase of capital goods diminishes, German complacency is likely to prove short-lived.

So who now "personifies capital," to use Marx's phrase? Marx said that capital is a social force. If you own or control capital, you are obliged to seek profit. You can do that by investing in industry, if you think there is a market for your products; or, if production seems too risky, you can invest in financial instruments. In other words, G E Capital can pick up where G E leaves off. But, either way, the person or team with responsibility for capital is obliged to maximize profit.

With respect to corporations in this country, there has been an endless discussion since Berle and Means published their famous book on the corporation in 1931. The question is, who really runs the corporation. The managers or the shareholders? It seems to me that a nice way to short-circuit that discussion is to state the obvious: that top managers *and* major shareholders run the corporations.

Today there are few capitalists in the old-fashioned sense. When Marx wrote *Capital*, the average firm had just a few dozen employees and the owners, the capitalists, were identifiable individuals. You could walk into a factory and see them: "There are the capitalists, there are the workers." They were constrained to pursue profit if they hoped to survive, but only exceptionally did they even have shareholders or "middle managers." They personified capital, but with real authority and without anonymity. Today maters are very different. Most notably, decision-making is a team effort. Even when the CEO is famous, like Jack Welch of General Electric, that leader has much less unbridled authority over investment than capitalists had in Marx's day – and when the celebrity CEO retires, the business press always has someone else to talk about. Nothing fundamental changes as a consequence of the leadership transition, since it was never just Jack Welch who ran the show anyway, it was always Welch and the top managers and major shareholders.

With respect to China: You're right, the party has primary responsibility for guaranteeing the profit rate. That fact conforms in an interesting way to Marx's famous dictum that the state is the executive committee of the ruling class. In China, that is true almost without qualification. Still, even in China there is a tension, since the state can act on behalf of capital *as a whole* or serve different sectors of capital. Lately, in China as well as the West, there has been a tussle between forces that want the state to deregulate or regulate capital. So even the Chinese state is no solid crystal.

Question: Brandeis said, "This is the moment when emerging giant firms – like the railroad companies in 1915 – need middle managers who are engineers and not investors." [Investment] need not be [coordinated] inside the firm. The state can be just as good an epistemic system for the maintenance of the free return on investment capital as can the firm itself.

Smith: A small comment about Marx first. It is often said that Marx wanted a state-controlled economy. Anyone who reads Marx's essay on the Paris Commune, "The Civil War in France," knows that the truth is the opposite. Marx actually opposed having an executive branch of government at all. Engels's famous phrase "the withering way of the state" reflects the wish to see the state lose its executive functions. Engels and Marx wanted government to have only a representative branch with rotating members who would hold delegated power only briefly and would receive only an average income. They would gain nothing from serving as representatives and they would remain representatives only for a while.

Here's another point. In his commentary on the so-called "Ricardian socialists," Marx discussed John Gray, who wanted the state to run the economy. Marx said, well, but that would make the nation into a corporation; that's possible, but it isn't desirable. If you want society run, not by a consortium of small corporations, but by a single mega-corporation with an army under its control, well... be careful what you wish for. Many people, including influential later "Marxists," actually wanted that. But Marx wanted the opposite – a society run democratically from below, not dictatorially from above.

Question: You brought up the Iowan who was president. Hoover also said that the only problem with capitalism is that some capitalists are greedy. But you're talking about many, many ills: people without jobs, the Fed having to pump so much money monthly in trillions of dollars. If the Fed has to do that, hasn't capitalism failed?
Smith: There are signs of failure. The world's leading business consulting firm, McKinsey Global, does tremendous research. McKinsey says that, if the rate of industrial investment in the U.S. in 1975 had remained constant until 2005, $20 trillion would have gone into production than actually went elsewhere. Let me repeat: $20 trillion. Those dollars exist. But they were not invested in industry. So where did they go?

Beginning in the early 1980s, they went into junk bonds. In the late 1990s, they went into dotcoms. In the early 2000s, they went into derivatives. Those dollars went nearly everywhere, in other words, except into manufacturing – and now, fewer people have jobs and even many people with steady jobs have shrinking paychecks.

Here's another key point. You may have seen Andrew Kliman's good new book, *The Failure of Capitalist Production.* In his fifth chapter, he discusses whether the profit rate is falling. This is not theoretical; rather, Kliman spent a lot of time raking through U.S. Commerce Department data. He concludes that we will never know whether the profit rate is declining globally. It does appear to be falling in the continental United States, but capitalism is a global system and we just don't have reliable data for most other parts of the world. So, yes – profit rates might be falling. But we need hard empirical data, not just theory, to establish that.

It's probably best not to worry too much about whether the profit rate is falling. What matters most, it seems to me, is whether the rate of industrial investment is falling. That isn't hypothetical. You don't have to troll through obscure data to find out whether the rate of industrial production is declining. Each month the business press analyzes the latest Purchasing Managers' Index, which reports what companies say when they are polled about their productive investments. Often that news is not positive.

Is capitalism failing? It certainly doesn't seem to be thriving. And I have yet to hear anyone offer a good reason to think that investors will regain confidence in industry or that global demand will revive.

Question: Have you seen Robert Reich's movie and book *Inequality for All?* He basically says that capitalists and governments took away the middle class wages, which therefore prevents people from being consumers. They don't make enough money to buy goods. He also says that outsourcing manufacturing has also specifically hurt the United States.

Smith: Here's a telling way of framing this. Graham Cassano gave a talk earlier today in which he said that one of FDR's goals during the Great Depression was to enable workers to become homeowners. Actually, for Marxian theory, that simple point is quite significant, because Marx says that the working class consists by definition of those who own only their own labor power. So what FDR wanted was a working class that owned *both* labor power *and* homes. So, think ahead to the first decade of the century in this country. What happened in the housing market? We had a mortgage crisis, in which millions of people lost their homes.

In a way, we seem to be reverting to pre-Rooseveltian times. Even in this country, where workers are relatively affluent, the working class is increasingly back to square one. Workers still own labor power, but they are less likely to own homes; and even their labor power is less saleable, and at lower prices. If they tilt towards fetishism, they might think, "That's just life. Sometimes wages rise, sometimes they fall. That won't change." Really? Is that just society's nature, now and forever? Or is it, perhaps, an outgrowth of the way we treat and regard each other and our products?

Question: Just to follow up on that. Remortgaging homes to finance was also a big part of what happened after 2001. It wasn't just a credit bubble in new homes, it was also refinancing – Get your house down to 75% and borrow back at 100% to consume again. That bubble burst too. So, is speculation still viable? Or has it reached its limit?

Smith: Right now, China appears to have a huge speculative bubble, and the regime is trying to stimulate production, but indirectly. China has a "shadow banking system" of poorly regulated lenders, and the Chinese government has been permitting risky loans from shadow banks as a way to momentarily pump up consumer demand. What's the underlying problem? A deficit of consumer demand. You can temporarily alleviate this deficit by persuading people to buy on credit or to accept subprime loans. That's what happened in the U.S. and Europe before 2008, and now a white-hot asset bubble is forming in China's coastal cities, which is where managers and better-paid workers live. But Chinese wages are still modest and well over 100 million people are floating in suspended animation, with neither land nor jobs. Will shadow loans help them?

China has a kind of class apartheid, in which ex-farmers are kept out of the cities. Without permission to settle in a city, you can be ejected or jailed. And the bottom line is that employers are not hiring the floating millions. That reduces overall demand, despite the coastal asset bubble and unbridled shadow lending. Some economists worry that a "hard landing," a major recession, will begin in China.

Question: That's fascinating. I've had a research project in China the last few years – but now I want to raise two points. Marx argues that the value of the commodity is what we impose on it socially. In his *Elementary Forms [of the Religious Life]*, Durkheim spends a lot of time trying to understand how religion became what it is due to everyday social interaction. In the end, it gains from collective effervescence and becomes a social fact. Second, with respect to what Graham Cassano said earlier in his talk about race. I wonder if he thinks the racialization of southern and eastern Europeans was regional or national. Because my understanding is that the majority of Italian immigrants from the north came earlier, were more educated, were lighter skinned and so forth and came as individuals. So Italian is simply referring to southern Italians, not necessarily Italians...

Cassano: My grandfather was from Turin, which is far north, but he had olive skin, and he was treated as a racial other. The Italian ambassador before fascism had a great line. In Louisiana, he found northern and southern Italians working alongside Black workers, and he asked, "Don't these Americans realize that Italians are white?"

We need to link racialization to the big story David is telling about capitalism. Here I point to David Roediger's work, both *Wages of Whiteness* and *Working Toward Whiteness*, where Roediger puts the story of racial transformation into the broader story of capitalism and also colonialism. We need to keep in mind what Arendt brings out so clearly in the second part of her totalitarianism book, the section on imperialism – that racialization and colonialism are related. That relationship seems to be both internal within nations as well as external so that racialization and capitalism are intimately connected to internationally.

Smith: I agree completely, and there's also another dimension here. Marx says that capital takes two principal forms in investment. As "constant capital," money buys means of production and as "variable capital" it buys labor power. (Marx also says that, in a certain sense, labor power *is* variable capital.) So what are we talking about? The ability to work, which has a price tag on it. Labor power sells for a wage. Now, one of the things that DuBois and Roediger focused on, as Graham mentioned earlier – and this is also discussed in feminist literature – is that labor power is not abstract. Labor power is concrete, and this concreteness includes ethnic and gendered dimensions.

I remember vividly when the slogan "Equal Pay for Equal Work" became popular. At that point women were paid 59¢ per hour for the same work that men did for a dollar. It's clear that labor power is unequally valued for reasons of race and gender. Marx said that labor power is valued, not in line with an external standard, but along axes of moral and historical judgment. The question is how people treat and regard *labor power*. That "treating and regarding" can reflect many kinds of prejudices. Nothing prevents society from *differently* regarding, and treating, units of labor power which, in terms of skill and strength, are virtually identical. Two equally competent and productive workers can be paid unequally simply because they differ in race, in gender, or in some other way.

This returns us to fetishism, or essentialism. Many people once thought that women are paid less than men because their labor power is intrinsically less valuable. Rarely did they wonder why women get paid differently for the same work at different times and places, or ask themselves why female labor power at one point appears to be exactly 41% less valuable than male labor power, but a different percentage at another time.

That lack of curiosity is striking, and it stems, in Marx's terms, from a form of capital fetishism – we can call it the fetishism of variable capital. We could also call it essentialism. Just as there is a wage for whiteness, there is a wage for maleness. Units of labor power that are very similar in terms of productivity can be forcibly *unequalized* in the market, just as different labor products can be forcibly *equalized*. Society has vast mysterious powers. It can make the like *unlike*. It can also make the unlike *identical*.

If we hope to abolish these constructed statuses – racialized, gendered, and commodified – we need to demystify them. In my opinion, Marx's critique of political economy helps us enormously. If Marx is right, part of our dilemma is that people find it hard even to imagine a future without commodities, money and capital. Many people are also psychologically invested in inequality, along lines of race, ethnicity, gender, religion, and class. I believe that, to understand that commitment, we need a critique of political psychology. That will help us judge the authoritarian and socially dominant tendencies that bind people to inequality and tilt them towards reaction when capitalism stumbles. It will also help us better understand how to work for equality and against reaction.

Critical theory, in the hands of Fromm and Adorno, was inspired by the wish to probe capitalism's future with reference to psychology as well as to economics. But Fromm and Adorno wandered into other fields. If we hope to remake critical theory, I think we need to return to their questions, their agenda, and dig deeper.

References

Adorno, T.W. ([1943] 2000). *The psychological technique of Martin Luther Thomas' radio addresses*. Stanford: Stanford University Press.

———— ([1955] 2010). *Guilt and defense: On the legacies of National Socialism in post-war Germany,* excerpted from Pollock. F. (ed.), *Gruppenexperiment,* translated by A.J. Perrin & J.K. Olick Cambridge, MA: Harvard University Press.

Adorno, T.W., Sanford, R.N., Frenkel-Brunswik, E., & Levinson, D.J. (1950). *The authoritarian personality*. New York: Harper & Brothers.

Altemeyer, B. (1981). *Right-wing authoritarianism*. Winnipeg: University of Manitoba.

———— (1988). *Enemies of freedom: Understanding right-wing authoritarianism*. San Francisco: Jossey-Bass.

———— (1996). *The authoritarian specter*. London and Cambridge, MA: Harvard University Press.

———— ([1998] 2004). The other authoritarian personality. In *Political psychology,* edited by J.T. Jost & J. Sidanius Pp. 85–107. New York: Psychology Press.

American National Election Studies. (2013). *Preliminary release ANES 2013 internet recontact study*, Stanford University and The University of Michigan, Accessed at: http://www.electionstudies.org/studypages/anes_panel_2013_inetrecontact/anes _panel_2013_inetrecontact_PrelimDoc.pdf; cf. the questionnaire at http://www .electionstudies.org/studypages/anes_panel_2013_inetrecontact/anes_panel_2013 _inetrecontact_qnaire.pdf.

Anti-Defamation League. (2014). *ADL Global 100: An index of anti-semitism,* Accessed at: http://global100.adl.org/public/ADL-Global-100-Executive-Summary.pdf.

Arendt, H. (1951). *The origins of totalitarianism*. New York: Harcourt, Brace and Co.

———— (1953). Ideology and terror: A novel form of government. *The Review of Politics,* 15(3), July, 303–327.

———— (1958). *The origins of totalitarianism,* second enlarged edition. New York: Meridian.

Asch, S. (1952). *Social psychology*. New York: Prentice-Hall.

———— (1961). Issues in the study of social influences on judgment. In *Conformity and deviation,* I. Berg & B. Bass (ed.). B. Pp. 143–158. New York: Harper.

Berle, A.A., Jr. & Means, G.C. (1932). *The modern corporation and private property*. New York: Macmillan.

Bettelheim, B. & Janowitz, M. (1950). *Dynamics of prejudice: A psychological and sociological study of veterans*. New York: Harper & Brothers.

Binet, A. (1887). Le fétichisme dans l'amour. *Revue philosophique* (24), 143–167; 252–274.

Brosses, C. de. (1760). *Du culte des Dieux fétiches, ou parallèle de l'ancienne religion de l'Egypte avec la religion actuelle de la Nigritie.* Chantilly: Bibliotheque S.J. See: http://reader.digitale-sammlungen.de/resolve/display/bsb10434753.html.

Christie, R. & Cook, P. (1958). A guide to published literature relating to the authoritarian personality through 1956. *Journal of Psychology*, (45) 171–199.

Cruickshank, B. (1853). *Eighteen years on the gold coast of Africa.* London: Hurst & Blackett.

Dicks, H.V. (1950). Personality traits and National Socialist ideology: A war-time study of German prisoners of war. *Human Relations* 3(2), June, 111–154.

——— (1973). *Licensed mass murder: A socio-psychological study of some SS killers.* New York: Basic Books.

Durkheim, É. ([1912] 1947). *The elementary forms of the religious life,* translated by J.W. Swain, Glencoe, IL: The Free Press.

Elms, A.C. & Milgram, S. (1966). Personality characteristics associated with obedience and defiance toward authoritative command. *Journal of Experimental Research in Personality* (1), 282–289.

Engels, F. (1847). Karl Beck, *Lieder vom Armen Mann,* or The poetry of true socialism. Accessed at: https://marxists.anu.edu.au/archive/marx/works/1847/true-socialists/poetry.htm.

——— [1895] 1974). Einleitung zu Karl Marx' *Die Klassenkämpfe in Frankreich* 1848 bis 1850. In *Marx-Engels Werke* (MEW), Bd. 22. Pp. 509–527. Berlin: Dietz.

Freud, S. ([1927]1963). Fetishism. In S. Freud, *Sexuality and the Psychology of Love,* edited by P. Rieff. Pp. 214–219. New York: Collier.

Fromm, E. ([1933] 1997). Robert Briffault's book on mother right. In E. Fromm, *Love, Sexuality and Matriarchy: About Gender,* edited by R. Funk. Pp. 76–84. New York: Fromm International.

——— ([1936] 1980). Sozialpsychologischer Teil. In M. Horkeimer, ed., *Schriften des Instituts für Sozialforschung,* Vol. 5: *Studien über Autorität und Familie: Forschungsberichte aus dem Institut für Sozialforschung.* Pp. 77–135. Paris: Librairie Félix Alcan.

——— (1941). *Escape from freedom.* New York: Farrar and Rinehart.

Geithner, T.F. (2014). *Stress test: Reflections on financial crises.* New York: Crown.

Gierke, O. ([1868]1881). *Das deutsche genossenschaftsrecht,* Vols. 1/3: Berlin: Weidmann.

——— (1900). *Political theories of the Middle Ages,* a translation by F.W. Maitland of "Die publicistischen Lehren des Mittelalters" in *Das deutsche Genossenschaftsrecht,* Vol. 3. Cambridge: The University Press.

——— (1957). *Natural law and the theory of society 1500–18,* a translation by E. Barker of five subsections in *Das deutsche Genossenschaftsrecht,* Vol. 4. Boston, Beacon.

Harrison, J.E. (1912). *Themis: A study of the social origins of Greek religion.* Cambridge: The University Press.

Hegel, G.W.F. ([1837] 1902). *Lectures on the philosophy of history,* translated by J. Sibree. London: G. Bell & Sons.

Hocart, A.M. (1927). *Kingship.* Oxford: Oxford University Press.

———— (1936). *Kings and councilors: An essay in the comparative anatomy of human society.* Chicago: University of Chicago Press.

Horkheimer, M. ([1937] 1999). Traditional and critical theory, translated by M.J. O'Connell. In Horkheimer, M. *Critical theory: Selected essays.* Pp. 188–243. New York: Continuum.

———— & Adorno, T.W. ([1944] 2002). *Dialectic of enlightenment,* translated by E. Jephcott. Stanford: Stanford University Press.

Institute for Social Research. (1944a). *Studies in anti-semitism.* American Jewish Committee and Institute of Social Research. Manuscript.

————. (1944b). *Anti-semitism among American labor.* Manuscript.

Kantorowicz, E.T.H. (1957). *The king's two bodies: A study in Mediæval political theology.* Princeton: Princeton University Press.

Kliman, A. (2011). *The failure of capitalist production: Underlying causes of the great recession.* London: Pluto.

Lenin, V.I. (2012). *Essential works of Lenin: What is to be done? and other writings* (Google eBook). Courier Corporation.

Levenstein, A. (1912). *Die Arbeiterfrage: Mit besonderer Berücksichtigung der sozial-psychologischen Seite des modernen Grossbetriebes und der psycho-physischen Einwirkung auf die Arbeiter.* Munich: Verlag Ernst Reinhardt.

Leviné, E. (1909). *Typen und Etappen in der Entwicklung gewerkschaftlich organisierten Arbeiter;* cited in *Leviné by* Rosa Leviné-Meyer (Glasgow, 1973) and other sources.

Lukács, G. ([1924] 2009). *Lenin: A study on the unity of his thought.* London: Verso.

Luxemburg, R. (1915). Rebuilding the International. In *Die Internationale,* 1, Accessed at: https://www.marxists.org/archive/luxemburg/1915/xx/rebuild-int.htm.

Marx, K. & Engels, F. ([1848] 1994). The Manifesto of the Communist Party. In H. Draper, *The adventures of the Communist Manifesto.* Pp. 105–185. Berkeley, CA: Center for Socialist History.

Marx, K. ([1859] 1987). *A contribution to the critique of political economy,* translated by S. Ryazanskaya. In *Marx-Engels Collected Works,* Vol. 29. Pp. 257–420. New York: International.

———— (1867). *Das Kapital. Kritik der Politischen Ökonomie. Erster Band. Buch I: Der Produktionzprozess des Kapitals.* Hamburg: Otto Meissner.

———— ([1867] 1976a). The Commodity, translated from the first edition of *Das Kapital* in *Value: Studies by Marx,* edited and translated by A. Dragstedt. London: New Park.

———— ([1867] 1976b). The Form of Value, translated from an appendix to the first edition of *Das Kapital* in *Value: Studies by Marx,* edited and translated by A. Dragstedt. London: New Park.

———— ([1867] 1976c). *Capital. A critique of political economy,* vol. 1: *The production process of capital,* translated by B. Fowkes. London: Penguin/New Left Books.

———— ([1870] 1972a). Letter on Ireland to Siegfried Meyer and August Vogt, April 9, 1870, in Marx and Engels, *On colonialism.* New York: International.

———— ([1880] 1989). Workers' Questionnaire. In *Marx-Engels Collected Works,* Vol. 24. Pp. 328–334. New York: International.

———— (1883). *Das Kapital. Kritik der politischen Ökonomie.* Erster Band. Buch I: *Der Produktionzprozess des Kapitals.* Dritte, vermehrte Auflage. Hamburg: Otto Meissner.

———— ([1885] 1981). *Capital. A critique of political economy,* Vol. 2: *The process of circulation of capital,* translated by D. Fernbach. London & Middlesex: Penguin/New Left Review.

———— (1887). *Capital. A critical analysis of capitalist production.* London: Swan Sonnenschein. [This is the first English translation of the third German edition, translated by S. Moore and E. Aveling and edited by F. Engels].

———— (1971). The civil war in France, in K. Marx, *Writings on the Paris Commune,* edited by H. Draper. New York: Monthly Review Press.

———— (1972b). *Theories of surplus value,* vol. 3, translated by J. Cohen. London: Lawrence & Wishart.

McKinsey Global Institute. (2011). *Farewell to cheap capital? The implications of long-term shifts in global investment and saving.* Accessed at: http://www.mckinsey.com/insights/mgi/research.

Michels, R. ([1915] 1966). *Political parties: A sociological study of the oligarchical tendencies of modern democracy,* New York: Free Press.

Milgram, S. (1974). *Obedience to authority.* New York: Harper & Row.

Mills, C.W., with Schneider, H. (1948). *The new men of power: America's labor leaders.* New York: Harcourt, Brace.

———— (1959). *The sociological imagination.* New York: Oxford University Press.

Moseley, F. (2002). Hostile brothers, in *The culmination of capital,* ed. M. Campbell & G. Reuten, Houndmills & New York: Palgrave.

Oberschall, A. (1965). *Empirical social research in Germany, 1848–1914.* Paris and The Hague: Mouton.

Ostrogorski, M. ([1902], 1910). *Democracy and the organization of political parties, Vols. 1 & 2,* translated by F. Clarke with a preface by J. Bryce. New York: Macmillan.

Pollock, F. (ed.). (1955). *Gruppenexperiment. Ein Studienbericht. Frankfurter Beiträge zur Soziologie,* Bd. 2. Frankfurt am Main: Europäische Verlagsanstalt.

Pollock, F., Adorno, T. *et al.* ([1955] 2011). *Group experiment and other writings: The Frankfurt School on public opinion in postwar Germany,* translated and edited by A.J. Perrin and J.K. Olick. Cambridge, MA: Harvard University Press.

Postone, M. (1980). Anti-Semitism and National Socialism, *New German Critique* 19, Special Issue 1: Germans and Jews, Accessed at: http://www.oocities.org/cordobakaf/postone_holcaust.pdf.

Rigaudias-Weiss, H. (1936). Die Enquête Ouvrière von Karl Marx, *Zeitschrift für Sozialforschung* 5. Paris: Librairie Félix Alcan.

Roach, S.S. (2010). *Stephen Roach on the next Asia: Opportunities and challenges for a new globalization.* New York: John Wiley & Sons.

———(2011-the present). Project Syndicate columnist, Accessed at: http://www.project-syndicate.org/columnist/stephen-s--roach.

Roediger, D.R. (1991). *The wages of whiteness: Race and the making of the American working class.* London & New York: Verso.

———(2005). *Working toward whiteness: How america's immigrants became white: The strange journey from Ellis Island to the suburbs.* New York: Basic Books.

Rousseau, J.J. (2012). *Of the social contract and other political writings.* London and New York: Penguin.

Sassen, S. (2014). *Expulsions: Brutality and complexity in the global economy.* Cambridge, MA: The Belknap Press of Harvard University Press.

Sidanius, J. & Pratto, F. (1999). *Social dominance: An intergroup theory of social hierarchy and oppression.* Cambridge, UK, and New York: Cambridge University Press.

Smith, D. N. and C. W. Gunn. 1999. "Authoritarian aggression and social stratification." Pp. 95–112 in *Social Thought and Research*, 22 (1–2).

Smith, D.N. (1988). *Authorities, deities, and commodities: Classical sociology and the problem of domination.* Ph.D thesis, University of Wisconsin.

———(1992). The beloved dictator: Adorno, Horkheimer, and the critique of domination. *Current Perspectives in Social Theory,* 11, 195–230.

———(1996). The social construction of enemies: Jews and the representation of evil. *Sociological Theory,* 14 (3), 203–240.

———(1997). Judeophobia, myth, and critique. In *The Seductiveness of Jewish Myth,* ed. S.D. Breslauer. Pp. 123–154. Albany, NY: SUNY Press.

———(1998a). Faith, reason, and charisma: Rudolf Sohm, Max Weber, and the theology of grace. *Sociological Inquiry,* 68 (1), 32–60.

———(1998b). The ambivalent worker: Max Weber, critical theory, and the antinomies of authority. *Social Thought & Research,* 20 (3), 35–83.

———(2001). The spectral reality of value: Sieber, Marx, and commodity fetishism. *Research in Political Economy,* 19, 47–66.

——— 2006a. Authority fetishism and the Manichæan vision. In *The evolution of alienation,* ed. L. Langman and D.K. Fishman. Pp. 91–114. Lanham, MD: Rowman & Littlefield.

———— (2006b). Time is Money. *The hegemony of common sense*, D.W. Manders. Pp 19–91. New York and Frankfurt: Lang.

———— (2009). Solidarity in question: Critical theory, labor, and anti-Semitism. *Critical Sociology*, 35 (5), 601–628.

———— (2011a). Charisma and critique: Critical theory, authority, and the birth of political theology. *Current Perspectives in Social Theory*, 29, 33–56.

———— (2011b). Mapping the great recession: A reader's guide to the first crisis of 21st-century capitalism. *New Political Science*, 34 (4), 577–583, with appended book reviews by 13 collaborating authors (pp. 583–601).

———— (2013). Charisma disenchanted: Max Weber and his critics. *Current Perspectives in Social Theory*, 31, 3–74.

———— (2014a). Slashing at water with a knife? Durkheim's struggle to anchor sociology in first principles. *Contemporary Sociology*, 43 (2), 165–171.

———— (2014b). *Marx's Capital illustrated*, revised with a new epilogue: The crash and after: Capitalism in crisis? Illustrated by P. Evans. Chicago: Haymarket.

———— (2015a). The adventures of Professor Piketty, illustrated by T. Johnson. *Critical Sociology*, 41 (2), March.

———— (2015b). Charisma and the Spirit of Capitalism. *The Anthem Companion to Max Weber*, edited by A. Sica. London: Anthem Press, forthcoming.

———— (2016). *Marx's World: Asia, Africa, the Americas, and Global Capitalism in Karl Marx's Late Manuscripts*. New Haven: Yale University Press, forthcoming.

Trotsky, L. ([1904] 1980). *Our political tasks,* part 2. London: New Park. Accessed at: https://www.marxists.org/archive/trotsky/1904/tasks/.

Wagenvoort, H. (1947). *Roman dynamism: Studies in ancient Roman thought, language and custom.* Oxford: B. Blackwell.

Weber, M. ([1904–05] 2002). *The protestant ethic and the 'spirit' of capitalism and other writings,* edited and translated by P. Baehr and G.C. Wells. New York & London: Penguin.

———— ([1906] 1946a). The protestant sects and the spirit of capitalism. In *From Max Weber*, edited and translated by H. Gerth and C.W. Mills. Pp. 302–322. New York: Oxford University Press.

———— ([1916a] 1946b). The social psychology of the world religions. In *From Max Weber*, edited and translated by H. Gerth and C.W. Mills. Pp. 267–301. New York: Oxford University Press.

———— ([1916b] 1964). *The religions of China.* Glencoe, IL: The Free Press.

———— ([1916c] 1946c). Religious rejections of the world and their direction. In *From Max Weber*, edited and translated by H. Gerth and C.W. Mills. Pp. 323–359. New York: Oxford University Press.

———— ([1916–17]1967). *The religions of India.* Glencoe, IL: The Free Press.

———— ([1919]1948). Politics as a Vocation. In *From Max Weber*, edited and translated by H. Gerth and C.W. Mills. Pp. 77–128. New York: Oxford University Press.

———— ([1920a] 1958). *The protestant ethic and the spirit of capitalism,* translated by Parsons, T. New York: Scribners.

———— ([1920b] 2009). *The Protestant ethic and the spirit of capitalism with other writings on the rise of the west,* translated by S. Kalberg. New York and Oxford: Oxford University Press.

———— ([1922] 1978). *Economy and society.* Berkeley, Los Angeles and London: University of California Press.

———— (1946d). *From Max Weber,* edited and translated by H. Gerth and C. W. Mills. New York: Oxford University Press.

Worrell, M. (2008). *Dialectic of solidarity: Labor, anti-Semitism, and the Frankfurt School.* Leiden & Boston: Brill.

PART 2

*Capitalism's Future and the Critique of
Political Economy*

∴

Beyond Left Liberalism: A Critical Look at Proposals to Reform the Capital/Wage Labor Relation

Tony Smith

Introduction

Marx began writing in a period of reaction, after the defeat of Napoleon gave every petty aristocrat and monarch in Europe an invitation to suppress liberal currents. Yet Marx had relatively little to say about reactionary views, dismissing them as 'beneath all criticism'(Marx, 1975b, p. 177). His attention was focused instead on the gulf between the political emancipation called for by leading progressive movements and theorists of the time and the far deeper transformation required for universal human emancipation (Marx, 1975a).

Today the social world is again dominated by a perspective 'beneath all criticism,' neoliberalism, whose theoretical bankruptcy and pernicious practical consequences are transparent for all who wish to see. Once again progressive forces are told that all would be well if only the correct political reforms were put in place. Once again critical theorists must ask whether a far deeper transformation is required.

Most prominent left liberal critics of neoliberalism (Joseph Stiglitz, Robert Reich, etc.) accept some version of *liberal egalitarianism,* whose central principle can be formulated as follows:

> If we agree that citizens are all worthy of concern and respect...then we ought to conclude that policies.... should treat each of them as ends, as sources of agency and worth in their own right, with their own plans to make and their own lives to live, therefore as deserving of all necessary support for the equal opportunity to be such agents.
>
> NUSSBAUM, 2001, p. 58

Marx embraced a variant of this *normative* individualism as well, calling for 'a society in which the full and free development of every individual forms the ruling principle' and in which 'the free development of each is the condition for the free development of all' (Marx, 1976, p. 739; Marx & Engels, 1976,

p. 506; see Callinicos, 2000).[1] He believed, however, that it would be impossible in principle for a capitalist market society to institutionalize equal concern and respect. In his view human well-being will necessarily be sacrificed for the sake of the good of capital, with the structural coercion, domination, and exploitation associated with the capital/wage labor relation providing especially important illustrations of that dynamic.

Unlike classical liberals and contemporary libertarians, liberal egalitarians agree with Marx that capitalism does *not* automatically tend to function in a normatively acceptable manner. In sharp contrast to Marx, however, they hold that with the proper background conditions in place matters would be different. This brings us to what can be termed their 'core thesis':

> A capitalist market society is compatible with the institutionalization of the moral equality principle so long as the systematic tendencies of markets to generate results incompatible with that principle are put out of play by effective political regulation.[2]

For many critical social theorists it is tempting to dismiss liberal egalitarianism as also 'beneath all criticism.' Given the horrific brutality of capitalism, the naivety of calls for 'moral equality' might seem to warrant sarcastic dismissal. The problem, of course, is that calls for a rupture from capitalism also have a strong whiff of unreality in the present historical moment. Under these circumstances it is not sufficient to simply point out how capitalist regimes continue to use every legal and extralegal coercive and co-opting power to maintain normatively unacceptable practices. The continuing power of the capitalist utopian imaginary must be fully acknowledged and confronted. Part of that project includes considering that imaginary 'from the inside,' a task to which I now turn.

---

1   *Normative* individualism is not to be conflated with either *methodological* or and *metaphysical* individualism, both of which Marx vehemently opposed.

2   Some liberal egalitarians follow Rawls in calling for some form of 'property owning democracies' distinct from capitalist welfare state (Rawls, 2001, 135 ff.). It is unclear, however, whether this is simply a social order in which the least advantaged have more access to primary social goods than the welfare state provides, combined with a bigger role for 'stakeholders' in decision making. If so, it would be a variant of capitalism. Perhaps the term is meant to refer to some vision of a renewed 'Jeffersonian democracy' (minus the slavery), that is, a world of family farms and small independent firms. Jefferson's world mutated into today's corporate capitalism. If we could somehow imagine its return (and good luck on that), what would prevent a similar mutation? These issues need not be pursued here. The vast majority of liberal egalitarian theorists either explicitly or implicitly affirm a suitably regulated form of capitalism (Murphy & Nagel, 2004 and Honneth, 2014 provide exemplary illustrations).

Part 1

The 'capitalist utopian imaginary' is based on a set of general claims and includes a set of particular policy proposals. We may begin with the former.

The Critique of 'Economism'

Liberal egalitarian theorists recognize that capitalist market societies necessarily tend to generate normatively unacceptable states of affairs in normatively unacceptable ways. They insist, however, that a capitalist market society could in principle function in a just manner and generate just results. In their view Marx arbitrarily rules this out, illicitly jumping from the shortcomings of capitalism in his day to the conclusion that no acceptable form of capitalism is possible, a hasty generalization rooted in his 'economism.'

'Economism' comes in a variety of forms. The least plausible holds that the political sphere is a mere epiphenomenon, mirroring developments in the economy while lacking distinct causal powers of its own. One variant of this view is the 'instrumental' theory of the state, holding that the state apparatus is a tool used by the capitalist class to further its perceived interests.[3] This simplistic view does not withstand scrutiny. For one thing, the capitalist class is not homogenous in its views; different members have different interests and different understandings of these interests. Modifying the position so that only the dominant faction of the capitalist class uses the state as its instrument will not do either, given the occasions when state policy diverged from what dominant factions of capital most wanted. In modern regimes with the democratic accountability of state officials, the presence of a reasonably open and dynamic public sphere, a system of checks and balances within the state apparatus, constitutional protections of fundamental political rights, and similar measures, the interests of other classes and non-class-based groups come into play. Political leaders must now worry about being elected and re-elected, forcing them to mediate among divergent economic interests. This mediating role creates a space for autonomous action by state officials, further complicating matters.

---

3   An important debate within liberal egalitarianism today concerns the relative weight of states and a regime of global governance within a normatively acceptable institutional framework. The issues at stake in this paper are not affected by the answer. For the sake of convenience I shall usually restrict the discussion of the 'political sphere' to the state, although in my view states are incorporated within the higher order unity of the capitalist world market (see T. Smith, 2009).

We must also recall that the state is a coercive apparatus. Legislation and regulations in tension with the perceived self-interests of the owners and controllers of capital may generate resistance. But those who control the state's coercive apparatus in principle have ample power to overcome this resistance.[4] If there is sufficient political will to pass laws and formulate regulations, there will be sufficient power to enforce them.

A perhaps more plausible version of economism appeals to functionalist imperatives. The argument begins by noting that members of the capitalist class invariably focus their attention primarily on short term particular interests. For capitalism to prosper over time, however, there must be some mechanism for articulating and implementing the long term requirements of capital in general. This is the state.

The state is conceptualized here as independent from the direct control of particular capitalists. Nonetheless, this view too counts as a form of economism, since the content of state policies is reduced to what is functional in the long run for capital in general. Here too other interests besides those of capital are excluded. Here too that is a serious omission; once democratic mechanisms are in place, state officials cannot simply see themselves as agents of capital in general, any more than they can see themselves as simply agents of particular factions of capital. Successful political coalitions will generally include a variety of factions from a variety of classes, alongside a variety of other interest groups not organized on a class basis at all (e.g. religious associations). There is a strong element of contingency with respect to what specific coalitions are successfully formed, the specific content of the policies those coalitions pursue, and the effectiveness with which they pursue their objectives in particular contexts, all of which implies an ineradicable element of contingency in the content of state policies. The claim that policies are always reducible to what is functional for capital as a whole seems absurd in the face of this contingency. Further, as already noted, state officials have interests of their own, not least their interest in being re-elected. If there were a sufficiently strong political will among the citizens of a democratic state for certain policies, it would be in the interests of state official to respond to that sentiment, whether or not anyone thought those policies were functional for the long term interest of capital in general.

The most serious difficulties for a functionalist economism remains to be considered. Even if state officials were solely dedicated to the long term interest of capital, how could they possibly know what it was? The inherent uncertainty of the future rules out such knowledge in principle. Even worse, there

---

4   I abstract from the special case of 'failed states.'

isn't a long term interest of capital to know. Capital is radically open-ended. There are an indeterminate number of possible paths it could take, each with its own long term requirements.

If neither instrumentalism nor functionalism provides an adequate account of the state, liberal egalitarians conclude, 'economism' must be rejected. The political realm must be seen as a separate sphere, with considerable autonomy from the economy and considerable power to regulate economic activity. If this autonomy and power is combined with democratic political institutions, a space is created for reforming capitalism. Meaningful reforms have in fact been implemented in the past, making capitalist market societies more normatively attractive from the standpoint of the normative commitments shared by liberal egalitarians and Marxists alike. Further reforms are not inevitable. But if they have occurred before, they can occur again. No one can determine their limits a priori. If normative advances can be continued and deepened, liberal egalitarians assert, surely there must be some point past which the normative adequacy of an institutional framework incorporating capitalism can be affirmed.

A Reform Agenda

An adequate defense of the core thesis of liberal egalitarianism requires more than a critique of economism. Specific proposals must be made to check tendencies that might otherwise undermine normative acceptability. Tendencies associated with wage labor provide a representative and especially important case.

Marx's account of the capital/wage labor relation concentrates on three aspects that appear incompatible with equal concern and respect: coercion, domination, and exploitation. When one set of social agents privately owns both a critical mass of the non-human productive resources of the society and the goods and services required to meet human needs, while another set of social agents owns hardly more than a capacity to act, the members of the latter group are in effect *coerced* to sell their labor power as a commodity to members of the former set. How, Marx would ask, could we possibly speak of equal concern and respect when some are forced to serve as a means to the ends of others for most of their waking adult life? Similarly, when one set of social agents has the power to impose its will unilaterally on the members of another set in the labor process, this *domination* is not obviously compatible with equal concern and respect. Labor power, finally, will only be purchased if it can be foreseen that living labor is likely to create more value than what workers receive back in the form of wages ('surplus value,' in Marxian parlance). For Marx, then, structural coercion in labor markets and domination in labor processes culminate in *exploitation*.

The liberal egalitarian response is that coercion, domination, and exploitation would not be associated with the capital/wage labor relation if the proper background conditions were in place, checking the tendencies that Marx correctly discerned.

Coercion

According to the standard liberal view, institutionalizing workers' right to form labor organizations is sufficient to eliminate the worst abuses in labor relations. Left liberals, in contrast, hold that eliminating the coercive element in wage contracts requires in addition a much more equitable distribution of resources than markets tend to generate.

Different theorists have proposed different rules for this distribution. Rawls, assuming that inequalities provides incentives furthering economic growth, insists that economic inequalities are normatively acceptable if members of the least advantaged groups share in the benefits of any resulting economic growth (with the additional condition that inequality cannot undermine an equal claim to basic liberties, the equal worth of political liberties, or fair equality of opportunity, see Rawls, 2001, Part II). Ronald Dworkin (1981) calls for a distribution of resources to compensate for bad brute luck (as opposed to the bad 'option luck' that can result from choices we have made). For Nussbaum (2001) and Anderson (1999) the equality that matters is being able to stand as an equal in social and political life, from which a universal right to be above that baseline follows. Ackerman (1980)recommends that all individuals receive upon reaching maturity a 'stakeholder grant' (in the range of $80,000) that could be used for advanced education or for investment (Ackerman & Alsott 1999; Ackerman, Alstott, & Van Parijs, 2006). Philippe Van Parijs (1998) has proposed that a basic level of guaranteed income sufficient to enjoy an acceptable quality of life be granted, providing 'real freedom for all.' Other liberal egalitarians assert that a progressive tax system could roughly approximate the normatively required distribution of resources (Murphy & Nagel, 2004; Kymlicka, 2001, pp. 79–87).

These proposals may refer to an ideal that may never be fully attained in capitalism. But New Deal programs and the Earned Income Tax Credit in the U.S., the successful income assistance programs of Scandinavian countries, the effectiveness of the *Bolsa Família* program in reducing poverty in Brazil, among other examples, have already proven that it is possible to make the distribution of income more equal in capitalist market societies. There is no reason to think these programs cannot be extended further, and new, even more effective, programs added.

Policies establishing and maintaining full employment must also be mentioned in this context. The higher the employment rate, the more the labor market is a seller's market, reducing the element of coercion in wage contracts. Rawls's theory of justice accordingly includes the demand for a 'stabilization branch of government' with the task of maintaining full employment (Rawls, 1971, p. 276).

The technical details of these programs are less important in the present context than the claim that a capitalist economy with, say, a sufficiently high basic income guarantee and full employment would eliminate coercion in labor markets due to an extreme asymmetry in bargaining power. Liberal egalitarians argue that if the political will were present to establish and maintain a sufficiently egalitarian distribution of resources and effective full employment were present, wage offers would not be coercive offers. With the proper background conditions in place workers' agreements to labor for a wage would then tend to actually be what they otherwise cannot be: truly free choices to give up some leisure in return for the means to purchase additional goods and services.

Domination

Liberal egalitarians agree with Marx that when managers function exclusively as agents of investors there is a strong tendency for members of the work force to be treated as mere means to further the ends of others. New technologies and forms of social organization tend to be introduced in the workplace without adequately taking into account the fundamental interests of the workforce. Workers tend to feel alienated from their own activities, and to suffer normatively unacceptable levels of physical and psychological stress in labor processes.

The right to organize can at best somewhat mitigate these problems. Overcoming them, liberal egalitarians assert, demands a 'stakeholder' society where managers have a legal obligation to take into account the interests of subordinates in the workplace (as well as communities, customers, and the public at large). Further, members of the workforce must possess enforceable rights to partnership in management. This could take the form of workers' councils with whom managers must consult whenever major decisions are taken. It could include extensive worker representation on a firm's Board of Directors along the lines of the German system of codetermination, where forty-nine percent of the members of the Boards of Directors of the largest firms represent the workforce. If workers have substantive rights of codetermination in the workplace, liberal egalitarians ask, how could the category of 'domination' still be applicable to labor processes?

Exploitation

For left liberals if coercion stemming from asymmetrical bargaining power in labor markets were eliminated, and codetermination removed domination in labor processes, the systematic tendency to exploit wage labor would immediately dissipate. They also insist that exploitation in capitalism is not due to private ownership of the means of production per se, but rather to the excessive concentration of private property. If capital ownership and its benefits were widely and fairly dispersed, the category 'exploitation' would lose any normative force. The establishment of pension funds complicated the issue of exploitation greatly by dispersing capital ownership and its benefits. 'Neoliberal' policies have reversed this dispersal in recent decades. But the future is not foreordained; reversals can be reversed. If sufficient political will were present, the dispersal of the benefits of capital ownership could be renewed and expanded. The 'stakeholder grant' proposed by Ackerman, for example, would provide a substantive fund to all young adults that they could invest in capital assets. It would still be the case that a social surplus beyond the returns flowing to workers would be produced. But the appropriation by some of a surplus produced by others is not necessarily wrong. The very young and the very old do not 'exploit' working adults when they are cared for, nor do the infirm 'exploit' the healthy in any normatively relevant sense of the term.

No liberal egalitarian believes it is inevitable that coercion, domination, and exploitation will be abolished, making the capital/wage labor relationship normatively acceptable. The difficulties of implementing significant reforms are immense. Unfortunately, even cautious optimism for the short term prospects of meaningful reforms may not be justified. When evaluating the 'core thesis' of left liberalism, however, that is not the issue. The question is whether a normatively acceptable variant of capitalism is possible in principle. If we reject 'economism' it would seem to follow that some combination of constitutional rulings, legislation, and regulatory policies could establish background conditions eliminating the coercion, domination, and exploitation that would otherwise afflict the capital/wage labor relationship. The fact that significant normative advances have been made before, including advances that had at one time seemed utterly unimaginable, should make us hesitate before pronouncing the impossibility of further positive transformations. If slavery can be abolished, and equal citizenship rights granted to women, then it would seem foolhardy to dogmatically insist that the injustices besetting capitalism today must inevitably beset it tomorrow. In democratic societies a civil society is in place, providing space for individuals and associations to advocate reforms. Cultural values endorsing fair opportunities are present too, along with democratic political mechanisms capable of bringing state officials to account. Last but not least, public policies based on the assumption that markets always and everywhere generate maximally optimal results have quite obviously and spectacularly failed. The capitalism of today need not be the capitalism of tomorrow.[5]

Part 2

For many social theorists, including most left liberals, it is self-evident that Marx was an economic reductionist of some sort or other. How could a social theory proclaiming capital the dominant 'subject' in society not be guilty of granting the economic sphere primacy over other dimensions of social, political, and cultural life (Marx, 1976, p. 255)? And are there not numerous passages in his corpus where Marx discusses the state in clearly instrumentalist or functionalist terms?

Marx never wrote the Book on the State he originally intended, and so we are left trying to fit together scattered passages as best we can. I shall argue that the best 'all things considered' reading absolves Marx of the charge of economic reductionism. Liberal egalitarian proposals for the reform of the capital/wage labor relation will then be considered.

Towards a Marxian Theory of 'The Political'

However one-sided and ultimately inadequate it may be, there is an undeniable element of truth in instrumentalism. History and contemporary social science document numerous cases where those who control capital have successfully directed state officials to further their private interests through corrupt payouts, private funding of campaigns, the capture of regulatory agencies, and so on. There are numerous other cases where state agents have operated as the de facto representatives of the class interests of holders of capital (or a particular faction of capital) without any personal control having to be exerted, due to shared cultural ties, educational backgrounds, ideological assumptions, or the hope of future lucrative employment in the private sector. Also, while ruling blocs may include various non-capitalist group interests, ruling blocs in capitalist societies tend to be dominated by hegemonic factions of capital, as

---

5   Marxists should not be too quick to proclaim that significant reforms are impossible on the grounds that capitalism necessarily socializes individuals 'all the way down' to ensure compliance with the good of capital. It would then be impossible to explain significant progressive reforms of the past, most of which were strongly opposed by representatives of capital at the time. Even worse, it would be impossible to give a plausible account of how agents can arise with the capacity and motivation to undertake a world historical break from capitalism in the future.

Gramsci explained in his *Prison Notebooks*. And it is close to a tautology to assert that in the long run successful regions of capitalist development tend to be those where political authorities provide what is 'functional' for capital in general (basic research, infrastructure, education, enforcement of property rights, and so on). Recognizing the causal influence of the economy on political apparatuses is simply good empirical social theory, not dogmatic 'economism.'

That said, not a sentence in Marx's critique of political economy, his political essays, or his journalistic endeavors, implies that concrete political policies will be adopted in a particular context can be reliably predicted from a list of economic determinants, no matter how long such a list might be. Marx notes that state policies sometimes strongly opposed aristocratic enclosures of common lands, on the grounds that destroying the yeoman class would harm the backbone of the British infantry, while at other times the British government fostered enclosures. Sometimes state officials supported restrictions on the length of the work day; other times they did not. Sometimes workplace practices transgressing state legislation were ignored; other times state officials were sent into factories to document illegal abuses. Sometimes state officials responded to financial crises in ways that served the immediate interests of bankers; at other times they allowed those interests to be harmed. Sometimes military excursions were clearly intended to bring economic benefits to favored groups; in other cases military strategies were implemented on the geopolitical 'chessboard' regardless of foreseeable effects on domestic economic interests.

In Marx's framework it is not just the case that the content of state policies exhibits a high degree of autonomy and indeterminateness vis-à-vis the economy. *The causal arrows go in both directions,* from the political realm to the economy no less than the reverse. No one who has read Part VIII of the first volume of *Capital,* could fail to be struck by the absolutely central causal role Marx assigned the state in the historical emergence of capitalism in Britain. No one who has read *The Eighteenth Brumaire,* or Marx's journalistic writings for the New York Tribune, could fail to be struck by the important causal role granted the state at other moments of capitalist history (e.g. Marx, 1980).

This emphasis on the independence of state activity is fully compatible with Marx's concept of capital. The homeostatic processes by which capital is maintained and expanded over time are astounding in their flexibility; an indefinite number of different and incompatible concrete paths are compatible with capital accumulation (De Angelis, 2007). An essential part of this flexibility is the capacity to adjust to state policies. A vast range of state policies can stimulate capitalist development, including policies perceived at a given time to go against the short and even long term interests of capital. Ironically, the strongest advocates of capital drastically underestimate it when they automatically resist these policies, overlooking capitalism's astounding flexibility. Capital is pure form; there is no one content that the capital accumulation process must take. And there is no one content the capitalist state must take to be consistent with capital accumulation. The content of both is radically open-ended. It was long thought, for example, that political restrictions on the length of the working day were fundamentally incompatible with the reign of capital. But adjustments to state legislation restricting the work day provided a tremendous spur to what was perhaps the single most significant moment in capitalist development, the transition from manufacturing to machinofacture.[6] It would not be an overstatement to say that Marx's writings establish that the historical development of capitalism *requires* external spurs from the political sphere.

If the content of state policy is radically indeterminate, if the state can have a strong causal effect on the economy, and if capitalism is capable of adjusting flexibly to state policies, then the case in favor of the thesis that a series of incremental reforms can push capitalism down normatively acceptable path would seem quite strong. Can this thesis be questioned without falling into an unacceptable 'economism'?

Given the all but universal acceptance of the economistic reading of Marx, it is a bit ironic to realize that the heart of his theory of the state is not a dismissal of the importance of 'the political.' It is instead the assertion that the structures and practices of capitalist market societies systematically generate an impoverished political sphere. The political dimension of social life has a far greater scope than has been recognized; to talk of 'economism' here is to miss the point entirely.[7]

In pre-capitalist class societies social relations were reasonably transparent. On the one side, there were slave owners; on the other slaves, producing a surplus appropriated by their masters. Or there were lords and serfs, with serfs producing a social surplus appropriated by lords. In yet other contexts elites demanded tribute from independent peasant households. In all these cases it was fairly clear to all concerned that the surplus extraction process was based on a political relationship of domination, based on a complicated mixture of an overwhelmingly disparity in the capacity for physical coercion, the dead weight of custom, religious world views condemning disobedience to superiors as heinous impiety, the pursuit of self-interest within given constraints,

---

6   The systematic subordination of science and technology under capital (the so-called 'knowledge economy'), and the associated real subsumption of living labor under systems of machinery embodying the 'general intellect,' both emerged in the period of machinofacture.

7   What follows has been greatly influenced by Murray (1988, Chapter 17); Lacher (2006); Rosenberg (1994); and the writings of Ellen Meiksins Wood, e.g. Wood (2002).

an inability to imagine alternatives to the given constraints, and so on. It is too weak to simply say that in pre-capitalist societies there was no distinct 'economic' sphere separate from the 'political' realm. The very idea of there being an economic relationship of classes distinct from political relations of domination was unintelligible.

In capitalist market societies matters appear to be quite different. The process of producing and distributing goods and services is mediated by the decisions of individual persons to exchange commodities and money. State officials provide the background conditions for these choices and then step aside. With these structures and practices in place there appears to be a 'natural' separation of the economic sphere and the political sphere, however much each complements the other.

Two questions must be posed. First, is capitalism a class society, in other words, is there a class that produces a surplus appropriated by another? The answer must be 'yes,' whatever the number of complicating factors.[8] The private ownership of money capital and productive resources, the fact that means of subsistence generally take the form of commodities, and the fact that the vast majority of individuals have no other commodity to bring to the market besides their labor power, taken together reproduce a social world in which those who do not own or control money capital are generally forced to sell their labor power to those who do. The latter will not purchase labor power unless they anticipate that setting living labor to work on the means of production is likely to result in commodity outputs that can be sold for more than their initial investments. In other words, wage laborers will not be employed over time unless their living labor produces a surplus in the form of surplus value [the difference between M, the initial money capital invested at the beginning of a capital circuit, and M,' the amount appropriated at its conclusion] appropriated by those who own and control money capital. This class relationship is not transparent in capitalism. It is reproduced through exchanges of commodities and money among (formally) free and equal individuals, rather than through the sort of direct personal subjugation imposed on slaves, serfs,

---

8   Complicating factors include: (1) holding a particular class position does not automatically lead to a sense of personal identity centering on that position; (2) there are intermediate positions where class classifications are not completely clear; (3) the top level of executives in corporations may be able to appropriate an increasing share of surplus value through inflated salaries and stock options (Duméniel & Lévy, 2011); and (4) relatively small amounts of financial assets can be owned by wage laborers (these should be seen primarily as deferred wages; their ideological import is far more significant than their effects on the structures and processes of class relationships). Other complicating factors will be mentioned presently.

or tribute-paying independent producers. While this is a profound difference, it does not change the fact that the capital/wage labor relationship is a class relationship of surplus production and expropriation.

Nor can this state of affairs be denied on the grounds that the physical process of producing the surplus invariably involves other inputs besides labor. The fact that those who own/control money capital supply living labor with access to the objective preconditions of human life (means of subsistence and the means of producing them) is similarly irrelevant to the point at hand. They are in a position to make this 'productive contribution' solely because of their ownership/control of money capital, and so this ownership/control cannot be either explained or justified by these 'contributions' without falling into the crassest of circular arguments. The ability to appropriate surplus value must be explained instead by the power over the social labor embodied in money capital.

This brings us to the second question. Could a macro level relationship between a class producing a surplus and a class appropriating it be 'private' and 'non-political' in any truly meaningful sense of those terms? Of course words can be defined however we wish, and so it is always possible simply to define the 'political' in terms of state institutions, state policies, the actions of state officials, the actions of agents outside the state apparatus to influence the constitution, legislation, or specific policies of the state, the extension of all these matters to international agencies, and so on. But such a definition is arbitrary and question-begging. The macro-level social division between a surplus producing class and a surplus appropriating class is absolutely central to the organization of the polity. From this standpoint it could hardly be more mistaken to assert that Marx's theory emphasizes the 'economic' sphere while ignoring (or even just downplaying) the 'political' realm. Marx's primary emphasis is instead on how the standard notion of 'the political sphere' is illegitimately restricted in capitalism, institutionalizing the profound category mistake of treating what is inherently political as a private matter. Far from being a defender of 'economism,' then, Marx is *the* great critic of conceiving 'the economic' as a separate 'sphere' or 'realm' of society. The 'bifurcation of the political' into separate 'political' and 'economic' spheres is an illusion, albeit one necessarily generated by the social relations of a capitalist society.[9]

We are now finally in a position to state why Marx insisted that the state in a capitalist society must be thought of as a *capitalist* state, despite the irreducible contingencies in the relationship between the state and the economy documented in his writings. The radical indeterminateness of the capitalist

---

9   The phrase 'bifurcation of the political' is taken from Rosenberg (1994).

state is not unrestricted. *The indeterminateness of the content of state policies is conjoined with a determinateness of form, imposing a restriction on the 'form-determined' content.*[10]

One side of the 'bifurcation of the political' is a depoliticization of the inherently political class relations of the economy. The other is a 'political' realm impoverished by the exclusion of inherently political matters. The historical process that resulted in the formation of an (apparently) depoliticized sphere of economic transactions simultaneously constitutes the state as (apparently) separate from the economy. There is only one set of social relations underlying both capitalist economy and the state, defining both the state form and the capital form. The state form restricts the (nonetheless indeterminate) range of state policies in the following sense: *the capitalist state cannot introduce reforms that overcome the bifurcation of the political without dismantling itself.* The bifurcation of the political allows the causal arrows to go from the state to the economy no less than from the economy to the state. It even allows state activities to play a profoundly determining role in capitalist economic development. But it does *not* allow the depoliticized economy to be politicized, or the impoverished political realm to encompass the entire range of the inherently political. These things cannot occur short of a radical rupture from the social relations defining a capitalist market society. No tinkering with background conditions suffices.

Any adequate social theory needs to distinguish between reforms that threaten the perceived short or long term interests of capital, but to which capital can adjust within some reasonable time frame, and policies that threaten the very bifurcation of the political that is constitutive of capitalist society itself. At first the representatives of capital can be expected to resist instances of the former no less fiercely than instances of the latter. Over time, however, if sufficient political will to impose the former is present capital will adjust like the homeostatic system it is, and develop down a new path of accumulation. Enterprising entrepreneurs will eventually seek ways to profit from state decrees, just as manufacturers in the nineteenth century eventually responded to restrictions on the length of the working day by introducing more sophisticated machinery.

In contrast, resistance to policies eradicating the bifurcation of the political will be unrelenting over time. Continuing ownership and control of investment capital grants the owners/controllers ample resources to make this resistance effective, however strong the public support for reform might be. At some point a stark choice must be faced. Either policies overcoming the

---

10   See Arthur, 2002, pp. 204–207 and Reuten & Williams, 1989 on 'form determination.'

bifurcation of the political must be abandoned, or capital's power to resist must be recognized for what it is, an inherently public power that cannot be left in private hands. Both paths abandon the core thesis of liberal egalitarianism.

These general considerations will now be applied to liberal egalitarian proposals for the transformation of the capital/wage labor relation.

A Critical Examination of Liberal Egalitarian Proposals

Liberal egalitarians call for the state (and higher-order political agencies) to push capitalist market societies onto normatively acceptable paths. Specific proposals regarding the capital/wage labor relationship have been mentioned above. I shall argue that they overlook the inherently political nature of class rule and make the specifically capitalist nature of the (capitalist) state opaque. More specifically, I shall argue that implementing these proposals would either be ineffectual and leave the normative problems in place, or would require dismantling the form of the state in capitalist societies. Intellectual honesty demands acknowledgement that the latter would provoke unrelenting resistance from the representatives of capital, including an investment slowdown that, if not successful at reversing the proposals, would eventually turn into an all-out investment strike.[11]

Coercion

It is easy enough to proclaim that if a basic income were granted to all, and employment provided for all who wish it, the extreme asymmetry in bargaining power that turns formally free agreements into substantively forced agreements would be removed from labor markets. It is easy enough to add that the democratic state structures already in place would lead to the adoption of these proposals as soon as arguments in their favor won sufficient assent in civil society, and that the sovereign power of the state would be sufficient to compel recalcitrant economic elites to comply if such reforms were adopted.

A first difficulty arises when we note that a serious attempt to implement the proposals would likely set off an inflationary spiral. Basic income guarantees and full employment would result in an initial rise in real wages. Given that liberal egalitarian reforms of the capital/wage labor relationship would still leave units of capital with the power to set prices, what would stop price increases aimed at keeping the profit/wage ratio stable? If nominal increases left real wages unchanged, the proposals would be ineffectual. Most social agents would still find themselves still forced to sell their labor power to others

---

11   I ignore extreme forms of resistance available to capital such as death squads, despite the lack of historical justification for doing so.

to gain access to required means of subsistence; labor markets would still be characterized by a serious asymmetry of bargaining power. Maintaining the substance of the reform would require another jump in basic income provision, another jump in expenditures to provide full employment, and another jump in real wages. But this could simply lead to a new round of price increases, leaving the proposals to transform the status quo ineffectual. And so on.[12]

Suppose, however, we imagine for the sake of the argument that strong price controls somehow allowed a reasonably generous basic income guarantee to be provided and full employment to be maintained without inflation. To assume that this is compatible with capitalism is to assume that persons would agree to work for wages even if they were no longer forced by economic compulsion to do so. It is easy to imagine particular cases where this would happen, since these wages would allow sellers of labor power to enjoy additional consumption opportunities (and purchasers of labor power could to accomplish tasks they could not achieve on their own). But Marx did not propose a transcendental critique asserting that each and every particular instance of wage labor that might ever occur is necessarily coercive, oppressive and exploitative. His critique was directed at *generalized* commodity production and exchange, where capital and wage labor are the dominant *social forms*. If I agree to help someone move for some pizza and beer, this hardly shows that labor power as a commodity is normatively justified as a central mechanism of social reproduction!

The capital/wage labor relationship is not based on a series of separate wage agreements that may or may not take place depending on contingent assessments of mutual benefits. The systematic reproduction of capitalist society *requires* the systematic reproduction of the capital/wage labor relationship. Without the systematic commodification of labor power capitalism does not exist as a historically specific mode of production. The correct question, then, is not why people might agree to contribute to others' projects when they did not have to. The real issue is whether agents would treat their capacity for acting for most of their adult waking lives as a commodity available for others to use if they were not compelled to do so. The answer is not obvious.

Suppose we simply assume that a critical mass of people would recurrently consent to engage in wage labor. Why should we assume that they would then agree to create a surplus product that was then appropriated by the holders

---

12   The financial sector and central banks would have to accommodate these price increases, but in a social world where the capital/wage labor relation remained in place, and where accommodating these price increases appears necessary to maintain this relationship, it would seem reasonable to expect such accommodation to occur.

of capital and their representatives? If basic income and employment guarantees somehow removed the extreme asymmetry in bargaining between labor and capital underlying coercive agreements, a significant portion of what would otherwise have been surplus would tend to be appropriated by workers in the form of higher wages. There is some level of wage increases that would reduce surplus value to the point where funds for expanded investments were depleted. A point could even be reached where depreciation funds, that is, funds for replacement investment, were threatened. As Marx explained in *Capital,* the formation of a reserve army of the unemployed poor has provided a mechanism ensuring that wage rates do not threaten capital accumulation (Marx, 1976, Chapter 25).[13] Liberal egalitarian proposals for basic income and full employment eliminate this mechanism. What would take its place? Surely workers would understand it was in their interest and the interests of their children and their communities that resources be available for replacement and appropriate expanded investments. But if the asymmetry of bargaining power between capital and labor were truly eliminated, wage laborers would have the power to deny ultimate power over the surplus to a class of owners (or their agents) who aren't accountable to them. Establishing substantive accountability, however, would go far beyond merely modifying the 'background conditions' of the labor market. The 'bifurcation of the political' that is constitutive of capitalism would be undermined, as the inherently political nature of surplus production and allocation would be institutionally recognized.

Would representatives of capital abide a situation threatening to leave them without a compliant labor force, and without confidence that a surplus value will be produced that they can appropriate and control? Whatever liberal egalitarian theorists might hope, those who own and control capital would not share the delusion that the capital/wage relation can be the dominant form of social reproduction without structural coercion in the labor market. It is reasonable to foresee that they would employ every possible resource at their disposal to prevent such proposals from being accepted, or to reverse them if they were somehow accepted. The bifurcation of the political granting them private control over society's productive resources also grants them the power to make this resistance effective through capital strikes and other measures. A point would be reached when the reforms would either have to be rescinded or the power to effectively resist those reforms would have to be taken away – in other words, investment decisions (such as the decision to bring the economy to a screeching halt through a capital strike) would have to be treated as the

---

13   Patnaik explains how this mechanism has worked on the level of the world market in
      Patnaik (1997).

exercises of public power they inherently are. Either choice requires abandoning the core thesis of liberal egalitarianism, the first by conceding that there are significant and irresolvable normative problems in capitalism, the second by overcoming the bifurcation of the political defining the social relations of capitalism.

Domination

It is easy enough to call for a mixture of constitutional guarantees, legislation, and regulations to bring about a 'stakeholder economy' in which labor is a true 'partner' in management, eliminating domination in the workplace (and providing the democratic accountability that basic income and full employment do not provide). If new technologies and forms of social organization were introduced after consultation with workers, rather than imposed on them externally, any systematic tendency for workers to suffer alienation at the workplace, or normatively unacceptable levels of physical and psychological stress in the labor process, would appear to be put out of play. But there are serious limits to this proposal. They can be illuminated by exploring three forms of 'partnership.'

A first type of partnership grants workers mere rights of consultation. Such rights are in principle compatible with the capital/wage labor relationship, even if representatives of capital would predictably fight their introduction tooth and nail in most historical circumstances.[14] These rights, however, would not allow workers to 'stand as equals' to owners and managers in capitalist firms, as the following thought experiment shows. Suppose all citizens in a (very much imaginary) polity are convinced of the benevolence of a ruling stratum, its expertise in all relevant matters, its ability to recruit future members who will be equally benevolent and competent, and so on. Suppose further that citizens of this special regime were willing to renounce any and all rights to more extensive rights of participation than the mere right to be 'consulted,' content to let the trained and well intentioned experts rule without interference. In this imaginary world, would the left liberal defense of a fundamental right to participate as an equal in the political processes of their community be irrelevant? No. Without the full democratic accountability of those exercising authority citizens cannot develop the self-esteem that is so important to a healthy sense of self, or be able to mutually recognize each other as substantively free.[15]

---

14   Would co-determination rights been granted in West Germany had it not been for the
      need for rapid reconstruction after the devastation of a world war, combined with the
      existential threat posed by East Germany?

15   The reasons for this conclusion are set out at length in Pettit (2012).

Without rights to participation extending beyond mere consultation even the best intentioned and informed ruling strata will regularly make mistakes regarding both the interests of the citizenry and the public policies that would best further those interests. Without full democratic accountability mistakes made by ruling strata will tend to not be noted for extended periods, let alone quickly corrected. Now imagine that workers somehow win a right to be 'consulted' on all decisions taken by managers. Why would this arrangement be any more adequate from a liberal egalitarian perspective?

In a second case rights of participation exceeding merely formal and symbolic rights to consultation are granted to the workforce. This might well lessen some normatively problematic forms of domination in the workplace. But there are good reasons to think that many other matters would remain substantially unchanged. In capitalist economies competitive pressures necessarily tend to force all units of production and distribution to internalize the valorization imperative ('M must become M'!'), however they are internally organized. As a result labor processes that are 'independent,' that is, not formally subsumed under the capital form, tend to 'self-exploitation,' paralleling the treatment of wage laborers within units of capital.[16] This dynamic would come into play if truly equal partnership in the workplace were somehow instituted. Units of production and distribution whose members best internalized the logic of capital would generally tend to be most successful.[17] We could expect, for example, speed-ups to increase production at the cost of health-undermining stress, and lengthy work days despite productivity gains. A truly fundamental change within workplaces requires a dismantling of the valorization imperative on the macro-level of society as a whole, and no mere adjustment of the 'background conditions' of its operation.

In the cases considered thus far left liberal proposals would be ineffectual in the sense that the normative problems of concern would remain. We can next try to imagine a third case where truly substantive rights to participate in decision making are somehow instituted without 'self-exploitation.' Decisions regarding the introduction and use of technologies in the workplace,

---

16   Who has the worse work conditions, a trucker for a unionized firm, or an 'independent' trucker depending on temporary contracts?

17   In this context it is worth considering the thesis that the key to the ongoing Eurocrisis is the increase in the rate of exploitation agreed to by German labor, which gave 'their' capitals a competitive advantage in the E.U. at the cost of placing other regions in unsustainable positions (Lapavitsas et al., 2012). Germany's labor costs relative to the euro area declined by 16% in the decade before the Great Recession setting off the Eurocrisis (Benoit, Baigorri, & Ross-Thomas, 2013, p. 12).

for example, are made by persons fully accountable to those over whom this authority is exercised. Normatively problematic exercises of domination in capitalist workplaces – deskilling to reduce wages, speed-ups to increase stress, the use of technologies to break strikes or implement effective 'divide and conquer' strategies against labor, and so on – would then be lessened to the point of insignificance. But in the past precisely these sorts of measures have furthered the production of surplus value and its appropriation by capital. If they were eliminated, what sort of alternative mechanisms would ensure that the social surplus remained under the control of the holders of capital and their agents? Even more to the point, why would a workforce allow managers who were delegated and revocable by them to simultaneously be agents of external investors, let alone have a fiduciary duty to grant the interests of investors special priority when directing the production and allocation of surplus value? Whatever liberal egalitarian theorists might hope, those who own and control capital would not share the delusion that the capital/wage relation can remain the dominant form of social reproduction for long without domination in labor processes. Any proposal that truly threatened to eliminate that domination would be viciously opposed by the holders of capital and their representatives. At this point we must recall once again that control over money capital is a tremendously effective weapon of resistance. Investments can be shifted from enterprises that do not submit to extensive self-exploitation to those that do. Or it could be used to create social chaos through a capital strike. It is theoretically myopic and practically irresponsible for left liberals to abstract from this rationally foreseeable reaction when calling for substantive participation rights in the workplace, no less than it would be when proposing reforms for overcoming coercion in labor markets. Private control of investment funds in effect grants a veto power over social change.

Once again a moment of decision would arise. Either the reforms must be rescinded, or the inherently political power granted by large-scale private ownership of investment capital must be dismantled. Either path implies abandonment of the core thesis of liberal egalitarianism. If investment decisions were democratized, we could no longer speak of an adjustment to the 'background conditions' of the labor process. Institutionalizing a form of political activity outside the confines of the capitalist state would overcome the bifurcation of the political defining capitalism as a historically specific type of society.

Exploitation

Guaranteed income at a level sufficient to make the choice to sell your labor power truly free in a substantive sense, lasting full employment, and participating as an equal in the management of the workplace are not compatible with either coercion in labor markets or domination in labor processes. They are also not compatible with exploitation, that is, the production and appropriation by capital of surplus value that necessarily tends to follow from coercion in labor markets and domination in labor processes.[18] For reasons that have already been considered, implementing proposals that would be truly effective in eliminating exploitation would lead to the same moment of decision described in the previous paragraph, with the same consequences for the status of the core thesis of liberal egalitarianism.

There is no need to repeat points made previously. But a brief observation on the proposal to overcome exploitation by dispersing capital ownership is in order. Measures such as Ackerman's 'stakeholder grant' would increase individuals' access to funds that could be in principle be used for investment. But this increase would surely be met with a corresponding increase in the cost of food, education, medicines, housing, and other sorts of non-'discretionary' spending for basic needs. The end result would in effect be a public subsidy to the sectors producing those goods and services, leaving most persons hardly less vulnerable to exploitation. If the grants were made more generous in response, prices would simply increase again.[19]

In Part 2 of this paper I have argued that the state is not a mere epiphenomenon of the economy, or a mere instrument for economic elites to use at their whim. The content of state policies is not determined by what is functional for capitalism in the long term. The political sphere can causally affect the economic sphere as much as the content of state policies can be determined by economic factors. Reforms that no faction of capital really wants can be implemented. There is no one set of specific policies functional for capitalism in either the short or the long run. Capitalism is open-ended; there is an indeterminate plurality of possible paths consistent with capital accumulation. The range of state-imposed reforms to which capital can adjust, and which may open new paths of capitalist development, is in fact radically indeterminate. All of this is consistent with the core thesis of liberal egalitarianism, which rests on the hidden premise that both capital and the state are unrestrictedly open-ended. But *radical indeterminacy is not the same as unrestricted open-endedness.*

---

18   This point was argued forcefully by Kalecki in the 1940's, in a classic essay somehow overlooked by the most prominent liberal egalitarian theorists writing on related topics today (Kalecki, 1971).

19   Increases in disposable income due to cuts to property taxes in the U.S. may serve as a rough analogy. Hudson has convincingly argued that these cuts did not lead to a significant increase in disposable income. The funds were instead absorbed by the real estate and financial sectors in the form of higher housing costs and increased debt (Hudson, 2012).

Capital's flexible homeostatic processes cannot just adjust to any disturbance in its social environment whatsoever; the state form in a capitalist society does not allow policies to have just any content. A transformation of the capital/wage labor relationship cannot be undertaken while that imperative remains in force. The implementation of proposals to eliminate structural coercion in labor markets, and domination and exploitation in labor processes, would either be ineffective or effectively put the valorization process and the capital/wage labor relation out of play.

There are more and less humane forms of the capital/wage labor relation. But the liberal egalitarian thesis asserting that the normatively problematic features of this relationship can be eliminated while leaving the relationship in place cannot be maintained. To remove those features is to eliminate that relationship. Similarly, no reforms undertaken by the capitalist state can fully politicize the depoliticized (but inherently political) capital/wage labor relation without undermining the capitalist state itself. Legislation and regulations of the labor market are certainly possible that do not call into question the hidden political nature at the core of capitalism, that is, its existence as a class society with a surplus produced by one group and then appropriated by another. The liberal egalitarian position, however, unwittingly calls for a transformation of the capital/wage labor relation that can only be effective with a radical break from this form of social organization. In the terminology of the Marxian critique of political economy, in capitalism the collective powers of social labor take on alien forms: the value of commodities; money, 'the god of commodities'; and capital, the 'subject' of social reproduction. This is due to the historically specific form of social relations of generalized commodity production. Liberal egalitarian proposals incoherently call for a transformation of those social relations that would leave the social forms of generalized commodity production in place. This is incoherent.

Once the incoherence of calling for a transformation of the capital/wage labor relationship that requires abolishing this very relationship is recognized, liberal egalitarians face a choice. They could rescind the parts of their agenda incompatible with the capital/wage labor relationship. Or they could acknowledge that institutionalizing the normative principles of liberal egalitarianism requires a different form of human sociality than that manifested in the capital/wage labor relation. Either way, the core thesis of liberal egalitarianism must be abandoned.[20] As long as the 'bifurcation of the political' remains in place, state imposed reforms will be profoundly partial and precarious, rooted

---

20   The bifurcation of the political defining capitalism also explains why liberal egalitarian proposals to overcome industrial crises, financial crises, environmental crises, and

as they are in the governing social forms of our society. This implies that capitalist market societies will continue to be unable to adequately realize the normative principles espoused by liberal egalitarian social theorists.

A Concluding Note

This paper has remained on a fairly abstract level of discussion thus far. In this conclusion I would like to sketch a historical narrative of the decades following the conclusion of World War II. There can obviously be no question of providing a comprehensive narrative of this period. The goal instead is to suggest that there was a liberal egalitarian moment, so to speak, and that this moment has passed.

In the decades after the devastation of World War II capitals could expand and grow rapidly as demand expanded. In this context public policies supporting the consumption of some categories of worker households were not in fundamental tension with capital accumulation. Also, decades of labor struggles had successfully built labor organizations in the U.S. and elsewhere capable of maintaining pressure for increased real wages. Ideological competition with so-called 'really existing socialism' placed pressure on capitalist countries to lift workers' conditions during the Cold War as well. This was the historical moment of left liberalism, a period in which there was at least some material basis in at least some regions of the world economy for thinking that 'capitalism with a human face' was a realistic possibility. This moment did not last.

In 1945 the Japanese economy was roughly a century behind the U.S., while Germany lagged a half century or so (McNally, 2010, p. 27). By the 1970's both regions had more than caught up. In many of the most technologically sophisticated and economically crucial sectors of the world market – consumer electronics, autos, motorcycles, chemicals, business machines, steel – Japanese and European capitals were more efficient producers of higher quality products than established U.S. firms. The latter, however, did not withdraw from these sectors at a corresponding rate. Productive capacity in the global economy increased faster than the growth of markets to absorb it. The result was *an overaccumulation crisis*, manifested in excess productive capacity and a corresponding decline in the rate of investment, profits, and growth (Brenner, 2006; Harmon, 2010; Desai, 2013). The post-WWII 'long boom' had also been characterized by relatively low levels of unemployment and relatively high levels of labor organization in the U.S. and other regions of the 'center.' The ability of workers to win wage increases and partial control of the labor process

---

severe global inequality and poverty also cannot accomplish their objectives. See T. Smith (forthcoming), Chapter 8.

squeezed profits. The rate of investment necessarily tends to decline when surplus value is threatened. Left liberals see the rise in inequality in recent decades as a failure of political will to tax, redistribute, and regulate sufficiently. But this ignores both the significant fall in the rate of profit in the world market set off by the overaccumulation crisis of the 1970's and capital's need to discipline labor.

The standard response by capital to overaccumulation is the destruction and devaluation of excess capacity of through a major downturn. Ruling strata across the globe had every reason to avoid this. Members of the ruling circles in the u.s. had an additional reason in the 1970s to avoid a severe global recession or depression: destroying or devaluing previous capital investments on the scale required would have inflicted massive harm on u.s. capitals in particular, due to their weaker competitive positions in key sectors of the world economy. The material foundation for the geopolitical hegemony of the u.s. would have been profoundly threatened. Another way forward for capital was sought.[21] 'Neoliberalism' has become the accepted term for the path that was eventually followed. It included increased coercion in the labor market due to levels of unemployment that were previously considered politically unacceptable; generalized precariousness in employment; speed-ups in labor processes; extensions of the work day, and other direct efforts to increase the rate of exploitation. But other dimensions of neoliberalism affected laborers more indirectly, including:

(1)   An unprecedented explosion of credit money, reaching $50 trillion of debt in the u.s. by 2007 (Duncan 2012, p. 34). This level of debt enabled productive capacity to be valorized that would otherwise have been destroyed or devalued, while simultaneously disciplining labor through new forms of debt bondage.

(2)   The rise of 'globalization,' which simultaneously enabled a partial and temporary 'spatial fix' for overaccumulation difficulties by providing new outlets for investment and increased pressures on labor (due, for example, to capital flight to regions where wages were 20% of u.s. levels, as in Mexico, or even just 5%, as in China).

---

21   In the industrial heartland of the u.s. there was brutal deindustrialization in the 1970's and early 1980's, and the situation in the United Kingdom was even worse. But it was not sufficient to remove excess productive capacity in most major sectors of the world economy; there was no '"slaughter of capital values" on a scale sufficient to end [overcapacity and overproduction]' (Desai, 2013, pp. 24–25; Harmon, 2010, pp. 231–233, 282).

(3)   The rise of 'financialization'; with overcapacity problems continuing to plague most sectors of the world market credit money tended to flow to and remain within the financial sector, leading to serial bubbles in various categories of financial assets. Working men and women did not share significantly in the benefits of these bubbles, while suffering a wildly disproportionate share of the social costs of their bursting (Krier, 2009).

(4)   The emergence of massive global imbalances, with global growth generated by surplus regions exporting to regions with ever-growing deficits. Exacerbating deflationary pressures on real wages was a major component of both strategies to maintain the advantages of surplus regions and strategies to escape the disadvantages of deficit regions.

Neoliberalism was a tremendous success from the standpoint of capital. Profit levels significantly recovered after the slowdown of the 1970s. While levels of growth in the global economy may not have reached those of the post-WWII 'golden age,' they did not diverge significantly from what had been attained in previous periods of capitalist expansion (McNally, 2010; Duménil & Lévy, 2011). The value of financial assets in general, and the U.S. stock market in particular, trended steeply upwards for an unprecedented period of time. A case could be made that the technological dynamism of this period was unsurpassed; at least it is doubtful whether there has ever been a technology trajectory with the steepness of the information technology revolution, or one that has spawned new firms and industries at a faster rate. The explosion of trade and foreign direct investment facilitated historically unprecedented rates of growth in East and South Asia. In poor regions of the global economy, by official measures, at least, more people were lifted out of poverty than in any previous period of human history. Most of all, *a destruction and devaluation of capital on anything approaching the scale the previous history of capitalism suggested would be necessary to address the overaccumulation crisis of the 1970's did not occur.* But the revival of capital accumulation came at immense social costs, one sign of which was the declining share of labor income in the G.D.P. of nations throughout the globe.

Immense indebtedness, higher rates of exploitation, recurrent financial bubbles, extreme global imbalances, and a declining wage share were not accidental occurrences that could have been avoided if only political elites had fulfilled their normative responsibilities.[22] *Measured by the standards of capitalist rationality, neoliberalism was a 'rational' response to the overaccumulation crisis*

---

22   The risk of environmental catastrophe must be added to this list as well. See R. Smith, 2013.

of the 1970's. In the present moment, when overcapacity continues to afflict the major sectors of the world economy, a renewal of neoliberalism remains capital's best hope even now, after its madness has been revealed for all who wish to see.

Capital's apologists desperately hope for a new technological revolution generating new sectors and new firms, providing an outlet for the trillion plus in cash and other liquid assets U.S. firms are sitting on. We may well be on the cusp of such a revolution; the doubling of computing power per dollar invested every two years has brought us to the point where machines of ever-more astounding capacities are becoming ever-more astoundingly inexpensive. The technological dynamism associated with artificial intelligence and robot technologies, however, is not likely to bring about a corresponding dynamism of capital accumulation, as the proliferation of effective national innovation systems compresses the time in which high profits can be won from innovation (T. Smith, 2015). It may well, however, irrevocably transform the wage labor relation. In a study of over 700 occupations Frey and Osborne concluded that no less than 47% of employment in the United States is at high risk of being automated within two decades (Frey & Osborne, 2013). If anything approaching that figure is reached, then capital's always fraudulent claim that human flourishing is best served by subsuming living labor within capital's process of self-valorization will be unequivocally undermined by capital's own historical development.

To call for a more humane variant of the capital/wage labor relationship in these historical circumstances is to compound a general failure to recognize the sort of beast capital is with a failure to recognize that the beast is now foaming at the mouth. The historical moment of liberal egalitarianism has concluded. Normative social theory in the twenty-first century must advance beyond a critical assessment of a particularly irrational variant of capitalism to the critique of capitalist 'rationality' in general (T. Smith, forthcoming). Quickly.

References

Ackerman, B. (1980). *Social justice in the liberal state.* New Haven, CT: Yale University Press.

Ackerman, B. & Alstott, A. (1999). *The stakeholder society.* New Haven: Yale University Press.

Ackerman, B., Alstott, A. & Van Parijs, P. (2006). *Redesigning distribution: Basic income and stakeholder grants as cornerstones for an egalitarian capitalism.* New York: Verso.

Anderson, E. (1999). What is the point of equality? *Ethics* (109), pp. 287–337.

Arthur, C. (2002). *The new dialectic and Marx's Capital.* Leiden: Brill.

Benoit, A., Baigorri, M. and Ross-Thomas, E. (2013). 'Ich bin Ein Madrileño?' *Bloomberg Businessweek,* Jan. 7: 11–12.

Brenner, R. (2006). *The economics of global turbulence.* New York: Verso.

Callinicos, A. (2000). *Equality.* London: Polity Press.

De Angelis, M. (2007). *The beginning of history: value struggles and global capitalism.* London: Pluto Press.

Desai, R. (2013). *Geopolitical economy: After US hegemony, globalization and empire.* London: Pluto.

Duménil, G. & Lévy, D. (2011). *The crisis of neoliberalism.* Cambridge, MA: Harvard University Press.

Duncan, R. (2012). *The new depression.* Hoboken: Wiley.

Dworkin, R. (1981). What is equality? Part 2: Equality of resources. *Philosophy and Public Affairs* (10:3), 185–246.

Frey, C.B. & Osborne, M.A. (2013). *The future of employment: How susceptible are jobs to computerisation?* Oxford: Oxford Martin Publications.

Harmon, C. (2010). *Zombie capitalism.* Chicago: Haymarket Press.

Honneth, A. (2014) [2011]. *Freedom's right: The social foundations of democratic life.* New York: Columbia University Press.

Hudson, M. (2012). *The bubble and beyond: Fictitious capital, debt deflation, and global crisis.* Dresden: ISLET-Verlag.

Kalecki, M. (1971) [1943]. Political aspects of full employment. In *Selected essays on the dynamics of the capitalist economy.* Cambridge: Cambridge University Press. Verso.

Krier, D. (2009). Speculative Finance Capital, Corporate Earnings and Profit Fetishism. *Critical Sociology* (35: 5), 657–675.

Kymlicka, W. (2001). *Contemporary political philosophy: An introduction.* New York: Oxford University Press.

Lacher, H. (2006), *Beyond globalization: Capitalism, territoriality and the international relations of modernity.* New York: Routledge.

Lapavitsas, C., et al (2012). *Crisis in the Eurozone.* London: Verso.

Marx, K. (1975a) [1844]. On the Jewish question. In Marx, K. & Engels, F. *Collected works: Volume 3.* New York: International Publishers.

Marx, K. (1975b) [1844]. Contribution to the critique of Hegel's philosophy of law. Introduction. In Marx, K. & Engels, F. *Collected works: Volume 3.* New York: International Publishers.

Marx, K. (1976) [1867]. *Capital, Volume I.* New York: Penguin.

Marx, K. (1980) [1851–52]. *The Eighteenth Brumaire of Louis Napoleon.* In Marx, K. & Engels, F. *Collected Works. Volume 11.* New York: International Publishers.

Marx, K. and Engels, F. (1976) [1848]. 'The Communist Manifesto', in Marx, K. and Engels, F. *Collected Works*, Volume 6, New York: International Publishers.

McNally, D. (2010). *Global slump*. Oakland: PM Press.

Murphy, L. & Nagel, T. (2004). *The myth of ownership: Property and justice*. New York: Oxford.

Murray, P. (1988). *Marx's theory of scientific knowledge*. Atlantic Highlands, N.J.: Humanities Press.

Nussbaum, M. (2001). *Women and human development*. New York: Cambridge University Press.

Patnaik, P. (1997). *Accumulation and stability under capitalism*. Oxford: Clarendon.

Pettit, P. (2012). *On the people's terms: A republican theory and model of democracy*. New York: Cambridge University Press.

Rawls, J. (1971). *A theory of justice*. Cambridge, MA: Harvard University Press.

Rawls, J. (2001). *Justice as fairness: A restatement*. Cambridge: Harvard University Press.

Reuten, G. & Williams, M. (1989). *Value-form and the state*. New York: Routledge.

Roemer, J., et al (1996). *Equal shares: Making market socialism work*. London: Verso.

Rosenberg, J, (1994). *The empire of civil society: A critique of the realist theory of international relations*. New York: Verso.

Smith, R. (2013). Capitalism and the destruction of life on earth: Six theses on saving the humans. *Real-World Economics Review* (64): 125–50.

Smith, T. (2009) [2005]. *Globalisation: A systematic Marxian account*. Chicago: Haymarket Books.

Smith, T. (2015). The Future of U.S. Capitalism. In *The future of capitalism after the financial crisis: The varieties of capitalism debate in the age of austerity*. Westra, R. (ed), New York: Routledge.

Smith, T. (forthcoming). B*eyond liberal egalitarianism: Marxism and normative social theory in the twenty-first century*. Leiden: Brill.

Van Parijs, P. (1998) *Real freedom for all*. Oxford: Oxford University Press.

Wood, E.M. (2002). *The origin of capitalism: A longer view*. London: Verso.

CHAPTER 3

Left Thatcherism: Recent Critical Theory and Post-Marxism(s) in the Light of Marxian Social Ontology

Christian Lotz

> As Marxists, we believe that politics, in the end is derivative of the mate-
> rial reality of economic and class relations. That's a very, very profound
> statement by Karl Marx, so long as it is understood properly, so long as it's
> not mechanical. The bottom line is this statement means that not every-
> thing is possible through politics.
>
> KOUVELAKIS 2015

Introduction

By now it has become the central aim of French post-Marxist thought and critical theorists of the Frankfurt School alike to develop critical theory further towards overcoming central features of Marxian theory, especially his critique
of political economy. What is at stake in post-structuralist inspired philosophy
and post-Adornian Frankfurt School theorizing is the rejection of a dialectical
conception of society that operates with strong assumptions about both the
reconstruction of the totality of society as well as the foundations of social ontology in social-economic terms. Arguing against these assumptions two other
foundations of the social have been put forward, namely, on the one hand, the
claim found in post-structuralist inspired thought (Badiou, Ranciere, Laclau)
that the social is founded on the political, and, on the other hand, the claim
advanced in recent Frankfurt School inspired thought (Habermas, Honneth,
Jaeggi, Forst) that the social is founded on the ethical. Both philosophical
schools advance a position that ultimately leads to the rejection of any dialectical conception of society and to the idea, even if not always explicitly stated,
that the social is constituted by something *external* to the social. This, in turn,
leads to the consequence that Marx's conception of the capitalist world as a
specific world constituted by the value form gets lost and is replaced by universal and, at least tendentiously, a-historical concepts. As a consequence, the
critique and analysis of capitalism is no longer the central task of recent phi-
losophies in the critical tradition(s), since the principle of valorized labor gets

replaced by other concepts, such as recognition, communication, and rhetoric. It is the concept of capital, accordingly, that is lacking from current social
and political philosophy, which leads to an idealization of the political itself
by pushing either power and discourse or identity into the center of Marxist
theory. The dividing line, accordingly, is the question of whether we can philo-
sophically defend dialectics over ontology and ethics. This dividing line especially applies to Badiou's currently very popular attempt to present a militant
politics beyond capitalism. As Badiou argues, the question of the political is
not a question about classes, movements and other agents; rather, as he especially argues against Negri, it is a question of how to organize a mass under the
heading of an idea to which each militant political individual subjects herself.
This idea, according to Badiou, is the communist idea. This position, as I will
argue, falls back onto an empty and abstract determination of a political subject (and capitalism) that is stripped of her social position, and, we might say,
is the sad expression of what could be called *left Thatcherism*.

Against this move, in the following I will try to recover some of the basics
of a Marx-inspired social ontology by arguing that only the principle of labor
and its social form can help us see the finitude of this social form. Only if we
operate with a dialectical concept of society, are we able to come to a concept
of society that is in its very form finite. Any other position, I submit, remains
ultimately positivistic. Following Adorno, I also argue that a theory of society
necessarily needs to assume a principle under which the totality of society, i.e.
"society," can be thought (i.e., exchange, capital, money, etc.). With this position I am in sharp disagreement with philosophers such as Laclau. According
to Laclau, who primarily understands by "society" the political antagonisms
contained in it, the plurality of contemporary struggles and social antagonisms
always transcend social totality, and, hence, society becomes "an ultimate
impossibility" (Laclau 2014, 165). The deconstructivist idea of the *impossibility of society*, has, by now, become something like a mantra for almost an entire generation of post-Marxist philosophers, with, perhaps, the exception of
Negri and Zizek. Almost all contemporary "post-Marxist" philosophers reject
the primacy of the relations of production, and the "standpoint of reproduction"
(Althusser). Post-Marxist philosophers like to argue that there are principles
that are independent from social reproduction, such as the "constituent pas-
sion of the multitudo," "agonistic action," "direct action," the "people," or other
speculative roots of social reality. As a consequence, these speculations about
the political make the social a secondary principle, and it is precisely this thesis
that is in conflict with the standpoint of reproduction. In my view, the major
problem is that most post-Marxists no longer ask for the condition of the possibility for thinking about political agents *within* a society unified by a specific

form of thinghood [*Gegenständlichkeitsform*] (Lukács). Against post-Marxists I advance a rather classical position by arguing that we need to return to Marx's thesis that political and ethical possibilities depend upon the historical level of productive forces and its immanent social relations (on this point I agree with Negri).

The Primacy of the Political: Badiou, Ranciere, Laclau[1]

The most prominent candidate of the aforementioned new left Thatcherism, despite its political radicalism and Maoist background, is Alain Badiou's attempt to think politics as philosophy, which is to say, as truth related. Badiou's ontology is characterized by the central concept of the event. Events are truth related occurrences that restructure the entire reality. Badiou assumes that there are four such events that constitute truth, namely, politics, art, science, and love. Events cannot be foreseen strategically and they bring about a "truth procedure" that carries with it a radical restructuring of everything that exists in historical situations, which, as such, remain singular. Events cannot be planned or instrumentally brought about, but if they occur, the reality of a singular situation changes in its relations and its utterances, as well as with respect to the things that make up this singular situation. As we can see already here, the social does not appear on Badiou's list of truth relevant events and it is treated particularly in relation to politics, as a secondary area, given that for Badiou political events are ultimately constituted *outside* of existing social-economic frameworks. Politics, accordingly, is an event that functions as the ultimate ground of the social, *external* to the social, because social organization always is rooted in historically relevant (re)organisations of the social reality through events that are truth related.[2] As Marchart puts it, Badiou's true politics operates within the "register of the real" and cannot be translated into social relations (Marchart 2010, 160). It comes at no surprise, then, that for Badiou [a] classes only exist in concrete practical confrontations, but are nothing in themselves, and [b] Marxism is neither a philosophy nor a theory, but primarily a political praxis that is constituted through the idea of equality:

---

1   Parts of the following section appeared in German in Lotz 2014b.

2   Similarly, as Laclau has it, we need to take into account a "heteregenous" element that escapes the logic of socio-economic formation: "Heterogeneity only enters the game if of it can be shown that the very logic of totality – behind dialectical or semiological – fails at some point as a result of an aporia that cannot be resolved within that totality's structuring principle" (Laclau 2014, 162).

"Genuine Marxism, which is identified with rational political struggle for an egalitarian organization of society, doubtless began around 1848." (Badiou 2012, 8):

> Marxism [...] is neither a branch of economics (theory of the relations of production), nor a branch of sociology (objective description of 'social reality'), nor a philosophy (a dialectical conceptualization of contradictions). It is, let us reiterate, the organized knowledge of the political means required to undo society and finally realize an egalitarian, rational figure of collective organization for which the name is 'communism'.
>
> BADIOU 2012, 8

Independent from the question of whether Marxists need to be committed to egalitarianism, with this extreme view of Marxism as "movement of history," the entire theoretical side of Marxist theorizing falls apart and becomes a secondary aspect in Badiou's Manichean worldview. This radical political definition of Marxism remains, however, dissatisfactory, which is especially visible in Badiou's reduction of capital, capitalism, and other categories of society to empirical data about which one needs to be "informed" (Badiou 2008, 8), but, since the data are well known, about which we do not need theory, dialectics or conceptual clarity. In short, society for Badiou has no reality and does not belong to the reality because in all of its aspects society is the *effect* of politics, which brings about social organization. Society, in this vision, we might add, is *only* political organization. Consequently, Marxism must be taken as a movement that – independent from all socially determining factors – reorganizes the entire reality, or it is meaningless. Any theorizing about capitalism remains within the existing paradigm, as it only analyses what is taken to be untruth, whereas Marxism as a praxis (already) exists outside of the existing paradigm. The empirical data that Badiou deals with are, unsurprisingly, not very Marxian: according to Badiou, capitalism, for example, is a "regime of gangsters" (Badiou 2012, 12), driven by profit and greed, and characterized by privatization (Badiou 2012, 13). Capital is simply defined as a "nihilistic" principle through which the market expands globally, formalizes communication, and leads to US hegemony (Badiou 2005, 120). Capitalism, in other words, is here taken to refer to a set of "facts." These facts are as such not wrong, but, as I argue below, these facts as facts remain empty as long as they are not genetically reconstructed in their relation to social totality; otherwise society remains for philosophy as opaque as it appears to agents within the society.

Badiou's position, in an odd reversal, shows some similarities with Chomsky's positivism for whom theory in social and political things is unnecessary, insofar as social and political problems are self-transparent and accessible to everyone. This entirely anti-Marxian position should be rejected from the viewpoint of a critical theory of society. As Adorno nicely puts it: "theories and sentences focus on society, insofar as these cannot be found in the Baedeker" (Adorno 2008, 39).[3] The current social formation, according to Badiou, need not be thought of as a different social organization of labor and society; rather, it purely reorganizes itself in political terms, which is based on the "force of an idea" (Badiou 2012, 15), of communism. This idea constitutes and interpellates individuals as political subjects that project the egalitarian idea into a non-existing history and thereby militantly reorganizes the reality (Badiou 2010, 3–5). Indeed, according to Badiou, the political subject is "a militant of this truth" (Badiou 2010, 3) through the "incorporation" of the idea. The individual goes through a process of "subjectivation" (Badiou 2010, 3): "The communist idea is what constitutes the becoming-political Subject of the individual as also and at the same time his or her projection into history" (Badiou 2010, 4). According to Badiou's idealism, through this political baptism and renewal of isolated and "animalistic" bodies these bodies now belong to a new order:

> Without the idea, the only thing left is an animalized humanity. Capital-ism is the animalization of the human beast, who no longer lives except in terms of its interests and what it deems to be its due. This animaliza-tion is extremely dangerous because it is devoid of values and laws.
> BADIOU 2010b, 35

This reduction of capitalism to an anthropological unit, to an apocalyptic ni-hilist system, and to a life without idea, reminds us of a mix of Christian theol-ogy and Heideggerian metaphysics. Capitalism is a system characterized by a spiritual downfall and meaningless life, which only *the* idea can bring back. Here Communism becomes an empty placeholder for the good. Instead of sol-diers of the hidden church, we now have our communist soldiers who liberate us from the downfall of civilization.

Badiou's attempt to present a militant politics beyond capital positions him also in opposition to Negri. As Badiou argues, the question of the political is not a question about classes, movements and other agents; rather, as he argues against Negri, it is a question of how to organize a mass under the heading of an idea. The anti-globalization movement, for example, is rejected as operating within the system. Instead, Badiou promotes "an autonomy and heterogeneity of politics, which exists at a remove from any relational dialectic" (Toscano

---

3   The "Baedecker" is a famous German travel and cultural guide.

in Bidet/Kouvelakis 2009, 532). Badiou's thesis that the form of politics in the form of (a) party has been exhausted and his rejection of Negri's attempt to think the political subject as the movement of the multitude, in combination with his rejection of social-economic categories and social reality, leads him to an empty militant subject who is constituted by an abstract idea that, as such, can contain anything. Nothing *exists* between the universal truth and the singular individual in Badiou's schema. Put differently, in his schema between the "two" (love) and the "all" (politics), nothing exists that is *constitutive* for reality. The image of a *philosophical soldier* might be of interest for activists that have lost their party and hope, but it is, as I submit, insufficient for developing a critical theory, as Marx already warned: "Do not say that social movement excludes political movement. There is never a political movement which is not at the same time social" (MEW 4, 182).

Though in their political positions they disagree, other post-Marxists, such as Ranciere and Laclau, operate in close proximity to Badiou. In recent publications Ranciere has recovered a radical anarchist notion of democracy as the "ungoverning" element in all government and as an event that underlies *all* attempts to organize social reality politically. According to Ranciere, democracy is the ultimate source of all social organization, insofar as all political reorganizations of society need to control the very uncontrollable element that sets any political control and organization in motion. Society, as it were, becomes "bracketed" by events of democracy, as the latter is the very word for the fundamental instability of the entire social order. Politics, as in Badiou, here turns into the *ontological* ground of the social, and, since it remains *external* to this order, it is also a deconstructivist "reminder" that cannot be described in social terms. This move leads, as in Badiou, to an uncanny return to historically universal concepts, which is nicely visible in the following statement: "The power of the people is not that of a people gathered together, of the majority, or of the working class. It is simply the power peculiar to those who have no more entitlements to govern than to submit" (Ranciere 2006, 46). Ranciere offers even the most radical formulation of the "autonomy" theorists by claiming that the political in the form of radical democracy does not depend on *any* social, ethical and historical forms:

> Democracy is as bare in its relation to the power of wealth as it is to the power of kinship that today comes to assist and to rival it. It is not based on any nature of things nor guaranteed by any institutional form. It is not borne along by any historical necessity and does not bear any. It is only entrusted to the constancy of its specific acts.
>
> RANCIERE 2006, 97

The problem with this position is not that it reintroduces a strong concept of politics; rather, the problem with this vision is, as in Badiou, that it is unable to conceptualize the political agent as a *historically specific* and social-economic agent who, as I argue below, can only *be* a political agent because its being is social. In Ranciere's schema, although he does not go as far as Negri's multitude, the political agent is "people." These "people," however, remain as empty as Badiou's subject; for "people" is a substance without form. If Ranciere's thesis would be true, then we should be able to apply this concept of democracy and politics to all forms of society, including nomadic societies, indigenous societies, or ethically and religiously divided societies, which does not make sense, unless, as Ranciere *presupposes*, there is a (modern) social-historical form under which his concepts are intelligible. Accordingly, the real battle that we are currently fighting is based on the problem of whether we want to remain faithful to Marx's later position and its standpoint of reproduction, or whether we indeed want to return to a metaphysically or anthropologically based autonomy of the political. The frontline of this battle was already nicely summarized by Poulantzas in an interview given in 1970:

> One must know whether one remains within a Marxist framework or not; and if one does one accepts the determinant role of the economic in the very complex sense; not the determination of forces of production but of relations of production and the social division of labour. [...] The conceptual framework of Marxism has to do with this very annoying thing which is called 'relations of production' and the determinant role of relations of production. If we abandon it then, of course, we can speak of the autonomy of politics or of other types of relations between politics and economy.
>
> POULANTZAS 2008, 396

In other words, almost all contemporary political left philosophers ranging from anarchists like Ranciere to Maoists like Badiou, reject the primacy of the relations of production, which, going back to Marx's position in *The German Ideology*, is based on what Althusser calls the "standpoint of reproduction" (Althusser 2008, 1–8). Instead of the *reproduction* of life, these political philosophers argue that there is a principle located before the reproduction of life. The problem, then, is to construct a concept of society that remains "authentic" to its root, and to the creativity and self-determination of life or the people, which, on a side note, brings back central problems of Marx's early humanism. This problem is most visible in Negri's speculations about constituent power, as he, similar to Abensour, claims that constituent power is ultimately an ontological principle of life itself. "As a form of dystopia," Negri claims, "constituent power shows a singular and irreducible concept of the political, but at the same time it construes and connects a methodology, a philosophy of history, and an ethics that are equally singular" (Negri 1999, 320). As a consequence, ontological speculations a la Negri about the multitude and its intrinsic capacities, such as desire, love, and enjoyment, conceived as the *ontological* foundation of reality, make the social a secondary principle, and it is precisely this thesis that is in conflict with the standpoint of reproduction. To be fair, though, Negri is somewhere in the middle in this picture, as he tries to argue that constituent power understood as the "strength" of the multitude finds its echo in the social through living labor: "Living labor constitutes the world, by creatively modeling, *ex novo*, the materials that it touches" (Negri 1999, 326). Whether Negri's attempt to move between the two camps is successful remains an open question, especially since he tends to underplay, on the one hand, the historical aspect of social reproduction (which, if taken seriously, would not allow us to move directly from life to labor), and, on the other hand, the role of capitalist relations of production and state apparatuses that lead, as Poulantzas has argued, to a distribution of bodies *before* they can express themselves in labor (Poulantzas 2000, 28–30). Accordingly, it is highly questionable whether we can simply start with an abstract conception of life that expresses itself *immediately* in labor, especially since this leads to an a-historical view of society. As Zizek points out, expressed in traditional philosophical dualities, a strong defense of the autonomy of the political implies a return to "idealism" (Zizek 2002, 272). Instead, I propose against all these left neo-idealisms, that we assume that labor always has a social form, i.e., a mode that depends upon the presupposed organic whole of social relations expressed in social categories. In our case this is capital. Here I am in agreement with Zizek, who underlined that it is precisely the lack of a rigorous analysis of the socio-economic sphere that gets lost in their Deleuzian redescription of life and politics (for this, see Zizek 2002, 331). This critique can be expanded to virtually all contemporary political philosophers, as almost all of them overlook Marx's analysis of capitalism. As Zizek has it:

> The problem with the deconstructionist or Deleuzian poetry of capital is that it totally suspends Marx's intention to provide an actual economic analysis of existing capitalism, not simply a critical philosophy of commodity fetishism and reification.
>
> IBID., 279

This lack is also visible in Laclau's semiotic and Derrida inspired political philosophy. As Toscano has argued with Zizek, Badiou's metaphysics shows a "family resemblance" with Laclau's thought (Toscano in Bidet/Kouvelakis 2009, 530). Similar to Ranciere, though with an eye to the plurality of antagonisms in our contemporary social order, Laclau also assumes "that there is a heterogeneous 'outside' preventing political economy from closing itself around its internal categories, and thus constituting the *fundamentum inconcussum* of the social." (Laclau 2014, 153). Laclau argues that all contemporary social antagonisms and struggles in their plural variety cannot be reduced to a single and unified struggle against capital; rather, as he puts forward, the unification of these struggles can only come out of these struggles, but in their diversity they remain outside of a unified social-economic framework that Marxist theory tries to place as the meta-framework above all other factors that determine social agents: "forces opposing capitalism are not just the result of a capitalist logic, but *interrupt* it from the outside, so that the story of capitalism cannot result from the unfolding of its internal categories" (Laclau 2014, 154). Though not as militant as Badiou, for Laclau the political is no longer a dialectical category that can be grasped through the existing relations of production; rather, the political is in principle *external* to the entire social order, and only because it is external to it, is it possible, As Laclau argues, the political can break through the existing orders: "the antagonism presuppose a radical outside, there is no reason to think that locations within the relations of production are going to be privileged points of their emergence" (Laclau 2014, 166). Given the primacy of the political, which leads to a pluriverse of social "formulations," society in the abstract becomes something absolutely contingent: "For me, the 'political' has a primary structuring role because social relations are ultimately contingent, and any prevailing articulation results from an antagonistic confrontation whose outcome is not decided beforehand" (Laclau 2014, 160). Consequently, he argues that a position that operates with the primacy of the economic, even in a wider and complex sense, presupposes "that at no point does social reality overflow what that matrix can determine and control" (Laclau 2014, 161), the consequence of which is giving up on the concept of class. It becomes clear that Laclau's concept of a theory of society is extremely reductive, insofar as he lays out Marxist theory from the begining on as a *political* theory with a focus on class and revolution, which leads him to reject the concept of society itself. Society, however, is the condition for the possibility of making any social distinctions, such as class or antagonism. As I will argue below, there is a difference between social relations, institutions, or group-related dynamics and the *form* under which all of these relations can be thought of as belonging to *society* and, as such, as being than more than the sum of all empirical relationships.

The Primacy of Ethics: Honneth

Let me briefly discuss another shift that we can currently observe in post-Marxist thought, namely, the shift towards a normative or ethical foundation of society. In contradistinction to philosophers discussed in the last section, recent critical theorists in the Frankfurt School tradition have argued for a turn towards communication, as well as towards recognitional and normative considerations in critical theory. This turn is posited in particular against Adorno, since Adorno still maintains that we need to develop a concept of society that is a totality and based on a principle of synthesis, which, for Adorno, is exchange. As he puts it in his *Introduction to Sociology* (1968):

> What really makes society a social entity, what constitutes it both conceptually and in reality, is the relationship of exchange, which binds together virtually all the people participating in this kind of society. [...] Ladies and Gentlemen, the abstraction we are concerned with is not one that first came into being in the head of a sociological theoretician who then offered the somewhat flimsy definition of society which states that everything relates to everything else. The abstraction in question here is really the specific form of the exchange process itself, the underlying social fact through which socialization first comes about. If you want to exchange two objects and – as is implied by the concept of exchange – if you want coexchange them in terms of equivalents, and if neither party is to receive more than the other, then the parties must leave aside a certain aspect of the commodities. In discussing equal exchange, I must for the moment disregard the question whether a violation of equivalence is not implied in the concept of exchange itself; for the present we are concerned only with constructing the concept to the extent that it is constitutive of society. In developed societies the exchange takes place, as you all know, through money as the equivalent form.[4]
>
> ADORNO 2003, 58

---

4   Though I agree with Adorno in principle, I have criticized his position by arguing that he does not go far enough insofar as he traces exchange back to money and labor (for this, see Lotz 2013 and Lotz 2014a).

The recent turn away from Adorno implies (even if not always admitted) a fundamental *ontological* assumption, namely the assumption, that "normativity" or ethics is the true foundation of the social, a thesis that we also find in philosophers such as Levinas. In Honneth's philosophy the turn is most visible in his return to a Hegelian inspired theory of democratic ethics [*Sittlichkeit*] which is driven by a set of recognitional relations that structure all aspects of society normatively (Honneth 2011). Similar to Habermas, Honneth leaves the "production paradigm" (Habermas) behind in order to replace it by a model of social recognition. Recognitional relations and processes are thereby understood as relations that are determined by ethical background assumptions, claims about these assumptions, and their social-psychological consequences. Rather surprisingly, Honneth has paid more attention to economic issues in recent years (Honneth 2011) and, in a contribution to a large conference on Marx in Berlin 2011, he criticized the Marxian Critique of Political Economy on the grounds of his theory. Honneth's attack is, mildly put, wrongheaded, insofar as he claims that Marx reduces social agents to utilitarian agents that only function in accordance with "economically functional imperatives" (Honneth 2013, 350) and within their self-interests. This starting point is a non-starter, however, because Marx is not terribly interested in utilitarian market agents; rather, his theory *is about the social form, under which the talk of self-interested market participants makes sense*. In addition, as Honneth argues, must we not confuse social conflicts with conflicts that are the result of the logic of capital. According to Honneth, Marx did not understand that historical, political, and normative conflicts cannot be reduced to conflicts that emerge out of a narrowly defined social principle, such as capital.

Honneth varies an age old critique advanced against Marx, namely, that Marx reduces social agents to economically determined agents unable to understand normative conflicts and the complexity of modern social life. Moreover, Honneth claims, the "temporal schema of a non-stoppable and uninterrupted expansion of capitalist valorization interests" (Honneth 2013, 356) does not help us understand that social progress as a *normative* process of social agents who fight for their interpersonal and for social recognition on the bases of claims that presuppose equally applicable normative assumptions. Put differently, according to Honneth, classical critical theory does not understand the advancements of capitalist society. As we know, though, Marx celebrates the civilizing achievements of capitalism, but – and this is the difference – he does not lay this out in terms of justice and norms, which, according to recent Frankfurt School philosophers, is its defect. Agents, such as classes, accordingly, already presuppose an ethically-defined framework under which social conflicts can appear as normatively defined exchanges. But we are unable to grasp this dynamic with Marx's Critique of Political Economy, so the story goes, and as such, we are asked to start with the assumption that social relations are founded on the basis of social-ethical assumptions, instead of asking first whether this basis is made possible by the concept and analysis of capital. It is precisely this claim that brings Honneth close to other post-Marxist philosophers, insofar as he proposes a shift in social ontology. Honneth's formulation of a "reality constituting ethics" [*wirklichkeitsbildender Moral*] (Honneth 2013, 358) should not be underestimated, inasmuch as the social *reality* here is founded upon something that remains external and foreign to the social as such, namely, in this case the ethical framework. Though Frankfurt School thinkers like to talk about our post-metaphysical age, they cannot avoid making certain tacit assumptions that reveal their commitments in regard to the being and reality of the social. In Honneth's case it is without doubt the idea that that which traditional critical theory had called "the" society is in truth Hegelian *Sittlichkeit*, of which civil society only partakes and parasitically feeds upon. It is of no surprise, then, that Honneth tends to downplay theories that operate with concepts and categories, and, instead, foregrounds intersubjective relations between agents. The thesis that all social relations are ultimately constituted by ethics is identical with the claim that the actuality of all entities that can be addressed as "social" already fall under the form "ethics." According to Honneth, this is also true for capital itself. The "capital relation," as he puts it, is "shot through" with normativity (Honneth 2013, 359). The consequences of this theoretical shift are obvious: instead of analyzing social reality as the result of a collective productivity that appears under a specific social form (=value), Honneth returns to idealist principles, insofar as he no longer assumes that the social reality is unified under such a form. Instead, he needs to argue that the normative frame that underlies social relations, including capitalist market relations, are based upon a *universally* defined ethics and morality. With this, however, we lose *precisely* the Marxian basis for analyzing society as a unity that frames everything that falls under it. The historically specific character of capitalism, we might say, is no longer visible in Honneth's ethicism because he needs to found a historically specific form on *universal* assumptions that, as such, remain historically neutral. The basic problem with our post-Marxist contemporaries becomes visible at this point: instead of taking human productivity as the central concept for a critical theory of society, Honneth takes *moral claims* to be the central concept, which, consequently, leads to a rejection of a substantial concept of money, capital, value and class, as class conflicts are now replaced by a pluriverse of social conflicts that are *all* based on "normative conflictuality" (Honneth 2013, 361). With this, the genesis of social relations from their origin in value, capital, and labor gets lost and social totality disappears behind a postmodern veil of a myriad of discourses, claims, arguments, and normative exchanges.

Even empirically Honneth's position leads to odd and at times cynical consequences: social pathologies are mainly interpreted as psychological, i.e. subjective, phenomena. However, being faced with the fact that 98% of the world's population is excluded from the wealth of the other 2%, Honneth's claim that market agents are equally determined by a "prior consciousness of solidarity" (Honneth 2011, 329) and the recognition of a shared value system (Honneth 2011, 341) remains ideological, to say the least. Given the fact that the three richest individuals on our planet control as much wealth as 600 million individuals at the bottom, Honneth's claim that *all* "economic agents need to recognize themselves as members of a cooperative community" (Honneth 2011, 349) is nonsense, as it is precisely the other way around. As Marx argues in the *Grundrisse*, the monetization of all social relations leads to the externalization of society, which today is mostly visible in the fact that people who profit most from collective productivity take themselves to be totally disconnected from society. The assumption of a quasi-transcendental morality that regulates all economic exchanges misses the fact that such an ethics would need a different social-economic form of society. Honneth's odd claim that with the "market-mediated division of labor social relations emerge in which all members of society can develop an 'organic solidarity' because they reciprocally recognize themselves in their contributions to their shared wealth" (Honneth 2010, 97) sounds nice, and Hegel would have clapped, but ideologically it simply repeats and affirms the widespread "social violence" (Adorno 1998/8, 383) that we find in our contemporary global order. As Marx has it in his arguments against this Hegelian position:

> what is forgotten, finally, is that already the simple forms of exchange value and money latently contain the opposition [and inequality, C.L.] between labour and capital. Thus, what all this wisdom comes down to is the attempt to stick fast at the simplest economic relations, which, conceived independently, are pure abstractions; but these relations are, in reality, mediated by the deepest antagonisms, and represent only one side, in which the full expression of the antagonisms is obscured.
>
> MEW 42, 173

Be that as it may, in my view the shift away from a social ontology founded upon human productivity towards the political or the ethical leads to paradoxes, given that with the foundation of the social upon something that remains external to sociality the task of a (critical) theory becomes impossible, inasmuch as post-Marxist theories reject the idea that social phenomena can be traced back to their underlying social form and that it is the task of theory to make the genesis of social categories transparent. Social transparency, however, can only be reached if we assume that all social categories ultimately go back to and take part in a unified social form. This task, however, can only be achieved if these social categories can be brought together in a *coherent* unity so that social totality as a historically specific form becomes apparent. As I will argue in the following: only the assumption of society as a social totality can lead to an understanding of capitalism as a *finite* social form. This systematic character of what we call "capitalism" as a *form* gets lost in economic, sociological, and positivist accounts of capitalism. In Marx's own words (that he removed after the first edition of Capital),

> The value-form of the product of labor is the most abstract but also most general form of the bourgeois mode of production, which hereby is characterized as a specific type of social mode of production and thereby likewise historical. Therefore, if one misperceives it for the eternal natural form of social production, one, then, naturally also overlooks what is specific in the value-form, thus the commodity-form, and, further developed, the money-form, the capital-form, etc.
>
> MEGA II/5, 44; translation from MURRAY 2013

This finite form is based on valorized labor and, accordingly, I reject Laclau's claim that "there is no ultimate *substratum*, no *nature* (*sic!*) *naturans*, out of which existing social articulations could be explained" (Laclau 2014, 169). To repeat this simple point, it is clear that all politics, all ethics, and everything else human would disappear if we would stop being productive and would stop laboring; life is primary, and it cannot be grasped without the production of needs, its cooperative element, and its relation to the earth. The organization of these relations into an existing whole, a form, is necessary for the reproduction of this whole. *Society does exist*, but it does not exist in the universal. Since production as such cannot exist, society as such cannot exist either. This finitude gets lost in post-Marxist thought: in Badiou we are forced to wait for some incalculable and unforeseeable event (which, since it cannot explain the finitude of capitalism from the inside, *in principle* expands the existing system towards an infinite future) and in Honneth we are forced to assume that capitalism is based on a universal normativity that escapes any finitude. As a consequence, only internal advancements are possible. We always end up with a conception of society that remains capitalist in its essence, i.e., its proponents either argue that capitalism does not exist because we only find a plurality of different social forms and "antagonistic points are going to be multiple" (Laclau 2014, 167) and remain heterogeneous to each other, or its proponents argue that only certain aspects of capitalism can be changed, but not its "good and just" framework. The loss of finitude as a *social* concept as underlying political finitude in post-Marxist thought is finally also visible in the loss of a Marxian concept of critique. Let me therefore finish my critique of post-Marxist thought with a brief analysis of what is meant by "critique" in a Marxian theoretical horizon.

The Marxian Concept of Critique

German and Anglo-American Frankfurt School theorists since Habermas have repeatedly argued against older authors within the same tradition that the concept of critique needs to be backed up by normative concepts. In addition, as Habermas argued, social reality cannot be derived from the "production paradigm," as the latter is in need of normativity. Instead, as is well known, he introduced a communicative paradigm, which Honneth further expanded into a recognitional paradigm. As I will argue in this section, the argument that critical theory is necessarily in need of normative foundation is wrongheaded, as the concept of critique should be conceived of as the attempt to reveal the *inner limits* of its object through an analysis of what is essential to its object. As the object of social critique is society, a critical theory of society is or becomes critical whenever it reveals its object as *limited*. Only if we understand that the object of critical theory is *finite* and historically limited, can we understand that the concept of totality is a *critical concept* and has nothing to do with what philosophers from Lyotard to Laclau conceive as "totalizing."

The concept of "immanent critique" has often been discussed in the secondary literature on Marx. It seems to me, however, that one important aspect has often been overlooked, namely, the Kantian origin of the concept of critique that Marx combines with a genetic theory of social relations. In a central passage on Hegel, Marx writes:

> [T]rue philosophical criticism of the present state constitution not only shows the contradictions as existing, but explains them, grasps their genesis; its necessity. It comprehends their peculiar and characteristic significance. However, this comprehension does not, as Hegel thinks, consist in everywhere finding the determinations of the logical concept, but rather in grasping the peculiar logic of the specific object.
> MEW1, 296; transl. altered

Decisive in this quote are three aspects of Marx's concept of critique, name-ly: [1] critique is a procedure that leads to a comprehension of its object, [2] critique is essentially a genetic procedure, and [3], critique comprehends the *inner* logic of *its* object, and in this way, as we will see, it grasps its essence. We can easily see that here critique is introduced by Marx as an analytic activ-ity that attempts to define its object through grasping the *inner limits* of its object by tracing its elements back to their origins. Genesis is here identical with *finitude*, insofar as an object with *its* genesis can no longer be located in an abstract logical space that is characterized by an atemporal structure. Instead, a genetically determined object has a temporally limited horizon and therefore a finite (and historical) origin. Only an object that can be determined by its own inner logic can be *separated* from another object, as the difference between objects comes about through that which "makes them up" as pre-cisely this and not another object. A determination of an object in its being, accordingly, introduces a limit through which the particularity of the object is revealed. Marx's connection of critique and analysis has a phenomenological character, as he traces that which makes an object a particular object back to its inner categorical determinations. As we know, this idea is central for Kant's *First Critique* in which Kant criticizes existing metaphysics no only by *limit-ing* the scope of what could legitimately fall under metaphysics, but also by *limiting* the scope and essence of reason and rationality itself. The concept of critique, as Kant knew, goes back historically, on the one hand, to "making a se-lection," and, on the other hand, to "judgment." "Judgment" originally means to "say that something is such and such," and, accordingly, it has a positive sense. Moreover, Heidegger reminded us that *categorein* literally means to *say what something is*. So, a successful judgment is a judgment that reveals the scope and limits of the object of the judgment.

Accordingly, it should become more transparent how Marx uses the con-cept of critique for the analysis of capitalism. The *Critique of Political Economy* is critical because the Marxian critique does not deal with *any* social forma-tion; instead, it has a *specific* object, which is capitalist society (i.e., a social formation determined by valorized labor). A critique of capitalist society, con-sequently, tries to analyze this specific sociality as a specific *form*, and, hence, tries to analyze capitalism in such a way that its *inner limits* become visible by revealing its essential categorical determinations. As we said above, deter-mining a social formation in its inner logic and inner limits is identical with revealing it as a historically finite social formation. From this it follows imme-diately that the specific categories that belong to the object of critical analysis [a] must be related to each other through their inner genesis and coherence (i.e., they must be traced back to valorized labor) and [b] must be analyzed

in their historical genesis by revealing their historical origin. That is why dialectics means both method and history. This is nicely visible in a distinction
that Marx makes at the beginning of the chapter on "original accumulation."
There he draws a distinction between two concepts of origin and argues
against political economists of his time that they identify origin [*Ursprung*]
with past [*Vergangenheit*]. Whereas bourgeois political economists determine
the "origin" of economic development as something that remains *external* to
the economic development itself, i.e., as a thing of the past that is over and no
longer is part of the development itself, Marx's own analysis reveals the origin
of the economic development as a *moment of* this development. The origin, in
the Marxian sense, accordingly, is a genetic concept, insofar as the origin is a
category of the *inner* structure and logic of the object in question. One could
also say that the origin of capitalism is not like a cause that brought capitalism about, which would presuppose two separate entities (cause and effect);
rather, the origin of capitalism is an essential moment of this form of sociality
itself. As Lukács has argued, the main category for Marx is "interaction" [*Wech-
selwirkung*]. Consequently, in every one of its stages the development of capitalism depends on this original element. For example, the violence contained
in the original accumulation of capital is not something that can be left behind with the further development of capitalism (as some of its contemporary
proponents would claim); instead, we need to grasp the (specific) violence of
capitalism as an inner and intrinsic moment of this (specific) social formation
itself. The chapter on primitive accumulation, accordingly, does not deal with
something that belongs to the past; rather, it deals with the past as something
contemporaneous. As a consequence of the foregoing, we need to claim that
within the Marxian framework it is not only the case that "production as such"
cannot exist, but also, that "society as such" does not exist, insofar as critical
theory deals with a specific social formation that is not taken to be universal
(though it is based on a universal). As there is no universal economic science,
there is no universal social science.

Critique of Political Economy is critical because it reveals its object, capitalist
society, as a *finite* form of sociality that, because it is finite, can also be overcome, can fall apart, or can be replaced by a different form of sociality. This
consideration already contains a concept of totality that is in itself and as such
critical; for the analysis of the essence of capitalist sociality necessarily presupposes a unity of its object and, since it is a specific unity, a negative concept
of this unity. The origin of Marx's concept of contradiction is to be found in
its concept of totality, as this very totality can only exist in its unity because
it is limited *through itself*. The essence of an object is not this specific essence
because it is not another essence; rather, as Marx says in the quote above, as a

social phenomenologist, it is *this* essence because it contains *its own* peculiar logic. Consequently, we need to assume that the negativity of the unity of this essence is an *internal negativity* (for this see Adorno 2008, 47). In this sense, all critical theory is based on what Adorno called "negative dialectics." In sum, Marx's concept of critique, as I just outlined it, is nicely visible in a famous quote from a letter to Lassalle written in February 1858:

> The work I am presently concerned with is a *Critique of Economic Categories* or, if you like, the system of the bourgeois economy critically presented. It is at once a presentation of the system and because of the presentation a critique of the system.
>
> MEW 29, 550

Conclusion

We can conclude from the foregoing the reasons for why the "theme of detotalization" (Toscano in Bidet/Kouvelakis 2009, 562) and the "suspicion towards the very idea of a totality of social relations" (Toscano in Bidet/Kouvelakis 2009, 563) that we find in post-Marxist thought goes into the wrong direction, as it is *precisely* the concept of totality that leads to a *detotalization* of history, to an anti-teleological concept of history, and to the possibility of rupture based on the negativity of the capitalist totality, which leads to a fundamental *finitude* of this specific social organization. In sum, the political, as Badiou, Ranciere, Laclau, and Mouffe claim, *cannot* be the first principle of social totality because it disconnects the social agent from the achieved historical level of social reproduction. The return to the political and, perhaps, the return to an *abstract* and empty form of Leninism in contemporary radical philosophy is based on the disconnection of philosophical speculation about the root of social reality *from* this reality, insofar as post-Marxist thinkers tend to no longer look at the social reality as a dialectical relationship, i.e., as a mediated relation, which constitutes the social agent as an agent who is only able to *be* a social agent because she exists through and as a historically achieved level of social mediation and externalization. As Marx has it, the individual is *determinate* and, accordingly, the possibility of politics *must*, according to my counter-position, be determined and can only evolve out of social existence, now understood as social form. Every act, I contend, depends upon the externalized reality as its mediation and it can therefore not be thought of as a total break, as Badiou seems to assume. A historical break can only be successful if the *conditions for the political* switch are *present* in the situation of the break in both intellectual and imaginative ways of how to go on and material ways of reorganization of the social relations of production. None of the post-Marxist philosophers says anything about how we *concretely* would move towards a different way of production, communication, and a reality not determined by capital. The latter presupposes the idea of a post-growth society, highly developed and highly creative individuals, as well as an associatively organized means of production. The idealist positions of our post-Marxists remain abstract and do not offer any concrete ways of a different productive life. Accordingly, their concepts of politics remain empty.

References

Adorno, T W. (1998), *Gesammelte Schriften*, Darmstadt: Wissenschaftliche Buchgesellschaft, Lizenzausgabe Suhrkamp.

Adorno, T W. (2003): *Einführung in die Soziologie*, Nachgelassene Schriften, Abteilung IV, Vorlesungen, Band 15, Berlin: Suhrkamp.

Adorno, T W. (2008): *Philosophische Elemente einer Theorie der Gesellschaft* (1964), Nachgelassene Schriften, Abteilung IV, Vorlesungen, Band 12, Berlin: Suhrkamp.

Althusser, L. (2008), *On ideology*, London: Verso.

Badiou, A. (2005), *Infinite thought*, tr. O. Feltham & J. Clemens, New York: Continuum.

Badiou, A. (2008), *Conditions*, tr. Steven Corcoran, New York: Continuum.

Badiou, A. (2010), "The idea of communism", in: *The idea of communism*, ed. C. Douzinas & S. Zizek, London: Verso, 1–14.

Badiou, A. (2012), *The rebirth of history*, tr. G. Elliott, London: Verso.

Bidet, J. & Kouvelakis, S. (eds). (2009), *A critical companion to contemporary Marxism*, Chicago: Haymarket Books.

Honneth, A. (2010). *Das Ich im Wir. Studien zur Anerkennungstheorie*. Berlin: Suhrkamp.

Honneth, A. (2011). *Das Recht der Freiheit. Grundriss einer demokratischen Sittlichkeit*, Berlin: Suhrkamp.

Honneth, A. (2013). Die Moral im ‚Kapital. Versuch einer Korrektur der Marxschen Ökonomiekritik, in: *Nach Marx. Philosophie. Kritik. Praxis*, hg. Rahel Jaeggi und Daniel Loick, Berlin: Suhrkamp, 364–394.

Kouvelakis, S. (2015). Interview with Bunden, *Jacobin*, 3/12/2015, Accessed at: https://www.jacobinmag.com/2015/03/lapavitsas-varoufakis-grexit-syriza.

Laclau, Ernesto (2014), *The Rhetorical Foundations of Society*, London: Verso 2014.

Lotz, C. (2013). "Capitalist schematization. Political economy, exchange, and objecthood in Adorno," *Zeitschrift für Kritische Theorie* 36/37, 110–123.

Lotz, C. (2014a). *The capitalist schema. Time, money, and the culture of abstraction*. Lanham Lexington Books.

Lotz, C. (2014b). Klasse und Gewalt. Kritische Anmerkungen aus Marxistischer Sicht zum Verschwinden des Klassenbegriffs in Kritischer Theorie und Post-Marxismus. *Prokla. Zeitschrift für kritische Sozialwissenschaft*, 176, 383–403.

Marchart, O. (2010), *Die politische Differenz. Zum Denken des Politischen bei Nancy, Lefort, Badiou, Laclau und Agamben*, Berlin: Suhrkamp.

Marx, K. & Engels, F. (1952ff). *Marx Engels Werke*, Berlin: Dietz [=MEW].

Murray, P. (2013). "Unavoidable crises: Reflections on Backhaus and the development of Marx's value-form theory in the *Grundrisse*." in *In Marx's laboratory: Critical interpretations of the Grundrisse*, Chicago: Haymarket Books, 121–148.

Negri, A. (1999). *Insurgencies: Constituent power and the modern state*, tr. by M. Boscagli, Minneapolis: University of Minnesota Press.

Poulantzas, N. (2000). *State, power, socialism*, tr. by P. Camiller, intr. by S. Hall. London: Verso.

Poulantzas, N. (2008). The Poulantzas reader: Marxism,law, and the state, London: Verso.

Postone, M. (1996). *Time, labor, and social domination: A reinterpretation of Marx's critical theory*. Cambridge: Cambridge University Press.

Ranciere, Jacques (2006), *The Hatred of Democracy*, London: Verso.

Zizek, S. (2002). *Revolution at the gates: Selected writings of Lenin from 1917*, London: Verso.

CHAPTER 4

Capital's Reach: How Capital Shapes and Subsumes

Patrick Murray

Introduction

Alasdair MacIntyre's *After Virtue* begins: "Imagine that the natural sciences were to suffer the effects of a catastrophe" (MacIntyre, 1984, p. 1). MacIntyre is setting up his claim that modern moral discourse has suffered a catastrophe, though one that has gone largely unnoticed. My point of departure is that social theory (social philosophy and the social sciences) has undergone such a catastrophe – also largely unrecognized. Moreover, this catastrophe is being exacerbated by developments such as the usurpation of social theory by "economics imperialism." This catastrophe encompasses the fragmentation of modern moral discourse that MacIntyre bemoans. The social theory of the modern world that informs MacIntyre's historical account of the breakdown of moral discourse derives largely from Max Weber.[1] My account of the catastrophe of social theory derives from Karl Marx's critique of political economy.

Simon Clarke, in his book *Marx, Marginalism and Modern Sociology*, states:

> There was a scientific revolution in nineteenth-century social thought... It was inaugurated by Marx's critique of the ideological foundations of classical political economy, which he located in the political economists' neglect of the social form of capitalist production which was the basis of their naturalisation of capitalist social relations. For Marx society could not be explained abstractly, on the basis of the confrontation between abstract individuals and an abstract nature... Capitalist society is a society based on a particular social form of production, within which the production and reproduction of material things is subordinated to the production and accumulation of surplus value, and within which the participation of the individual in society is conditional on the individual's insertion into the social relations of production. Thus Marx's critique of political economy established an alternative foundation on

---

1 "The contemporary vision of the world, so I have suggested, is predominantly, although not perhaps always in detail, Weberian" (MacIntyre, 1984, 103).

which to build a theory of capitalist society whose fundamental concepts would be those of *value, surplus value* and *class.*

CLARKE, 1982, p. 240

Clarke goes on to point out, rightly I believe, that Marx's "scientific revolution" was missed – including by most Marxists, who mistook Marx for a radical Ricardian economist. Marx's idea that capitalist society is "based on a particular social form of production" disappeared.

Neoclassical (mainstream) economics is oblivious to or dismissive of the topic of specific social forms, in particular, specific social forms of wealth, labor, production, distribution, etc. Instead, neoclassical economics conceives of itself as a generally applicable social science. Consider Lionel Robbins's widely-cited definition: "Economics is the science which studies human behavior as a relationship between ends and scarce means which have alternative uses" (Robbins, 1994, p. 85). For neoclassical economics, the capitalist mode of production reduces to the production and distribution of use-values by entrepreneurs and laborers employing use-values. Everything else is just so much "hocus pocus." With the first sentence of *Capital*, Marx rebukes any such approach; he tells us that his topic is not "the wealth of nations" but rather those societies in which wealth generally takes the social form of the commodity. For Marx, the very idea of a generally applicable science of economics is bogus.

Clarke goes on to argue that this foreshortened horizon of neoclassical economics was adopted by Max Weber (who was trained as an economist before there were sociologists in German universities), Talcott Parsons, and others into modern sociology, thereby incorporating into sociology's basic outlook obliviousness to specific social forms of needs, wealth, labor, production, and distribution, in particular, obliviousness to the specific social forms constitutive of production on a capitalist basis. Modern social theory has been put onto a procrustean bed. Nonetheless, Clarke opens the door to dialogue with the skewed disciplines of economics and sociology; he notes the incompleteness of Marx's project and credits the accomplishments that mainstream economic and sociological analyses have made:

> Marx did not provide a complete theory of capitalist society that can be offered as a ready-made alternative to the theories of modern economics and of modern sociology. There are many questions in response to which economics and sociology have developed concepts and methods of analysis, to say nothing of empirical investigation, that transcend the ideological limitations of those disciplines. What Marx did was to establish

new conceptual foundations on which a more adequate understanding of capitalist society could be built.

CLARKE, 1982, p. 209

This chapter begins to map out these foundational concepts for a Marxian theory of capitalist society; extends them; and repositions disciplinary boundaries, especially the boundaries separating economics, sociology, and moral philosophy. This chapter challenges the conceptual horizons of mainstream sociology and economics, as a social philosopher's attempt to work out a coherent set of basic critical concepts for understanding and investigating modern capitalist societies. By focusing on capital and the specific social forms that belong with it, this chapter seeks to disclose the vast potential of Marx's theory to contribute to our understanding of capitalist modernity.

Marx's Breakthrough to Historical Materialism

The historical materialist conception is that human needs, wealth, and labor always involve specific social forms and purposes. Marx's major work, *Capital*, develops concepts that grasp the characteristic social forms and purposes of the capitalist mode of production, above all, the concept of capital as value that increases its value – roughly, money that makes money. From the opening sentence of the book, Marx makes it clear that he is writing about societies where wealth generally takes the commodity form (and does so because wealth is produced on a capitalist basis), not about "the wealth of nations." I argue against discarding Marx's theory of value; it carries his mature theory of the social forms and purposes that define the capitalist mode of production and the way of life that it constitutes. The commodity, exchange-value, value, surplus-value, capital, wages, and profit are all value forms; they are co-constitutive social forms of the capitalist social order. Marx contrasts these specific social forms with generally applicable categories such as wealth, use value, concrete labor, and the labor process.[2] Economics errs gravely by failing to recognize the difference between specific and general categories; it slurs value into wealth, capitalism into "the economy." The problem is compounded when, as Simon Clarke argues, the faulty horizon of mainstream economics is adopted by modern sociology. Because Marx's critique of political economy has been overlooked, the significance of Marx's theory of capital for social theory (its "sociological" importance) has been bottled up. This chapter seeks

---

2 Marx also contrasts the form that the commodity, exchange-value, value, surplus-value, capital, wages, and profit take within modern capitalism from forms they take outside that totality.

to release the "sociological" power of Marxian value theory and encourage dialogue between a renewed Marxian theory and the going social sciences of economics and sociology.

The historical materialist phenomenology of the human situation that Marx developed constitutes a revolution in human self-understanding comparable to Charles Darwin's theory of evolution. However, this revolution in human self-understanding, so fraught with implications for social theory, has largely been missed. In part this is because historical materialism has been widely misunderstood by treating the "forces of production," "relations of production," and "superstructure" as separable strata, like layers of a cake.[3] Marx condenses the phenomenological insight of historical materialism as follows: "All production is appropriation of nature on the part of an individual within and through a specific form of society" (Marx, 1973, 87). Production is a thorough-goingly social phenomenon; moreover, it always involves specific forms of sociality and specific social purposes. There is no production in general; neither is there any society in general. Since humans are creatures whose needs are met, for the most part, by the production of new use-values (goods and services), there must always be some (sustainable) mode of production in place. This obvious presupposition of human history ceases to be trivial when we adopt Marx's insight that production always takes place "within and through a specific form of society." The breakthrough insight of historical materialism for social theory is that to understand any society one must identify the specific social forms and purposes belonging to its mode of production and investigate their content, consequences, and possible contradictions. Overlooking this necessity gets social theory off on the wrong foot.

In their unfinished attack on Hegelianism, *The German Ideology*, Marx and Engels put the spotlight on the "mode of production," which, they say, always involves a "way of life":

> This mode of production [*Weise der Produktion*] must not be considered simply as being the reproduction of the physical existence of the individuals. Rather it is a definite form of activity of these individuals, a definite form of expressing their life, a definite *way of life* [*Lebensweise*] on their part.
>
> MARX & ENGELS, 1976, p. 31

---

3 For a criticism of the conventional view, as defended by G.A. Cohen in Cohen (1978), see Sayer (1987).

They make the generally applicable observation of production that it always has a double character, natural and social:

> The production of life, both of one's own in labour and of fresh life in pro-creation, now appears as a twofold relation: on the one hand as a natural, on the other as a social relation – social in the sense that it denotes the cooperation of several individuals, no matter under what conditions, in what manner and to what end.
>
> MARX & ENGELS, 1976, p. 43

So, the production of useful things to meet human needs is always a joint endeavor that is undertaken under specific conditions, in a specific manner, and oriented to specific ends. Production is always social, but there is no sociality in general, no general form of social cooperation: production always involves specific social forms and purposes. Moreover, as a particular way of life, a mode of production possesses a particular moral character. Morality for Marx is like the weather, the question is not will we have any but what will it be.

That production and wealth always have a double character means that they always have *constitutive social forms and purposes*. This conception of constitutive social forms has its roots in Aristotle, whom Marx praises as "the great investigator who was the first to analyse the value-form, like so many other forms of thought, society and nature" (Marx, 1976a, p. 151). Unlike modern thinkers caught up in what he calls "the bourgeois horizon," Marx is a neo-Aristotelian; he takes forms seriously, in particular, social forms. Social forms do not stand apart; they do not enjoy an independent existence as Platonic forms do. They are always *forms of*; thus, capital is a specific social form of wealth and the production of wealth.

Capital is Marx's answer to a question few think to pose. Two questions about wealth are widely asked: How much wealth is there? and How is wealth distributed? Marx takes up the question that lies outside the horizons of most social theorists: *What is the specific social form and purpose of wealth and the production of wealth in this society?* To answer this question involves identifying a specific measure of wealth. For capitalism, that measure (and purpose) is surplus-value (profit); more precisely, the measure is the rate at which capital is accumulated. The prevalent concept of capital is that of a *resource* (usually, but not always, a produced resource, as contrasted with undeveloped land or water resources) that can be employed in the production of new wealth. Today, we find this idea of capital as resource proliferating in every imaginable direction, trampling the needed socially specific concept of capital to death: thus, we have human capital, social capital, political capital, intellectual capital, concept capital, natural capital, and more. The Trinity Formula's way of thinking of capital goes viral.[4] The trouble with this conception of capital as a produced resource useful in the production of new use-values (or, simply, as a resource) is that it is generally applicable. Instead of recognizing that capital is all about money and moneymaking, in this popular conception of capital as a resource, there is no reference to money. Produced resources useful for the production of new goods and services (much less resources without such qualifications) are a feature of any imaginable human society. Ironically then, the prevalent conception of capital has nothing to tell us about what is distinctive to capitalism. For that, we need the kind of concept of capital that Marx provides, one that grasps capital as a specific social form of wealth and the production of wealth with a specific social purpose, namely, making and accumulating money, an imperious social form whose momentous consequences reverberate throughout society and the world. Without "the exact development of the concept of capital" as a specific social form of wealth, social theory is at a loss to investigate its consequences: the very idea of this project lies beyond its conceptual horizons.

Marx, then, adopts Aristotle's metaphysics of formal causality: social forms have their specific contents and powers.[5] They are consequential, and in the case of capital as a social form of wealth and the production of wealth, momentous. We cannot pretend – as neoclassical economics does – to understand any actual mode of production or way of life in abstraction from those constitutive specific social forms and purposes. A mode of production is inseparable from its constitutive specific social forms and purposes, which make a mode of production at the same time a way of life. Therefore, to treat production as if it could stand alone, as production-in-general, devoid of any constitutive specific social forms or purposes, is to engage in bad abstraction.[6] There is no production-in-general and no general way of life. To suppose that there is, is to fall into what I call "the illusion of the economic."

While there is no production-in-general, we can – and Marx does – investigate general features of needs, wealth, and the production of wealth, "It is entirely certain that human production possesses definite *laws* or *relations* which

---

4   What Marx calls the Trinity Formula has a few versions, but the basic one links the three
    factors of production, means of production (capital), land, and labor with the three revenue
    forms interest/profit of enterprise, rent, and wages, respectively. See further Chapter 48,
    "The Trinity Formula," in Marx 1981; for a commentary, see Murray (2002).

5   For more on this topic see Murray (1997).

6   This bad abstraction is not the same thing as treating a particular mode of production in
    abstraction from its specific social forms and purposes in order to identify general features of
    production. That sort of abstraction is unobjectionable and useful.

remain the same in all forms of production. These identical characteristics are quite simple and can be summarized in a very small number of commonplace phases" (Marx, MECW 34, p. 236). Picking out these "identical characteristics," however, involves no claim that there is production-in-general, only that there are some shared features of particular modes of production. The different fruits have characteristics in common, but "the Fruit" does not exist. Identifying and organizing common features has a role to play in scientific accounts of material production, but it does not add up to a science.[7] There are only particular social formations, particular modes of production with their particular ways of life. To understand any of them, scientific inquiry needs to develop, and make ingredients of their theories, the concepts that grasp the specific social forms and purposes constitutive of any actual mode of production.

Recovering the "Qualitative Sociological Side" (Rubin) of Marx's Theory of Value, Which Includes His Theory of Capital

Rubin has observed: "The basic error of the majority of Marx's critics consists of...their complete failure to grasp the qualitative sociological side of Marx's theory of value" (Rubin, 1972, p. 72). In fact, by identifying Marx's theory of value with the classical Ricardian theory – only thought through to radical conclusions – most Marxists have likewise failed to grasp this "qualitative sociological side of Marx's theory of value." Where the reduction of capital to resources aborts the enormous significance of the Marxian conception of capital as a specific social form of wealth, reducing Marx's theory of value to the classical Ricardian labor theory of value, which pays no heed to specific social forms and reduces value to embodied labor, cancels the vast social import of Marx's theory of value, which represents his mature theory of the alienation and domination of wage-labor. This chapter outlines the shape and scope of this "qualitative sociological side" of Marx's theory of value and all the specifically capitalist social forms, the value forms, that go with it, for example, the commodity, money, capital, and wage labor.

We may wonder why the "sociological content" of Marx's theory of value has been overlooked. Let me suggest several reasons, all of which are rooted in the dominance of "the bourgeois horizon": (1) Marx's theory of value has been identified with the classical, Ricardian theory of value, when, in fact, Marx's theory is cut from different cloth; it is a theory of the specific social form of the labor that produces value.[8] It is not a theory of "labor" taken in a transhistorical sense;

---

7   For more on these general abstractions, see Chapter 10 of Murray (1988).

8   "According to the 'traditional' interpretation, Marx's theory of value is not essentially different from Ricardo's" (Saad-Filho, 2002, p. 21).

rather, Marx argues that value is socially and historically specific – specific to the capitalist mode of production.[9] Indeed value is "purely social," a necessary outcome of the generalization of a particular social form of labor, namely, commodity-producing labor – labor that is socially validated *as* abstract labor inasmuch as it is privately undertaken labor that produces goods for sale. Since capital is value that increases in value, this means that Marx's concept of capital has likewise been misunderstood. (2) In one of the most significant, but still disputed, lines of argumentation in *Capital*, Marx goes on to show that this generalization of commodity-producing labor occurs only where production is on a capitalist basis (Campbell, 2013). Marx begins *Capital* by saying that wealth "appears" to take the commodity form in societies where the capitalist mode of production predominates because he shows that the truth of the commodity is that it is not merely a use-value for sale, a simple commodity; the commodity is *commodity capital*, that is, a commodity produced on a capitalist basis, pregnant with surplus-value. No surplus-value, no value. (3) Marx has been treated as a radical economist rather than as a radical critic of economics for its failure to include specific social forms among its fundamental concepts. (4) Marx's theory of the value-form, that is, his account of money as the necessary form of appearance of value, which is – bizarrely – "purely social" and supersensible, has been ignored, misunderstood, or parroted back, even though, as Hans-Georg Backhaus points out, "The analysis of the logical structure of the value form is not to be separated from the analysis of its historical, social content" (Backhaus, 1980, p. 107). (5) Marx's concepts of subsumption, beginning with the formal and real subsumption of labor under capital, force the topic of specific social forms into the open – since subsumption refers to subsumption under specific social forms – but they have been overlooked. (6) Readers of *Capital* have failed to appreciate that the focus of Marx's investigation is the content and consequences of the *specific social forms* constitutive of it as a mode of production.

It is not surprising, then, that Marx's colorful ways of calling attention to peculiarities of capitalist social forms are widely ignored, dismissed, or misinterpreted. They include (1) the commodity is the "cell" form; it begins the systematic dialectical development of the constitutive categories of the capitalist mode of production (use-value is not a cell form); (2) magnetism (a use-value that is not also a value has no polarity): the polarity of the value form – commodities and money are in different value-forms (relative and equivalent) – accounts for the necessity of the value of the commodity to be expressed in money: magnets are not ordinary metal bars; (3) gravity

---

9   Moishe Postone argues that what he calls "Traditional Marxism" understands Marx's labor
    theory of value in that transhistorical way. See Postone (1993).

(use-value may be lost – I may spill my milk, but, insofar as a use-value is not also a value, it is not subject to devaluation): Marx compares the law of value to gravity; when the accumulation of capital goes into crisis and massive devaluations occur (assets prove "toxic"), it is like your house collapsing around you; and, of course, (4) the fetish character of the commodity, money, and capital, whereby things are possessed with peculiar social powers not based on their natural powers (use-values that are not values are not fetishes, at least not of this kind).

How Capital Shapes the Spaces of Sociality

Capital shapes society in many ways, including by not subsuming, by delineating capital's negative spaces, so to speak. (Even these negative spaces, however, are not free of capital's powers.) Marx's plans for his "Economics," show that he largely follows Hegel's account of "ethical life" [*Sittlichkeit*] in the *Philosophy of Right*, which identifies three social spheres: (1) the family or domestic sphere; (2) what he called "civil society," which includes the whole sphere of commerce and industry as well as voluntary associations often identified with civil society today; (3) the state, which includes constitutional law [*innere Staatsrecht*], international law [*äussere Staatsrecht*], and world history [*Weltgeschichte*], the international stage on which all of social life is played out.[10] Capital presupposes and reproduces both the family (the domestic sphere) and the state as social realms that, necessarily, are not under capital's *direct* control.

Capital shapes class structure by eliminating formally recognized classes, estates, or castes. Iris Marion Young observes that Marx's genius was to shows how class persists as a feature of the capitalist mode of production, despite its elimination as an official, legally recognized distinction.

Capital shapes space and time and our experience of them. David Harvey suggests that we can distinguish effects of *money* and *capital* on time and space: "I argue that the very existence of money as a mediator of commodity exchange radically transforms and fixes the meanings of space and time in social life and defines limits and imposes necessities upon the shape and

---

10   In fact, in one of his first plans in the *Grundrisse* (Marx. 1973, p. 264), Marx follows Hegel as far as including "foreign trade" and the "world market" under "the state," but he soon adopts the plan of treating foreign trade and the world market as books separate from the book on the state. Of course foreign trade and the world market are not exactly the same as international law and world history in the first place. Even in the earlier plan Marx includes a telling phrase that suits the present essay well and separates him from Hegel: "Encroachment of bourgeois society over the state" [*Übergreifen der bürgerlichen Gesellschaft über den Staat*] (Marx, 1973, p. 264).

form of urbanization. The particular use of money as capital hardens these connections at the same time as the dynamics of accumulation...render them less and less coherent" (Harvey, 1989, p. 165). The shaping of time by capital is a major theme of Moishe Postone's *Time, Labor, and Social Domination* and has been taken up recently by Amy Wendling in her chapter on time in *The Ruling Ideas: Bourgeois Concepts* (Postone, 1993; Wendling, 2012). Today the investigation of how capital shapes climate and the physical environment has become especially urgent (Foster, 2000; Burkett, 2005).

The Constitutive Forms of the Capitalist Mode of Production

The critical theory of the capitalist world order that Marx planned at the time of writing the *Grundrisse* (1857–58) and the *Contribution to the Critique of Political Economy* (1859) called for six "books": "I examine the system of bourgeois economy in the following order: capital, landed property, wage-labour; the State, foreign trade, world market" (Marx, 1970, p. 19). Marx wrote only the first of these six books, and he did not complete it in his lifetime.[11] All of the socially specific categories that Marx would have developed in this six-book work would have been constitutive social forms of the capitalist world order. Constitutive forms enable social formations to reproduce themselves, even if not indefinitely – as Achinua Achebe wrote: "things fall apart" – as opposed to forms by which no actual social formation can be organized or reproduced. When Marx wrote in the *Grundrisse*,

> While in the completed bourgeois system every economic relation presupposes every other in its bourgeois economic form, and everything posited is thus also a presupposition, this is the case with every organic system. This organic system itself, as a totality, has its presuppositions, and its development to its totality consists precisely in subordinating all elements of society to itself, or in creating out of it the organs which it still lacks. This is historically how it becomes a totality.
>
> MARX, 1973, p. 278

I believe that the totality he meant, "the completed bourgeois system," included everything he intended to cover in the projected six books. If so, then

---

11   The significance of Marx's incorporation of material on landed property and wage-labor into the three volumes of *Capital* is debated. I believe that, for the most part, Marx included in *Capital* what he did regarding landed property and wage-labor because it was necessary to the systematic development in that (first) book but that room remained for separate books on landed property and wage-labor that he never wrote.

there are many specific social forms and purposes constitutive of the capitalist world order that Marx never developed in a systematic way. The social forms systematically developed by Marx, those constitutive of the capitalist mode of production, are those found in the three volumes of *Capital*. For that reason, when speaking of the constitutive social forms of the capitalist mode of production, I will generally refer to those developed in *Capital*, keeping in mind that they are far from an exhaustive list of all those constitutive of the capitalist world order. From the *Grundrisse* and other works of Marx, we can work out a broader picture of the way that capital shapes the social order. I will return to that in the next section.

The first task, then, is to identify the many, and inseparable, value forms, namely, the commodity, exchange-value, value, money, capital, surplus-value, wage-labour, profit, interest, rent, and more, as *constitutive* forms of the capitalist mode of production and to explore the social significance of each, the social "content of the form."[12] In *Capital*, Marx demonstrates that these social forms constitute the capitalist order by showing – through a systematic dialectical presentation – how they belong together and how they are capable of reproducing themselves.[13] This capacity for self-maintenance – and growth and development through the process of capital accumulation – entitles these value forms to be called constitutive of the capitalist order. It is Marx's singular achievement to have identified and systematically presented the dialectic of the value forms as the constitutive social forms of the capitalist order. Paul Mattick Jr., emphasizes the scientific originality of Marx's categories, "Marx's critique – his 'scientific revolution' – therefore involved not merely a reworking of economic categories but the construction of another set of concepts, explicitly social and historical ones" (Mattick Jr., 1993, p. 124).[14] As already noted, Marx recognizes the place for generally applicable abstractions, and, generally applicable abstractions such as use-value and the labor process have a role to play in *Capital*.[15] These are not the categories that are constitutive of the specifically capitalist mode of production; all too often these generally applicable

---

12   "The categories of bourgeois economics...are forms of thought which are socially valid, and therefore objective, for the relations of production belonging to this historically determined mode of social production, i.e. commodity production" (Marx, 1976a, p. 169).

13   See Marx's brief summary of the three volumes of *Capital*, Marx, 1981, p. 957.

14   Likewise, Martha Campbell concludes 'there are no counterparts to Marx's economic concepts in either classical or utility theory' (Campbell, 1993, p. 152).

15   In fact, in Marx's first plan for his "Economics," in the *Grundrisse*, he had in mind to begin with "the general, abstract determinants which obtain in more or less all forms of society" (Marx, 1973, p. 108). On use-value, see Marx, 1976a, pp. 125–126. On the labor process, see Marx, 1976a, pp. 283–292.

categories are confused and/or conflated with the constitutive categories, a point to which I will return shortly.

First let us consider some of the social content of the commodity form of wealth and social forms immediately involved in it, namely, commodity-producing labor and commodity exchangers, who are property owners in the social roles of buyers and sellers. Unlike use-value taken in abstraction from all specific social forms, the commodity, as a specific social form of wealth, is not innocent, even when we set aside the point that the commodity is the "cell" out of which more complex and fraught social forms, such as capital, can be dialectically developed. Let us explore some of the content of the commodity form at the level of simple commodity circulation. As a value in addition to being a use-value, a commodity is a weird "socio-natural" hybrid, "a thing that transcends sensuousness (*ein sinnlich übersinnliches Ding*)" (Marx, 1976a, p. 163). The commodity is a fetish, that is, it is possessed with a peculiar social power that "has no connection with the physical nature of the commodity"; we may call it purchasing power, that is, command over the goods and labor power of others (Marx, 1976a, p. 165). "Whence, then arises the enigmatic character of the product of labour, as soon as it assumes the form of a commodity?" asks Marx. In answering, Marx appeals to the causal power of social forms, "Clearly, it arises from this form itself" (Marx, 1976a, p. 164). Marx follows up, again invoking the power of social forms, this time the social form of the labor that produces commodities: "this fetishism of the world of commodities arises from the peculiar social character of the labor which produces them." This fetish character, which just is the value character of the commodity, arises not from its being the product of "labor," but from being the product of labor of a "peculiar social character." It is no wonder, then, that social theories that breeze past the commodity form of wealth and the specific social character of the labor that produces commodities, lack the conceptual space for thinking about the fetish character of the commodity. Consequently, they dismiss the strange social objectivity of value that makes a commodity a fetish. This impersonal social objectivity, manifested in the system of commodity prices, lords it over participants in commodity exchange:

> The value character of the products of labour becomes firmly established only when they act as magnitudes of value. These magnitudes vary continually, independently of the will, foreknowledge and actions of the exchangers. Their own movement within society has for them the form of a movement made by things, and these things, far from being under their control, in fact control them.
>
> MARX, 1976a, pp. 167–168

Think of how the financial assets (themselves commodities) that suddenly, and uncontrollably, turned "toxic" sent the world into a global slump. How ironic it is that the Enlightened world of simple commodity circulation is haunted by the "ghostly" objectivity of value. To bring home how capitalist Enlightenment boomerangs into a peculiarly abstract new religion (of capital), Marx observes:

> In order, therefore, to find an analogy we must take flight into the misty realm of religion. There the products of the human brain appear as autonomous figures endowed with a life of their own, which enter into relations both with each other and with the human race. So it is in the world of commodities with the products of men's hands.
>
> MARX, 1976a, p. 165

Here we have some of the more disturbing content of the commodity form; let us turn to some brighter aspects.

In its peculiar, roundabout way, the generalization of the commodity form involves the treatment of human labor as equal, establishing a footing for an egalitarian society: "The social character of the equality of the various kinds of labour is reflected in the form of the common character, as values, possessed by these materially different things, the products of labor" (Marx, 1976a, p. 166). The social equality of labor is expressed, then, in the pricing of products. But commodities are produced privately for others to purchase; the commodity form, then, posits private property and the basic social roles of buyer and seller as the agents of commodity circulation. These social roles involve a high-minded conception, that of the freely-acting person:

> In order that these objects may enter into relation with each other as commodities, their guardians must place themselves in relation to one another as persons whose will resides in those objects, and must behave in such a way that each does not appropriate the commodity of the other, and alienate his own, except through an act to which both parties consent.
>
> MARX, 1976a, p. 178

So, the commodity form is doubly implicated in social equality; in commodity exchange there is effected a roundabout recognition of the social equality of the producers and, in the social roles of buyers and sellers, the exchangers recognize one another as equally persons, whose wills must be respected. At the same time, this elevated mutual respect is but one aspect of the kind of social relations brought about in the sphere of commodity exchange, for what motivates exchanges in this sphere is narrow self-interest, thus Marx summarizes the socio-moral character of this sphere of commodity exchange as follows:

> The sphere of circulation or commodity exchange...is in fact a very Eden of the innate rights of man. It is the exclusive realm of Freedom, Equality, Property and Bentham. Freedom, because both buyer and seller are determined only by their own free will. They contract as free persons, who are equal before the law... Equality, because each enters into relation with the other...and they exchange equivalent for equivalent. Property, because each disposes only of what is his own. And Bentham, because each looks only to his own advantage. The only force bringing them together, and putting them into relation with each other, is the selfishness, the gain and the private interest of each.
>
> MARX, 1976a, p. 280

No wonder, then, that Marx sees the social consequence – in this, he is hardly alone – of the generalization of the commodity form of wealth to be a high-minded, respectful social atomism: "Men are henceforth related to each other in their social process of production in a purely atomistic way" (Marx, 1976a, p. 187). Since the society that appears this dissociated proves to be a class society, this atomism is not the whole story.

Within the social forms constitutive of the capitalist mode of production, Marx distinguishes between "appearance" forms and "essential" forms, though, following Hegel's logic of essence, where *essence must appear as something other than itself*, Marx recognizes that "appearance" and "essence" are inseparable, hence both are essential. Marx makes this point in the first chapter of *Capital* in arguing that the readily-observed phenomena of generalized commodity circulation, in which use-values with the social form of commodities are priced and sold, can be explained only if there is some "third thing" – Marx calls it "value" – which is the basis for pricing commodities.[16] But this "third thing," value, whose substance is congealed abstract labor, is "purely social" and "supersensible." As such, it cannot appear as itself – what would congealed abstract labor look like! – rather, following the logic of essence as Hegel

---

16   Once we see that the (simple) commodity form is really an appearance form of the more complex form commodity capital, we see that the commodity form as it initially appears creates the illusion that a capitalist society is merely a commercial or market society.

recognizes it, value must appear as something other than itself, namely, money. That is the line of argument Marx develops in Section 3 of Chapter 1, "The Value-Form, or Exchange-Value," in answering the third of the three questions about value that he poses: What is the substance of value? What is the magnitude of value? How is value expressed?[17] The fact that value must appear as price and that the price form can be extended to use-values, such as undeveloped land, that are not products of labor,[18] makes it appear that Marx's claim that congealed abstract labor is the substance of value is untenable.[19]

Just as Marx explains price by bringing in value, he explains profit by bringing in the concept of surplus-value, which has as its sole source the surplus labor of wage-workers. That is so, argues Marx, even though the division of the "working day" into necessary and surplus labor does not, and cannot, appear. Moreover, the wage-form makes it seem as though there is no such division in the first place: "On the surface of bourgeois society the worker's wage appears as the price of labour, as a certain quantity of money that is paid for a certain quantity of labour" (Marx, 1976a, p. 675). This makes the wage-form one of many constitutive appearance forms that make Marx's explanation of profit by surplus labor seem to be wrong. By drawing the critical distinction between labor-power and labor, however, Marx recognizes the wage as the price of labor-power, dismissing the very idea of the price of labor as nonsense. This is why Chapter 19, on wages, bears the title "The Transformation [*Verwandlung*] of the Value (and Respectively the Price) of Labor-Power into Wages."[20] Profit and the rate of profit, which are forms that Marx does not take up until the beginning of *Capital* III, are important constitutive "appearance" forms. They make it appear that profit is based on the sum of capital invested, irrespective of how

---

17 On Marx's dialectic of the value-form, see Murray (2013), which contains an extended criticism of Backhaus's criticism of Marx's dialectical development of the value-form.

18 "The price-form, however is not only compatible with the possibility of a quantitative incongruity between magnitude of value and price, i.e. between the magnitude of value and its own expression in money [A bubble involves this sort of "quantitative incongruity."], but it may also harbor a qualitative contradiction, with the result that price ceases altogether to express value, despite the fact that money is nothing but the value-form of commodities" (Marx, 1976a, p. 197).

19 For a reply to that objection, as made by Chris Arthur (Arthur, 2002), see Murray (2005).

20 This appearance that wages represent full compensation for the value-added by wage-workers is one leg of the Trinity Formula, which makes it seem as though each of the revenue forms, wages, profit, interest, and rent are compensations for the value added by wage-workers, capitalist entrepreneurs, lenders of capital, and land owners. This feature of the revenue forms of the capitalist mode of production reinforces the proclivity to factor out aspects (notably subjective vs. objective aspects) of a phenomena that actually are inseparable.

that capital is constituted, which makes the distinction between constant and variable capital that Marx draws seem pointless and once again makes Marx's theory of surplus labor as the sole source of profit seem to be wrong.[21]

Marx's presentation of the constitutive social forms in *Capital*, then, involves two, inseparable, levels, namely, supersensible essence (value/surplus-value) and sensible appearance (money/price/profit). As these examples of the appearance forms of value and of surplus-value show, the constitutive "appearance" forms of the capitalist mode of production figure heavily into capital's discursive effects, notably in the creation of various illusions. Capital covers its tracks. The fact that the scientific account of the capitalist mode of production requires the sort of bifurcating categories that belong to the logic of essence in Hegel's logic, is already a critical commentary on that mode of production, a point that Tony Smith has long and rightly stressed.

Marx's Subsumption Concepts

Formal subsumption and real subsumption of labor under capital are Marx's two primary and best-known subsumption concepts. Since it actually involves the material reshaping of products and labor processes for the purpose of increasing profits, "McDonaldization" counts as the real subsumption of wealth and its production under capital. "Mc" is the prefix of real subsumption. Marx has several other subsumption concepts; they include: hybrid subsumption in a "transitional form" (transitional to formal and real subsumption) and an "accompanying form"; ideal subsumption; what I call non-formal subsumption, e.g., when, under conditions of capitalist agriculture (where seeds are generally in the commodity form), I use my own seeds to plant the next crop, they are subsumed under capital without taking on the "value-form," that is, without ever having been sold; non-productive laborers are subsumed under the wage form; some unproductive labor, notably, by government employees, which is paid for by taxes, is subsumed under capital and even enters into the formation of prices (Marx, 1976b, pp. 1,042–1,043); and the subsumption of non-capitalist commercial forms under specifically capitalist forms that generally bear the same name, such as the commodity, money, even capital itself:

---

21   In fact, as Marx argues, the tendency toward an average rate of profit cannot be reconciled with commodities selling at their "individual values" and profits matching "individual surplus-values." Marx recognized that the classical labor theory of value, which was a theory of individual values, was simply untenable. One of Marx's remarkable scientific feats was to defend a new labor theory of value on a new conceptual basis directed not at individual commodities and capitals but at the total social capital and its aliquot parts. See further Murray (2014).

"We see here how even economic categories appropriate to earlier modes of production acquire a new and specific historical character under the impact of capitalist production" (Marx, 1976b, p. 950). Marx's subsumption concepts are among his ways of articulating the power of capital to shape society; each is a specification of capital's reach.

Extending Marx's Subsumption Concepts

One direction here is to vastly extend Marx's subsumption rubric by setting up a conceptual matrix that cross-references the many different value forms – not only capital – with various aspects of social life – not only labor. From Marx's basic rubric of the formal (or real) subsumption of labor under capital, I propose an *extension* of Marx's approach to subsumption by following the pattern: **the _____ subsumption of _____ under _____**, where some type of subsumption fills in the first blank, some pertinent domain the second, and some value form the third slot. So, for example, we can consider the formal subsumption of use-values under the commodity form. That is a way of approaching some of the issues taken up in Michael Sandel's *What Money Can't Buy* in terms of understanding limits to the proliferation of commodification. Sandel takes up Fred Hirsch's concept of "the commercialization effect" in challenging what Sandel calls one of the "tenets of market faith," namely, "that commercializing an activity does not change it" (Sandel 2013). The idea that subsuming something under a value form, in this case the commodity form, changes it. Capital's reach includes, but goes far beyond the effects of commodification.

Another direction is to stretch the subsumption concepts. One example is *ideal subsumption with real consequences*. Ideal subsumption ordinarily means treating a phenomenon that does not formally come under the relevant value-form as if it did. An example of ideal subsumption is the curious notion of "self-employment." Here an individual person is subsumed, ideally, under the value-forms of capitalist (employer) and wage-laborer (employee). Ideal subsumption with real consequences involves more than just classification. Within a large capitalist firm, or even within a not-for-profit corporation such as a hospital or university, subunits of the firm – different departments or profit centers – may be ideally subsumed under the form of the capitalist firm and treated, up to a point but with real consequences, as if they were independent capitalist units. This practice has a name, "internal outsourcing."

Another stretching of Marx's thinking on subsumption is to introduce the idea of *real subsumption without formal subsumption*. Governmental and not-for-profit institutions, notably those in healthcare and higher education, are increasingly adopting measures developed by for-profit institutions – in some cases ones competing with them – in the course of their real subsumption under capital. At Iowa Western Community College, the graphics for the on-line course registration imitate online shopping, for example, shopping at Amazon. com. When you select a course, a symbol of the course is dropped into a shopping basket. When you have selected all of the courses that you want to take, you are ready for checkout. What is so disturbing about this imagery, especially when you consider that students pay to take courses? I think that this example involves ideal subsumption, real subsumption without formal subsumption, and discursive effects of capital all at once.

Capital's Shadow Forms

Shadows are not to be confused with the physical objects that they are the shadows of. As Plato indicated in his famous "divided line," shadows depend on physical objects; they are not physical objects that come only in gray. *Peter Pan* begins with a metaphysical joke when Wendy sews Peter's shadow back on. Though shadows are dependent on physical objects, they are omnipresent in experience, and they have their own kind of reality and efficacy. Though dependent, they are not to be dismissed. The Peter Pan gaffe comes up frequently in social theory, when shadow forms are not recognized for what they are, namely, social forms dependent upon other social forms that are constitutive of social orders but, instead, are thought to be free-standing constitutive social forms themselves. To recognize the dependent nature of shadow forms; however, is not to dismiss them. In capitalist society shadow forms are ubiquitous and have real effects.

This notion of capital's shadow forms has its basis in Marx. In his criticism of the Ricardian socialist John Bray; Marx writes:

> Mr. Bray does not see that this equalitarian relation, this *corrective ideal* that he would like to apply to the world, is itself nothing but the reflection of the actual world; and that therefore it is totally impossible to reconstitute society on the basis of what is merely an embellished shadow ["*ombre*"] of it. In proportion as this shadow ["*ombre*"] takes on substance again, we perceive that this substance, far from being the transfiguration dreamt of, is the actual body of existing society.
>
> MARX, 1963, p. 79

This amounts to Marx saying that egalitarianism ["*égalitaire*"] is a shadow form, specifically a shadow of the circulation of capital. Marx's point is that the market, the sphere of simple commodity circulation, is in actuality an inseparable aspect of the circulation of capital, so that it is not an independent actuality – there is no generalized commodity production *apart from* production on a capitalist basis. Taken on its own, then, simple commodity circulation, and the ethos of equality that comes with it, is only a shadow.

Utility is a shadow of the social sort of wealth characteristic of capitalism, that is, the commodity. As Marx and Engels observe in the *German Ideology*:

> The apparent absurdity of merging all the manifold relationships of people in the *one* relation of utility, this apparently metaphysical abstraction arises from the fact that in modern bourgeois society all relations are subordinated in practice to the one abstract monetary-commercial relation.
>
> MARX & ENGELS, 1976, p. 409, translation amended

I propose to develop this rubric of capital's shadow forms in a more explicit and expansive way. I contrast capital's shadow forms with the constitutive forms, the value forms, of which they are the shadows. If we fail to draw the distinction between constitutive forms and shadow forms, then we are likely to find ourselves tilting at windmills. George Ritzer's (2000) attack on "McDonaldization" – instead of real subsumption under capital – is a case in point. These shadow forms include: utility, technical rationality, the "economic," secularism, egalitarianism, nihilism, indifference (what Georg Simmel calls "the blasé attitude"), the calculative mentality, punctuality, giganticism, and the Protestant work ethic (workaholicism). Developing this rubric of capital's shadow forms allows for a more complex and comprehensive social theory of capitalist society, and it opens doors to dialogue between Marxian theory and various social scientific investigations of capitalist modernity, which are often directed at capital's shadows. Referring to these as shadow forms is meant to contrast them with the social forms that are constitutive of capitalist society; it is not intended to dismiss them. They have their own efficacy in the life of capitalist societies. Shadow forms are further manifestations of capital's power, extensions of its reach.[22]

Capital's Discursive Effects
Capital shapes the public and scientific discourse about the society that it subsumes. Perhaps the most profound way that it shapes discourse is the support it gives to what Marx calls "the bourgeois horizon." Marx challenges the

---

22   Tony Smith points out that shadow forms fall into different groups. Some, at least in some form, predate capitalism; some would be specific to capitalist society; and others, say egalitarianism, would presumably cross over to a post-capitalist social order.

"bourgeois horizon," which he identifies as the philosophical orientation that structures political economy, much of modern philosophy, and many forms of socialism. Marx's critique of the "bourgeois horizon" renews Hegel's criticism of the mindset of the "reflective understanding" (*Verstand*).[23] In the patterns of bourgeois thinking, Marx finds a series of bifurcations: mind versus world, subjective versus objective, form versus content, concept versus object, passive versus active and immediate versus mediated.[24] The factoring philosophy – characteristic of the bourgeois mindset – which rashly treats as separable whatever can be distinguished in thought, trades in these dualisms.

A second, related, major discursive effect of capital is "the illusion of the economic," a concept that I have been exploring as a way to think about the crooked discourse of mainstream economics and sociology. The failure to recognize that a mode of production involves a way of life results in the truncated view that I call the "illusion of the economic." The idea of "the economic" is the idea of production that is no particular mode of production, is production-in-general, and, by the same token, involves no particular social forms and no particular way of life. The peculiar social forms and purpose of a capitalist society make it appear to be the economy-in-general, such that the "illusion of the economic" comes naturally to participants in capitalist societies. Martha Campbell puts it this way: capitalism "claims to create wealth pure and simple and [to be] organized by this purpose" (Campbell, 2004, p. 86). The "illusion of the economic" closes off the questions that drive Marx's inquiry in *Capital*: What are the specific social forms and purposes of wealth and the production of wealth and what are their consequences? The result is the now familiar narrowing of the horizons of scientific and public discourse to questions about how much "wealth" there is and, perhaps, how it is distributed.

The idea here is to undertake a socio-epistemological inquiry into the horizons of discourse of mainstream economics and sociology revealing that, due to its abstractness and impersonality, capital creates the illusion that capitalist

---

23   One indication of Marx's sweeping criticism of the "bourgeois horizon" is his enthusiasm, which he shared with Hegel, for Aristotle, that "giant of thinking" [*Denkriese*] (Marx, 1976a, p. 175, n. 35). Thinkers functioning within the "bourgeois horizon" generally are hostile to Aristotle.

24   The bifurcation between form and content is one of many that Hegel rejects: "Form and content are a pair of determinations that are frequently employed by the reflective understanding, and, moreover, mainly in such a way that the content is considered as what is essential and independent, while the form, on the contrary, is inessential and dependent. Against this, however, it must be remarked that in fact both of them are equally essential" (Hegel, 1991, §133, addition, 202). Marx employs this thought over and over in criticizing the political economists.

society is the economy-in-general, a notion that resembles Karl Polanyi's (1957; 1968) ambiguous characterization of the capitalist mode of production as the "disembedded economy." It is ambiguous because, on the one hand, Polanyi identifies the capitalist mode of production as historically specific, yet, on the other hand, he identifies it with "the economy" pure and simple, free of the admixtures characteristic of pre-capitalist societies, as if it, for the first time in history, instantiated the economy-in-general. This final topic, then circles back to the beginning, except that now the problematic discourses of economics and sociology are disclosed as discursive effects of capital. These mainstream social scientific discourses, too, belong to capital's reach.

References

Arthur, C.J. (2002). *The new dialectic and Marx's "Capital."* Leiden, the Netherlands: Brill.

Backhaus, H.G. (1980). On the dialectics of the value-form. *Theses Eleven*, 1, 99–120.

Burkett, P. (2005). *Marxism and ecological economics: Toward a red and green political economy.* Leiden, the Netherlands: Brill.

Campbell, M. (1993). Marx's concept of economic relations and the method of *Capital*. In *Marx's method in "Capital": A reexamination*, Moseley, F. (ed.). Atlantic Highlands: Humanities Press.

Campbell, M. (2004). Value objectivity and habit. In *The constitution of capital: Essays on Volume I of Marx's 'Capital'*. Bellofiore R. & Taylor, N. (eds.). Basingstoke, Hampshire: Palgrave Macmillan.

Campbell, M. (2013). The Transformation of Money into Capital in Marx's *Capital*. In *Marx's laboratory. Critical interpretations of the "Grundrisse."* Bellofiore, R. Thomas, P. & Starosta, G. (ed.). Leiden; Boston; Koeln: Brill Academic Press.

Clarke, S. (1982). *Marx, Marginalism, and Modern Sociology*. Basingstoke, England: Macmillan.

Cohen, G.A. (1978). *Karl Marx's theory of history: A defense*. Princeton: Princeton University Press.

Foster, J.B. (2000). *Marx's ecology*. New York: Monthly Review Press.

Harvey, D. (1989). *The condition of postmodernity*. Oxford: Basil Blackwell.

Hegel, G.W.F. (1991 [1821]). *Elements of the philosophy of right*. Wood, A.W. (ed.) and translated by Nisbet, H.B. Cambridge: Cambridge University Press.

MacIntyre, A. (1984). *After virtue*. Notre Dame: University of Notre Dame Press.

Marx, K. (1963 [1847]). *The poverty of philosophy*. New York: International Publishers.

Marx, K. (1970 [1859]). *A contribution to the critique of political economy*. Dobb, M. (ed.) and translated by Ryazanskaya, S.W. New York: International Publishers.

Marx, K.(1973 [1857–58]). *Grundrisse*. Translated by Nicolaus, M. Harmondsworth: Penguin.

Marx, K. (1976a). *Capital, volume 1*. Translated by Fowkes, B. from the 4th edn (1894). New York: Harmondsworth: Penguin/NLB.

Marx, K. (1976b). *Results of the immediate production process*. Translated by Livingstone, R. in Marx, K. *Capital, volume 1*. Translated by Fowkes, B. from the 4th edn (1894). New York: Harmondsworth: Penguin/NLB.

Marx, K. (1981). *Capital, volume 3*. Translated by Fernbach, D.. Harmondsworth: Penguin/NLB.

Marx, K. & Engels, F. (1976 [1845–6]). *The German ideology*. In Marx, K. & Engels, F. *Collected works, Volume 5: Marx and Engels: 1845–47*. New York: International Publishers.

Mattick, P. Jr. (1993). Marx's dialectic. In *Marx's method in "Capital": A reexamination*, Moseley, F. (ed.). Atlantic Highlands: Humanities Press.

Murray, P. (1988). *Marx's theory of scientific knowledge*. Atlantic Highlands, NJ: Humanities Press International.

Murray, P. (1997). Redoubled empiricism: The place of social form and formal causality in Marxian theory. In *New investigations of Marx's method*. Moseley, F. & Campbell, M. (eds.). Atlantic Highlands, N.J.: Humanities Press.

Murray, P. (2002). The illusion of the economic: The Trinity Formula and the 'religion of everyday life.' In *The culmination of capital: Essays on volume III of Marx's Capital*. Campbell, M. & Reuten, G. (ed.). Basingstoke, Hampshire: Palgrave.

Murray, P. (2004). The social and material transformation of production by capital: Formal and real subsumption in "Capital," Volume I. In *The Constitution of Capital: Essays on Volume I of Marx's "Capital."* Bellofiore, R. & Taylor, N. (eds.). Basingstoke, Hampshire: Palgrave Macmillan.

Murray, P. (2005). The New Giant's Staircase, *Historical Materialism*, 13, 2, 61–83.

Murray, P. (2013). Unavoidable crises: Reflections on Backhaus and the development of Marx's value-form theory in the "Grundrisse." In *Marx's Laboratory: Critical interpretations of the "Grundrisse."* Bellofiore, R., Thomas, P., & Starosta, G. (eds.) Leiden, the Netherlands: Brill.

Murray, P. (2014). The secret of capital "laid bare": How Hegel helped Marx overcome Ricardo's theory of profit. In *Marx's "Capital" and Hegel's "Logic."* Moseley, F. & Smith, T. (eds.). Leiden, the Netherlands: Brill.

Polanyi, K. (1957 [1944]). *The great transformation*. Boston: Beacon Press.

Polanyi, K. (1968). Aristotle discovers the economy. In *Primitive, archaic, and modern economics: Essays of Karl Polanyi*. Dalton, G. (ed.). Garden City: Doubleday.

Postone, M. (1993). *Time, labor, and social domination: A reinterpretation of Marx's critical theory*. Cambridge: Cambridge University Press.

Ritzer, G. (2000). *The McDonaldization of society*. Thousand Oaks: Pine Forge Press.

Robbins, L. (1994 [1935]). An essay on the nature and significance of economic science. In *The philosophy of economics*, Hausman, H.M. (ed.). Cambridge: Cambridge University Press.

Rubin, I.I. (1972). *Essays on Marx's theory of value*. Detroit: Black & Red.

Saad-Filho, A. (2002). *The value of Marx*. London: Routledge.

Sayer, D. (1987). *The violence of abstraction*. Oxford: Basil Blackwell.

Sandel, M. (2013). *What money can't buy: The moral limits of markets*. New York: Farrar, Strauss & Giroux.

Wendling, A. (2012). *The ruling ideas: Bourgeois political concepts*. Lanham, MD: Lexington Books.

CHAPTER 5

Easing the Encumbered Subject: Security, Speculation, and Capitalist Subjectivity

Kevin S. Amidon and Daniel Krier

Introduction: Universal Capital, Alienation, and Critique

Capitalism has, across its history, often seemed a single and coherent object. Not only within Marxist historical narratives that have critiqued capital, but also within histories and critical analyses that focus on the global elaboration of capital, capitalism has appeared to be a unitary – if not historically invariant – phenomenon (Hall & Soskice 2001; Esping-Andersen 2013; Streeck 2010). Furthermore the capitalist *homo oeconomicus* has, despite recent critiques from the standpoint of behavioral economics, seemed similarly isomorphic across geographic, cultural, and even historical boundaries (Feldner & Vighi 2015). Karl Marx's foundational critique of capital is a major source of strategies of representation that render capitalism into a unitary global force. Marx's arguments furthermore trace the accumulation of all capital to the specific phenomenon that enables it: the alienation of surplus value from productive labor. Thus the history of critical theory down to the present day has been a history of the conceptual power of universal capital, within which the forces of alienation stand at the center (Marx [1844]1980); Adorno & Horkheimer [1947]2002; Marcuse ([1964] 2012).

Major critical theorists today take a variety of approaches to the analysis of universal capital. Slavoj Zizek focuses, in his critiques of the "naturalization of capitalism" derived from his reading of elements within Alain Badiou's thought, on how capitalism ontologically subsumes other forms of being, particularly in their political stakes. In doing so, he emphasizes capitalism's global reach:

> Badiou thus recognizes the exceptional *ontological* status of capitalism whose dynamic undermines every stable framework of representation: the task that should normally be performed by critico-political activity... is already performed by capitalism itself.... Badiou gets caught here in an inconsistency: he draws the "logical" conclusion that, in a "worldless" universe (which is the contemporary universe of global capitalism), the aim of emancipatory politics should be the precise opposite of its "traditional" *modus operandi*....
>
> ZIZEK, 2008, p. 398

For Zizek, critique of one mode of argument about the universality of capital thus undergirds claims that it is universal in other ways.

Frederic Jameson, engaging in direct and close reading of Marx in his *Representing* Capital: *A Reading of Volume One*, explores how, in the chapter from *Capital* on "The General Law of Capitalist Accumulation," Marx's narrative construction of the originary moment of the alienation of value from labor seems to generate the universal character of capital that appears to surmount historicity itself:

> So here too with capitalist production (whose systematicity Marx often names "totality").... It is not capital but labor which is at the origin of the process; when the wages finally materialize and the act of exchange of money and labor power actually takes place, it is an "always-already...." This is then the way in which the present of capitalism as a system "extinguishes" its seemingly constitutive moments and elements in the past. This is the sense in which capitalist production is an infernal machine, an autotelic system; even though it is often exchange or the market that its critics and enemies identify in this manner (particularly in the age of globalization).
>
> JAMESON, 2011, pp. 106–7; see also Jay, 1984

Capital, it seems, erases its own historicity, and not according to any Hegelian *telos* of an "End of History" (Zizek, 2008, p. 405), but within itself and through the forms of alienated being that it generates and exploits.

In search of new ways to pursue the history of capitalist development with additional nuance, including through its attendant social dynamics of alienation up to today, this paper therefore turns to the reception and critique of a canonical sociological text that has made a uniquely significant contribution to the analysis of the emergence and development of capitalism: Max Weber's (1930) *The Protestant Ethic and the Spirit of Capitalism*. Weber's text is read here with its critics and against itself with the goal of developing a differentiated theory of capitalist subjectivity that reflects something of the diversity of the social forms that accrete to capital in different regions, nations, and periods.[1] Central here is an analysis of an internal dialectic within the history of capitalism – and perhaps especially of that nebulous thing that Weber calls

---

1   Steinert (2010), in a careful and revealing critique of Weber's essay, goes further to suggest that Weber's conclusions, while contributing to the universalization and de-historicization of capitalism, are themselves deeply historically contingent, and thus that the evidence upon which Weber based his conclusions must necessarily resolve into different arguments today. The authors, however, still see value in close engagement with Weber's categories of analysis.

capitalism's "spirit" – which conceptually counters unitary narratives of the emergence of capitalism and the forms of subjectivity adequate to it.[2] This is the complex and mutually constitutive relationship between speculation and securitization, a problem that has received comparatively little attention in the theoretical literature on the social forms that accrete to capital. Capitalism, indeed, is no monolith. It has, across its history, been polyvalent and polymorphic, resolving into widely varying local, regional, and national forms (Hall & Soskice, 2001). Through a re-reading of Weber's narrative of capitalism's roots and "spirit," this paper suggests a historical and conceptual framework that can advance critical theory by linking the analysis of capitalism to the consequences it has for the subjects who act and transact within it.

Capitalism and Subjectivity

Since the parallel disciplinary emergence of political economy and Enlightenment epistemological and moral thought in the later eighteenth century, analyses of capitalism have tended toward two poles to which the discipline of economics still often hews in the discourses of "macroeconomics" and "microeconomics": macroscopic focus on large-scale political-economic forms (cf. the focus on national forms of political economy in Smith, Spencer, Malthus, Ricardo, List, and many more, including much Marxist thought and analysis); and closer microscale attention to individuals and their sometimes collective proxies as firms or corporations (derived similarly from later eighteenth century arguments, but diverging toward the disciplinary economics of the Anglo-American liberal marginalist tradition associated with Marshall). This macro–micro divergence has often distracted from close analysis of the dynamics of subjectivity within capitalism, not least because of the ways in which the discipline of economics has tended to build models on the basis of a universalized, rational, utility-maximizing individual subject and its common institutional proxy, the profit-maximizing firm. Recent critical theory of globalization (cf. Zizek, Badiou, Hardt & Negri) has further reduplicated

---

2   H.H. Gerth and C. Wright Mills, in the wide-ranging introduction to their extensive 1946 collection of Weber's writings in English, emphasize the ways in which Weber himself, in contrast to Marx, tends to see capitalism as unitary: "The further back Weber goes historically, the more he is willing to see capitalism as one feature of a historical situation; the more he approaches modern industrial capitalism, the more willing he is to see capitalism as a pervasive and unifying affair" (Weber, 1946, p. 66). "Unlike Marx, however, Weber is not interested in investigating the problems of capitalist dynamics" (p. 68).

this conceptual tension by treating capitalism as a global and globalizing phenomenon.[3]

Foucault's later work, sketched out especially in the College de France lectures of the later 1970s (and therefore partly invisible to scholarship until recently because never fully elaborated in published work during his lifetime), proposes a vocabulary that can assist in mapping the historical dynamics and variants of capitalist subjectivity. Foucault's arguments in the lectures published in English in the mid-2000s as *Security, Territory, Population* and *The Birth of Biopolitics* represent "security" as supervenient upon the structures of juridico-legal and disciplinary organization and institutionalization of the political through knowledge that emerged in the 16th/17th and 18th/19th centuries respectively (and which receive famously close attention in his books like *Discipline and Punish* and *The History of Sexuality, Volume 1*). For Foucault, security means the ways in which knowledge-apparatuses organize, enumerate, and collectivize subjectivity after its historical emergence through law and discipline: individuals become populations, lands become territories, and subjects emerge carrying a double loading (Foucault, 2007, pp. 20–21). They are subject *to* the dynamics of disciplinary-institutional power (domination; exploitation; state authority), but at the same time they can understand themselves as subjects *of* a range of concepts that resolve as forms of autonomy (ideas; political action; economic behavior; self-fashioning).

This double loading of the modern subject has had many analysts. Perhaps the *locus classicus* of this discursive sphere is Kant's elaboration of "enlightenment" as the "emergence from self-incurred tutelage": the emergent autonomous subject becomes so by realizing that subservience to power is itself the scaffolding of any autonomy. The dialectical emanations of Hegel's thought placed that insight at the core of systematic political, legal, historical, and moral philosophy (Franco, 2002; Patten, 2002). Freedom – for Kant, for Hegel, and also in Foucault's narrative – is therefore a complex and emergent artifact of processes and apparatuses of power (Foucault, 2007, p. 48). In contrast to its framing within so much liberal-capitalist thought, freedom understood this way has no originary or natural form. A further artifact of this historical emergence of coterminous moral forms of subjective autonomy in the later 18th century is the concept of race: race is the concept which allows some human populations to be excluded from the potential for autonomy to be exercised (Eigen & Larrimore, 2006). The trajectory of the psychoanalytic analysis of the

---

3 Symptomatic is the rhetoric found, for example, in David Harvey's description of the rise of free trade and manufacturing outsourcing in the 1980s: "Capital now had access to the whole world's low-cost labour supplies." (2011, p. 16).

layered subject that culminates in Zizek's Lacanian-inflected reading of today's globalized neoliberal capitalism is perhaps the most elaborate, even baroque, form of exploration of these complex dynamics (Amidon & Sanderson, 2012). The subject, in Zizek's understanding, is contingent upon a dynamics of symbolic and imaginary ordering so complex as to render the subject everywhere contingent and foreclosed even in and through the possibility of its emergence.

What, then, is the status of subjectivity under the condition of contemporary capitalism? Does it inhere radical moral, political, or economic freedom? Or is the subject powerless and contingent before vast impersonal forces? Were either representation to dominate, the subject would be made to recapitulate the ways in which capitalism itself has been rendered unitary and isomorphic in so many discourses. Rather, we argue, the subject exists between poles of representation that tend toward the individual resolved through market forces as speculation and the collective resolved through securitization.

Varieties of (Finance) Capitalism: Securitization/Speculation

Within the emergent forms of capitalism going back to the 16th and 17th centuries, practices can be mapped in a way parallel to that of the contingently "free" or "autonomous" subject described above: some practices appear to adhere conceptually to groups or populations, and some appear to adhere discretely or autonomously to individuals. The former, in particular, can be understood as conceptually contiguous with Foucault's "security": these are social practices of capital that create instruments that pool and collect, through knowledge and enumeration, the "securities" based on networks of "trust."[4] These dynamics we call "securitization." The correlative concept that focuses on the individual gains and losses that derive from processes of exchange and flows of securities and currencies within populations: "speculation." In contrast to forms of securitization in which participative dynamics prevail, allowing the pooling and spreading of risk in ways that can insure and secure, speculation appears as an artifact of the autonomous agency of the participating subjects, for whom securities are representative instruments of the potential for profit – whether or not such profit carries moral, ethical, or normative loading. Securitization and speculation, therefore, are not disjunct concepts. They are, rather, mutually implicated processes that focus on phased dynamics within capitalism, and that therefore further enable a mapping of varying forms of capitalism.

---

4 Compare the focus on the "security of property" in Clark (2007).

Speculation is used here in a sense generally congruent with common usage, one that throws the focus of analysis upon the actions of capital-holding individuals (or institutions) "speculating" about the future value of their assets. In seeking profit, those individuals place some of their own financial capital at risk. We extend this usage, however, to argue that speculation generates conceptual power because it secondarily alienates value from objects that have accreted it in a variety of ways. Especially in the past 150 years as asset markets have gained sophistication, the value that forms the basis of the assets traded within them has become increasingly rarefied. Speculation has come to transform objects that carry value (real estate, commodities, government debt, corporate stocks and bonds) into instruments with fictitious or fantasy-like character (derivatives, interest-rate and credit-default swaps, futures). Keynes classically represented this point in his (1936) *General Theory of Employment, Interest and Money*:

> If I may be allowed to appropriate the term *speculation* for the activity of forecasting the psychology of the market, and the term *enterprise* for the activity of forecasting the prospective yield of assets over their whole life, it is by no means the case that speculation predominates over enterprise. As the organisation of investment markets improves, the risk of the predominance of speculation does, however, increase. In one of the greatest investment markets in the world, namely, New York, the influence of speculation (in the above sense) is enormous.... Speculators may do no harm as bubbles on a steady stream of enterprise. But the position is serious when enterprise becomes the bubble on a whirlpool of speculation. When the capital development of a country becomes a by-product of the activities of a casino, the job is likely to be ill-done.
>
> KEYNES, 1964, p. 159

Krier (2005), developing Keynes's logic further with reference to more recent capital market mechanisms, argues that from these proliferating forms of speculation a kind of "dark capital" emerges, one that projects value into the sphere of fantasy, and thus generates the kinds of systemic risk that became so widely discussed during the financial crisis and Great Recession of 2007–2009.

Securitization, on the other hand, is deployed here in a sense somewhat counterintuitive with respect to recent usage. Since the financial crisis beginning ca. 2007, this term has entered common parlance to refer to the bundling of assets that became, for example, so problematical in the issuing of mortgage-backed securities that masked risks both that the underlying asset was mispriced in a bubble economy, and that the underlying security, the mortgage, was insufficiently underwritten and therefore at high but unacknowledged risk of default. These financial market dynamics surrounding the Great Recession reveal how securitization depends conceptually upon market processes that can themselves be represented as speculative, and also, vice versa, how speculation can be driven by innovations in securitization. We nonetheless extend the conceptual space of securitization historically to focus upon the ways in which the development of financial instruments secured the positions and livelihoods of individual subjects within their communities. Since the rise of neoliberalism, the term securitization has in fact became synonymous with speculation. The two terms, and the concepts they signify, have collapsed into one another. Here, we revive earlier usage in which each designated a specific mode of ethically-legitimated economic action.

Fundamentally, securitization represents the possibility that economic subjects can act in concert to create means of addressing and mitigating risk: securitization is the creation of risk pools. It takes shape in a proliferating range of transactional forms. Francois Ewald's claims – and Ewald was Foucault's student and the general editor of the College de France lectures – that a society emerges into modernity in that it becomes an "insurance society" are further congruent with these arguments (Sørensen & Christiansen, 2013, 16). Weber's attention in "The Protestant Ethic" to specific German, Dutch, and Anglo-American religious communities is particularly revealing here, especially in how those communities tended toward the development of practices that theologically and institutionally sanctioned either the individual and personal stakes of economic activity (thus driving speculation), or attended more significantly to the possibility that community action could generate security (driving securitization). From the simplest personal guarantee to the most complex credit default swap, from the state-granted privilege of limited-liability incorporation to the vast emanations of modern welfare states, individuals and institutions have sought to shape the future more securely. Securitization is thus always and everywhere both social and political.

The subject under the condition of capital always participates in these dynamics of securitization and speculation. The subject is therefore circumscribed within a sphere in which necessity and autonomy are at once contiguous and contingent. Just as freedom cannot be understood historically without the recognition of its status as an artifact of apparatuses of power, and is therefore generated as a kind of excess of the emergence of those apparatuses, so too are securitization and speculation linked, both conceptually and in practice. As markets have emerged historically, they have cycled through periods in which the one or the other has risen to symbolic primacy, only to be recycled into the other through perceptions of collapse, crisis, depression, or decline. Secondary conceptual accretions like "social capital" or "human capital" serve to further embed and reify these dynamics.

Protestant Master Narratives and the Re-Reading of the Weber Thesis

Understanding of the layered dynamics of capitalism has been set back over many decades by misreadings of Weber's theses on "The Protestant Ethic." Weber's claims that are usually emphasized in the literature, those about Puritan-Calvinist capitalist traditions and the ways they emphasize the links between theological salvation and (usually) individually conceived, speculative economic practices are in fact accompanied by a line of argument that focuses on parallel capitalist traditions ordered around not primarily around speculation but rather securitization. Alastair Hamilton's essay on "The Protestant Ethic" in the (2000) *Cambridge Companion to Weber* is classically symptomatic of the overemphasis on the Puritan-Calvinist trajectory within Weber's ideas about the "spirit of capitalism." After a few biographical reflections that focus on the "Reformed faith" of Weber's mother and many of his close colleagues, and which stretch credulity by dubbing the Heidelberg of 1903 a "Calvinist university" – the period of Reformed dominance of the university ended permanently at the outset of the Thirty Years War in 1620 – Hamilton reduces Weber's thesis (a few largely dismissive reflections on Pietism and the "authoritarianism and passivity" of Lutheranism notwithstanding) to the following: "He looked above all at the system in England and concluded that the economic success both of England and America could be traced back to a Puritan or Calvinist tradition" (2000, p. 153).

We argue that alongside arguments about Puritan-Calvinist moments, close attention must be paid to the Pietist-Quaker traditions within capitalist development. Weber himself gave them – Pietism in particular – at least as much, and likely more, analysis in his essay, particularly in the extensive footnotes that he appended in 1920 to the original essay written in 1904–5 (Ghosh 2014, pp. vii–viii). Nonetheless he organized his essay in a way that masked their significance by dividing varieties of Pietism too strongly from Quakerism, especially in the ways their branches developed in the United States.[5] In a reading of Weber adequate to his focus on these multiple varieties of capitalism, the Puritan-Calvinist trajectory emphasizes the moral-theological loading of speculative profit and the at-risk character of salvation as a representation of capital. It therefore focuses on the ways in which the subject is encumbered by the stakes of capitalist practice: capitalism is an avatar of salvation, and the subject is always and everywhere encumbered with these stakes. The Pietist-Quaker

---

5   For an extended discussion of the academic controversies that Weber's claims about Protestantism have unleashed both during his lifetime and after, see: Steinert, 2010, pp. 219–260.

traditions, on the other hand, emphasize the pooling of risks within the religious community (cf. the Quaker "meeting house"), and the ways in which salvation can be mapped through forms of community or congregational participation. They therefore instantiate a subject potentially eased of the encumbrances of moral-theological and economic uncertainty.

Our view of Weber parallels Peter Ghosh's (2014) thorough reading of Weber's scholarly biography through close analysis of "The Protestant Ethic," and reveals the level of care necessary to understand the differentiated levels of Weber's argumentation. Ghosh carefully explicates Weber's statements about the various branches of Protestantism, noting regularly how Weber's close scholarly and personal relationship with Ernst Troeltsch shaded his claims (as does Steinert). Central here is Weber's placement of Pietist thought in relation to the "spirit" of ascetic accumulation-work through a "calling" or "vocation" that represents the core element of the capitalist "spirit." Ghosh explains how Pietism works as a foil to Calvinism in Weber's text. Importantly, the focus turns from the individual toward the social:

> The Pietist emphasis on the *praxis pietatis* (practical piety) and group organization in the conventicle offered an alternative stimulus. Its consequences for social behaviour might not be entirely predictable, but normally the "effect of Pietist principles was simply a still *stricter* ascetic control of conduct within the vocation, and a still firmer religious anchorage for vocational ethics than could be engendered by the mere, worldly 'respectability' of the normal, Reformed Christian...." In short, Pietism in its social aspect could trump dogmatic Calvinism if the latter was simply predestinarian and individualistic.
>
> GHOSH, 2014, p. 351; the internal quote is from Weber, 1930, p. 131

Weber clearly charts a tension between two streams of the capitalist spirit: individualistic Puritan-Calvinism and socially-engaged Pietist-Quakerism. Throughout Weber's writings on economic ethics, the socially-engaged Pietist-Quaker variants of Protestantism fare as well, or better, than their individualist Calvinist counterparts as spirits conducive to capitalism. Indeed, socially attuned business practices among Quakers, Baptists and Methodists meant that – as Weber stated in his *General Economic History*, "piety [was]...the surest road to wealth" (Weber, [1927] 1992, p. 367; see also Weber, 1946, p. 302–22).

Ghosh further reflects upon Weber's interest in the ecstatic blood theology of Count Zinzendorf and his Herrnhut community, a complex embranchment of the Pietist tradition usually marked as "Moravian." In doing so, he trenchantly dismisses traditionally reductive readings of Weber that attend only to (Calvinist) individualistic elements:

> If we take the *PE* at face value, as an account of the individual psychology of ascetic Protestantism..., the amount of attention devoted to the emotionalism and outright silliness of Zinzendorf and the *Herrnhuter* must appear perplexing. However, Weber was not interested in Zinzendorf because of his *"childlike quality"* or his irrational reliance on random *"lots"*... – i.e. his relative failure to reproduce Calvinism's psychological hardness and rigour – but as the pioneer of a distinctive, communitarian form on German soil that went beyond the conventicle....
>
> GHOSH, 2014, p. 347

The Herrnhut community, and the sometimes bizarre theological and organizational emanations of it through Zinzendorf's activities both in Europe and in America (including substantial influences upon Anglo-American Methodism), point to the ways in which "vocation" could become not a just driver of individual striving, but more significantly the basis of social practice.[6]

Ghosh further recognizes the tension in Weber's treatment of the Quakers, who were so important to the development of finance capital in America, particularly in Philadelpha. He frames this in the context of a short discussion of Weber's own statements about the two most glaring deficits of "The Protestant Ethic": inadequate discussion of the issue of credit, and, in Weber's own words, an undifferentiated "discussion of the social policy of ascetic Protestantism" (Ghosh, 2014, 358). The latter issue relates specifically to how Weber analyzes the Quakers. As Ghosh describes it:

> ...In the *PS* [Weber's essay on "The Protestant Sects and the Spirit of Capitalism" that Talcott Parsons excluded from his translation of "The Protestant Ethic," but which Gerth and Mills included in their 1946 collection] this [discussion of social policy] is reduced to a single reference to the "highly developed" and indeed overdeveloped "support system of the Quakers." Now it must be assumed that Weber wanted to discuss the hostility of a deliberately impersonal ascetic Protestantism towards what he regarded as an enfeebling and sentimental "welfare policy" here.... But this brief utterance cannot be construed here. Instead it raises an unsolved mystery: how did the Quakers whom he admires so much come to take such a wrong, anti-individualistic turning?
>
> GHOSH 2014, p. 358

---

6 For a reading of Weber's interest in Zinzendorf that further emphasizes the significance of social practice in the Herrnhut theological community see Smith (2013). Pietism and its communitarian yet ascetic economic ethics were addressed, with considerable success, to working classes who had remained resistant to the individualist ethos of Calvinism.

Thus Ghosh points to the core of the tension in Weber's text between speculation and securitization by showing how the question of social relations in
Weber's "spirit" of capitalism remains oddly fragmentary and mysterious:
Weber's text itself contains a tension that makes Puritanism and the forms of
speculative practice associated with it appear to be a purer form of the "spirit"
of capitalism. Groups in the Pietist-Quaker traditions that were associated with
more socially complex, securitized forms of capitalist practice, while clearly and
unmistakably capitalist, seemed less purely an embodiment of that "spirit."
This issue forms a central moment in Steinert's (2010) critique of Weber as well.

Two further aspects of Weber's analysis highlight how speculation overs-
hadowed securitization as a result of his vocabulary and interpretive practices.
The first of these is the treatment of "free labor"; the second is the question of
Weber's treatment of finance capital as an aspect of capitalism. For Weber, a
precondition of the emergence of capitalism and its spirit is freedom from coerced and corvee systems of labor, as within slavery, patriarchy, patrimonialism
and feudalism. Unlike coerced labor, "formally-free labor" is dominated by
market practices and speculative dynamics. These reflections particularly col-
or Weber's 1920 essay on the sociology of religion that Parsons translated as the
first section of "The Protestant Ethic" (Weber, 1930, pp. 21, 22, 24).[7]

While Weber, in his *General Economic History*, identifies speculatively determined, formally free labor as a condition of capitalism's emergence, his list of
preconditions does not, curiously, include speculative financial markets.[8] In an
additional correlative of his analysis of labor, Weber does not explore how individual capitalists act in financial markets. In fact, the institutions of finance
capital seem to exist outside the spirit of capitalism (Ghosh 2014, p. 164). Weber

---

7 This essay concludes with Weber's reflections upon how another scholarly form of social
   taxonomy, that derived from "the importance of biological heredity" and "comparative
   racial neurology and psychology" may provide additional answers in the future (Weber, 1930,
   pp. 30–31). For discussion of Weber's criticism of the ideas of Alfred Ploetz, founder of the
   German Society for Race Hygiene, see Proctor, 1991, pp. 110–111.

8 Weber's list of preconditions includes: "appropriation of the physical means of production
   by the entrepreneur, freedom of the market, rational technology, rational law, free labor,
   the commercialization of economic life"([1927]1992, p. 286). While he adds speculation as
   a "further motif," its causal contribution to capitalism as such is negative. The significance
   of speculation is bounded by "the great economic crises which it called forth" ([1927]1992,
   p. 286). Through speculation, "crises became an imminent factor of the economic order," and
   hence, as Krier (2005) suggests, a form of "dark capital" or anti-capital frequently destructive
   of value. Crucially, although speculative markets (bourses) appear as early as the 16th century, the trade in industrial securities does not develop until late in the 19th century, more
   than a century after the "spirit of capitalism." ([1927]1992, p. 293–294). See also Amidon, 2008.

thus implicitly shows how the tensions between securitization and speculation affect both capital and labor.

The Bismarckian Welfare State and the Stakes of Pooled Risk

Many moments in the historical development of European states and economies, particularly in the German-speaking world of the eighteenth and nineteenth centuries, demonstrate how the mapping of capitalist practice onto moments of securitization and speculation enriches and clarifies the classical Weberian narrative. One significant example is found in the relations between the Prussian state and the emergent forms of economic and intellectual practice found in Pietist circles centered in the city and university of Halle.[9] Gawthrop (1993) emphasizes how for a short period in the middle of the eighteenth century, the ways in which the Halle Pietists approached the education and discipline of the religious community intersected with the emergent interests of the Prussian state.

As European nation-states expanded their imperial and economic purview and developed their institutional infrastructures during the nineteenth century, the complex interplay between securitization and speculation became increasingly manifest. As institutions like railways demanded newly extensive sources of capital, financial markets and their regulatory schemes grew in tandem throughout the industrializing world (McCraw 1984; Amidon 2008). Different nations and different regions, however, accreted varying emanations of these varieties of capitalism. Similarly, critiques of capitalism developed in widely varying ways. A particularly revealing moment in the institutional dynamics of finance and politics during the later nineteenth century is the moment often referred to as the birth of the welfare state. This was the establishment during the 1880s by the German empire, under the chancellorship of Otto von Bismarck, of three forms of social insurance still central to many forms of welfare-state capitalism: health insurance (the Workers' Health Insurance Law, 1883), workers' compensation (the Workers' Accident Insurance Law, 1884), and pension insurance (the Old-Age and Invalid Insurance Law, 1889).

---

9 In his writings on economic ethics, Weber did not consistently distinguish between the rationalist, institution-building, bureaucratic, proto-scientific Pietism centered in Halle and the more emotional, voluntarist communitarian Pietism of Zinzendorf and the Hernhutters. Though both counter Calvinist individualism with social groupings and foster "pooling," their modes of sociality are quite distinct and worthy of separate conceptualization (Weber, 1930, pp. 244–252).

The goals of these innovations in German social policy brought together three elements of Bismarck's policy program during the 1870s and 1880s: firstly, to undermine through positive policy the political power of socialism (in concert with the legislation banning socialist organizations that was in force between 1878 and 1890); secondly to reveal the bankruptcy of liberalism, which itself seemed unable to approach the questions of socialism and national unity with coherence; and thirdly to provide a positive foil to the Empire's conflicts with the Catholic Church (the so-called *Kulturkampf*), by creating a national empire that could claim to enact Christian charity in the industrial age more effectively than Catholic institutions. These three social insurance laws successfully became the abiding foundation of German social policy in the twentieth century (Reinhardt, 1989, pp. 614–17).

The rise of the Bismarckian welfare state has been understood by many major historians as a form of policy with direct links to Pietist traditions. Indeed, all three of these forms of pooled risk were prefigured in the 18th and 19th centuries on a smaller scale and with mostly voluntary participation among Pietist-Quaker groups (the "social support" noted by Weber above). While remaining mindful of historian John E. Rodes's (1964) admonishment against overstating Bismarck's power, it is clear that important lines of influence run through Bismarck himself (p. 383). At the simplest biographical level, James J. Sheehan – a scholar hardly prone to overstatement – argues that Bismarck was exposed as a young man to "a particularly potent blend of pietist religiosity and aristocratic sociability" (1989, p. 562). Two of the most significant historians of German social policy, Hermann Beck and Gerhard Ritter, emphasize the continuities between pietist thought, cameralist policy, and the Bismarckian social state. Several figures with personal influence on Bismarck himself were significant here. Beck emphasizes how Hermann Wagener's "conservative socialism" prompted Bismarck to think of the state as the benevolent protector of the population (1995, pp. 107–9), and Ritter calls Wagener "one of Bismarck's closest advisers on social policy" (1989, pp. 71–2). Ritter further claims that another of Bismarck's close advisers (who nonetheless broke with Bismarck over the politics of the social insurance laws in 1883), can specifically be seen as one of the figures who brought Pietist thought into nineteenth-century social policy (1995, p. 37).

These ways in which the German state developed and emphasized practices of securitization alongside speculation have had a lasting legacy. Furthermore, German cultural codes became – and remain today – fraught with complex representations of individuals and groups associated with speculation. The most dramatic of these, of course, has been through antisemitism, which of course, while hardly limited to Germany, took on unique forms there.

The longstanding tension in German culture between securitization and speculation, heightened by the rise of finance capital in the later nineteenth century, gave that period's new forms and institutions of political antisemitism a particularly powerful symbolic and representational instrumentarium (Pulzer 1988, pp. 42–46; Wistrich, 2010).

Conclusion: 21st Century Capital, Class, and the Stakes of Subjective Autonomy

This chapter has framed a conceptual scaffold whose central beams, speculation and securitization, provide theoretical access to two interrelated problems: (1) the historical and contemporary relationships between subjectivity and capitalism; and (2) tensions in the internal dynamics of capitalism between social and individual forms of action that resolve today as questions of income distribution, social policy, and economic justice (Krier & Amidon, 2015). The ongoing scholarly resonance of Max Weber's foundational narrative of the "spirit of capitalism," and the critical sparks that his ideas continue to generate, show how significant these issues remain in contemporary society.

Political discourse in the United States today carries significant tension generated by the problems broached here of the relationships between individual freedom, risk pooling, and the (welfare) state. A logic of economic ethics that remains vested largely in the field of speculation, one in which imagined returns remain linked to both individual freedom and rectitude, while the pooled risks characteristic of securitization can be represented as a diminishment of the same freedom, provides a potential for explanation of many current political controversies. Two examples from recent American politics demonstrate these symbolic stakes: (1) the powerful derision expressed toward the policy initiative that overtly raised, perhaps the first time in American politics, the idea that individuals should perceive themselves consciously as part of risk pools: the Affordable Care Act; and (2) the seemingly evergreen idea that both individuals and American society would benefit from a transfer of some of the financial flows of the Social Security system more directly into the financial markets.

Both of these contemporary American political controversies show that even today welfare state policies retain and heighten the conceptual and symbolic tensions between securitization and speculation. In *Economy and Society*, Weber himself criticized the Bismarckian policy initiatives that established the German welfare state because he saw them as creating a double perversion in the functioning of the capitalist economy. Firstly, they ran the risk of damaging the state's cohesiveness by evacuating the moral stakes of economic behavior, particularly for the working class, a point Weber makes by directly and ironi-cally contrasting the German state's goals in both military and social policy:

> A state that wants to base the spirit of its mass army on honor and soli-darity must not forget that in everyday life and in the economic struggles of the workers the sentiments of honor and solidarity are the only deci-sive moral forces....
>
> WEBER, 1978, p. 1391

Secondly, the Bismarckian welfare policies could reduce to an attempt to recre-ate affection for the state through bribery rather than moral logic:

> To be turned into demagoguery, and very bad demagoguery at that, was also the fate of the Imperial welfare legislation in Bismarck's hands.... Bismarck, in imitation of certain American practices, believed that he could create a positive attitude toward the state, and political gratitude, by granting welfare benefits out of the public funds or compulsory pri-vate funds... (1978, pp. 1390–1).

Additionally, in a revealing passage in the *General Economic History*, Weber shows the ways in which he perceives speculative finance capital to be some-thing separate from the "spirit of capitalism," but that at the same time accretes to the forms of securitization found in welfare state policies: he argues that one of the major problems of financial speculation is that it leads to economic cri-ses that further generate a desire for rational socialism among working classes: hence, the primary evil of pooled capital is that it generates speculative excess which leads to a demand for pooled risk in socialism ([1927]1992, p. 291).

Weber's negative views regarding both the Bismarckian welfare state and the capitalistic social support systems found in the Pietist-Quaker traditions are all of a piece: wherever pooling emerges, it tends to undermine the bourgeois sub-ject characterized by its relationship to speculation: autonomous individuality is placed at risk by liquidation into the pool. For Weber, then, risk pooling is not a firm ground upon which autonomous individuals can stand, but a mire into which they sink. Thus Weber's implicit theory of alienation emerges. Weber, shaped by his concerns with bureaucracy, domination, and disenchantment, and by his investment in bourgeois ethics, represented the modern world as one in which only a kind of rigorous self-discipline could generate sufficient meaning to ground individual life. His two famous Munich lectures on "Politics as a Vocation" and "Science as a Vocation," delivered in 1918, thus necessarily recapitulate the language of "The Protestant Ethic" by representing both social fields as spaces in which subjects must, if they wish to act meaningfully, pursue their calling in a carefully self-disciplined manner (Weber, 1946, pp. 77–156).[10] Those individuals are therefore intellectual-moral speculators: they may not be able to realize for themselves the intangible benefit of their activity, but only when they act according to their vocation, can future generations benefit from their political or scientific activity. Today's political subjects may face challenges different from those that Weber metaphorically captured within that *stahlhartes Gehäuse* that comes down to English-speaking readers translated as the "iron cage," but they continue to exist within capitalist forms and practices that map onto speculation and securitization. This, it seems, remains one of the characteristic and lasting moments of vigor in the capitalist political-economic order: the future is always in play, and always unknown, but the future can be shaped, ordered and valued by both social and individual action. Capitalism's diversity is this double potential for future meaning.

References

Adorno, T.W. & Horkheimer, M. ([1947] 2002) *Dialectic of enlightenment.* (E. Jephcott, Trans.) Stanford: Stanford University Press.

Amidon, K.S. (2008). The visible hand and the new American biology: Toward an integrated historiography of railroad-supported agricultural research. *Agricultural History* 82.3: 309–336.

Amidon, K.S. & Krier, D. (2009). On rereading Klaus Theweleit's *Male Fantasies. Men and Masculinities* 11.4: 488–496.

Amidon, K.S. & Sanderson, Z.G. (2012). On subjectivity and the risk pool; or, Zizek's lacuna. *Telos* 160: 121–138.

Beck, H. (1995). *The origins of the authoritarian welfare state in prussia: Conservatives, bureaucracy, and the social question, 1815–1870.* Ann Arbor: University of Michigan Press.

Clark, G. (2007). *A farewell to alms: A brief economic history of the world.* Princeton: Princeton University Press.

Eigen, S. & Larrimore, L., (Eds.). (2006). *The German invention of race.* Albany: SUNY Press.

---

10   Weber's scholarly and political subjects of 1918 Germany resonate here with Klaus Theweleit's analysis (in *Male Fantasies*) of the severely self-disciplining "soldierly men" who served in the German Free Corps units during the revolutionary period at the close of the First World War, and subsequently wrote about their experiences during the 1920s (Amidon and Krier, 2009).

Esping-Andersen, G. (2013). *The three worlds of welfare capitalism*. Cambridge: Polity.

Feldner, H. & Vighi, F. (2015). *Critical theory and the crisis of contemporary capitalism*. London: Bloomsbury.

Foucault, M. (2007). *Security, territory, population: Lectures at the College de France 1977–1978*. New York: Palgrave Macmillan.

Franco, P. (2002). *Hegel's philosophy of freedom*. New Haven: Yale University Press.

Gawthrop, R.L. (1993). *Pietism and the making of eighteenth-century Prussia*. Cambridge University Press.

Ghosh, P. (2014). *Max Weber and The Protestant Ethic: Twin histories*. Oxford, UK: Oxford University Press.

Hall, P.A., & Soskice, D. (2001). *Varieties of capitalism: The institutional foundations of comparative advantage*. New York: John Wiley.

Hamilton, A. (2000). The Protestant Ethic. In Turner, S.P. (Ed.), *The Cambridge Companion to Weber,* (pp. 151–171) Cambridge, UK: Cambridge University Press.

Harvey, D. (2011). *The enigma of capital and the crisis of capital.* New York: Oxford.

Jameson, F. (2011), *Representing* Capital: *A reading of volume one*. London: Verso.

Jay, M. (1984). *Marxism and totality: The adventures of a concept from Lukács to Habermas.* Berkeley: University of California Press.

Keynes, J.M. ([1936] 1964). The general theory of employment, interest, and money. New York: Harcourt, Brace.

Krier, D. (2005). *Speculative management: Stock market power and corporate change.* Albany, NY: State University of New York Press.

Krier, D. & Amidon, K.S. (2015). Critical theory and the limits of academic economics: Resolving the political in Piketty's *Capital in the Twenty-First Century. Critical Sociology,* 41 (2): 349–358.

Marcuse, H. ([1964] 2012). *One-dimensional man: Studies in the ideology of advanced industrial society.* Accessed at: https://www.marxists.org/ebooks/marcuse/one-dimensional-man.htm.

Marx, K. ([1844] 1980). *Economic and philosophical manuscripts of 1844.* Trans. and Ed. by D. Struik. New York: International Publishers.

McCraw, T.K. (1984). *Prophets of regulation.* Cambridge: Harvard University Press.

Patten, A. (2002). *Hegel's idea of freedom.* Oxford UK: Oxford University Press.

Proctor, R.N. (1991). *Value-free science: Purity and power in modern knowledge.* Cambridge, MA: Harvard University Press.

Pulzer, P. (1988). *The rise of political Anti-Semitism in Germany and Austria.* Rev. ed. Cambridge, MA: Harvard University Press.

Reinhardt, K. (1989). *Germany: 2000 Years,* New York: Frederick Ungar.

Ritter, G.A. (1989). *Der Sozialstaat: Entstehung und Entwicklung im internationalen Vergleich.* Munich: Oldenbourg.

Rodes, J.E. (1964). *Germany: A history.* New York: Holt, Rinehart and Winston.

Sheehan, J.J. (1989). *German history: 1770–1866.* Oxford, UK: Oxford University Press.

Smith, D.N. (2013). Charisma disenchanted: Max Weber and his critics. *Current Perspectives in Social Theory* 31: 3–74.

Sørensen, M.P. & Christiansen, A. (2013). *Ulrich Beck: An introduction to the theory of second modernity and the risk society.* London: Routledge.

Steinert, H. (2010). *Max Weber's unwiderlegbare Fehlkonstruktionen: Die protestantische Ethik und der Geist des Kapitalismus.* Frankfurt/Main: Campus, 2010.

Streeck, W. (2010). E pluribus unum? Varieties and commonalities of capitalism. Accessed at: http://www.econstor.eu/bitstream/10419/43292/1/64070493X.pdf.

Weber, M. (1930). *The protestant ethic and the spirit of capitalism.* (T. Parsons, Trans.) London: Allen and Unwin.

Weber, M. (1946). *From Max Weber: Essays in sociology.* (H.H. Gerth and C.W. Mills, Trans. and Ed.) Oxford: Oxford University Press.

Weber, M. (1978). *Economy and society: An outline of interpretive sociology.* G. Roth and C. Wittich (Eds.). Berkeley, CA: University of California Press.

Weber, M. ([1927] 1992). *General economic history.* (F. Knight, Trans.) New Brunswick, NJ: Transaction.

Wistrich, R.S. (2010). *A lethal obsession: Anti-Semitism from antiquity to the global jihad.* New York: Random House.

Zizek, S. (2008). *In defense of lost causes.* London: Verso.

PART 3

Capitalism's Future and the Critique of Political Psychology

∴

The Idolatry of Mind: Durkheim's Critique of Idealism

Mark P. Worrell

Whitney Pope's (1976) analysis of *Suicide* placed a tombstone on Durkheim's seminal work, concluding that, while historically interesting, the book was, despite a few croutons of enduring relevance and insight, an antiquated and colossal failure. Pope went to so far as to suggest that the concept of 'force' (as well as a few other central ideas) could be flushed from Durkheim's work with no appreciable loss whatsoever (pp. 201–204).[1] The problem with Pope, however, was that he was mired in postwar, positivistic and behavioristic assumptions that precluded grasping Durkheim's work.[2]

We should recall that by the 1970s, when there was a last gasp of terrible, retrospective works dedicated to Durkheim, sociology was already in a state of advanced intellectual decay. The 1950s and 1960s witnessed sociology parasitically ingratiating itself with the bloating welfare state and managerial capitalism. A new opportunity arose with the student antiwar movement and the emergence of a current of anti-positivism during the late 1960s but these trends did little for Durkheim's reputation.[3]

---

1 It went unrecognized that Durkheim's conception of 'force' (if not the terminology) was not derived from mechanics. Force was not a physical thing, but, rather, was a further development of the idealist move that transformed substance into subject. For Durkheim, though, substance was not merely subject as it was with German idealists but intersubjective. Force was something that lived in the imagination, not merely of individuals, but a shared or collective imaginary. Betraying his nominalism, Lukes dismisses 'forces' and 'currents' as "...distinctly inappropriate analogical language..." (1973, p. 215). As an aside, the Lukes biography has its merits, however, the chapter on suicide is highly problematic and misleading.

2 Worth noting is that, after WWII, strains of European social thought that veered away from methodological and ontological individualism and empirical methods were suspect and implicated, even if only implicitly, in romantic reaction at best and proto-authoritarianism at worst. Witness the bashing that Hegel took in 1950s America.

3 A rising tide does not lift all boats. Only after the behemoth of Parsonian structural functionalism began to dissolve, did Durkheim have a chance at a fresh hearing and, indeed, a few took up the task – but only a few. Even into the 90s, relatively few had any inclination to reexamine Durkheim. Recall that the major onslaught against functionalism in the late 60s and early 70s was carried out by multi-disciplinary neo-Marxists who had virtually no interest in reclaiming Durkheim. Moreover, to this day, Durkheim plays almost no role in the world

There have been a few attempts to rehabilitate Durkheim in the 1980s and 1990s but he still remains the *ne plus ultra* of bad sociology and a chimera of positivism and obscurantist Realism.[4] A recent and interesting development finds Durkheim cast as a secret Hegelian (Strenski, 2006).[5] While there is a certain element of truth to this I hope to demonstrate that while Durkheim was indebted to the legacies of absolute and speculative idealism, he was not only a staunch critic of these intellectual currents, but, additionally, their coordinates can be precisely mapped out within a topography of pathologically disaggregated society – Durkheim would not have seen himself as an "Hegelian" so

---

of critical social theory which is too bad since, in my estimation, we need a 'Marxheimian sociology' more than ever.

4 No surprise, the harshest attacks emanate from neo-Marxist positions. The standard criticism against Durkheim's notion of the externality of social facts (his anti-psychology and anti-subjectivism) is that there is no "such thing as a unified social subject" of the kind promulgated by Durkheim (Adorno, 2000, p. 44). Adorno proffers an alternative view of social dynamics such that "the totality of society is maintained not by solidarity but by the antagonistic interests of human beings, by its antitheses..." (2000, p. 44). This is reminiscent of Sartre's view that "if we do not wish the dialectic to become a divine law again, a metaphysical fate, it must proceed *from individuals* and not from some kind of supra-individual ensemble" (2004, p. 36). These two comments from Adorno and Sartre are, ironically, totally in line with both the spirit *and* word of Durkheim. It is certainly true that Durkheim was prone to phrases such as "collective personality" and society as a "sentient being" and so on but a careful reading of *Suicide* reveals that any conception of static solidarity, or some kind of preexisting solidified substance ruling over people, is unwarranted. Indeed, with Durkheim, one gets a fairly good sense of how societies can be artificially or mechanically maintained (at least temporarily and always as a monstrosity) in the absence of solidarity and his model of social organization, as it is worked out in *Suicide*, is predicated on equilibrium as a product of synthesizing contradictory moral currents (what Adorno would call a 'field of forces'), or, in the absence of equilibrium, the *superimposition* of contrary forces (in worse case scenarios we arrive at bad on top of bad twice over). His work is full of social 'monstrosities' and contradictory superimpositions, alternations, and quasi-sublime formations where there are clear absences of solidarity and clashes of antagonistic forces (e.g., his swarming bees and tumbling molecules metaphors).

5 One might argue that Durkheim's sociology was 'Hegelian' but it would be the kind of 'Hegelianism' we find in Marx – inverted, demystified, and thoroughly socialized. Hegel's sociological flaw was seeing the long-range development of the odyssey of *Geist* in terms of the inexorable triumph of the Idea and Reason and the realization of a realm of absolute human freedom. Humans, here, became instruments of the divine Idea. While a few writers have recently argued for a connection between Hegel and Durkheim, and I think there is one, no one has, in my opinion, really hit the ball out of the park with regard to their convergences and divergences.

much as one who had sublated the entire idealist program, if he indeed even ever thought in these terms.[6]

Here, we will examine two things presently: (a) the occluded identity of Durkheimian sociology relative to its ontological commitments as a precursor to the second part, namely, (b) locating the precise coordinates of idealism within Durkheim's critique of social self-destructiveness and demonstrating along the way that dogmatic, skeptical, and transcendental idealism each contain the seeds of self-annihilation, and that notions such as the Idea as absolute, a teleological odyssey of spirit across time, or a triumphal actualization of any concept (Reason, etc.) would strike Durkheim as symptomatic of diseased society in its reflective and seeking activities.

A   The Identity of Durkheimian Sociology

Durkheim has been labeled many things (realist, positivist, etc.) but none of the standard tags genuinely fit his sociology. The paradigms and positions Durkheim casts aside as one-sided errors include:

> Empiricism: "Classical empiricism leads to irrationalism; perhaps it should be called by that name" ([1912] 1995, p. 13). Notice the qualification, leaving open the necessity for emersion in empirical reality and history as opposed to abstracted rationalism.
>
> Materialism: "It is...improper to characterize our method as materialist" ([1895] 1982, p. 163). Material practices were obviously central to Durkheim's sociology but social facts were not reducible to materiality. Mana, for example, has physical effects but is itself ideal in nature. Interestingly, the mature Marx was also not a 'materialist' – note the famous line in chapter one of *Capital*, volume one where "not an atom of matter" enters into things as value.[7]
>
> Realism: "To be sure, it is...true that society has no other active forces than individuals..." ([1897] 1951, p. 310). If the only active forces are

---

6   I am extending a previous claim that, for Durkheim, even though philosophy is the "collective consciousness" of science as a whole, sociology represented the sublation of philosophy (Worrell, 2010). Durkheim's sociology was the crowning achievement whereby idealism and materialism were sublated, raised up, so to speak, to an entirely new form of critical engagement with the world.

7   See the works of David Norman Smith for the definitive analyses of the intersection of mana (Durkheim), value (Marx), and charisma (Weber).

individuals than there is no transcendental subject or entity operating behind the backs of people. Totems, mana, suicidal currents, etc., are the products of individuals in association. Totems are irreducible, true, 'Big Others' if you will, but people do not worship totems because they are sacred, rather, totems are sacred by virtue of being worshipped. But take heed: Durkheim's sociology includes, but does not stop with, the inter-subjective construction of sacred objects such that reification and alien-ation are given their full weight.

Nominalism: Social facts are not merely verbal whimsy. Even if social facts are representations the sign is not the same as the thing signified, which, for Durkheim, is force or, in other words, authority, the sacred.[8]

Positivism: "Yet beneath these superficially different appearances, the es-sential features of the phenomenon are the same" ([1897] 1951, p. 283). What you see is not what you get. So far was Durkheim from positivism that the above quote is nothing less than the definition of Hegel's (nega-tive) speculative method: "For since the rational, which is synonymous with the Idea, becomes actual by entering into external existence, it emerges in an infinite wealth of forms, appearances, and shapes and sur-rounds its core with a brightly colored covering in which consciousness at first resides, but which only the concept can penetrate in order to find the inner pulse, and detect its continued beat even within the external shapes" ([1821] 1991, pp. 20–21). We would have to substitute "Idea" for "so-ciety", however, for Durkheim's 'absolute' was society not an hypostatized model of an odyssey of self-moving consciousness heading toward trium-phal actualization.

Idealism: society is not reducible to a system of ideas. Durkheim, like the mature Marx (1858 and beyond) explored the interdigitated nature

---

8 Nominalistic positions are entirely inadequate to the task of analyzing language. Everyday social reality is only ultimately possible on the basis of the externality of social facts because communication and thinking on the basis of signs would lose coherence otherwise. For ex-ample, a well-known metaphor such as the lion being the king of the jungle "implies the existence of both /king/and/lion/ as functives of two previously codified sign-functions. If signs (expressions and content) did not preexist the text, every metaphor would be equiva-lent simply to saying that something is something. But a metaphor says that *that* (linguistic) thing is at the same time *something else*" (Eco, 1984, p. 25). "Because language itself is a nec-essary condition of reflection, because philosophical awareness arises only in and through language, the human spirit always finds language present as a given reality, comparable and equal in stature to physical reality" (Cassirer, 1955, p. 117). Not only, though, does a fact (like language or a metaphor) confront the individual as a pre-existing reality but these facts have the power to impose themselves over personal inclinations.

of material practices (the real) and the ideal. Durkheim's 'social realism' was identical with Marx's 'historical materialism' or what we would refer today as 'constructionism' – if by that word we reject the varieties of constructionism that neglect alienation, reification, and structure.

Conceptualism: I have seen it argued, completely in reverse, that Durkheim began as a social realist and ended as a 'conceptualist.' This is not true. Nor is it even true that he was a 'Realist' in the normal sense of the word. Initially, Durkheim championed Abelard's 'conceptualism' as providing an adequate solution such that "general ideas are neither words nor substances but exist in our minds and thus have a subjective existence. General [universal] ideas also exist substantively in each individual object – by the very fact that the individual object belongs to the class, the class is realized in the individual. So general ideas are more than just words" (2004, p. 135). Abelard was not the best example he could have chosen but neither did he come to rest there. His later formulation shifted to classifications and typologies and then, in *Rules*, he focused on the comparative analysis of 'species' of societies or social facts.

Rationalism: Durkheim certainly thought that apriorist rationalism was "more attentive to the facts" compared to empiricism but he was also not a rationalist. In fact he said, about both currents of thought: "Such are the two conceptions that have competed for centuries. And if the debate has gone on and on, it is because the arguments back and forth are in fact more or less equivalent. If reason is but a form of individual experience, then reason is no more. On the other hand, if the capacities with which it is credited are recognized but left unaccounted for, then reason apparently is placed outside nature and science. Faced with these opposite objections, the intellect remains uncertain. But if the social origin of the categories is accepted, a new stance becomes possible..." ([1912] 1995, p. 14).

At one time or another, Durkheim has been packed up into all of these boxes. According to Lukes, Durkheim was a Realist; Cassirer claimed he was a nominalist; after groping in the dark, Nye and Ashworth admit defeat and conclude that Durkheim was both a realist and a nominalist (1971, p. 133). Likewise, Jay says "Durkheim's struggle to devise a method to analyze this generic reality [social facts as *sui generis* realities] is now generally conceded to have produced a brilliant failure; his defense of an epistemology at once positivist and idealist, empiricist and a priori has not stood the test of time" (1984, p. 280). What, then, was Durkheim's paradigmatic pose if, as I argue, all these commentators are in error?

Durkheim writes in three separate dimensions simultaneously and was a chameleon constantly undercutting his own claims by presenting multiple lines of argument for distinct audiences: mechanical, organic, and dialectical. One can most clearly see this presentational multiplicity at work in *Suicide* where, for example, he notes that contrary forces may combine their influences. Egoism may combine with its opposite, altruism, forming the combination of egoism-altruism (here we get the social forces for dummies version that says $A + B = A + B$) but when we explore further we find that egoism fuses with altruism to form irreducible, synthetic forms, e.g., mysticism and stoicism that blend with an unnamed imaginary construct, the *sage*. Here, we find that Durkheim has a slightly hidden theoretical account of sagacious devotional alienation and moral self-subjugation. It is common to find Durkheim prescribing a dose of altruistic action to cure self-absorption or melancholy, for example, but the resulting compound is not equal to its parts $(A + B)$. Egoism + Altruism may be expressed, poorly, as Egoism-Altruism but the underlying idea is that the resulting alloy is something new entirely emerging from one of three distinct forms of interaction: (a) alternation; (b) mechanical or juxtaposed superimposition; and (c) fused superimposition or synthesis resulting in a sublimation (either positive or negative). Why speak in three voices at all times? Why muddy the water? Was Durkheim confused, ambivalent, simply lack terminology, or did he have a conscious strategy in mind when he fell back on clunky phraseology?

At the end of *Rules* we find Durkheim vowing to forego further attempts to reach the public with old terms and retreat to an esoteric, scientific position that will garner more prestige and respect for the new discipline at a later date. However, it is also true, I think, that Durkheim simply had difficulty giving a name to his new approach other than forcefully and repeatedly insisting upon *what it was not*: psychology (reductionist individualism) or history (nominalistic). The closest he came to giving his sociology a fresh designation was when he referred to it as a "spiritualist" approach. However, even here, he appears to undercut this moniker by noting that the current of spiritualism had come and gone. Notice the difference, though: spiritualist versus spiritualism. Durkheim was keen to note that verbal similarities do not mean similar things, e.g., the radical difference between "individual," "individualism," and "individuality" in his work.[9] Durkheimian sociology was, in short, spiritual in a way that a speculative idealist would understand the concept of *Geist*, if, that is, *Geist* was not construed as a transcendental ego hidden behind the moon transmitting

---

9 The American mentality finds individuality and intense collective life mutually exclusive but, as Durkheim notes, the words "individual" and "individuality," though obviously similar and related, mean radically different things and are even opposed to one another in some respects (Durkheim, 1973, pp. 54–55). America is not the land of real individuality but anti-social egoism (cf. Simmel, 1971, p. 259).

its ideas from on high but an immanent and ebullient intersubjectivity that bubbles upward. As we shall see later, though, where Hegel subsumed *Geist* or Spirit under the Idea, Durkheim places *Geist* (collective consciousness) on a purely social footing and approaches it with new methods. If this were true, then, it would also be true that Durkheim was a realist. After all, the development of idealism was one toward growing realism (Beiser, 2002) but we must recall that the claim that Durkheim was a "social realist" was one applied to him by critics, even though he did identify with the phrase because a better label was not at hand. Keep in mind, though, that *social* realism is not identical with Realism and *sociological* realism is also distinct from social realism. It was not until the 1960s that the term "constructionism" and the idea of "the social construction of reality" entered the sociological vocabulary (and was a good fit for Durkheim with some qualifications) but most of the proponents of "constructionism" were interested in 'micro' sociological endeavors and, again, Marxists and other critical practitioners were averse to relinquishing materialism and realism (they would rather wrestle with alligators in the swamp of surplus value than, with the mature Marx of *Capital*, drain the swamp altogether) so they could find no common ground with Durkheim, still, or the constructionist paradigm as a whole. So, here we are all these decades later, and Durkheim is still, generally, pigeonholed as a positivist, realist, etc.

However, Durkheim's constructionism is alive and well, even if rejected or disguised. Examine Zizek's 'transcendental materialism' rooted in some kind of Hegelian, Marxist, and Lacanian composite:

> We are dealing here with the interconnection between anamorphosis and sublimation: the series of objects in reality is structured around (or, rather, involves) a void; if this void becomes visible 'as such,' reality disintegrates. So, in order to maintain the consistent edifice of reality, one of the elements of reality has to be displaced on to and occupy the central Void – the Lacanian *objet petit a*. This object is the 'sublime object [of ideology],' the object 'elevated to the dignity of a Thing,' and simultaneously the anamorphic object (in order to perceive its sublime quality, we have to look at it 'awry,' askew – viewed directly, it looks like just another object in a series).... We can see...why anamorphosis is crucial to the functioning of ideology: anamorphosis designates an object whose very material reality is distorted in such a way that a gaze is inscribed into its 'objective' features (2002, pp. 149–50).

Zizek is right when, in many places, he correctly identifies the intersubjective nature of Marx's historical-materialist theory of the commodity as a sublime objectification. What few care to see is that Durkheimian social facts are sublime, phantom-like objectivities in exactly the same way and that we can mine *Capital* for descriptions of commodities that are virtually indistinguishable from Durkheim's characterizations of social facts in general: external, coercive, and sui generis.[10]

We arrive, then, at a weird point in the intellectual development of the West: a place where idealism and materialism, realism and nominalism, rationalism and empiricism, etc., are sublated into a new form of thought: Marx's "historical materialism" and Durkheim's "social realism." We can clearly see how sociological intersubjectivity (and the interplay between the imagination and material) is radically removed from the old paradigms by locating them within a 'social octahedron' at the heart of *Suicide*. Here we will limit ourselves to just one side of this 'octahedron' that is applicable to idealism.

B   *German Idealism within the Topography of Durkheim's* Suicide

We can locate Durkheim's critique of idealism in its key manifestations as they unfold through the conceptual matrix on display in Durkheim's *Suicide*. Idealism is, from this perspective, a one-sided or defective paradigm that has secret affinities with ascetic self-mortification, especially in the Kantian transcendental and critical forms. What we will find, ultimately, is that pre-Hegelian idealism, from the Durkheimian perspective, is a symptom of resignation, the unity of egoism and fatalism, and the impulse for self-destruction. Later we will see that Hegelianism (a condensation of Absolute Idealism) offers solutions to its predecessors but falls short of what is required for sociology. First, we will pinpoint key moments in this diagram:

Egoism (positively, egoism is identical with excessive individuation and, negatively, it is identical with insufficient attachment to others, i.e., lack of integration or solidarity): we must avoid the obvious inclination to one-sidedly equate idealism with Stoic intellectualism because we find that both Stoicism and Epicureanism blending into a synthetic alloy of indifference here (it takes

---

10   Where Zizek goes horribly wrong is in his persistent post-structuralism that finds nothing positive in what we would call collective representations (the Lacanian 'master signifier') or the *objet petit a* that prevents the totalization of the master signifier. The reason behind this defect in Zizek's thought lies in the logic of spectalization whereby, to use Marx, the "particular equivalent," though operational, is occluded (remains eclipsed) giving rise to the illusion that the moments of individuality are directly related to universality. Post-structuralism does not explain late capitalism so much as it is itself explained by late capitalism.

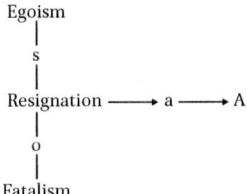

both dimensions to account for idealism). Recall, for Durkheim, genuine Epicureanism is not what we would today call hedonism, but, rather, a negative orientation to materialism and the *minimization* of material needs such that needs are easily satisfied and the proliferation of wants is extinguished. A family resemblance to cynicism (a dog's life) is noticeable.

Fatalism: over-regulation or de-termination as in completely limited (a theologically extreme or pure ideal-typical form is predestinationism).

Resignation represents the unity of egoism and fatalism, or a convergence point. Do not be fooled, resignation is not just a form of social inertia but, as Simmel indicates, a form of resistance and an attempt to solve deadlocks. The notion of rejection in theory, acceptance in practice (RITAIP) should be noted (Bhaskar, 2008, p. 143). Resignation, here, is not wholly passive but contains a tension that potentially drives some subjects toward the energetic 'side' of the social field.

S: Skeptical or Subjective Idealism (Descartes and Berkeley are prime examples). This subjective form is also associated with Jacobi's "Nihilism" where all we have are doubts about the existence of anything beyond our own subjective representations (see Beiser, 2002).

O: Dogmatic or Objective Idealism: this form, that denies the reality of empirical stuff, is more or less identical with a Transcendental Idealism minus a subject and both Leibniz as well as Spinoza are suitable examples. Objective idealism leads, inexorably, to fatalism (see Beiser, 2002).

Subjective and Objective Idealism are forms of what is called "Empirical Idealism" and they presuppose Transcendental Realism (Beiser, 2002). For Kant, idealism degenerates into egoism and a third way beyond the double impasse of skepticism and dogmatism was needed. However, Kant does not solve the misery of doubt and *denial* embedded in idealism because his transcendental idealism, and later his critical idealism, were woven with threads of ascetic self-punishment.[11]

---

11   It is entirely possible to view idealism as a vast enterprise involving of psychotic breaks, paranoid delusions, hysterical reactions, autism, and sadism.

a: Kantian Transcendental Idealism, located at "a" (asceticism) was the sublation of the twin dead ends of S and O (they terminate in egoism and fatalism respectively).[12] However, the contradiction of Transcendental Idealism meant the presupposition of an Empirical Realism and what Nietzsche would call the "sacrifice of the intellect": Kantianism, in this form, was a road to the renunciation of reason and, to put it bluntly, intellectual 'suicide.'[13] How so?

When we turn to Hegel's account of Kantianism in his *History of Philosophy* we should be profoundly struck by the Durkheimian timbre as we juxtapose the conceptual structure found in *Suicide* with Hegel's criticism:

> Kantian philosophy does not go on to grapple with the fact that it is not things that are contradictory, but self-consciousness itself. Experience teaches that the ego does not melt away by reason of these contradictions, but continues to exist; we need not therefore trouble ourselves about its contradictions, for it can bear them. Nevertheless Kant shows here too much tenderness for things: it would be a pity, he thinks, if they contradicted themselves. But that mind, which is far higher, should be a contradiction – that is not a pity at all. The contradiction is therefore by no means solved by Kant; and since mind takes it upon itself, and contradiction is self-destructive, mind is in itself all derangement and disorder....
>
>   HEGEL, [1840] 1995, p. 451

This is an expression of Hegel's anti-asceticism and his unwillingness for mind to resign itself to misery and permanent alienation. Oddly enough, this idealist demand for resignation toward contradiction and foisting asceticism onto the subject is alive and well in orthodox quantum theory:

> The orthodox view of quantum mechanics, known as the "Copenhagen interpretation" after the home city of Danish physicist Niels Bohr, one of its architects, holds that particles play out all possible realities simultaneously. Each particle is represented by a "probability wave" weighting these various possibilities, and the wave collapses to a definite state only when the particle is measured. The equations of quantum mechanics

---

12   See Durkheim (1973, p. 44) where the idealism of Kant and Rousseau are pinned to an abstract form of individualism.

13   Not every form of suicide is total, hence the concept of embryonic suicide or "partial" suicides in the work of Menninger or even "moral suicide" or symbolic devaluation (Durkheim 1897, p. 54). Note also the connection between the embryonic or partial with the idea of a contract representing a kind of partial slavery (1993, p. 85) – an idea Marx would certainly agree with ([1867] 1976, p. 416).

do not address how a particle's properties solidify at the moment of measurement, or how, at such moments, reality picks which form to take. But the calculations work. As Seth Lloyd, a quantum physicist at MIT, put it, "Quantum mechanics is just counterintuitive and we just have to suck it up."

SIMONS SCIENCE NEWS, 2014

We see, here, also the idea of reality as the "burnt offering" to spirit in his lectures on the philosophy of religion – all of nature and reality as spirit crystallized and objectified in material.[14] Nothing could be further from the Kantian imperative to inflict the mind with turmoil while sparing nature. There is a parallel expression in *Suicide* where Durkheim says that social facts include more than individuals and include materializations such as architecture, modes of communication, industrial machines, and so on ([1897] 1951, p. 313–14).[15]

A: Absolute Idealism and It's Absolute (Hölderlin, Schelling, Hegel).

The torment of actuality leads to the pure ego's turning inward to the inner domain of universality where the world is no longer "an object of dread" (Hegel, 1956, p. 439). The promise of idealism was contentment in "theoretical abstraction" (Hegel, 1956, p. 444) but Kantianism undermined the languorous repose of subjectivist resignation by drawing out its fatalistic implications, leaving the understanding at the level of pure identity, and delivering the subject over to autocracy (Hegel, 1956, pp. 455–59). Kant failed to move idealism beyond the impasse of egoism: "Great popularity has from one point of view been won for Kantian philosophy by the teaching that man finds in himself an absolutely firm, unwavering center-point; but with this last principle it has come to a standstill" (Hegel, 1956, p. 459). It was up to the Absolute Idealists to move spirit beyond the self-torturing aspects of transcendental idealism. However, the elevation of the Idea to the status of the Absolute, the autogenesis of the concept, brings with it the conflation of nature and spirit as well as a vitalism and the prospect of Geist overshooting its destination into bourgeois will-mania (anomie) and self-destruction:

---

14   In stark contrast to the fanatical destruction of actuality for the benefit of abstractions, a la, the Terror.

15   The criticism that Bhaskar levels at Hegel on this point is incomprehensible: "Unfortunately, locally and globally theory/practice inconsistency...or incoherence is always for Hegel resolved in thought, in theory. Transformative negation is confined to thought.... Once again, Hegel is untrue to his theory of truth. If reality is out of kilter with the notion of it, it is reality which should be adjusted, not its truth. The unity (or coherence) of theory and practice must be achieved in practice. Otherwise the result is not autonomy, but heteronomy and the reappearance of a Kant-like rift" (2008, p. 26–27).

> Ideation and movement are really two hostile forces, advancing in in-
> verse directions, and movement is life. To think, it is said, is to abstain
> from action; in the same degree, therefore, it is to abstain from living.
> This is why the absolute reign of idea cannot be achieved, and especially
> cannot continue; for this is death.
>
> DURKHEIM, [1897] 1951, p. 280

Speculative idealism, even though it rejected the ascetic self-torture of earlier
forms of idealism, was nonetheless besieged by this same reign of the Idea
over the individual pushed around by the cunning of Reason. Hegel's speculative idealism represented a more 'realistic' philosophy but realism leads away
from life. The current fad known as "Speculative Realism" provides a perfect
example of this intellectual suicide.[16]

Durkheim's position was neither the idealism of Kant, nor, as some claim,
neo-Kantianism. Kant rescued the mind from the crude empiricism of the
British Enlightenment by positing an active and projective mind whereby
sensible intuitions were synthesized with concepts by the imagination. Far
from a passive system of sense perception, the mind was responsible for con-
structing experience by means of the a priori categories of understanding that
are already present within the mind (Kant, 1929, pp. 42–43). Where, then, do
these a priori categories originate? Are we born with them? Durkheim's genius
is to locate the a priori categories within social immanence:

> There is an aspect of every religion that transcends the realm of specifi-
> cally religious ideas. Through it, the study of religious phenomena pro-
> vides a means of revisiting problems that until now have been debated
> only among philosophers....At the root of our judgments, there are certain
> fundamental notions that dominate our entire intellectual life. It is these

---

16   One of the great ironies, of course, is that it is the petit bourgeois male academic who
      is regularly tasked with figuring out problems like ontology which means that they are
      already at a disadvantage, abstracted as they often are, from the living pulse of social
      life, relegated to the entropic fringes of self-absorption, materialism, or pining for contact
      with some vital energies and running off into vitalism or superstition and mystical devo-
      tion to imagined realities. The current fad known as "speculative realism" that excites
      young white male academic types is a good example of a kind of mystical vitalism (the
      hunt for "substance X") and represents an intellectual 'suicide' whereby the ego attempts
      to imagine a world in-itself (without us). The starting point to unraveling speculative re-
      alism is the "dreamy melancholy" associated with Stoicism and its devotion to the con-
      structed Other that terminates in the realism of altruistic self-abandonment.

ideas that philosophers, beginning with Aristotle, have called the categories of understanding: notions of time, space, number, cause, substance,
personality. They correspond to the most universal properties of things.
They are like solid frames that confine thought. Thought does not seem to
be able to break out of them without destroying itself, since it seems we cannot think of objects that are not in time or space, that cannot be counted,
and so forth. The other ideas are contingent and changing, and we can conceive of a man, a society, or an epoch that lacks them; but these fundamental notions seem to us as almost inseparable from the normal functioning
of the intellect. They are, as it were, the skeleton of thought. Now, when one
analyzes primitive religious beliefs methodically, one naturally finds the
principal categories among them. They are born in and from religion; they
are a product of religious thought. This is a point that I will make again and
again in the course of this book. Even now that point has a certain interest
of its own, but here is what give it its true significance. The general conclusion of the chapters to follow is that religion is an eminently social thing.
Religious representations are collective representations that express collective realities; rites are ways of acting that are born only in the midst of
assembled groups and whose purpose is to evoke, maintain, or recreate
certain mental states of those groups. But if the categories are of religious
origin, then they must participate in what is common to all religion: They,
too, must be social things, products of collective thought ([1912] 1995,
pp. 8–9).

Moreover, Kant's transcendental subject was always a mystery and undeter-
mined: it had no physical existence and could not be individuated and his empirical realism meant that individuals were relegated to experiencing reality
as a play of appearances (Beiser, 2002, p. 209) which splits the world into the
knowable realm of phenomena and a realm that we have difficulty accessing
even indirectly, the noumenal. Durkheim's 'transcendental' substance-subject-
object was just society, it was real, it could be physically experienced, and it
did individuate itself in its members. His picture of society was rooted in the
fusion of two older paradigms: society was simultaneously 'transcendental' in
the sense that is metaphorically 'above' the individuals that constitute it (i.e.,
sublime) but also purely immanent, just as his ontology, if we can speak of an
ontology at all, represented a sublation of materialism and idealism.

Perhaps Cornford (a card-carrying Durkheimian) summarizes best the suicidal tendencies of egoistic reflection and idealism at the conclusion of his
From Religion to Philosophy, where we find nearly every element presented in

the foregoing analysis, which I was delighted to find, I might add, after I had constructed the foregoing analysis, as it seemed to me to neatly pull together the various threads and confirm, at least to myself, that I was indeed on target with respects to the self-destructive qualities of idealism:

> The ideal for the individual, then, is to escape from society.... He will withdraw like the Stoic, into autonomous self-sufficiency and Olympian contemplation.
>
> It is only a step further to the mystical trance of neo-platonism, in which thought is swallowed up in the beatific vision of the absolute One, above being and above knowledge, ineffable, unthinkable, no longer even a Reason, but 'beyond Reason' ... 'the escape of the alone to the alone.' In this [passive] ecstasy, Thought denies itself; and Philosophy, sinking to the close of her splendid curving flight, folds her wings and drops into the darkness whence she arose – the gloomy Erebus of theurgy and magic ([1912] 2004, p. 263).

It is true that, like the idealists, reality is a system of representations but, for Durkheim, the sign was not to be confused with the thing signified ([1897] 1951, p. 315). Under the representation was collective energy and a system of moral drivers determining social action by virtue of their practically infinite forms of interpenetration. I'm not sure if anyone has realized that, as far as Durkheim goes, every qualitatively unique form of action, thought, and feeling is a particular combination of two, three, or four primary spirits (Worrell 2014) – the 'four horsemen of the apocalypse' (egoism, anomie, altruism, and fatalism). Rather than conceptual autogenesis we get the twin pillars of Durkheimian sociology: surplus moral energy produced through association, its projection and signification, and its partial crystallization where the products of social interaction reign as authoritative forces over their creators.

Conclusion

Sometimes we look at a phenomenon and think idealism or rationalism holds the keys or, in contrast, that materialism is the right attitude to take. We look again and do not see what was previously seen and nominalism seems to hold insights, then, we look again and realism seems to suggest itself as obviously true. It is not quite so mysterious, then, why Durkheim (as just one example) has been accused of being so many different and contradictory things. It all depends upon how, when, and from where we look. Our mistake is in confusing any one traditional paradigm or viewpoint (one-sided and finite, i.e., 'abstract') for an 'absolute' view. All the various motivations that drive different paradigms emerge from the paradoxes and contradictions associated with judgments made from within a particular symbolic universe or from a particular sector of society[17] where comprehension is hobbled by reflected distortions that provide only an illusion of grasping the 'big picture' – distorted or fetish interpretations recur because they mistakenly attempt to universalize their particular point of view rather than attempting the very difficult task of encircling a phenomenon – this is not the 'view from nowhere' or everywhere "the absolute gaze of the omniscient, omnipresent spectator, who, thanks to his knowledge of the social mechanics, is able to be present"[18] but the admittedly impossible task of working our way up to a dialectical ubiquity – the true sense of 'objectivity.'[19] As my colleague Dan Krier would say, this is trying to "see like a society." This is not identical with imagining society as a unitary subject, i.e., Hegel's speculative rendering of history as the self-conscious movement of an organism (Marx,

---

17   One-sided and thereby flawed perspectives are still important as "valuable sources of information in that they convey some part of the underlying social reality, but each only expresses one aspect and not always very faithfully" (Durkheim, 1974, pp. 63–64). Orthodox Marxism, for example, has a terrible time talking about 'value' without consciously or unconsciously falling into the trap of transcendental realism.

18   Here, Bourdieu takes structuralism to task for reducing "agents to the status of automata or inert bodies moved by obscure mechanisms toward ends of which they are unaware" (1990, p. 98). Yet he also recognizes (1990, p. 108) that the definitions of social reality from the standpoint of collective misrecognition (the natural, everyday attitude of group members) runs the risk of sanctioning fetishism. I think it is entirely possible to aim for ubiquity (i.e., the systematic view) without necessarily reducing humans to the status of robots.

19   Dialectics shares with money the 'occult' capacity to be in more than once place at any given time. Relativists discarded 'objectivity' long ago as a monomaniacal delusion but in my estimation relativism is not mutually exclusive with objectivity and perspectival ubiquity so long as we distinguish between mere intelligence and reason. "Although biologically the brain capacity of the human race has remained the same for thousands of generations, it takes a long evolutionary process to arrive at objectivity, that is, to acquire the faculty to see the world, nature, other persons and oneself as they are and not distorted by desires and fears. The more man develops this objectivity, the more he is in touch with reality, the more he matures, the better can he create a human world in which he is at home. Reason is man's faculty for grasping the world by thought, in contradiction to intelligence, which is man's ability to manipulate the world with the help of thought. Reason is man's instrument for manipulating the world more successfully; the former is essentially human, the latter belongs also to the animal part of man" (Fromm, 1981, pp. 10–11).

[1859] 1970, p. 199) but taking a systematic view of the interdigitated nature of structures and processes in any society. For example, any sociology that fails to consider the 'spiritual' aspects of politics or economy will never know much about politics and economy. Likewise, what political sociology could possibly succeed without an economic and spiritual eye? Whether a lofty goal like this is entirely possible is beside the point; the 'absolute' (a.k.a., society) is a regulative ideal that keeps us moving toward a goal, self-consciously aware of our own co-ordinates in the world and using methods and theory to help surmount our limitations. Not that we are aiming at failure but even failed attempts of these kinds are essential and indispensable (see Pinkard, 2002, p. 256).[20] Does this mean, then, that we have approach everything from a bunch of different perspectives (Mannheim or Mills) as if they were all at least partially correct and that we can blend them to form a picture of the whole?[21] No, the point is not to 'see' with a multiplicity of differing 'instruments' even though that sounds like a common sense approach and it certainly does not mean getting a bunch of people together with differing views and reaching some kind of synthesized consensus. We cannot simply 'be' idealists one moment and materialists another moment and hope to cobble together some coherent picture of reality nor can we mate an idealist with a materialist and hope for dialectical materialist offspring.

We are interested in 'seeing' from two or more 'locations' at once (seemingly a magic trick from the standpoint of empiricism) via the effective development and deployment of conceptual models united to form an intellectual constellation.[22] The reason this kind of project seems so implausible today is because sociology has relinquished its theoretical legacy and, worse, we live in an age characterized by anti-intellectualism. Sociology has forsaken itself because you cannot write a grant proposal for this kind of science, you *cannot simply convert a concept into a variable*,[23] and you cannot simply pull a data set down off a shelf and crunch some numbers and hope for something true. Nor can you simply conduct a field study and hope to grasp anything like a sense of a social totality.

---

20   The 'absolute' view is a 'romantic' perspective, one filled with irony (negating at every turn), and more plausible from an egoistic, disinterested coordinate in the social system.

21   "In fact, the law that governs the divergent perspectives is the structure of the social process as a preordained whole" (Adorno, 1973, p. 37).

22   "The concept of totality is but the concept of society in the abstract form. It is the whole that includes all things, the supreme class that contains all other classes" (Durkheim [1912] 1995, p. 443).

23   This is worth amplifying: a sociology driven by "variables" (gutted and lifeless) is doomed to know nothing and will forever be mired in particularity but a sociology driven by the *concept* (here we are indebted to Hegel) and the project of a conceptual constellation as a 'living being' promises objective knowledge.

In other words, contemporary sociology has fallen back on naturalistic methods and statistical surveys for the sake of practicality and profitability. Then again, American society and sociology (excluding some Marxist varieties) have always had these orientations. Sociology, like the rest of bourgeois society, is roaming around aimlessly in a state somewhere between the living and the dead. The path back to the living is through *Suicide* – i.e., Durkheim's work on self-destruction (as well as his writings on archaic religious practices). A firm grasp of *Suicide* will enable us to read Marx's *Capital* in novel ways and give us new conceptual and theoretical insights ('Marxheimian Sociology') to better grasp the complexity of commodity-producing society and the anomic mania for surplus value.

References

Adorno, T.W. (1973). *Negative dialectics*, translated by E.B. Ashton. New York: Continuum.

Adorno, T.W. (2000). *Introduction to sociology*, translated by E. Jephcott. Stanford: Stanford University Press.

Beiser, F. (2002). *German idealism*. Cambridge: Harvard University Press.

Bhaskar, R. (2008). *Dialectic: The pulse of freedom*. London: Routledge.

Bourdieu, P. (1990). *The logic of practice*, translated by R. Nice. Stanford, California: Stanford University Press.

Cassirer, E. (1955). *The philosophy of symbolic forms, Vol. 1*. New Haven: Yale University Press.

Cornford, F.M. ([1912] 2004). *From religion to philosophy*. Mineola, NY: Dover.

Durkheim, E. ([1893] 1984). *The division of labor in society*, translated by W.D. Halls. New York: The Free Press.

Durkheim, E. ([1897] 1951). *Suicide*, translated by J.A. Spaulding and G. Simpson. New York: The Free Press.

Durkheim, E. ([1912] 1995). *The elementary forms of religious life*, translated by K.E. Fields. New York: Free Press.

Durkheim, E. (1973). Individualism and the intellectuals. In *Emile Durkheim: On morality and society*, edited by R.N. Bellah, pp. 43–57. Chicago and London: The University of Chicago Press.

Durkheim, E. (1974). *Sociology and philosophy*, translated by D. F Pocock. New York: The Free Press.

Durkheim, E. ([1895] 1982). *The rules of sociological method*, edited by S. Lukes and translated by W.D. Halls. New York: Free Press.

Durkheim, E. (1993). *Ethics and the sociology of morals*, translated by R.T. Hall. Buffalo: Prometheus.

Durkheim, E. (2004). *Durkheim's philosophy lectures: Notes from the Lycée de Sens Course, 1883–1884*, edited by N. Gross and R.A. Jones. Cambridge: Cambridge University Press.

Eco, U. (1984). *Semiotics and the philosophy of language.* Bloomington: Indiana University Press.

Fromm, E. (1981). *On disobedience and other essays.* New York: The Seabury Press.

Hegel, G.W.F. ([1840] 1995). *Lectures on the history of philosophy*, Vol. 3, translated by E.S. Haldane and F.H. Simson. Lincoln: University of Nebraska Press.

Hegel, G.W.F. ([1821] 1991). *Elements of the philosophy of right*, translated by H.B. Nisbet. Cambridge: Cambridge University Press.

Hegel, G.W.F. (1956). *The philosophy of history.* Mineola, NY: Dover.

Jay, M. (1984). *Marxism and totality.* Berkeley: University of California Press.

Kant, I. 1929. Critique of pure reason, translated by Norman Kemp Smith. New York: St. Martin's.

Marx, K. ([1859] 1970). *A contribution to the critique of political economy*, translated by S.W. Ryazanskaya. New York: International Publishers.

Marx, K. ([1867] 1976). *Capital: A critique of political economy, Vol. 1*, translated by B. Fowkes. New York: Penguin.

Nye, D.A. & C.E. Ashworth. (1971). Emile Durkheim: Was he a nominalist or a realist? *The British Journal of Sociology*, 22(2), 133–148.

Pinkard, T. (2002). *German philosophy, 1760–1860: The legacy of idealism.* Cambridge: Cambridge University Press.

Pope, W. (1976). *Durkheim's Suicide: A classic analyzed.* Chicago and London: The University of Chicago Press.

Sartre, J.P. (2004). *Critique of dialectical reason, Vol. 1: Theory of practical ensembles, new edition*, translated by A. Sheridan-Smith. London: Verso.

Simmel, G. (1971). *On individuality and social forms*, edited by D.N. Levine. Chicago: The University of Chicago Press.

Simons Science News. (2014). "Have We Been Interpreting Quantum Mechanics Wrong This Whole Time?" *Wired*, accessed at http://www.wired.com/2014/06/the-new-quantum-reality.

Strenski, I. (2006). *The new Durkheim.* New Brunswick: Rutgers University Press.

Worrell, M.P. (2014). "The Commodity as the Ultimate Monstrosity." Fast Capitalism 11.1: (https://www.uta.edu/huma/agger/fastcapitalism/11_1/worrell11_1.html). Accessed 24 September, 2015.

Worrell, M.P. (2010). "Dialectical Durkheim: From absolute idealism to the social fact." Symposium for New Directions in Critical Social Theory, Iowa State University, December 6–8.

CHAPTER 7

Social Character in Western Pre-Modernity: Lacanian Psychosis in Wladyslaw Reymont's *The Peasants*

Daniel Krier and Tony Allen Feldmann

Introduction: Social Character and Social Theory

Classical social theory sought to understand the social and psychological traumas unleashed by capital upon traditional Europe and its colonial territories. Concepts analogous to social character appear throughout these foundational texts. To Durkheim ([1893]1997), increasing social density associated with capitalist modernization shattered moral vacuums separating tribes, clans, feudal manors and peasant villages, dissolving collective consciousness and mechanical solidarity. Once traditional systems of ritually-supported beliefs and punitive social control were disrupted, traditional social character open to the moral energies of altruism and fatalism were displaced by more modern social character congruent with anomic and egoistic moral forces (Durkheim 1951). To Marx (1887), capital supplanted feudal society's direct production of real utilities with production of surplus value through alienated wage-labor production of commodities for market exchange. Capitalism generated subjectivities shaped by alienation and commodity fetishism. Weber (1978, 1981) and Simmel (2004) stressed the transformative effect of capital and money upon economic and social life, displacing magical, enchanted cultural forms with disenchanted subjects of rational calculation. Goffman (1959) and Elias (2000) stressed modernity's impact upon manners and morals. Traditional social life had been conducted in perpetual familiarity, with high levels of emotional and expressive volatility that made controlled self-presentations and role distance impossible. Modernity was marked by a civilizing process that increased subject's disciplined control of conduct and self-presentation, as discrepant emotions and behaviors were hidden behind a "shame frontier" of access-controlled, private backstage regions. In the effort to interpret capitalism's structural impact, classical social theory implicitly invoked social character.

Social character (or character structure) was a focal concept in critical social theory beginning in the 1930s, when Wilhelm Reich refashioned and extended his clinical approach to the analysis of individual character (Reich 1949) to the analysis of mass psychology and the rise of fascism (Reich 1946).

Reich began from the starting point of Freud's psychosexual theory of character, traced back at least to Freud's (1908) essay, "Character and Anal Eroticism," and developed analytic protocol for treating patients with *character armor*: psychic defenses against anxiety that become habitual, rigidified and embodied, preventing the formation of a therapeutic transference relationship with an analyst. Reich thought it essential to analyze/dissolve character armoring before psychoanalysis proper could begin, leading him to develop differential approaches to patients whose characters were labeled with sometimes bizarre names such as passive-feminine, aristocratic, hysterical, compulsive, masochistic and phallic-narcissistic. Reich's clinical experience led him to theorize that character armor (the structure of individual personality) was formed during the pre-genital stages of early childhood. This meant that families played a dominant role in the formation of character, hence critical theory's analytic focus upon family structure as a mediator between self and society.

When Reich turned to the analysis of mass character, he argued that masses attracted to fascism were drawn from social strata with authoritarian families in which child-rearing systematically went awry in the "first four or five years" of childhood "interlacing...the socio-economic with the sexual structure" in such a way as to build fascist characters. Reich wrote that "the authoritarian state develops its enormous interest in the authoritarian family: *the family is the factory of its structure and ideology*" (Reich 1946, p. 24). Authoritarian character structure resulted from sexual suppression of "natural" "genital sexuality" that "makes the child apprehensive, shy, obedient, afraid of authority, 'good' and 'adjusted' in the authoritarian sense... [thereby] producing an individual who is adjusted to the authoritarian order and who will submit to it in spite of all misery and degradation" (Reich 1946, p. 25). The family functioned as an "authoritarian miniature state" that broke the child like a horse-trainer, fitting a bit of submission whose reigns were picked up by the "general authoritarian" state throughout life (Reich 1946, p. 25).

Reich's Freudian analysis of social character was reconstructed and extended by Erich Fromm in *Escape from Freedom* ([1941]1994), *Man for Himself: An Inquiry into the Psychology of Ethics* (1990) and *Anatomy of Human Destructiveness* (1992). Fromm, agreeing with Reich, designates the family as the "psychological agent of society" ([1941] 1994, appendix) that begins the process of integrating the child into the social via the molding of character. Yet, Fromm focused more than Reich upon understanding how individuals reconcile themselves with the world, and argued that groups and classes develop a particular set of character traits, or social character, in response to the shared "economic, social, and cultural conditions" (1996, p. 17) they faced. To Fromm, the transition to capitalist modernity not only generated conditions for unprecedented freedom, democracy and human potential but also simultaneously created anti-democratic social conditions and life-thwarting character structures, including authoritarianism (moral sadomasochism), destructiveness and automaton conformity. Fromm traced the inner relationships between the social situation of the lower middle classes in Weimar Germany and authoritarian character ("hoarding, hating, sadistic"). Fromm's "analytic social psychology" was central to critical theory's urtext, the *Authoritarian Personality* (Adorno et al.,1950), the definitive study of authoritarian families as the factory of authoritarian personalities.

Critical theories of modern, capitalist social character developed alongside of historical and comparative analyses. Many comparative studies focused upon non-Western tribal peoples (Malinowski, 1927, 1929; Erikson, 1950) while others studied the premodern villages of Western peasantry (Parsons, 1969; Wolf, 1952, Foster, 1967). Fromm and Maccoby's (1970) *Social Character in a Mexican Village* is a particularly rich, careful, empirically-rich parsing of variant social character in a village of 800 residents in central Mexico.

Fromm and Maccoby's study confirmed the general portrait of peasant character traits found throughout peasant literature: "They are selfish, suspicious of each other's motives, pessimistic...fatalistic...submissive... [with an] overwhelming feeling of powerlessness" (1970, p. 37). Peasants "spread gossip about each other... [that is] damaging and not always true...[displaying] extreme distrust and fear of others...based on the experience of being cheated and betrayed" (1970, p. 38). Fromm and Maccoby identified three distinctive character structures in the village: (1) *oral receptive* characters who believed that good and goods were found outside the self who passively, non-productively awaited their reception from others, (2) *oral exploitative* characters who were also non-productive, but actively manipulated others to take good things from them, and (3) *anal hoarding* characters, also non-productive because their focus was upon miserly "hoarding and saving" the good and goods they possessed while stingily minimizing outflow (1970, pp. 69–71). The oral receptive type was the most frequently encountered in Fromm and Maccoby's village, especially among the peasants at the bottom of the village structure, and was marked by a strong, lifelong and multisided mother-fixation (1970, p. 111). These themes will be analyzed in greater detail below.

Though respectfully reviewed (see Foster, 1971), Fromm and Maccoby's empirically rich study received less attention than it deserved and was not, to our knowledge, replicated elsewhere. In the 1996 introduction to the text, Maccoby suggested that the book's acceptance was hampered by declining interest in psychoanalytic studies of character structure, which had been supplanted by survey analysis within the field of political psychology. Meisenhelder (2006) argued that Fromm and other Frankfurt School conceptions of social character were biologically reductionist and irredeemably tainted by Freud, and had been replaced by Bourdieu's *habitus* which he preferred because it was devoid of biology and the notion of the unconscious. Prominent critical theorists, like Habermas, also abandoned the analysis of character to focus upon social processes like communicative action. Even Adorno and Horkheimer left character analysis behind in their later cultural theory.

Geertz (1961) and Blum (1982) note that anthropologists turned away from the study of peasants at the very time when they were vanishing, preferring the study of holistic tribal societies, pristine in their self-referential completeness, rather than peasants: "part societies with part cultures" (Geertz, 1961, p. 23). Geertz's essay noted a mid to late 20th century resurgence of scholarly interest in peasants, but mostly in the global South. By the time peasants returned as objects of anthropological study, the opportunity to study them in the hearth societies of Western Modernity had already passed.

We pick up this lost thread of critical theory by reconsidering social character in the pre-capitalist peasant world of Europe, a world that had all but vanished during the 20th century, but was fortunately and sensitively captured in realist novels (Blum, 1961, 1978, 1986). We analyze what we view as the best of these novels (Reymont's *Peasants*) to reconstruct pre modern social character using classic critical theory and the structural psychoanalysis of Jacques Lacan.

Peasants in Classical Social Theory

To adequately analyze transitions to modernity, classical social theory paid close attention to peasants and their experiences. Before modernity, peasants constituted between 70 and 90 percent of the population of pre-modern Europe (Blum, 1978 p. 3). In the servile lands of Europe, peasant serfs possessed few civil rights or political representation until emancipated in the period between 1770 and 1870 (Blum, 1978, p. 356). Polish peasants, the subject of Reymont's novel, were freed from serfdom in stages throughout this period: emancipation occurred in the Polish Duchy of Warsaw in 1804, in the Prussian partition in 1807, the Austrian occupied territory in 1848 and in Russian territory in 1861. Emancipation was completed by 1864 so that the rural proletariat depicted in Reymont's novel were peasant but not serf (Blum, 1978, pp. 398–400). In the century before emancipation, the economic condition of Polish peasants under serfdom had declined (1961, p. 468), but in the partition occupied by Russia, Polish seigniorial customs continued so that fees and services due to masters were proportional to the size of the serf's holdings (Blum, 1961, p. 461). Peasants without the means to purchase land were also exempt from most state dues. Thus, although the services required of Russian-Polish serfs were extensive (up to 158 days of labor, half with a team of horses), on balance, Polish serfdom had been less onerous than elsewhere in Europe.

Marx viewed the European smallholding peasantry as "an enormous mass" who toiled in isolation on small plots without developing a division of labor, scientific agriculture, diversification or cooperative mutuality. Peasants produced use-values for their own consumption; hence their labor was "an interchange with nature [not] ...intercourse with society." Because they lacked a civil society or political organization, geographically-isolated smallholding peasants were unable to act in their class interest. To Marx, peasant households aggregated into villages but not into politically viable groups. Peasant society was formed by "the simple addition of homologous magnitudes, much as potatoes in a sack form a sack of potatoes." Unable to represent their interests, they sought political masters with unlimited authority to protect them from outside powers and to "send them rain and sunshine from above." Peasants were political reactionaries rather than revolutionaries who desired submission to authoritarian rule by an "executive power which subordinates society to itself." (Marx, 1852, n.p.).[1]

Gramsci (1919), like Marx and Durkheim, viewed peasants as political reactionaries who compared unfavorably with revolutionary urban workers. Gramsci viewed peasants in "capitalistically-backward" countries as survivals of "genuinely feudal economic forms and a corresponding psychology." Peasants were servile, confused, defensive, impatient, wildly violent, undisciplined and relatively useless in revolutionary action. Peasants were "incapable of posing a general aim and of pursuing it with perseverance and systematic struggle" (1919, n.p.). Foster echoes Gramsci's view, portraying peasants as dependent, powerless and politically authoritarian: "Peasants obey, they do not command. They wait to be told, they do not make major decisions themselves.... [they are] passive acceptors, for they lack the power and knowledge to be otherwise" (Foster, 1967, p. 8).

Durkheim also viewed the peasantry as reactionaries, but his analysis of peasant life was richer and formed a basic empirical referent of his sociology. To Durkheim, peasant villages were social segments that aggregated to cover large territories without organizing into economically specialized locales.

---

1   Marx and other Marxists writings on peasants culminated in an intensive interdisciplinary debate over the "peasant mode of production" (see Chayanov & Thorner, 1966). To Chayanov, the central feature of peasant production was the absence of wage-labor: subsistence production and (marginal) market production was performed by the immediate family members of the smallholding peasant rather than by hired hands. With qualifications, the villagers in Lipka approximate the peasant producers analyzed by Chayanov.

Durkheim had the peasantry in mind when developing the entire complex of ideas in the *Division of Labor in Society* ([1893]1997) related to mechanical solidarity: peasants live in moral isolation, overruled by collective conscious-ness, punitive morality and conformity to a collective type. Their religious life closely resembles the totemic tribes in Durkheim's *Elementary Forms of the Religious Life* ([1915]1965): their rituals mandated isomorphic alignment and mimetic actions, generating collective effervescence projected upon totems. In Durkheim's analysis of tribal and village life, social control was internalized in a collective consciousness that functioned differently than Freud's (modern) ego-ideal or superego. Outward conformity to group practices mattered much more than inward-responsiveness to the dictates of individual conscience: shame, not guilt, predominated. The peasant was altruistic – relatively selfless, with weak ego boundaries open to the flow of moral energies ([1897]1951).

Weber viewed peasants as Europe's socially less-favored strata that re-mained "engulfed in the massive and archaic growth of magic" (1946, p. 277). The magical orientation of peasants was rooted in their dependence upon nature and other "elemental forces" over which they sought some form of control. This need for control led peasants to "readily believe in a compelling sorcery directed against spirits who rule over or through natural forces" and in the direct purchase of spiritual favors (with sacrifice). Peasants were mysti-cal, favoring "orgiastic and ecstatic states of 'possession,' produced by means of toxics or by the dance" over intellectual mysticism of higher strata (1946, p. 283). Peasants were earthy in matters of the flesh, possessing "primal, natu-ralist, and unsublimated sexuality" (1946, p. 349). Weber emphasized that the peasantry led a "conservative way of life" (1946, p. 370) with cyclical, unchang-ing timeways: "The peasant, like Abraham, could die 'satiated with life' ...But the 'cultivated' [modern] man...cannot do this. He can become 'weary of life' but he cannot become 'satiated with life' in the sense of completing a cycle" (Weber 1946: 356). Weber viewed the peasant's hard economic "struggle for ex-istence" as a force that "selects for frugality" (1946, p. 368, compare to the "anal hoarding" peasant characteristics noted by Fromm and Foster).

Premodern Western Subjectivity and the Realist Novel:
Reymont's The Peasants

Viewing the past through the window of fiction seems like a dodgy procedure, yet one that is widely deployed and well-defended in cultural theory (Auer-bach, [1942]2003; Jameson, 1981; Jameson, 2013). Aydelotte (1948) compared contemporary literary representations of England to the economic writings of Marx and Mill, and found great discrepancies that he felt cast doubt upon fiction as a valid data source. Aydelotte finds novels to be suspect: "spotty, impressionistic and inaccurate." He argues: "the attempt to tell the social history of a period by quotations from its novels is a kind of dilettantism which the historian would do well to avoid" (Aydelotte, 1948, p. 43). We respectfully disagree. The novels that Aydelotte criticized were not realist novels of the late 19th and early 20th century, but romanticized fiction written as entertainment. We agree with Lukács, who viewed realist novels as an intellectual product akin to social theory. To Lukács, realism is more than naturalism: the "central aesthetic problem of realism is the adequate presentation of the complete human personality... [the] realistic creation of types" by which he means "a peculiar synthesis which organically binds together the general and the particular both in characters and situations" (1964, p. 6).

Like Weber, Lukács emphasizes that what "makes a type a type is not its average quality" but the representation of essential elements depicted "on their highest level of development, in the ultimate unfolding of the possibilities latent in them, in extreme presentation of their extremes, rendering concrete the peaks and limits of men and epochs." Realism emphasizes "three-dimensionality and all-roundedness" so that events and character are endowed with reality (1964, p. 6). To Lukács, realist novels allow theoretical interpretations of social character, including emerging modern bourgeois character (Lukács, 1978; Ridley, 1994).

The passing of peasant modes of production from Western modernity (Chayanov & Thorner, 1966) and the paucity of written peasant records means that peasant realist novels (*Bauernromanen*) may be the best access currently available to analysts of the social character of the European peasantry (Blum, 1982). Peasant realist authors produced works of exceptional quality, indeed, five such authors received a Nobel Prize for literature in the early 20th century: Pontoppidan 1917, Hamsun 1920, Reymont 1924, Deledda 1926 and Bunin 1933. Of these only Reymont and Hamsun were born and raised in peasant villages, and only Reymont lived in Poland, one of the last remaining servile lands of Europe.

The rich detailed texture of Reymont's peasant novels comes from his depiction of contemporaneous characters and experiences rather than romanticized events of the past (Blum, 1982, p. 124). The richness is further enhanced by his inclusion of details about regions of peasant experience repressed from official records: sex, death and the "jolly coarseness of life" (1982, p. 125). Reymont conducted ethnographic research when writing his books: his first book described a pilgrimage he undertook to the shrine to Our Lady of Chestohova, his industrial novel *Promised Land* (Reymont, 1928b) was based upon extensive site visits in Łódź, and he returned to live among peasants when writing his books about them (Blum, 1982, p. 126). Reymont's novels lack heroes: it is difficult for modern readers to fully identify with his characters or to idealize them, a mark of their accurate representation (1982, p. 126). To Blum (1982, p. 127), a crucial indicator of the reliability and validity of Reymont's novels as a narrative of premodern European subjectivity is the similarity they bears to other peasant realist novels (Zieliński & Dyboski, 1923; see also Lukács, 1964, p. 27) and to studies of peasant social character available to us. Even though the characters in Reymont's novel are not operating within a pure peasant mode of production (post-feudalism but prior to generalized commodity exchange), their action patterns and frames of reference reflect these studies of peasant social character more than the bourgeois subjectivity of modern capitalism.[2]

We argue that Wladyslaw Reymont's novels provide exceptional access to peasant social character. Reymont's The Peasants was written throughout the first decade of the 20th century and published in four volumes between 1904 and 1909 (Autumn, Winter, Spring, Summer): it is the longest (over 1400 pages) and most comprehensive of the peasant realist novels. Like Rabelais, whose writings captured the disappearing language and social forms of medieval carnival as they disappeared, Reymont's upbringing in a peasant village placed him inside a peasant world that he wrote about at the moment of its vanishing. Finally, Reymont's The Peasants is virtually unknown and unread in the English-speaking world, with scant secondary literature to mar the freshness of discovery upon reading it for the first time.

Wladyslaw Reymont was born 1867 in Russian-ruled Poland to a church organist. In his autobiographical essay written for the Nobel Prize ceremony (Reymont, 1924), an unpaginated document from which the following quotations are obtained, Reymont revealed that his uncle was the village priest, a "well educated and ascetic man," "the most ardent Catholicism ruled" the household and though not peasants, the family "led a hard life almost like the peasants." Reymont's childhood was spent in intimate contact with peasants providing

---

2 Reymont's Peasants is a *novel*, and as such, a mediated form of representation structured by conventions and genre markers of long development. Many cultural theorists note that, historically, the novel was less about valid representation of external reality than inner reflection upon bourgeois subjectivity. Realist novelists departed markedly from the typical "bourgeois novel" to emphasize mimetic representation, not just imitative copies of experience (naturalism), but thoughtful and apt typification of bounded social worlds. Some realists continued the bourgeois novel tradition to reflect aspects of bourgeois subjectivity, but peasant realists like Reymont hewed close to their first-hand intimate experience of (vanishing) agrarian village life. Following Blum (1982), we believe that similarities of the various peasant novels to each other, as well as congruence with the anthropological and sociological literature on peasants, leads us to accept them as a reasonably valid historical source.

him with a detailed view of their life patterns and social character. Reymont's family was politically active, having participated in the 1863 uprising. Reymont was sickly as a child. Reymont's education was informal but appears to have been of high quality under his uncle's tutelage. He had free access to a parish library where he read voraciously and took work as shepherd to allow extensive reading time. Reymont studied music to become a church organist like his father and also worked as a parish clerk. During this time, Reymont felt "vague enchantments, dull restlessness, and uncertain desires" and experienced hallucinations. He moved to Warsaw, became a socialist, was arrested, returned home, only to run away with a troupe of actors. Reymont later worked for the railway where he again lived in peasant village. He met a professor-spiritualist who encouraged additional study and writing. Reymont worked at a variety of odd jobs, including railway agent that paid modestly but allowed free time to write. For a time he wrote in Warsaw under conditions of extreme poverty, using the nearby heated cathedral as his study.

Reymont's literary career began when he published a memoir of a pilgrimage he made to Chestohova. Afterwards, he lived in Łódź, the "Polish Manchester," "to study conditions in heavy industry," culminating in the *Promised Land* (1928b), a two volume Buddenbrooks-like account of capitalist development and bourgeois ways. He was seriously injured in a railway accident in Poland, and received a settlement in 1902 that allowed him to write *The Peasants*. Other works include *The Vampire* (1911), set in London, that chronicles a dark, occult economy. In the critical essay for Reymont's Nobel Prize Presentation, Per Hallström (1924) praised Reymont as a realist who avoided "conventionalized, distorted, and coarse characterization of the class of society in which he had grown up and which he loved with all the warmth that had been cherished by his childhood memories." His writing was rooted in "abundant experience" of peasant life "from within, and with full understanding." Reymont's peasantry was depicted "in its reality, without any distortion through theories." By the time Reymont won the Nobel Prize, he was dying. English translations of his works "hardly outlived him." The u.s. edition of the Peasants (1924–5) has never been reprinted nor has the 1927 translation of the Promised Land (Krzyzanowski, 2011, p. 1097).

Reymont's *The Peasants* was translated into English in 1924. It ran through at least eight printings and was reissued in one volume in 1928, but went out of print and is now almost unread in English and nearly unavailable. As of this writing, there are no copies of *Promised Land* available for sale on Amazon (new or used) and interlibrary loan was necessary to obtain a copy. Johnston (2013) and Krzyzanowski (2011) both fault the English translator, noting that Reymont's works have "fared much better in translations other than English."

(2011, p. 1097). Reymont is well-known in Poland (the Łódź airport is named in honor of him), "his contribution to the genre of the novel still remains to be discovered in the English-speaking world...few Nobel Prize winners in litera-ture are so little known" (2011, p. 1097).[3]

Reymont's *The Peasants* is set in an unnamed year in the very late 19th century: a lack of specificity consistent with traditional cyclical time-ways, in which each year is much like another, a rotary unfolding of sacred and pro-fane ritual practices. The action is set in Lipka, an actual village located near Łódź in the geographic center of contemporary Poland. Lipka's population of approximately 150–200 people was augmented by residents of nearby ham-lets (small villages without a church), each with slightly distinctive folkways (unique dress and hamlet character). Characters from these hamlets swell the volume of people moving through scenes of the novel.

Poland maintained serfdom until very late by European standards (1864), and while Reymont's peasants are no longer serfs, they remain alive to pre-modern social distinctions and class hierarchies. At the top is the squirearchy, the noble remnant of Poland's military, religious and political leadership. This stratum was mostly absent from Reymont's diegesis, represented by the sole figure of "the Squire." Reymont depicts a number of officials in the village, including the parish priest, religious shepherd to the village and peasants in surrounding hamlets. Other officials include the church sexton, the *Voyt* and *Soltys* (village headmen and intermediaries with regional officials). Two "new men" of the bourgeois age, capitalists bent on acquisition and non-traditional profit-making through exploitation of wage labor in industry, appear in the figures of the Smith and the Miller. The peasants proper are divided into land-owning peasants (including the largest landowner, Boryna, whose fam-ily is at the center of the novel), small, near destitute land-owning peasants called *Komorniki* (Reymont, 1928a, *Winter,* p. 132) and *Dziads*, non-land owning peasants who either work for other peasants or wander as beggars. The novel depicts other social categories, including the local Jewish inn-keeper (referred to as "the Jew" throughout the novel), German Lutheran colonists, Russian

---

3   Perhaps more than most producers of award-winning literature, Reymont's narrative is
    rooted in his own memories and experiences of peasant life. All the same, these memories
    were undoubtedly transformed in the process of writing for publication and sale to a bour-
    geois novel-reading public. The political economy of publishing likely shaped the narrative
    structure, imagery and stylistic tone of Reymont's narrative. Rather than a pure mimesis of
    peasant life or an autoethnography of Reymont's childhood experiences, the novel should be
    read as a document shaped, in part, by strategic alignment with the values and projections
    of his book-buying public. This argument follows Cassano (2014), who makes a similar point
    regarding the production of New Deal cinema for a theater-going public.

soldiers and gypsies. As discussed below, these distinctions are often a source of rivalry, envy and aggression rather than simple obedience and respect.

The novel revolves around the Boryna family, headed by the hard-working widower Matthias, a widely respected former headman of the village and a large landowner with 36 acres. The Boryna family is prosperous by village standards. A central plot of the novel is the ongoing Oedipal triangle between the aging Matthias Boryna, his nineteen year old, sexually promiscuous, *femme fatale* bride, Yagna and his eldest, already-married but lascivious son, Antek. Antek and his wife, Hanka, have two children and are chafing under their economic dependence upon Matthias. Antek fights with Matthias over his decision to remarry Yagna, as much because she receives six acres of valuable land as a bride-price than because she is his mistress. Yagna is often controlled by her mother, Dominikova, an aging, widowed, shrewish woman who emasculates and dominates her two sons. Another gossipy, faultfinding, trouble-stirring "hag" in the village is Yagustynka, a character Reymont uses to embody negative, suspicious village social life. The embodiment of peasant virtue is a middle-aged, devout, valued servant in the Boryna household named Kuba. Lipka was located in Russian (Christian Orthodox) territory but was also being actively colonized by German Prussians (mostly Christian Lutheran, see Thomas and Znaniecki, 1927; Thomas, 1914). The embodiment of Polish nationalism, cultural resistance to Russian rule and economic resistance to German colonization is Roch, a learned, travelling mystic who teaches children and serves as a carrier of native folklore and folkways.

The twisted love triangle between Matthias Boryna, his wife Yagna and son Antek forms a major plot line of the novel, triggering envious demonization of Yagna, mostly inflamed by older married women, that grows wave-like with public exposure of sexual scandals with her son-in-law, the village headman and a popular young novitiate to the priesthood. The plot is further shaped by underground Polish resistance to Russian domination, mob action in response to enclosure of the village commons (primitive accumulation in which the Squire sells the trees for lumber), and post-serfdom colonization of the Squire's lands by German Lutherans. In the wake of these riots, Russian courts and state police control the fate of villagers. While these plot lines provide narrative tension and are of historical interest, the primary value of the novel for our purpose lies in its dense, descriptive narration of peasant social character and its detailed portrayal of the rotary motion of the ritual calendar intersecting with the agrarian cycles of work.

The realist novels analyzed by Blum (1982), including those of Reymont, consistently reveal peasants as stubborn, insensitive "great lumbering beasts" of pure materiality, who "dig their way through life with back breaking toil," producing use values without calculation or anticipation of exchange. The materiality of peasants is reflected in this description from Reymont:

> They sat there in a row, hoary-headed clean shaven old men, nearly of an age, hale as yet, though bowed down by years and labour; ponderous as moss-grown boulders in the fields, rugged, tough-sinewed, ungainly, but hard-headed and shrewd...they approached the matter in hand circuitously as sagacious sheep-dogs do a flock they aim at driving through a gate.
>
> REYMONT, 1928a, *Winter*, p. 107

Peasant life was "harsh, joyless, filled with unending labor, torn by quarrels, envy and misdeeds." Peasants were often "lewd, lazy...rough, dishonest, filthy" – sometimes bathing in and drinking water laced with cow urine (Blum, 1982, pp. 129–130). Suspicion, distrust and envy were central leitmotifs of peasant character: life was an "unrelenting struggle" with neighbors and outsiders who were equally hostile, envious and threatening. While peasants remained strongly connected to mothers throughout life, fathers appeared as strange, perverse patriarchs, often feared but rarely respected. Peasants lacked body shame and backstage privacy so that it was impossible for peasants to avoid the smells, sounds, fluids and views of other people's bodies. Peasants lacked strong guilt or guiding ethics. The ascetic, intellectualized religious ethos of Weber's modern West was absent from peasants: "cows had more religion than villagers" (Blum 1982, p. 134). Spiritual life was dominated by magic, superstition, folk demonology, hallucination, curses and incantations (Blum, 1982, p. 134). Priests were greedy and gossipy with little effective authority over community doings. Peasants were not egalitarian, but acutely aware of fine-grained differences in status, ranking, prestige and honor, and enforced deference and demeanor rituals with great severity. Such a portrait of peasant life diverges sharply from romanticized images of rural *gemeinschaft*.

Character Structure in Lacanian Psychoanalysis: Neurotics, Psychotics and the Paternal Function

Critical theories of social character developed in the 1930s to interpret support for and resistance to fascism, hence their focus upon the authoritarian personality and other anti-democratic manifestations of character (destructiveness, automaton conformity, marketing personality). We assert that many of the traits marking anti-democratic character are compatible with the symptomatic behaviors, emotions and thought processes that Jacque Lacan associated with *psychosis*. We develop a model of peasant character, informed by Lacan's writings on psychotic structure. This model is tested and refined through the interpretation of the peasants depicted in the realist novels of Reymont (and others). We find that Lacan's psychotic structure provides a powerful, provocative framework to analyze pre-modern Western subjectivity.[4]

In the same way that modernization – the rupture in traditional society caused by industrial capitalism – formed the central problematic of classical social theory, psychosis – the rupture separating psychotics from neurotics – formed the central problematic of classical psychoanalysis. Patients with psychotic structures did not respond to analytic techniques designed to treat neurotics. Psychotics undergoing analysis generally became worse, often suffering "psychotic breaks" with loss of reality and active production of delusions (Freud, 1924; Lacan, [1996] 2006, p. 251). Lacan, like Wilhelm Reich, specialized in treating these difficult cases.

Psychic Structure and the Paternal Function

To Lacan, psychotics are differentiated from neurotics by an essential lack: the *lack of the paternal function* (Lacan, [1996]2006, p. 476; 1993, p. 204; Fink, 1995, pp. 74–76; 1997, pp. 79–81; 2007, pp. 262–266). The paternal function is the fundamental precondition for the development of modern neurotic structure *homo normalis* in Reich's (1933, p. 399) terms. The paternal function is the agency of symbolic castration that installs the subject within the symbolic order of language and law. Lacan ([1996]2006, p. 264) follows Freud's original account of the paternal function as it appeared in the "myth of the murder of the primal father" in *Totem and Taboo* ([1914]1950, pp. 141–149). In Freud's reconstruction, prehistory was dominated by primitive hordes held together by primal males, each a "violent and jealous father who keeps all the females for himself and drives away his sons as they grow up" ([1914]1950, p. 141). These physically imposing men used violence to enforce a monopoly of enjoyment, until "one day the brothers who had been driven out came together, killed and devoured their father and so made an end of the patriarchal

---

4   This chapter constructs and disciplines a sociological ideal-type model of peasant subjectivity while recognizing that actually-existing peasant communities will display greater complexity and admixtures not captured in the model. Lacan's psychotic character is presented here as an ideal type in the Weberian sense, a logically-integrated, multi-dimensional hermeneutic that provides analysts with fixed points of comparisons to guide interpretative research (for a description of Weberian methodology in the construction of ideal types, see Krier, 2005, pp. 20–24). Lacan's model does not capture without remainder the overdetermined reality of peasant existence. Instead, the relatively pure type of psychotic character developed here exaggerates central tendencies, core features and logical connections.

horde" ([1914]1950, p. 141). However, the only way to prevent one of the brothers from dominating the others by assuming the primal father's place was for the guilty sons to jointly (1) elevate the dead father into a totemic god, the "Name-of-the-Father," honored as the giver of law and spiritual power that enforces the law, and (2) renounce the enjoyment of the dead father's women (symbolic castration). Though the real father's biological substance was gone, the "Name-of-the-Father," physically-absent but spiritually-present, enforced the symbolic order ([1914]1950, p. 143).

As a result, symbolic mandates were socialized and internalized: the sons internalized the dead father, prohibiting themselves from violating the law rather than be subject to a "real" father who would externally enforce compliance. The internalized power of the paternal function is especially strong in monotheistic religions that prohibit sacrifice and forbid the construction of totemic images, such as Judaism, Islam and Calvinist Protestantism (Freud, 1939; Lacan, 1993, pp. 214–215, 242). The murder of the "primal father" generates the Law as an external, symbolic system. Without the paternal function and symbolic castration, language and law remain external to rather than internally binding upon the subject, implicated in the subject's being (Lacan, [1996]2006, p. 464). Those with a psychotic structure "never enter the game of signifiers except through a kind of external imitation" (Lacan, 1993, p. 251).

The paternal function, symbolic castration and the resulting repression of drives are the preconditions of the neurotic structure: "neurosis without Oedipus doesn't exist" (Lacan, 1993, p. 201). Children who traverse the Oedipus complex experience fathers as agents of symbolic castration that enforce renunciation of maternal pleasures and repression of desires in conformity with the law (Lacan, [1996]2006, p. 465). These neurotic subjects become ethical, sublimating immediate drive satisfaction in the "real" while desiring recognition through the production of social values (Lacan, 1997, p. 94). To Lacan, relations with fathers are decisive in determining psychic structure, since "the god of each [subject] is formed in the likeness of his father...at bottom God is nothing other than an exalted father" (Freud, [1914]1950, p. 147). The paternal function is not fulfilled by a flesh-and-blood father but by a *symbolic father*, or *Name-of-the-Father*, condensed by the neurotic into "the figure of the law" (Lacan, 1993, p. 228). The Name-of-the-Father, the symbolic condensation of the Big Other, therefore determines neurotic subjectivity. The neurotic is the Big Other's quintessential subject, the subject called into question by the desire for the desire of the Big Other. "What am I there, in the Big Other?" "What does the Big Other want of me?" (Lacan, [1996]2006, p. 459). The Big Other is the "locus of memory Freud called unconscious" whose contours were determined by symbolic castration and repression ([1996]2006, p. 479). The neurotic subject does not primarily identify with and seek recognition from a real father (actual, embodied father of procreation), but of "what religion has taught us to invoke as the Name-of-the-Father" ([1996]2006, p. 464).

Lacan argues that the paternal function is the "red thread that passes through all of Freud's work," the enduring problem that structured his attempt to understand how the neurotic became possessed by a "system of signifiers" and "a form of reason of which he is more victim than master and by which he is condemned in advance" (Lacan, 1993, p. 242). The paternal function condemns the neurotic to suffer from a "literal logos" that takes "hold of an animal who doesn't need it and doesn't care about it – since it doesn't at all concern his needs" (1993, p. 242). The Name-of-the-Father is the "quilting point" that determines neurotic subjects' reality by stitching together and affixing the symbolic order, the imaginary and biological being-in-the-real (1993, pp. 260–261). The Name-of-the-Father is the neurotic's master signifier that ties together all other signifiers in the signifying chain, providing coherence to reality. The paternal function is the "quilting point between the signifier and the signified," by which the neurotic's "notion of father" is palpably experienced as akin to the "fear of god" (1993, p. 268).

In psychosis, the paternal function goes awry. An "accident" *forecloses* the Name-of-the-Father from the chain of signification leaving an empty space where the symbol of the Big Other should be (Lacan, [1996]2006, p. 479). In a psychotic, the symbol that ties together the neurotic's world does not exist. As a result, the psychotic's being-in-the-real bears no fixed relation to the symbolic order. Unlike neurotics, psychotics are not *installed* in the symbolic order, having avoided symbolic castration, repression of drives and sublimated desire for recognition. They lack neurotic insulation from *jouissance* in the real.[5] In psychotic structures, the "unconscious is present but not functioning" (Lacan, 1993, p. 143). The psychotic has "cancelled his subscription to the unconscious" (Fink 2007, p. 233).[6]

Freud's writings on psychosis emphasized "loss of reality" as a central trait (1924). Without the Name-of-the-Father in the symbolic space of the Big Other,

---

5   Feminization, especially of men, is a counterintuitive outcome of the avoidance of symbolic castration – "unable to be the phallus the mother is missing, there remained the solution of being the woman that men are missing" (Lacan, [1996]2006, p. 472).

6   Lacan's comment about psychotics having unsubscribed from the unconscious was made in reference to the novelist James Joyce. The current Lacanian literature on psychosis focuses heavily upon Lacan's writings about Joyce, whom he knew personally and believed to exhibit a psychotic structure (Lacan, 1975). Lacan's analysis of Joyce points towards psychotic structures as aberrant in modernity while we argue they were typical of the premodern West.

a psychotic ego lacks the symbolic anchor of identity. Depersonalization, a disintegration of the self known as psychotic break, occurs when a psychotic "can no longer even sustain himself in the position of Narcissus... The anima, like a rubber band, snaps back to the animus and the animus to the animal" (Lacan, [1996]2006, p. 460). Without the unconscious and the capacity to repress drives and psychic content in response to superego claims, the psychotic is overwhelmed. To cope with this, the psychotic ejects or "forecloses" discrepant psychic content and physical forces from "reality." Though conscious of them, the psychotic treats them as though they were not there. Lacking neurotic repression and a neurotic unconscious, psychotics defend against drives by masking them behind a psychic curtain projected as an "upsurge of hallucinatory phantasmagoria" ([1996]2006, p. 454). While outsiders view such delusions and paranoid projections as symptoms of suffering, the psychotic does not experience them as such: psychotics "love their delusion as they love themselves" (1993, p. 215).

Psychosis and Sinthomes

Psychotic delusions that effectively stabilize the relationship between signifier and signified sufficiently to restore a sense of reality are *sinthomes*: personalized, tenuous functional equivalents of the "Name-of-the-Father" that provide a "sort of island of...constancy... [but] that makes it uninhabitable for him" (Lacan, [1996]2006, p. 478).[7] During a psychotic break, delusions and speech can reach a level of "negative freedom" in which the subject gives up "trying to gain recognition." The subject becomes a prisoner of delusional speech and is "spoken instead of speaking" (1993, p. 229). The missing master signifier destabilizes the entire field of meaning and triggers extensive hallucination in an effort to reestablish consistency (1993, p. 203).

The psychotic subject is constituted by the activity of avoiding or "skirting" the hole left by the missing paternal signifier (Lacan, [1996]2006, p. 470). The paternal function plays a decisive role in the Oedipal complex as the agency of symbolic castration that breaks up the mother-child relationship, structurally

---

7   Lacan illustrated this by relating a case of *folie a deux* in which a mother-daughter pair generated and sustained a collective paranoid fantasy that their neighbor's boyfriend was harassing them, calling the daugher a "Sow!" and so on. Lacan suspects that the daughter had actually called the young man a "Pig!" but she recalls murmuring, "I've just been to the butcher's" though she could not say why or to whom she spoke. To Lacan the daughter was "possessed" by language, spoken by it, to sustain a fantasy shared by both mother and daughter that her former husband and in-laws were planning to "carve her up piece by piece" (Lacan, [1996]2006, p. 448).

separating the mother, child and father. Without this function, a psychotic remains a "prisoner of dyadic relationship" ([1996]2006, p. 448). The absence of the paternal signifier leaves intact, unrepressed, the desire of the child for the mother, the mother's desire for the child and the father's rivalry with the child. The father and pre-psychotic child are not separated onto different structural planes, but remain specular doubles of each other, rivals for the mother's affections (1993, p. 209). The lack of the paternal signifier not only leads to a "rivalrous relation" with the father, but the need to develop imaginary compensation to mask the lack of symbolic differentiation, often through a "series of purely conformist [external] identifications" with father figures (1993, p. 205). In short, the psychotic is incapable of inhabiting the symbolic position of Father (the signifier is missing) but learns to mimic the external appearance and behaviors of fathers. Psychotics often experience imaginary fathers who they mimetically copy (but never quite trust), rather than symbolic fathers inwardly understood as agents of duty and law (1993, p. 204).

Crucial for the analysis of peasant novels is Lacan's notion that a father who "manifests himself simply in the order of strength and not in that of the pact, [establishes to the child] a relation of rivalry, aggressiveness, fear" (Lacan,1993, p. 205).

What causes the paternal function to fail? Lacan lists all of the following as "paternal failings" that generate psychotic structures: "the thundering father, the easy-going father, the all-powerful father, the humiliated father, the rigid father, the pathetic father, the stay-at-home father, and the father on the loose" (Lacan, [1996]2006, p. 482). The content of these failings matters less than the following conditions: (1) the experience of paternal failure or hypocrisy, and (2) maternal denigration of the father or the father's authority. A father who claims to be an actual embodiment of the paternal function, a father who "presents himself as a pillar of faith, as a paragon of integrity or devotion, as virtuous or a virtuoso, as serving a charitable cause" is set up for conspicuous failure when later seen to be "at fault, to fall short, and even to be fraudulent – in short, to exclude the Name-of-the-Father from its position as signifier" ([1996]2006, pp. 482–483).[8] In the failure of the paternal function, the mother's "reverence

---

8   Lacan's reading of the Schreber case, Freud's only sustained analysis of psychosis, emphasized the hypocrisy of Schreber's father who was a public figure of immense proportion, an idealist who publicly and famously presented himself as educational expert to raise excellent children. Young Schreber was unable to negate the inconsistencies and discrepancies he witnessed in his father, unable to reconcile his private experience with the public "symbolic" image (Lacan, 1993).

is regarded as decisive" not only in the way that she "accommodates the father as a person" but even more in the "importance she attributes to his speech – in a word, to his authority–in other words, with the place she reserves for the Name-of-the-Father in the promotion of the law" ([1996]2006, p. 482). We shall see that both of these are omnipresent in Reymont's families.

By installing subjects in a symbolic order, the paternal function differentiates and specializes, which thereby reduces power struggles, conflict and competition. Psychotics manifest a fixation upon authority, power and control. With no Big Other to stabilize and adjudicate social relations, all others threaten to take the psychotic's place in the social order and the psychotic is liable to strike out in advance to ward off such threats. The psychotic is liable to project dark and evil intentions upon others, and psychoanalysts who work with psychotics go out of their way to provide innocent reasons for their actions lest dark motives be projected onto them (Fink, 2007, p. 250).

Simmel wrote that a *"pater familias"* who possessed "unlimited and wholly subjective power," who decided all "arrangements by momentary whim and in terms of personal advantage," operated with "arbitrary power," much like Lacan's "imaginary father" or Freud's obscene father of the primal horde. Their power appears absolute, but when a symbolic power embodied in a *"spiritus familiaris"* emerged, the patriarch "felt himself to be merely an executor and obeyer" because something other than "subjective preference determined his actions, his decisions and judicial decrees." The father was no longer the "unconditional master" but "administrator in the interest of the whole" whose "position had more the character of an office than that of an unlimited right" (Simmel, 1950, p. 262). To both Simmel and Lacan, when exclusive dyadic relationships between master and slave (or father and child) become triadic, the stabilizing "third" is "placed on an entirely different plane of reality" (the symbolic order in Lacan, the spiritual, ideal, objective order for Simmel). Simmel locates this triangulation of power in the symbolic order (as do Freud and Lacan with the Name-of-the-Father): "The patriarch can give orders to the other members of the family only in the *name* of that ideal unit" and the father thereby "subordinates himself to the law" so that "the law-giver, in giving the law, subordinates himself to it" (1950, p. 262).

The Failure of the Paternal Function in Peasant Society

Social science studies of peasant social character indicate significant troubles with the paternal function (Fromm and Maccoby, 1970; Wolf, 1952; Parsons, 1969; Foster, 1967). In Reymont, peasant fathers do not represent the law but flaunt it, violate it and stand at odds against it. The *Voyt*, the priest, the Squire, the "master" and the "father" are separate and misaligned nodes of social power. There is no "quilting point" that stitches together and anchors these imaginary and real sources of power into a united symbolic structure. Each node of power remains real, imaginary, free floating and disparate. Mothers – given the absence and perversity of fathers – take on many of the disciplining and control functions. The paternal function is disordered, if not absent: a world of psychosis.

Reymont's novel is replete with depictions of weakness and disorder of paternal function:

> "To the devil with the world as it goes on now! For everything, nay, even for a good word, you must pay! It is so bad that worse cannot be. Even children rise up against their parents; there is nowhere any obedience, and everyone would devour everyone else! The dogs!" "They are fools, not remembering that we shall all lie one day together in consecrated ground." "One has scarce begun to be a man, when he flies in his father's face, loudly demanding a portion of his land; and the young only scoff at the old. Scoundrels, for whom their own village is a hole, who despise all ancient rules, and who -some of them-are even ashamed of their peasant's dress!" "All because they have not the fear of God." "Because or not because of that, things are wrong." "And will surely not mend." "They must! But who can compel men to do right?" "God's judgments... He will punish them!"
>
> REYMONT, 1928a, *Autumn,* p. 59

Each psychic structure negates inconsistent affects and drives to maintain psychic consistency: neurotics repress into an unconscious lacked by psychotics. Inconsistencies of thought and contradictory drives coexist alongside each other without steps taken to create consistency or stability. An extended example of this from Reymont's novel is the sordid love affair of Antek and Yagna, whose sexual acts, emotional feelings and verbal expressions are inconsistent, not just between scenes but even within a single scene. Acts, emotions and words do not align: contradictory words, feelings and actions lie alongside each other without pains taken to identify any with a specific accent of reality. A neurotic takes pains to sort and classify acts and expressions, to identify and avow those that are ego-syntonic as "reality" while repressing the others. Such neurotic sorting and repression does not occur in psychotics: expressions of love and hate, feelings of desire and disgust, tenderness and violence intermix within a single span of time. Further, whereas a neurotic would apologize, explain or account for glaring situational inconsistencies, the psychotic characters in Reymont's novels do not.

Without repression and a functioning unconscious, psychotics rely upon primitive defenses such as splitting and projection to externalize blame for action. Yagna disavows her role in sustaining sexual affairs with her son-in-law and with a young curate. She projects blame onto others while foreclosing her own agency all the while imagining herself a passive victim of circumstance. Similarly, Antek does not accept his own guilt for sustaining a sexual affair with his father's wife, but splits off the blame for his behavior, projecting it onto the father while plotting revenge against him, all the while pursuing his mother-in-law for sexual encounters. Desires and psychic inconsistencies are not repressed but lie upon the specular surface of life like a non-functioning, non-repressed unconscious visible for all to see.

Even if a peasant would wish to repress acts and drives, the lack of privacy among peasants prevents it. Peasants know so much about each other's lives (someone, somewhere seems to observe every act) that they live in a state of perpetual familiarity. In Goffman's (1959) terms, peasants are stuck within a never-ending, geographically-distributed backstage: there is no social "outside" where discrepancies can be suppressed. After the smith coaxes Boryna into marrying Yagna, we would expect to see a Goffman-like performance by both men, but instead: "The two separated on good terms. But neither trusted the other a jot – Each was transparent to each as a pane of glass, each as easy to know as a horse with a star on the forehead" (Reymont, 1928a, *Autumn*, p. 112). Peasants are "transparent to each," rendering performances impossible and eliminating the modern game whereby performers seek to unmask each other to reveal the "real self" beneath.

Whatever rudimentary social backstage and personal privacy might have existed within peasant society was vulnerable to destruction by acidic gossip. Yagustynka embodies the omnipresent mutual surveillance, lack of privacy and destructive backbiting rampant in peasant communities. Throughout the novel, Yagustynka's gossiping disrupts and damages others but never completely or catastrophically. Living perpetually in a social backstage makes it impossible for peasants to stage a Goffmanesque performance because discrepant information and inconsistencies cannot be negated. Fathers must remain imaginary fathers whose inconsistencies, hypocrisies and perversions are visible to their children: they cannot function as symbolic fathers (Name of the Father) whose idealized presence is consistent, powerful and representative of law and language. Peasant fathers are often dark, obscene fathers-of-enjoyment whose children may fear and envy them but who cannot possess symbolic power or fulfill the neurotic's paternal function. In Reymont's novel, the paternal function fails at every turn: the hypocrisies and failings of fathers, civic leaders and church authorities are visible in great detail, clarity and frequency. Trusting no one, especially fathers and leaders, the peasants depicted by Reymont approach the *familial amoralism* Banfield (1958) noted in the towns of rural Italy in which the material interests of nuclear families served as the only haphazard ethical foundation for action.

Here, the Lacanian reading of peasant social character runs counter to most sociological framings of traditional society as social worlds marked by symbolic mandates that are absolute, unquestioned, and unquestionable. Sociologists tend to view traditional authority (patriarchal father over family, lord over peasant, master over slave) as absolute especially in relation to modernity, where authority appears comparatively weak and symbolic mandates disturbed by cross-cutting affiliations. Our Lacanian reading of peasant's certitude and absolute attachment to already-existing cultural patterns is not rooted in a mythically powerful paternal function. Instead, *peasant social character is determined by the absence of paternal function, its utter failure, requiring paranoid projections, hallucinatory delusions and imaginary constructs to mask its absence.* The peasant subject, like Lacan's psychotic, is constituted by the avoidance and skirting of the fearful lack of paternal metaphor, the hole where the master signifier should be that is defended from recognition by covering it beneath the four-corners of collective representation. We argue that traditional peasant submission is not caused by the overwhelming fear of all-too-powerful authority, but by the overwhelming fear that the absence of the paternal function will be revealed, destabilizing all symbolic power (law, language and social structure). The deep cultural conservatism of peasants and ritualistic, exacting repetition of unchanging ways maintains the mask concealing the absence of the paternal function. By holding fast to what always was, peasants sustain the illusion that symbolic power actually exists.

Psychotic Structure and Psychotic Break

Without the structural differentiation and separation of the paternal function, all relationships are "imaginary": others are specular doubles, rivals, competitors seeking to annihilate the subject or take their place in the social order. Positions that are structurally differentiated and non-competitive in homo normalis (normal modern neurotic) are fraught with open hostility and rivalry. Boryna and Antek, father and son, fight as enemies and rivals for a woman's affections and open competitors for a piece of land. Normative, neurotic relations between father and son, where each upholds structurally-determined reciprocal duties and obligations are inoperative in the novel (Reymont, 1928a, *Winter*, pp. 166–167). Even before the death of Boryna, while lying upon his deathbed, his children engaged in disrespectful treatment of his person and property and launched envious and deceitful attacks upon each other to secure advantageous division of his property and position. There was little recognized structural differentiation between the children and no symbolic authority: the outcome of the division was felt to be (and actually was) the pure result of the power struggle between the children, with each child locked inside of an unstructured, nearly absolute, struggle to the death with their family members.

Lacking a paternal function, social relations in the village remain at the level of the Lacanian imaginary. Duty and obligation are not internalized; hence, compliance to power requires its immanent immediate presence. Peasants can believe in an imaginary god, tangibly present in the dazzling brilliance of the monstrance or shining radiantly in an illuminated painting, but not in a symbolic, transcendent God. The priest is viewed as a man not unlike any other, gossiped about and gossiped with, selfishly concerned with his own farm and cattle: a man with scant special power or symbolic authority (Reymont, 1928a, *Summer*, p. 82). When villagers assembled to violently attack sexual deviants whom they thought were bringing a curse upon their village, they were dissuaded and dispersed by an encounter with the priest. But it was not the priest's person or office that stopped them "as if held back by a chain," but the gleaming, golden monstrance that contained within the immanent God. They went silent, many fell to their knees, kneeling and bowing their heads and eventually "slunk off...leaked away like water" (1928a, *Winter*, pp. 231–232).

Psychotics lack a functioning unconscious, which means that psychic content that neurotics repress remains visible and accessible to the psychotic's consciousness. Neurotics would tend to repress delight at the prospect of material gain attendant to the death of a sibling (or at least feel guilty about it), but when Gregory dies, his siblings and fellow villagers openly discuss and relish without shame their gains from his inheritance. Lack of an unconscious also means lack of repression of drives: a peasant in Lipka "concealed nothing, and could conceal nothing, for he could not help doing what he did then" (Reymont, 1928a, *Winter*, p. 148). Crass and crude behaviors, repressed by guilt-laden neurotics, are evidenced by psychotically-structured characters throughout the novel. When Kuba lay dying, Vitek begged the sexton to attend to him, and intercede with the priest to administer last rites. The sexton responded: "Oh let him die, then, and not prevent folk from eating their supper!" Further, the church and priest's orchard were used as places of sexual assignation and mob violence.

Lacan's psychotic structure is prone to psychotic breaks, generally triggered by struggles with fathers, lovers or authority figures who speak from the empty place of the Big Other, falling into the hole at the center of the imaginary world. This occurs after Antek was forced to renounce his mother-in-law as sexual partner, causing a flood of paranoid fantasies in which his father appears as persecutor. When Antek lowers a gun to kill his father, his paranoia triggers a break: "before he could pull the trigger...no shot came... A sense of unspeakable horror had entered his heart: he could hardly draw breath for the pain of it. His hands shook as with an ague; all his body trembled; a mist veiled his eyes." ..."My father! O Jesus! My father!" (Reymont, 1928a, *Winter,* p. 195)

Another instance of psychotic break occurs when Antek was being castigated by the village priest, who speaks as a stand-in for the missing Other, "calling him to repentance, beseeching, imploring, adjuring him." The priest admonished villagers to shun Antek, "For such a one would taint you all; ye would all grow foul at his touch; and, should he not mend his ways, atone for his misdeeds and do penance, then ought ye to pluck him out as ye weed stinging nettles, and cast him forth to his perdition" (Reymont, 1928a, *Winter,* p. 247). The priest spoke from the empty symbolic space, causing a psychotic break. "Every eye was cast upon Antek like a fiery dart. He, white as a sheet, and scarcely able to breathe, stood stiffly upright, the words smiting him as if the church were falling about his ears. He looked round, as though to find help, but there was now an empty space around him, lined only by menacing or terrified faces" (1928a, *Winter,* p. 246). Antek was "unheeding, bewildered, amazed, filled with unspeakable awe" (1928a, *Winter,* p. 247). Antek loses touch with reality triggering paranoia and persecution fantasies, blaming "that man...never will I forgive him! No, never!" (1928a, *Winter,* p. 248). Antek felt "a strange spell which somehow chained him to the spot. It was incomprehensible, but he experienced a resistless power that had seized hold of him with an inexplicable dread" (1928a, *Winter,* p. 249).

During psychotic breaks, paranoia deepens for Antek:

> He eyed those lamplit windows, and terror possessed his soul. They were all watching him, he thought; they were peering at him, following him, to fetter and enslave him with adamantine chains. He was no longer able to flee, nor to move, nor to cry out. He leaned back against a tree; and there, crushed with anguish, he listened...and heard – from all the homesteads, the shadows around them, the fields, nay even the heavens themselves – those same words of pitiless condemnation, now ratified by the whole population of Lipka.... Struck with mortal fear of that almighty Power, the Voice of the Many.
>
> REYMONT, 1928a, *Winter,* p. 249

Hanka experiences a psychotic break when Yagna speaks from the position of the empty space, sending Hanka into a psychotic break that lasts for days and is only overcome by producing a *sinthome* in the form of the imaginary presence of Our Lady of Chestohova and a pilgrimage pledged in payment of help:

> Her words pierced Hanka, wounded her almost to death. They struck her without mercy, crushed and trampled her down. She felt strengthless, mindless, almost as unconscious as a tree that falls struck by the thunderbolt. She was scarcely able to breathe; her lips grew very white, and she sank back on a bench. Her anguish, it seemed to her, was rending her to pieces – nay, crushing her to grains of barren sand: even the tears had vanished from her face, grown ashy...her bosom still was shaken with deep dry sobs. She stared out into space as if in terror – into the abyss which had opened suddenly before her eyes; and she trembled as trembles an ear of corn, that the wind whirls to destruction...unable to scream out, to defend...to flee any whither.
>
> REYMONT, 1928a, *Summer,* p. 75

Hanka's psychotic delusion grows to fill the empty space with a *sinthome*: "But heaven had pity on her and granted her a little relief. She came to herself again, knelt down before the holy pictures, and with abundant tears made a vow to go on pilgrimage to Chenstohova, if what she had heard should prove untrue" (Reymont, 1928a, *Summer,* p. 75). Hanka dreaded the sight or sound of her rival Yagna after this episode, and "hearing her voice now and then, crossed herself as if to keep of a fiend...more than once the thought of some awful revenge filled her mind" (1928a, *Summer,* p. 76).[9]

To Lacan, psychotics lack symbolic castration and remain in emotionally-cathected, dyadic relationships with mothers, relationships that are not

---

9 Psychotics do not ask the same existential questions as neurotics. Classic neurotic self-questioning seems to occur in the novel by Yagna, a character with otherwise psychotic traits. In the midst of a struggle between Yagna and Hanka over the disposition of Boryna's property, Yagna is treated poorly, is verbally abused and wishes to flee. Before she does so, she asks neurotic questions, almost Job-like: "Why are ye all – as many as dwell in Lipka – all of you against me?" "What have I done to them? Whom have I robbed or Slain?" (Reymont, 1928a, *Summer,* pp. 73–74). Crucially, she does not ask these questions of a Big Other but of the very small, dyadic other of the person she is struggling against, Hanka. The question is not asked because she wonders how she appears to others-in-general or because she wants to learn what the "big other" wants of her (the neurotic's constitutive question). Instead, she asks these questions to goad her opponent, Hanka, into a more intense struggle that she might win (a psychotic's purpose).

triangulated or limited by law-giving symbolic fathers. Peasants in Reymont's novels manifest these psychotically-structured, charged relationships to their mothers and to mother figures. Some are depicted with a strong Madonna-complex, in which the Big Other is figured in the form of a mother. Upon returning from captivity, men from Lipka bowed down and kissed the earth, saying "O most beloved Mother" ... "O Holy Mother... And how their eyes gloated over that land, their true foster-mother! Some even saluted it with doffed caps; all knelt down in spirit, mutely and fervently worshipping Her, the Hallowed Her, the Much-desired" (Reymont, 1928a, *Spring,* pp. 208–209). Later, when Antek is released from prison, he finds himself overcome with feeling for "the rush and mighty impetus of all growing things...the mysterious potency of that hallowed Mother, the Earth, who brings forth all in joy and gladness" (1928a, *Summer,* p. 102). Antek "was led somehow into a land of ecstasy...towards some garden where angels dwell, some happy land – Paradise, or Heaven...ready to fall prostrate on the earth, kiss her with burning kisses, and take her to himself in the most loving embrace... [to assume] his father's ways...the young should succeed the old and the sons the fathers, one by one" (1928a, *Summer,* p. 103).

Peasant cultures often manifest a Madonna complex in the form of visitations by and devotions to the Virgin Mary. Foster (1967), Fromm and Maccoby (1970), Wolf (1952) and Parsons (1969) all describe intense Virgin Mary worship among the peasants they study. While Mexican peasants worship Our Lady of Guadalupe and Italian Peasants pay homage to Our Lady of Sienna, in Reymont's Polish village, peasant's devotions are directed to Our Lady of Chestohova who appears so often in the novel that she is almost a minor character. While the Father God is feared and invoked when seeking vengeance, it is the Virgin, the "Mother of Mercy, Comforter of the Afflicted" who is called out in times of trouble and difficulty: "Madonna, Madonna, most Holy Madonna" is chanted as part of church service (Reymont, 1928a, *Summer,* p. 35). Peasants frequently light candles to the Virgin as "insurance" (Foster, 1967: 114), and the length of time necessary to recite one "Hail Mary" is used as a unit of time. Peasants often elide God-the-Father to pray to, worship and seek sacraments from the Madonna. Parsons (1969) reports that young women wish to stay pure so that they can be married before the Virgin, and Hanka confesses her sins to and seeks absolution from the Virgin rather than the priest. The devotion to the Virgin is felt with great intensity:

> Hanka was on her knees, glowing with gratitude, her heart almost bursting with gladness. Short broken sighs and whispered ejaculations seemed to be filling the room with flashes and pillars of flame, fed with the fire of her life- blood, and rising up to the feet of Our Lady of Chestohova.

The bliss of it was almost too much for her to bear: her tears flowed in torrents, washing away the memory of all her past sorrows and sufferings.
REYMONT, 1928a, *Spring*, p. 292

The Madonna often appears as a nurturing and maternal figure, and is invoked when asking for blessings: "May God and the Blessed Virgin of Chestohova grant him health!" (Reymont, 1928a, *Autumn*, p. 65); when seeking comfort: "gazing at the sweet dark maternal face of the Virgin of Chestohova, and with parched lips said prayer after prayer, and sang with such force and fervour, welling up from the inmost depths of his enraptured heart" (1928a, *Autumn*, p. 66); or when expressing surprise: "For the Lord Jesus and His Virgin Mother!" (1928a, *Autumn*, p. 66). Occasionally, even the Madonna can be inverted into a spirit of vengeance: 'May the Most Holy Mother grant you be struck dead unshriven!' the woman ejaculated, with a deep sigh, and a glance at an image of the Blessed Virgin that hung in a corner" (1928a, *Autumn*, p. 50)

Basic Psychotic Features of Peasant Social Character

Foster (1967) summarizes studies of peasant character collected from several continents that parallel psychotic symptoms: "suspicion, distrust, inability to cooperate in many kinds of activities, sensitivity to the fear of shame, proneness to criticize and gossip, and a general view of the people and the world as potentially dangerous" (1967, p. 89). Gossipy peasant discourse provides far greater opportunities to criticize negatively than to acknowledge goodness or speak positively (1967, p. 91). The prevailing tone of negativity contributes to an underlying deep mistrust of others and keeps villagers at a distance from each other, reserved, not wanting to share for fear of "betrayal...gossip and criticism" (1967, p. 94). The critical, oral sadistic quality of social life keeps people fearful and tense with worry for the "whole world is hostile...gossip is feared, eavesdropping is feared, envy is feared, anger is feared, fierce dogs are feared and sleeping alone is feared" (1967, p.103). Villagers are paranoid: they fear eavesdropping and build their dwellings with few windows to limit its occurrence (1967, p. 105).

Foster argues that a zero-sum "image of limited good" underlies peasant social life, a belief that "all desired things in life...exist in absolute quantities insufficient to fill even minimal needs of villagers" such that helping others harms the self (1967: 123–124). This belief undermines communality: villagers are aggressive, suspicious, and hostile toward their family and neighbors, limiting their ability to cooperate (1967: 133–136). In Reymont's village of Lipka, land is limited and viewed its possession is zero sum: land granted to new brides is taken from existing children. Foster's two rules of peasant life – hiding goods and "the good" to limit envy and aggression while yielding no ground to others (1967: 138) – is apparent throughout Reymont's narration of village life. The anal-hoarding character traits described by Fromm and Maccoby (1970) are replete in the behavior of Reymont's villagers who maintain secrecy and sus-piciously conceal possessions "lest envious people be tempted into aggressive acts" (Foster 1967: 13).

Reymont provides a detailed description of the negative, gossipy character structure of the older women of Lipka who had gathered for a working bee in mid-winter:

> Golab...with a vinegar-face, always bound up, who always complained of everything... Valentova the talkative – a huffy woman who cackled like a hen; Sikora's wife, a terrible gossip, thin as a broomstick, and much in-terested in all her neighbour's quarrels... Ploshka's wife, tubby red-faced, plethoric, always over-dressed, high and mighty to everybody, and gifted with rare powers of speech which made her generally disliked. Blacer-vokva, skinny, undersized, withered, and sly; an ill-tempered woman, and such a lawsuit-maker that she was on fighting terms with half the village, and went to the law-courts every month. Kobus...so malicious a gossip and so rank a shrew that folk shunned her friendship as they would fire... Gregory's wry-mouthed wife, a drunkard, a cheat, and given to practical jokes – especially such as did harm to her neighbours...there were others also, too hard to describe, being as like one another as geese in a flock, and indiscernible, save by their attire. ...they formed a large circle...and they looked like a clump of bushes, well-grown, mature and blighted by late autumn; for all were elderly, and all about the same age.
>
> REYMONT, 1928a, *Winter,* pp. 192–193

In the Mexican village studied by Foster, envy and the defensive dynamics to ward off envious aggression constituted a large portion of village social cus-toms, including the *remojo*, in which those receiving good make "payment" to others to fend off envy, as well as ritual actions to dispel the (envious) evil eye (Foster, 1967, pp. 153–166).

Envy was frequently on display in Reymont's novel, as one character says: "Gossips will gossip for gossiping's sake and for envy" (Reymont, 1928a, *Autumn,* p. 31). Another character chided a group of women saying: "Your un-bridled tongues are wagging, not for the sake of justice, but from envy and spite!... Worn-out old bosoms ye are, who would hate the very light of the sun!" (1928a, *Summer,* p. 80) Yagustynka, an old now-married "hag" functioned in the novel as an embodiment of envious village culture: full of suspicion, rancor and vile expressions of envy: she is described as "diabolically wicked...and possibly, as folk whispered, evil in a yet more unearthly sense" and "an evilminded beldame" (1928a, *Winter*, p. 166). She gained access to huts by fear and intimidation:

> In winter there was but little to do; so she used to go with her distaff from hut to hut, listening to the talk and setting folk by the ears and laughing with impartiality at everyone. None durst close their doors on her, partly out of fear of her tongue, partly because she was thought to have the evil eye (1928a, *Winter*, p.165).

At village gatherings Yagustynka is described as moving from "group to group, here with a word of mockery, there with a merry jest, or whispering some bit of gossip" (1928a, *Winter*, p. 135). She runs as a negative go-between to pick scabs or put lingering grievance onto a boil, such as between Boryna and Antek (1928a, *Winter*, p. 166) "Has not Yagustynka been here?" "She is not wanted: our company takes no pleasure in slandering and backbiting...a wicked hag she is!" "[so] why listen to her snarls?" "they all enjoy hearing her talk against someone else." (1928a, *Winter*, pp. 194–195)

Envy was often directed toward property:

> The house itself, to begin with, was the first in the whole village: large, conspicuous, tall, with rooms (they fancied) as good as those in a manorhouse: whitewashed, and with boarded floors! Then how numerous the household articles and utensils were! In the big room, too, there were a score of holy images: and all of them glazed! And then, the byre, the stable, the granary, the shed! Five cows were kept there, to say nothing of the bull—no small source of profit. And the horses, and the geese, and the swine—and, above all, the land! Eaten up with envy, they sighed deeply; and one said to another: "Lord! and to think that all this goes to one that is undeserving !" ..."Why should your Ulisia have missed this chance?" "Because she fears God and leads and honest life." "And all the rest do the same!"
>
> REYMONT, 1928a, *Autumn*, p. 249

Yagna, the beautiful young bride of Boryna and mistress of several men in the village, was a source of particularly strong envy: a long description of Yagna's beauty and expensive, showy dress as "for a wedding" ensured that "the women's tongues wagged against her with bitter reviling" (1928a, *Winter*, p. 144). While Yagna danced with her son in law, "folk were watching them, and whispering or even uttering aloud their disapproval" (1928a, *Winter,* p. 146), "women were loud in their amazement at such behavior and, while they censured it, expressed their pity for Boryna" (1928a, *Winter,* p. 147), "...the women, shocked at what was going on" fetched the husband (1928a, *Winter,* p. 148). "The village was thus alive and humming with continual gossip and scandal; invectives now and then, and bickering" (1928a, *Winter,* p. 169). The villagers' "fierce hatred for Yagna became still more envenomed. With cruel tongues, the women set themselves to...dragging her as through a wilderness of thorns and briers" (1928a, *Winter,* p. 234).

The paranoid fear that others will take the psychotic's place in the social structure is especially pronounced in relations to outsiders. Peasants in Lipka engaged in violent, projective outhating of Jews, *Tsiganes* (Gypsies) and Germans. When a group of gypsies passed through Lipka in Spring, the whole village locked up animals, and went into high alert, setting their dogs upon them: "the hag lifted her staff...and muttered sundry words and curses of magic might.... Our things would be stolen!! There is no safety against such a creature, then should your eyes follow her hands all the time!" (Reymont, 1928a, *Spring*, p. 164). Gypsies were viewed as "accursed heathens" with tremendous demonic powers, desiring to "kidnap children" and blacken them with a bath of alder-bark to make them look *Tsiganes*, and "take a brick and rub away the flesh – even to the bone – where the holy oil of baptism had been set: they simply make little fiends of them." Gypsies are feared because "they know charms and incantations awful even to name" "one would have but to breathe on you, and a moustache would sprout out to a cubit's length at once" – they can make dogs go blind, can shapeshift into animals and can cause demonic possession to farmers so that they run about "on all fours" and require formal exorcism to put right (Reymont, 1928a, *Spring*, p. 164).

Projective outhating of German Lutheran colonists was especially intense, and the Germans in the novel left after being threatened by villagers who refused to help them put out the fire that burned their village to the ground. A crowd of Lipka peasants gathered to watch them leave, mocking them while projecting hatred onto them: "on passing in front of the church, not one of them so much as doffed his cap. Their eyes were glaring, their beards bristling – with hatred, no doubt. And they eyed the people with murderous looks" (Reymont, 1928a, *Summer*, p. 40). The villagers verbally abused them with epithets "thick as hail": "Long-Trousers!...Carrion!...Ye horse-begotten ones!...Droppings of swine!...Who is forced to leave?...Our fists are too heavy... Not so fast, or your breeches will come tumbling down... A sudden death carry you off, ye ungodly hounds!... May all of you perish like mad dogs...Scum of the earth, dog-begotten miscreants!" (1928a, *Summer*, p. 40).

Projective outhating by peasants appears to be a harbinger of collective action. The peasants in Lipka rarely came together in constructive concerted action, but infused by collective consciousness and paranoid projection, they came together as destructive, violent mobs. The emotional volatility, ideational instability, paranoia and delusions of psychosis seem evident in this description of the mob attack upon Yagna:

> All the old offences which had caused their hatred, now again returned to their minds: a shower of epithets, reproaches, threats and evil spiteful words, were hurled at her; ant their fury was so hot that, had she appeared among them at that instant, she would surely have been attacked and beaten... Smith [who had an economic interest in Antek's demise] stirring them up, calling them to take revenge, ...wrought to the very highest pitch of rage...looking for sticks, intending to drag him from his cabin and give him such a thrashing as he would remember to his dying day... The clamor grew, with cries, threats, curses and a hullabaloo so great that the folk swayed hither and thither... Voices were lost in the uproar...swept along by the torrent...everyone dashed on, tore along, and shouted with all the force of his lungs: the whole band, carried forward by a tempest of hate, appeared like men possessed...married women, especially the poorest of all, took up the cry with a hideous bellow and, with arms stretched force...the mob rolled on with the din of a raging torrent. The howling and shrieking grew...the all pressed together, surging along, shrieking, shaking their fists, and lurched against one another, glaring with sinister glances, and a savage many-sounding voice, the cry of universal exasperation, burst from them as they hastened on, intent upon their purpose[10]
>
> REYMONT, 1928a, *Winter*, pp. 229–231

Hallucination and Certainty of Meaning

Neurotic subjects, disturbed by content repressed into the unconscious, are riddled with fundamental doubts and existential questioning. Uncertainty

---

10   The Polish characters in Reymont's novel are not peasants in a stable feudal society. Rather, they are survivors of disruptive military invasion, economic exploitation and political domination: a Durkheimian situation of anomie that would, by default, generate psychotic traits as a normal response. Perhaps Reymont's characters manifest psychotic traits not only because they are peasants, but also because they survived brutal colonization over a span of centuries.

propels neurotics upon a quest to uncover knowledge of the truth hidden within them. Psychotics lack both repression and a functioning unconscious and are marked by *certainty*. The disturbing content that neurotics repress into an unconscious remains accessible to psychotics. Psychotics have difficulty distinguishing between intra-subjective fantasy/hallucinations and objectively-ratified facts, and tend to place the same accent of reality upon all strongly felt psychic content. The neurotic subject is full of questions: their psychic life is structured by a desire to know what is repressed/unconscious. The psychotic subject, on the other hand, *lacks a question:* their psychic life is structured by avoidance of the hole in the symbolic order, the place of the missing master signifier (paternal metaphor). When someone or something speaks from the position of that impossible place or forces the psychotic to acknowledge it, the psychotic subject produces hallucinations or delusions that complete/sustain the imaginary fabric of reality. Hallucination is a *"perceptum* without an object" often experienced by psychotic subjects as voices and messages that mean something essential and certain (Lacan [1996]2006: 446).

Reymont's peasants hallucinate. Mystical communications and fantasies are a constant psychic admixture within the life of villagers. In *Autumn*, Boryna talks to his dead wife, Mary, about his prospect of remarriage (Reymont, 1928a, *Autumn*, p. 35), Kuba undergoes a mystic experience while attending a religious service, experiencing the sublime (p. 174), and Antek experienced intrusive thoughts about being with his father's bride, Yagna (p. 194).

Crucially, Reymont's peasants lacked neurotic doubt about the meaning of intra-psychic, free-floating messages. After digitizing Reymont's text, we searched for the word "doubt" in the narrative and found it was always preceded by the word "no." Reymont's peasants were only in the state of "no doubt" and were never in doubt. A search for the words "uncertain" and "uncertainty" revealed that they occurred infrequently and always in reference to a character who is unsure of unfolding events or who is uncertain as to the proper behavioral course to pursue in the moment. Reymont narrates no instances of peasant uncertainty regarding identity, beliefs, the nature of reality, or the meaning of fantasies.[11] For example, when Paul the messenger brings news to

---

11   On ambivalence: Psychotics lack a functioning unconscious and repression as a mechanism of psychic negation, so will not exhibit Freudian emotional ambivalence. Ambivalence results from the repression into the unconscious of emotional valences that contradict superego injunctions. It would be easy to misperceive the psychotic's lack of structure and emotional motility as evidence of ambivalence. Emotional inconsistencies and psychic fluctuations, including fluctuations of love and hate, is not a symptom of a repressed value emerging upon weakening of repression.

Hanka after visiting Antek in prison she is "uncertain" about what to do with
the envelope because she cannot read (1928a, *Spring*, p. 291). Matthew is "uncertain" how to appropriately react after witnessing a struggle between Simon
and Dominikova (1928a, *Spring*, p. 297).

Without the neurotic's unconscious keel of repression, psychotics exhibit
high levels of emotional volatility. Neurotic subjects tend to become ambiva-
lently fixated upon an object, generating *structured* emotional phase-shifting
between conscious love and repressed hate. Psychotic subjects lack such
fixation, displaying unstable ideation that generates unstructured emotional swings within the span of moments. For example, during a confrontation
between Yagna and Antek, a bewildering array of ideas, feelings, love, hate,
boredom, and nausea are expressed within a single episode of interaction.
Inconsistent emotions and ideas are not structurally differentiated from each
other, generating psychotic subjectivity whose boundaries are neither sensible
nor stable (Reymont, 1928a, *Winter*, pp. 262–266).

Several instances of hallucination in the novel were interpreted in terms of
folk beliefs about demons, spirits and souls that were widely held by villagers
but neither approved nor sanctioned by the village priest. For example, a peasant, Kuba, and other villagers congregated in a graveyard on the evening of
All Souls Day, imagining that they heard voices, saw shadows and experienced
the presence of long dead and forgotten ancestors of the village. Though for-
bidden by the priest, the villagers believed that the souls suffering in purgatory
were released by Jesus on this day, and wandered the earth. Villagers fed these
souls:

> Kuba took from his bosom several pieces of bread that he had put by.
> Kneeling down, he broke them, and threw the morsels among the tombs.
> "Food for you there is, O Christian soul!" he whispered, very earnestly.
> "I forget you not at eventide. – Food for you, O sufferer that was mortal! –
> Food for you!" "And will they take it?" Vitek asked in terror. "Beyond
> doubt! – Our priest forbids it – The others put the food into those barrels,
> and these poor creatures get nothing. But what? Shall the priest's and the
> Dziads' swine have to eat, and Christian ghosts stray starving." "Ah! Will
> they come hither?" "Yea, all who suffer the cleansing fires – all. Jesus lets
> them back to earth for today, to visit their people." "To visit them!" Vitek
> repeated, shuddering (1928a, *Autumn*, p. 175).

> A solemn silence, disturbed only by weird rustlings and thrilling
> whispers, now reigned among the tombs. The graveyard seemed filled
> with shadowy forms, the bushes bore questionable shapes; there were
> melodies of lulled soft moans, oceans of eerie tremors, movements of
> shapeless things in the dark, bursts of dread hushed sobs, mysterious

and horror-breathing alarms which made the heart sink. Throughout the village, the very dogs were howling with long despairing howls (1928a, *Autumn*, p. 177).

Outside the cabins, the folk glided about in fear; in fear did they listen to the quiet sighs of the trees; in fear they look towards the wind, lest there should appear to them one of those who, on this day, wander by God's decree and their own yearning – lest they should be heard lamenting where four roads meet – or be seen looking sorrowfully in through the window... Outside certain huts, the husbandmen – following ancient customs – set the remains of the evening meal for the hungry ghosts to partake of and crossing themselves, breathed such invitation: "O Christian soul that still abidest in the place of cleansing, lo! Here is refreshment for thee!" (1928a, *Autumn*, pp. 177–178).

After Kuba's death, a villager hallucinates his reappearance: "this place too is haunted... I know that Something walks the stable at night, and shakes out the provender, while the horses neigh... And then it passes out beyond the haystack." There is little doubt about the identity of this *Something*: "it must be Kuba's ghost" (1928a, *Spring*, pp. 165–166). Superstitions and magical beliefs and practices were shared widely as folk culture and lie upon the surface of life, unmarked by special accents of unreality. When things go awry, villagers are *certain* that "there is a curse upon Lipka...and it is heavier every week" (1928a, *Spring*, p. 168).

Inability to Create New Metaphors: Stereotyping of Language

One of the most obvious language disturbances of psychotics is the inability to create new metaphors (Fink, 1997, pp. 90–94). Because psychotics are not installed in the symbolic order, they do not live in and experience language in the same way as neurotics. The failure of the paternal metaphor – the "Name-of-the-Father" – means that psychotics lack a master signifier that facilitates the substitution of signifiers to express new, poetically metaphoric meanings. Hence, speech is wooden, imitative and stereotyped. The lack of "newness" operates at the level of meaning as well as mere words. Meaning remains fixed: new meanings cannot emerge even if new expressions or words could be found. One of the most striking qualities of discourse in Reymont is the frequency with which characters "quote" already-existing folk sayings and epigrams at the precise point when moderns might use a metaphor. They quote rather than create, closer to linguistic parrots than poets. In modernity, people speak the culture; in peasant society, the culture speaks the people.

Hundreds of folk sayings appear in the speech of Reymont's villagers, many are used more than once. Often, a folk saying is used to by a character to indicate that there is "nothing new under the sun," that the experience related in discourse fits readily within the already-existing, always-complete cultural meanings of peasant society. Often, when one character "quotes" a folk saying, it triggers other characters to do so in response, often choosing a folk saying with slightly different or even contradictory implications. Folk sayings cover a wide array of experience, including:

> "Suffering shapes the soul as the smith shapes iron"
> "Tis hard to lead an ox against its will"
> "Nobles in rags and tags, with naught but bundles and bags!"
> "Long lousy locks warrant well-born rights"
> "If a woman's tongue fail, she thinks tears ill prevail."
> "Gossip is like fire; ye shall not quench it with your hands, only burn them."
> "He that takes for a wife one that might be his daughter, for his pains gets a fiend who will scorn holy water."
> "One tainted sheep infects the flock"
> "When a wolf is your neighbor, you can only come to an understanding with a club or an ax"
> "For the authors of their fall, sinners have no love at all"
> "Man's happiness is a field to be sown with blood and sacrifice and labour"
> "The shepherd only cares for the sheep he can shear"
> "A promise is a toy made to give fools joy"
> "If sin you destroy, you kill all your joy?"
> "But for sin dearly cherished, long ago man had perished"
> "Sin must be good for something, just as a weed: Our Lord made them both" "Man, like swine, mars all things with his rooting snout."
> "Pot-making is for others than saints"
> "Who goes oft to the fair shall lose all he has there"
> "What must be will be"
> "When dogs have too much bread, each flies at t' other's head"
> "a priest's kith and kin will never grow thin"

The similarity of folk sayings across peasant cultures is remarkable, as noted in these examples from Mexico: "He who serves the common weal is paid by none for his trouble...no horse is so well shod it never slips...he who works in a soap factory should be prepared to slip...he who walks with the wolves will learn to howl..." (Fromm and Maccoby, 1970, p. 39).

The lack of the new is built into peasant experience of cyclical time. Experiencing time as the passing of seasons is intimately connected with the conservative outlook on life of the members of Lipka. The villagers move in a rotary motion, renewing the past in magic and ritual. Examples of time-worn, cyclical repetition include:

Candlemas (magic prevention of throat diseases with candles),
Kolendy (annual ritual of house, home and livestock blessing by priest),
Shrove Tuesday and Carnival, Palm Sunday, and "hallow-fare" (food and Easter eggs blessed by the priest on Holy Saturday),
Elaborate decorations for Easter Sunday,
Avoidance of warm food from Good Friday until Easter Sunday,
Easter Monday soaking rituals, in which young girls are soaked with water by boys,
Sobotki fires on St. John's Eve,
The village festival that surrounds the Feast of St. Peter and Paul

The cyclical view of time, linked to a stereotyped and unchanging symbolic order, contributes to a fatalistic worldview and extreme cultural conservatism. Psychotic cultural patterns guide life through the imaginary repetition of time-worn customs rather than the symbolic assumption of structural mandates and duty. When Antek inherits his father's farm, he makes no new plans for development or change, but rather intends to reproduce a stereotyped existence: "Now we have a farm of our own, we must behave as becomes our condition, and as our fathers have always done" (Reymont, 1928a, *Summer*, p. 107). Even after traumatic events, the inertia of peasant culture asserts itself to restore a sense of unchanging permanence:

In Lipka things went on according to the everlasting ordinance. He that was predestined to death died; whoso was to be glad rejoiced; he that was fated to be sick confessed his sins and awaited the end. And so, with the help of God, they continued to live on, from day to day, from week to week (1928a, *Winter*, p. 168).

The Invasion of *Jouissance*

Symbolic castration installs neurotics in the symbolic order and leads to the structuration/repression of drives. Psychotics, who lack symbolic castration and installation in the symbolic order, also lack drive repression. Without symbolic support, psychotics manifest weak body and psychic structures that readily break down and flood with *jouissance*. In psychotics, the "boundaries of the ego are not simply flexible, as they are sometimes described in neurosis, but virtually nonexistent" because "language that names and delimits" the flow of *jouissance* is absent (Fink, 1997, p. 90). In neurotics, symbolic castration creates socially-mapped erogenous zones that channel drives and contain *jouissance*. Psychotic subjects lack these structures and *jouissance* flows uncontrolled through the self, so that the body is experienced as "suddenly inundate[d] with it, invaded by it...an attack, an invasion, or forcible entry" of enjoyment (Fink, 1997, p. 97).[12] The psychotic is remarkably susceptible to inflows of moral energy and the breakdown of the ego during Durkheimian *collective effervescence*. Reymont's novels depict peasants who overflow with enjoyment during festivals, carnivals, wedding feasts, and especially during moments of ritual punishment, destructive collective action and mob violence.

Yagna, the amorous object of masculine peasant lust in Lipka, is depicted as particularly susceptible to the flooding of jouissance:

> He spoke so earnestly and with such kindness of her that every word of his sank into their minds with sweet mastery, and brought sunshine into every soul; and everyone felt consoled and radiant – except his hearers of Lipka. These quivered with anguish with the remembrance of the wrongs done them racking their minds. They burst out crying and groaning, and threw themselves down upon the pavement with outstretched arms, asking from the bottom of their hearts for mercy and relief in their woes.
>
> REYMONT, 1928a, *Spring*, p. 112

Yagna floods with *jouissance* when men gaze, flirt or otherwise display erotic interest in her. The physical streaming of energy (Reich) is especially strong when Yagna catches sight of the young novitiate with whom she is falling in love:

> Yagna was now growing more and more beside herself. Her heart throbbed madly, her eyes glowed with fire, her full lips were burning hot. Instinctively, she stretched her arms out to him...she felt a strange

---

12   Wilhelm Reich's long report of the treatment of a young psychotic from Ireland, "The Schizophrenic Split" bears striking resemblance to Lacan's portrait of the flooding of jouissance in psychosis, and to the character structure of peasants (Reich 1949: 398–508).

resistless agitation take hold of her, and had to lean against the fence...
What then took place within her, she was never able to understand. Such
a fire ran through all her limbs, and with such penetration, that she was
ready to cry aloud with the delicious pain of it. Shudders came over her
like swift lightning flashes; she felt a burning whirlwind rushing away
with her; wild cries, impatient to break forth, thronged all her being,
tense with an unspeakable longing. She wanted to crawl towards him –
nearer – nearer – but only to lay her lips on his white hands – kneel to
him – gaze on him close at hand – pray to him as to some holy image...a
feeling of mystic dread, and the vague fear of some horrible evil (1928a,
Summer, p. 61).

To psychotics, the symbolic dimension of language does not exist, hence words
are experienced as *real*: they are things that cause embodied reaction. Three
examples from Reymont's novel are especially telling in this regard. First, when
Antek was admonished by the priest, the words had little symbolic impact but
were experienced as body blows: "the priest's voice followed, smiting him as
with a scourge that drew blood at each stroke...he walked out as fast as he
could, fearing lest he should fall dead with agony – fearing those eyes that
glowed, fearing that awful voice" (1928a, *Winter*, p. 247). Second, when Yagna
proclaimed that Hanka was loathed by her own husband, Hanka experiences
the words as wounds: "Her words pierced Hanka, wounded her almost to death.
They struck her without mercy, crushed and trampled her down" (1928a, *Summer*, p. 75). Throughout the novel, curses and oath-swearing have real effects,
such as when Dominikova curses Hanka by saying: "'May the worst of all possible fates not pass you by!' Hanka winced under the curse...she was subdued
and depressed the whole evening...she worked with great diligence to shake
off old Dominikova's menaces from her mind; but unsuccessfully" (1928a, *Summer*, p. 78)

Lacan's Psychotics and Incomplete Modernity: New Directions in Critical Social Theory

In this chapter, we developed a Lacanian model of Western peasant subjectivity, refined through an interpretation of Reymont's *The Peasants*. The unifying
logic of this model is psychosis, defined by Lacan as a failure of paternal function. Peasant subjects are neither separated from the immediate (m)others
about them or alienated in the symbolic order of language and law. Without

this separation and the symbolic compensations that accompany alienation, peasants remain dependent upon and submerged within undifferentiated, agonistic dyadic relationships. Peasants struggle with others, paranoid lest they be displaced from the peasant community upon which they depend. Without a functioning unconscious or the psychic mechanism of repression, peasants place the same accent of reality upon fact and fantasy. Words are real and contain magical power. With weak psychic boundaries between self and other, peasants flood with jouissance. Peasant subjects must skirt the lack at the center of the symbolic order, generating hallucinatory delusions and mystical constructs as mechanisms of avoidance. As a result, their orientation to the symbolic order is deeply conservative.

This model is congruent with Freud, Reich and Lacan in viewing the modern bourgeois subject in terms of neurotic structure. The bourgeois subject has been separated from immediate dyadic relationships and has been alienated in language and law. They have undergone symbolic castration, but have acquired a symbolic phallus as compensation: they inhabit a position within the social order. Bourgeois subjects are capable of repression: drives and psychic inconsistencies are repressed and sublimated by a functioning unconscious. Perhaps most significantly, bourgeois subjects are animated by a question (what does the Big Other want of me?) that leads to uncertainty, doubt and ongoing inquiry. Rather than reproducing a stereotyped, ultra-conservative world, bourgeois subjects become an active force of change (for good and evil).

Lacan was rather pessimistic about the outcome of treatment for psychosis: no clinical protocol exists to transform a psychotic structure into a neurotic structure. Once a subject passes the developmental moment of paternal function/symbolic castration, a psychotic structure remains for life. With installation in the symbolic order precluded, treatment may alleviate symptoms or contain psychotic breaks, but it cannot generate a *post-hoc* neurotic structure. Perhaps the best outcome of treatment would be the creation of a benign *sinthome*, a personalized, tenuous knot that lacks inter-subjective recognition but nevertheless holds the psychotic's body and soul together. The mystical content of peasant religion – visitations by the Virgin, ghosts, demons, spirits, curses – functions as a collective *sinthome* binding peasant subjectivity in stereotyped ways strongly resistant to change.

Given the subjective similarities between contemporary anti-democratic characters (authoritarians, destructive personalities) and peasants, this model suggests that critical social theorists of alienation face enormous challenges. How could a mass of people with psychotic character be brought into democratic movements without forming them into a mass of "true believers" with doctrinaire ideology, charismatic leaders and ritual? If neurotic subjects are difficult to shake free of alienation and into left-liberal and social democratic movements (recall Deleuze and Guattari's view of Oedipus as Fascist), how much more difficult is the task of building a social democratic order with psychotics? Given the incomplete modernization of capitalist society, the Lacanian model of premodern Western social character suggests a new, albeit difficult, direction for critical social theory.

References

Adorno, T.W., Frenkel-Brunswik, E., Levinson, D.J., Sanford, R.N. (1950). *The authoritarian personality*. New York: W.W. Norton.

Auerbach, E. ([1942]2003). *Mimesis: The representation of reality in western literature*. Princeton, NJ: Princeton University Press.

Aydelotte, W.O. (1948). "The England of Marx and Mill as reflected in fiction." *The Journal of Economic History* 8(Supplement), 42–58.

Banfield, E.C. (1958). *Moral basis of a backward society*. Glencoe, IL: Free Press.

Blum, J. (1961). *Lord and peasant in Russia: From the ninth to the nineteenth century*. Princeton, NJ: Princeton University Press.

———— (1978). *The end of the old order in rural europe*. Princeton, NJ: Princeton University Press.

———— (1982). "Fiction and the European peasantry: The realist novel as a historical source." Proceedings of the American Philosophical Society 126 (2), 122–139.

Cassano, G. (2014). *A New Kind of Public: Community, Solidarity, and Political Economy in New Deal Cinema, 1935–1948*. Leiden and Boston: Brill.

Chayanov, A., & Thorner, D. (1966). AV Chayanov on the theory of peasant economy. B.H. Kerblay, & R.E.F. Smith (Eds.). American Economic Association.

Durkheim, E. ([1893]1997). The division of labor in society. New York: Free Press.

———— ([1897]1951). Suicide: A study in sociology. Glencoe, IL: Free Press.

———— ([1915]1965). *The elementary forms of the religious life*. New York: The Free Press.

Elias, N. (2000). *The civilizing process. Sociogenetic and psychogenetic investigations. Revised edition*. Oxford: Blackwell.

Erikson, E. (1950). *Childhood and society*. New York: Norton.

Fink, B. (1997). *A clinical introduction to Lacanian psychoanalysis: Theory and technique*. Cambridge, MA: Harvard University Press.

———— (2007). Fundamentals of psychoanalytic technique: A Lacanian approach for practitioners. New York: W.W. Norton.

Foster, G.M. (1967). *Tzintzuntzan: Mexican peasants in a changing world*. Boston: Little Brown.

——— (1971). Review of *social character in a Mexican village*. American Journal of Sociology 77(2), 336–338.

——— ([1914]1950). *Totem and taboo*. London: Routledge and Kegan Paul.

——— ([1920]1949). *Group psychology and the analysis of the ego*. London: Hogarth.

——— (1924). Loss of reality in neurosis and psychosis. *Freud complete works*. (pp. 4092–4098). Retrieved from http://www.valas.fr/IMG/pdf/Freud_Complete_Works.pdf.

——— (1939). *Moses and monotheism*. London: Hogarth.

Fromm, E & Maccoby, M. ([1970]1996). *Social character in a Mexican village*. Englewood Cliffs, NJ: Prentice Hall.

Fromm, E. ([1941]1994). *Escape from freedom*. New York: Macmillan.

——— (1990). *Man for himself: An inquiry into the psychology of ethics*. New York: Holt.

——— (1992). *Anatomy of human destructiveness*. New York: Holt.

Geertz, C. (1961). Studies in peasant life: Community and society. *Biennial Review of Anthropology*, 2, 1–41.

Goffman, E. (1959). *The presentation of self in everyday life*. New York, NY: Doubleday-Anchor.

Gramsci, A. (1919). *Workers and peasants*. Retrieved from www.marxists.org/archive/gramsci/1919/workers-peasants.htm.

Hallström, P. (1924). *Critical Essay: Nobel Prize in Literature 1924 – Presentation*. Retrieved from http://www.nobelprize.org/nobel_prizes/literature/laureates/1924/present.html.

Jameson, F. (1981). *The political unconscious: Narrative as a socially symbolic act*. Ithaca, NY: Cornell University Press.

——— (2013). *The Antinomies of Realism*. London: Verso.

Johnston, B. (2013). Szymek from the village and Joe from Missouri. *Perspectives on Literature and Translation: Creation, Circulation, Reception* 5, 47.

Krier, D. (2005). *Speculative management: Stock market power and corporate change*. Albany: State University of New York Press.

Krzyzanowski, J. (2011). Wladyslaw Stanislaw Reymont, 1897–1925. In Schellinger, P. (Ed). *Encyclopedia of the novel, vol. II*. (pp. 1096–1097). London: Routledge.

Lacan, J. (1993). *The seminar of Jacques Lacan, book III: The psychoses 1955–1956*. New York: W.W. Norton.

——— ([1996] 2006). *Ecrits*. New York: W.W. Norton.

——— (1997). *The seminar of Jacques Lacan, book VII: The ethics of psychoanalysis*. New York: W.W. Norton.

———(1975). *Joyce the symptom*. Retrieved from http://www.lituraterre.org/illiteracy_
and_psychoanalysis-Joyce_the_Symptom.htm..

Lukács, G. (1964). *Studies in European realism*. New York: Grosset and Dunlap.

———(1978). *Essays on Thomas Mann*. New York: Howard Fertig.

Malinowski, B. (1927). *Sex and repression in savage society*. London: Routledge and
Kegan Paul.

———(1929). *The sexual life of savages*. London: Routledge and Kegan Paul.

Mann, T. ([1901]1994). *Buddenbrooks: The decline of a family*. New York: Everyman's
Library.

Marx, K. (1852). *The 18th Brumaire of Napoleon Bonaparte*. Retrieved from http://www
.marxists.org/archive/marx/works/1852/18th-brumaire/ch07.htm.

——— (1887). *Capital: volume 1*. Retrieved from https://www.marxists.org/archive/
marx/works/download/pdf/Capital-Volume-I.pdf.

Meisenhelder, T. (2006). "From character to habitus in sociology." *The Social Science
Journal* 43(1), 55–66.

Parsons, A. (1969). Belief, magic and anomie. Essays in psychosocial anthropology. New
York: Free Press.

Reich, W. (1946). *The mass psychology of fascism, enlarged 3rd Edition*. New York:
Orgone Institute Press.

———(1949). *Character-analysis, third enlarged edition*. New York, NY: Orgone Institute Press.

Reymont, W. (1924). Biographical Essay prepared for Presentation of Nobel Prize.
Nobelprize.org. Retrieved from http://www.nobelprize.org/nobel_prizes/literature/
laureates/1924/reymont-bio.html.

———(1928a). *The peasants: A tale of our own times*. New York: Alfred A Knopf.

———(1928b). *The promised land*. New York: Alfred A Knopf.

Ridley, H. (1994). *The problematic bourgeois: Twentieth-century criticism on Thomas
Mann's Buddenbrooks and the Magic Mountain*. Columbia, SC: Camden House.

Simmel, G. (1950). *The sociology of Georg Simmel*. New York: Free Press.

——— (2004). *The philosophy of money, 3rd enlarged edition*. New York: Routledge.

Thomas, William I. (1914). The Prussian-Polish situation: An experiment in assimila-
tion. *American Journal of Sociology* 19(5), 624–639.

Thomas, W.I. & Znaniecki, F. (1927). *The Polish peasant in Europe and America*. New
York: Alfred Knopf.

Weber, M. (1946). *From Max Weber: Essays in sociology*. Oxford: Oxford University
Press.

———(1978). *Economy and society: An outline of interpretive sociology*. Berkeley, CA:
University of California Press.

———(1981). *General economic history*. New Brunswick, NJ: Transaction.

Wolf, K. (1952). Growing up and its price in three Puerto Rican subcultures. *Psychiatry* 15, 401–433.

Zieliński, T. & Dyboski, R. (1923). The peasant in Polish literature. *The Slavonic Review*, 85–100.

CHAPTER 8

Critical Pragmatism's Status Wage and the Standpoint of the Stranger

Graham Cassano

Introduction

Any attempt to make sense of complex historical realities requires a theoretical apparatus. In some disciplines, that apparatus takes the form of a more or less conscious theoretical introduction to empirical material. In the historical field, however, that theoretical organization of data sometimes takes a more implicit form, and the theoretical apparatus is embedded within a complex set of interrelated scientific formulae concentrated into descriptive tropes like "republicanism" or "wages of whiteness." It is this latter phrase, in particular, that draws the attention of these pages. Since the early 1990s scholars in a variety of fields have made use of David Roediger's phrase "wages of whiteness." Roediger, in turn, openly acknowledges his debt for that phrase to W.E.B. Du Bois. While Du Bois never uses the precise formulation Roediger coins, his seminal text *Black Reconstruction* (1935), provides the schema for Roediger's later neologism. At the same time, the schema that Du Bois provides has its own set of intellectual sources and influences, and its own context, American sociological pragmatism. On the one hand, *Black Reconstruction* represents the maturation of Du Bois' Marxist economic analysis. On the other, that economic analysis was supplemented by a social psychology and social phenomenology deeply rooted in pragmatic social theories also associated with Charles Horton Cooley and Thorstein Veblen. In the early twentieth century, Veblen, Cooley, and Du Bois each independently elaborated a pragmatic social theory of desire that attempted to connect quotidian social behaviors to the production and reification of broader patterns of social actions (structures). All three of these pragmatists built their theories of symbolic exchange upon a quasi-Hegelian quest for recognition. And all three used their theories to dissolve social structures into social processes.

Cooley's "looking glass self" serves a functionalist explanation of the manner in which subjectivity in search of recognition helps maintain social order and sustain dominant norms. Both Veblen and Du Bois also examine the problem of identification with systems of status and domination. But both reject Cooley's simple functionalist assumptions that consent and identification are immediate and automatic results of normative domination. And both reject his uncritical approbation of invidious norms. Veblen turns his critique upon the forms of hegemonic desire that potentially infect subjectivity and reinforce domination and working class division. And he situates these symbolic status systems in the context of economic and ideological tensions that potentially disrupt their easy operation. Du Bois adds to the Veblenian analysis of normative domination an examination of the counter-reaction of the repressed. The "double-consciousness" (Du Bois, 1907 [1903]) produced by estrangement from the normative racial system allows for the development of a critical, sociological imagination. While normative racism may secure accommodation from some colonized subjects, and Manichean rejection or self-destruction from others, this estrangement from the normative order also allows for a new perspective on the structures of domination that sustain normative values. Like Simmel's stranger, the excluded self remains remote from the group, yet "is an element of the group itself" (Simmel, 1950, p. 402). Through this combination of "distance and nearness," the stranger achieves an objectivity regarding normative conditions and desires (Simmel, 1950, p. 404). "Objectivity" in this context does not mean "value-neutrality." Rather, the stranger finds a critical distance and perspective (the critical perspective of the dominated) that allows her to recognize the forces of domination that fuel taken-for-granted norms. For Du Bois, "double consciousness" provides the gift of "second sight in this American world" (Du Bois, 1907 [1903]), the objectivity of Simmel's stranger – the ability to perceive the symbolic violence at the basis of normative desire.

Race as Social Fact and Dynamic Process

Let me begin by clarifying and defining the phrase "wages of whiteness" through a comparison to a related approach to the question of racial construction, Eduardo Bonilla-Silva's theory of structural racism. Bonilla-Silva (1999) defines race as both a social fact and a social construction. Race is a social fact, in that it presses upon the socialized subject like the invisible weight of the atmosphere (Durkheim, 1982). And like any social fact, race is a social construction, collectively elaborated over time and space. That Bonilla-Silva's definition is useful has been proven in scientific practice. But even a sensitive structuralism can sometimes reify the everyday interactions that produce race as active, lived, and shifting, identities. Metaphors are important scientific tools. But beneath metaphors like "structures" are interactive, realities, dissolving and reconstituting in transformed patterns. Thus, beneath race, as a social structure, there is race-making as a dynamic process of social exchange.

In order to get at the active dynamics that generate racialized social structures, Hannah Arendt employs the useful term "race thinking." And, indeed,
apart from Du Bois, it is in Arendt that we find one of the first uses of the
idea "wage in whiteness." Arendt's theory of "race thinking," focuses the analyst upon the perpetually renewed discursive and material practices that create and recreate racial boundaries, definitions, and identities. Thus, for Arendt,
whiteness and white identity are social constructs, social facts, and, consequently, social practices. In a language that anticipates David Roediger, Arendt
finds that the social construction of the white Boer had very definite social and
economic consequences.

> But in contrast to the natives who were immediately hired as cheap un-
> skilled labor, they demanded and were granted charity as the right of a
> white skin, having lost all consciousness that normally men [sic] do not
> earn a living by the color of their skin. Their race consciousness today is
> violent not only because they have nothing to lose save their member-
> ship in the white community, but also because the race concept seems
> to define their own condition much more adequately than it does that
> of their former slaves, who are well on the way to becoming workers, a
> normal part of human civilization.
>
> ARENDT, 1968, p. 194

Like Roediger (1999; 2005), Arendt is suggesting that the South African Boer
received a "wage in whiteness." Moreover, she even deploys a vaguely psychoanalytic argument, suggesting that violent racism depends upon white projections that, in turn, emerge from unconscious white anxieties about their
own social status. But for Arendt, while race thinking has complex causes, it
has definite and immediate economic consequences. The Boer received a very
material wage in whiteness, earning their "living by the color of their skin."
Whatever her differences with Marxism, Arendt shared the Marxist analysis
of the material consequences of race thinking. No doubt, in the context of
imperialism, such a rational analysis of the economics of white supremacy
helps further the understanding of racial construction. But part of the power
of the Du Bois/Roediger formulation is that it takes us beneath the rational-
material explanation of race-making, to the (unconscious) symbolic compensations provided by prestigious recognition.

Roediger argues that even when direct material benefits were absent, American whiteness still paid a kind of wage. In the 19th and early 20th century, American society was based upon a white supremacy that was both economic and
normative. Quoting Du Bois (1935), he writes the "avoidance of connection to

dependency and to blackness paid... 'public and psychological' wages" (Roediger, 1999, p. 55). Industrial proletarianization transformed artisans and farmers into wage laborers, with a consequent loss in social status. Industrial workers, now dependent upon a wage, fashioned a new concept of republican independence fused to their white racial identity. "*Herrenvolk* republicanism had the advantage of reassuring whites in a society in which downward mobility was a constant fear – one might lose everything but not whiteness" (Roediger, 1999, p. 60). Thus, in addition to perhaps ephemeral material benefits, this symbolic wage provides 'public and psychological' compensation for lost social status. Simmel (2011) argues that it is precisely this scientific focus upon interaction and exchange as "a sociological phenomenon sui generis" (p. 106) that allows for the "relativistic dissolution of things into relations and processes" (p. 126). And, indeed, Roediger's representation of normative whiteness as a symbolic wage directs analytic attention to the social *processes* that make social facts appear so stable.

At the same time, these processes of symbolic exchange are already implied even by the structural account of social facts. Since Bonilla-Silva draws upon Emile Durkheim's theory, let me turn to Durkheim's original outline of that scientific instrument. Social facts assert themselves upon the subject with invisible force. And, in Durkheim's initial description, social facts form a disembodied structure that automatically programs a seemingly passive subject.

> Not only are these types of behaviour and thinking, external to the individual, but they are endued with a compelling and coercive power by virtue of which, whether he wishes it or not, they impose themselves upon him. Undoubtedly when I conform to them of my own free will, this coercion is not felt or felt hardly at all, since it is unnecessary. None the less it is intrinsically a characteristic of these facts; the proof of this is that it asserts itself as soon as I try to resist.
>
> DURKHEIM, 198, p. 51

Based on these lines, we can understand the criticism so often leveled at Durkheim by micro-interactionists, that he reifies social structure and ignores the social processes of identification and exchange that enable the *illusion* of structure. Yet, later in that same passage, Durkheim acknowledges, and even emphasizes, the dynamic interactive processes that produce social facts. At first, he continues to deploy disembodied abstractions, like "the public conscience." "If purely moral rules are at stake, the public conscience restricts any act which infringes them by the surveillance it exercises over the conduct of citizens and by the special punishments it has at its disposal" (Durkheim, 1982, p. 51). Even so, Durkheim moves toward the concrete by specifying the mechanism through which "the public conscience" does its work: "surveillance." With this ocular and disciplinary conception of social control, the dynamics of desire and exchange beneath normative structures (like social facts) become apparent.

Durkheim concludes the passage with a very concrete and simple case illustrating the terms of social desire that condition social facts. "If I do not conform to ordinary conventions, if in my mode of dress I pay no heed to what is customary in my country and in my social class, the laughter I provoke, the social distance at which I am kept, produce, although in a more mitigated form, the same results as any real penalty" (Durkheim, 1982, p. 51). This prosaic illustration leads directly to the force behind social facts. To deviate from normative custom is to provoke laughter, social distance. To provoke laughter means awakening the disciplining *gaze of the other*. Through moral surveillance, the self receives pedagogical instruction in the proper paths of desire. Just as deviance provokes distance, so, too, in return for normative behavior the self receives the other's approbation. Thus, beneath Durkheim's seemingly structural account of the social fact is a dynamic theory of desire, and a social phenomenology premised upon the mediating power of the other's gaze. For Durkheim, the self is born a double, with an other within. The other's gaze mediates and guides the self's desire. In his theory of the social fact, Durkheim implies what Alexandre Kojeve (1969) – after Hegel – articulates with such force, *desire desires the other's desire.*

While Durkheim posits a set of social processes at the basis of so-called social structures and social facts, the path from structure to process in his work is tangled and concealed. On the other hand, Durkheim's contemporaries, the American pragmatists, were simultaneously developing a theory of social processes and organization that was deeply concerned with highlighting the link between micro processes and macro structures. Why did the ideas of Cooley, Veblen, and Du Bois intersect in the emerging twentieth century? Perhaps it was shared influence. Both Veblen and Cooley owe a debt to Adam Smith's *The Theory of Moral Sentiments* ([1759] 1976), and it seems likely Du Bois knew the text. Or their pragmatic theories of desire could be the result of Hegel's slow impact upon American thought. Perhaps the influence was mutual, though (lack of) evidence suggests otherwise. Whatever the cause, all three developed theories of the interaction between social psychology and dynamic social processes and structures of domination.

Sympathy in Smith and Cooley

Both European and American sociology were born out of the confrontation with the industrial revolution, but the European sociological tradition sprang more directly from history's impact upon the classical European philosophy of

Kant and Hegel. Karl Marx, Emile Durkheim, Georg Simmel, and Max Weber all owe systematic debts to this philosophical tradition. American sociology, while sometimes cognizant of these European writers and texts, owed its deepest debt to Adam Smith; or, more correctly, to the unique synthesis of Smith's writings and Emerson's transcendentalism. Smith's *The Theory of Moral Sentiments* (1976[1759]) provides a template for a new, problematic and sociological theory of selfhood. Perhaps it was this newly problematized self that Emerson had in mind in his deconstruction of individuality, "Self Reliance." While Emerson's essay is most obviously a plea for an independent individuality, the context for that plea is the author's recognition of the tyrannizing power of the other's gaze through the force of "sympathy."

> But the man is, as it were, clapped into jail by his consciousness. As soon as he has once acted or spoken with eclat, he is a committed person, watched by the sympathy or the hatred of hundreds, whose affections must now enter into his account. There is no Lethe for this. Ah, that he could pass again into his neutrality!... Society everywhere is in conspiracy against the manhood [sic] of every one of its members. Society is a joint-stock company, in which the members agree, for the better securing of his bread to each share-holder, to surrender the liberty and culture of the eater. The virtue in most request is conformity. Self-reliance is its aversion.
>
> EMERSON, 1866, pp. 38–39

While self-reliance may turn away from society, into solitude, there is no escaping the prison of consciousness, a prison with bars made of "the sympathy and hatred of hundreds." Emerson here uses "sympathy" in Adam Smith's sense of the term.[1] Indeed, he seems to humorously evoke Smith with metaphors of the self's "account," and society as a "joint-stock company." And for Emerson, as for Smith, even the independent self must account for the other within.

Smith's eighteenth century use of the term "sympathy" differs from current usage (Smith, [1759] 1976, pp. 9–26; for a broader interrogation of the eighteenth century meaning of "sympathy," see Marshall, 1988). According to Smith, through sympathy and imagination, we identify with the other, "we enter as it were into his [sic] body, and become in some measure the same person with

---

1 Throughout this chapter, I am primarily interested in the manner in which Emerson, Cooley and Veblen used Smith's work. Thus, while they may have misread some of his concepts (like "sympathy"), it is precisely that creative misreading I hope to elaborate.

him" (Smith, [1759] 1976, p. 9). Thus, following Smith, Cooley (1902) will define sympathy, "in the sense of primary communication, or an entering into and sharing the mind of someone else" (p. 102). And, as Cooley's open acknowledgement of his intellectual debt makes clear, Adam Smith's early work (at least as read by Cooley) marks the beginning of a new, problematic sense of self. After all, what is the "mind" if, through a kind of "primary communication," it can be shared among selves? Put another way, from Adam Smith's theory of "sympathy," the self emerges as a de-centered double, and society becomes the other within that makes selfhood possible (on Smith's influence in Cooley's work, see Jacobs, 2006, pp. 24–26).

Smith acknowledges this doubling when he writes: "When I endeavor to examine my own conduct, when I endeavor to pass sentence upon it, and either to approve or condemn it, it is evident that, in all such cases, I divide myself, as it were, into two persons... (Smith, [1759] 1976, p. 113) And Cooley, reading Smith through Emersonian spectacles" (Cooley 1998, pp. 35–38), develops the theory of this divided I into the "looking glass self."

Part of the power of Cooley's theoretical construction comes from the intuitive force of his initial proof that every self contains an other within. He confronts the reader with the direct experience of shame. And not any sort of shame, but the humiliation of a young boy caught by his mother (doing what, the reader is left to imagine).

> The reference to other persons involved in the sense of self may be distinct and particular, as when a boy is ashamed to have his mother catch him at something she has forbidden, or it may be vague and general, as when one is ashamed to do something which only his conscience, expressing his sense of social responsibility, detects and disapproves; but it is always there. There is no sense of "I," as in pride or shame, without its correlative sense of you, or he, or they.
>
> COOLEY, 1902, p. 151

With this invocation of maternal authority, Cooley situates the surveilling power of the other as a disciplinary power, like Durkheim's laughing crowd. And by reminding the reader of her own experiences of shame and social rebuke, he establishes an affective bulkhead for his radical proposition: the self exists as a double, desiring the desire of the (powerful) other.

> A social self of this sort might be called the reflected or looking-glass self... As we see our face, figure, and dress in the glass, and are interested in them because they are ours, and pleased or otherwise with them according as

they do or do not answer to what we should like them to be; so in imagination we perceive in another's mind some thought of our appearance, manners, aims, deeds, character, friends, and so on, and are variously affected
by it.

COOLEY, 1902, p. 152

The self is mediated by its imagined perception of the other's gaze. Cooley's
theory of the self depends upon the dynamics of the self's desire to please
the other. But while Cooley's initial introduction of the concept contains the
rhetorical hint of the normative power of the other's gaze, he does not fully
elaborate the link between "the looking glass self" and the fact that this self desires approval, in particular, from those invested with normative prestige. Nor
does Cooley systematically investigate the relationship between domination
and normative prestige and the way the desire for the other's approval reinforces invidious distinctions of rank and status. In short, however interesting
his theoretical articulation, Cooley never examines the critical implications
of his schema. Both Veblen and Du Bois produce parallel, but critical, extensions of this schematic sociology of desire. Veblen and Du Bois use critical
pragmatism to displace and deconstruct Cooley's functionalist approbation of
conventional norms and his implied acceptance of the invidious forms of symbolic violence that sustain them.

Veblen's Sociology of Desire

Although Veblen, writing before Cooley, never uses the latter's terminology, he
nonetheless elaborates a theory of the "looking glass self" in *The Theory of the
Leisure Class*. Most probably, this convergence represents the result of their
shared inheritance from Smith and Emerson (Watson, 2012). But whatever the
reason for their parallel arguments, Veblen provides an emphasis absent in
Cooley's formulation. For Veblen, as for Cooley, the self seeks the other's approbation, so that the other's desire becomes an internalized aspect of the self.
This desire for the other's respect is a desire to be recognized by the other. But
Veblen adds that the self desires recognition from those who are recognized,
that is, those invested with invidious prestige (Cassano, 2014, pp. 86–88).

As Matthew Watson (2012) has shown, Veblen owes a deep, and largely unacknowledged, debt to Smith's *The Theory of Moral Sentiments*. But while Cooley
reinvigorates Smith's use of "sympathy," Veblen concentrates upon another, related term in Smith's rhetorical arsenal, "approbation." Indeed, once, through
his use of sympathy, Smith introduces the idea that the self has an other within,

he is almost irresistible driven to posit a new schema for human motivation. The (seeming) arch materialist who authored *The Wealth of Nations*, argues that the fundamental motive behind all production and consumption is not material well-being, but the approbation of the other.

Does material necessity motivate consumption? he asks.

> Nay, it is chiefly from this regard to the sentiments of mankind, that we pursue riches and avoid poverty. For to what purpose is all the toil and bustle of this world? what is the end of avarice and ambition, the pursuit of wealth, of power, of preheminence? Is it to supply the necessities of nature? The wages of the meanest labourer can supply them.... To be observed, to be attended to, to be taken notice of with sympathy, complacency, and approbation, are all the advantages which we can propose to derive from it. It is the vanity, not the ease, or the pleasure, which interests us. But vanity is always founded upon the belief of our being the object of attention and approbation.
>
> SMITH, [1759] 1976, p. 50

Perhaps even more than by material necessity, human beings are driven by the desire for recognition (approbation). Smith's remarks become an important basis for Veblen's "conspicuous consumption" in *The Theory of the Leisure Class* (Watson, 2012). Expanding Smith's proposition, Veblen argues that "conspicuous consumption" is not itself a primary motivation in human life, but is the historically specific expression of a deeper desire for social recognition and prestige.

In (Veblen's) contemporary society, consumption and wealth become markers of prestigious normativity. Thus, echoing Smith, Veblen writes "those members of the community who fall short of this...*normal* degree of prowess or property suffer in the esteem of their fellow-men; and consequently they suffer also in their own esteem, *since the usual basis of self-respect is the respect accorded by one's neighbor*" ([1899] 1994, p. 20, emphasis added). Anticipating Cooley's "looking glass self," Veblen argues that the self is a social process emerging through interaction. I come to know myself through the gaze of an other. And precisely because of this phenomenological origin of self-consciousness, I desire the other's desire, the other's approbation, the other's respect. But Veblen goes further than Cooley. I don't desire the respect of any other, but of particular, respected others. These members of the community are designated as "normal" to the extent that *normativity itself is invested with social prestige*. Through desire for the other's approbation, the self identifies with an invidious schema of normative prestige that profits the powerful.

In return for the symbolic profits generated, the "normal" self receives a wage. That is, because social norms are invested with prestige, normative behavior and normative identity can provide the self with a kind of "status wage" in reflected prestige (Cassano, 2009b). With his theory of the status wage, Veblen anticipates Du Bois' parallel idea of a public and psychological wages in whiteness. And Veblen deployed this concept to answer a parallel question. Since his entire sociology is premised upon the unserviceability of human needs under capitalism, Veblen finds himself confronting the mystery of why exploited workers accepted the dominant system of normative behavior, or "scheme of life," rather than resisting the imposition an ideology and value system that served the interests of the leisure class.

Here again, Veblen echoes Smith. Smith ([1759] 1976) writes:

> When we consider the condition of the great, in those delusive colours in which the imagination is apt to paint it, it seems to be almost the abstract idea of a perfect and happy state. It is the very state which, in all our waking dreams and idle reveries, we had sketched out to ourselves as the final object of all our desires. We feel, therefore, a peculiar sympathy with the satisfactions of those who are in it. ...Upon this disposition of mankind, to go along with all the passions of the rich and the powerful, is founded the distinction of the ranks, and the order of society. Our obsequiousness to our superiors more frequently arises from our admiration for the advantages of their situation, than from any private expectation of a benefit from their good-will (pp. 51–52).

According to Smith, the powerful are often able to secure that power not through direct domination, but by dominating the desires of the dominated. Veblen expands this argument into a thorough-going theory of ideology. Because wealth provides a "good name" (Veblen 1994, [1899], p. 19), the behaviors, desires and norms of the leisure class become the dominant social forms and desires. It is "among [the] highest leisure class...decorum finds its fullest and maturest expression... [and] serves as a canon of conduct for the classes beneath" (1994, [1899], p. 33). The "members of each stratum accept as their ideal of decency the *scheme of life* in vogue in the next higher stratum, and bend their energies to live up to that ideal" ([1899] 1994, p. 52, emphasis added.). The society's "scheme of life" represents the system of broadly acknowledged invidious distinctions that provides the market architecture for the symbolic exchange of respect and recognition. Within this system, the values and practices endorsed by the respected, those normalized through prestige, become the values and practices dispersed (on the basis of rank) throughout the society.

This system is sustained when the common, powerless subject receives a status wage in reflected repute by accepting normative standards injected with prestige. Normative behavior provides the self with prestigiously invested recognition, while, simultaneously, legitimating invidious normative distinctions. Through normative behavior, the self partially identifies with the prestigious, and in that identification, accumulates a kind of cultural capital. But that capital remains a small "increment" of the symbolic surplus generated by the subject's participation in this unequal symbolic exchange. Thus it is that the "base-born commoner delights to stoop and yield" ([1899] 1994, p. 34) to the scheme of life offered by the leisure class because to "affiliate themselves by a system of dependence...to the great ones" provides an "increment of repute" ([1899] 1994, p. 48). By examining the dynamics of social desire, Veblen explains one particular, and particularly frequent, result of an invidious status system: "Emulation causes the oppressed to want to be as much like their oppressors as possible" (Dugger and Sherman, 2000, pp. 70–71). This emulation is simultaneously a form of "symbolic exploitation" in which the "base-born commoner" produces a symbolic surplus that legitimates the system of domination, and receives, in return, an "increment" of symbolic (reflected) repute (Cassano, 2009b).

In their recent study of mega-spectacles, Krier and Swart (2014) synthesize the Veblenian search for repute and the Freudian (repressed) desire for the other's desire. "The subjectivity of invidious consumers is fundamentally de-centered in that their own desires are structured by the desires of others. The hunt for trophies is in essence a search for collective representations that resonate with other people's fantasies and repressed desires" (p. 7). The trophies that haunt the imaginations of Krier and Swart's consumer-subjects are more material (though decidedly overdetermined and symbolic) than the status wages provided by leisure class identification. But Krier and Swart's investigations do the valuable work of situating Veblenian/Freudian identification within an empirical cultural sphere that mediates symbolic relations. Through my more diagrammatic examination of these symbolic exchanges, I intentionally evade any particular context in order to highlight the theoretical schema itself. What I hope I have shown is Veblen's general propositions: First, as Krier and Swart (2014), Dugger and Sherman (2000), and Watson (2012) also argue, the self emerges through the desire for the other's desire, *when the other is invested with prestige*, whether that prestige is derived from pecuniary power (the leisure class), mega-spectacle fame, or racial distinction (normative whiteness); Second, this is an unequal symbolic exchange, in which the subject accepts (symbolic and material) exploitation in return for an "increment of repute." This symbolic exploitation results in a status wage.

Veblen, Symbolic Exploitation, and the Status Wage

Equations are useful, but context matters and diagrammatic schema require content. History shifted Veblen's interests and his writings just after the First World War utilize the same theoretical schema, he applied to conspicuous consumption to explain the symbolic wage provided by national identity and nationalism. Although he may have initially supported u.s. entry into the First World War (Jorgensen and Jorgensen, 1999, pp. 149–150), by 1919 he had identified the war with imperialism, and American nationalism with a kind of collective psychosis (Cassano, 2009a). During this postwar period Veblen's open radicalism, his critique of American capitalism, and his support of the Bolshevik Revolution, appear in the pages of the New York periodical, *The Dial* (Jorgensen and Jorgensen, 1999, p. 158). In one of those articles, "The Divine Right of Nations," Veblen investigates the "psychic income" (Veblen, [1919] 1964, p. 127) provided by the reflected "honor and prestige" (p. 131) of national identity (Cassano, 2009b). And his interrogation of the nationalist self anticipates Du Bois' parallel argument concerning the "public and psychological" wage paid by normative whiteness.

As in his earlier work, Veblen's argument is premised upon a basic contradiction between the interest of pecuniary capitalism, which seeks profit, and the interest of the community at large, which seeks abundance and industrial efficiency. This so-called "business/industrial dichotomy" (Jorgensen and Jorgensen, 1999 p. 159) means that business must necessarily sabotage efficient production in order to maintain profits. Under the business system (capitalism), production is for profit, rather than for human need. In order to secure profits, business must interrupt production, and disrupt the efficiency of an interconnected economic system. In the same way, the nation state, in order to secure profits for the captains of finance and industry, sabotages the community's productive apparatus through war and imperial adventure. By pursuing national self-interest, the nation-state necessarily sabotages the interconnected, international industrial order. Veblen ([1919] 1964) argues that a "new order of industry has come into bearing, with the result that any disturbance which is set afoot by any one of these self-determining nations in pursuing its own ends is sure to derange the conditions of life for all the others" (p. 117). This derangement of the industrial system in turn "deranges the ordinary conditions of life for the common man [sic]" (p. 117). War, and the disorder brought to the production of human necessities by the production of armaments, fundamentally harms the ordinary American. Writing after one of the most brutal and wasteful conflicts in human history, Veblen uses his sociology of desire to explain how, in a democracy, the majority of working people could support a conflict so obviously against their rational-material self-interest.

Veblen begins with the American republican assumption that the "mantle of princely sovereignty has fallen on the common man." But, he adds, "In practical effect, as 'democratic sovereignty' it has been converted into a cloak to cover the nakedness of a government which does business for the kept classes" ([1919] 1964, p.125). Because of this democratic cloak, he argues, the "common man [sic] has to be managed rather than driven" (p. 127). The kept classes and vested interests, and the government that secures their profits, manages the common lot by compensating workers for material loss through symbolic wages. Just as the conspicuously consuming subject desires the (respectable) other's recognition, and through that approbation, attempts to accumulate prestige in the form of "an increment of repute," so the nationalist subject receives "imponderable" compensation through sympathetic identification with the nation's honor. "And the common man of the democratic commonwealth has at least come in for a ratable share in these imponderables of prestige and honor that so are comprised under the divine right of the nation. He has an undivided interest in the glamour of national achievement" (p. 126). The American polity is fundamentally divided by economic contradiction and social conflict. But through national identity these divisions fall away, in favor of an undivided interest in national glamour (a synonym for glory, honor, prestige, and thus recognition). At least one function of nationalism is to secure workers' loyalty to business interests and the profit of the kept classes. Class contradictions evaporate amid the "picturesque hallucination" of national solidarity (p. 133).

The symbolic status wage in honor preserves a nation state that serves the interests of the wealthy kept classes thus and vested interests. In one of the more humorous passages in this dark analysis, Veblen writes:

> The value of these collective imponderables of national prestige and collective honor is not to be made light of.... Indeed, they constitute the chief incentive which holds the common man to an unrepining constancy in the service of national interests. So that, while the tangible shell of material gain appears to have fallen to the democratic community's kept classes, yet the "psychic income" that springs from national enterprise, the spiritual kernel of national elation they share with the common man on an equitable footing of community interest ([1919] 1964, pp. 127–128).

This solidarity of interests in national honor may be an illusion, but "at least a profitable illusion, for the use of those who are in a position to profit by it"

(p. 131). With this invocation of "profits," Veblen reveals the symbolic exploitation behind this unequal relationship. Subjects produce a symbolic surplus (sustaining the invidious normative system through participation and consent), symbolic profits are appropriated (in the form of superior status for the vested interests and kept classes), and a symbolic state wage (or "psychic income") is paid. In the process, this symbolic exploitation also secures the *economic* profits of the kept classes. Here, as with conspicuous consumption, processes of symbolic exploitation contribute to the success of economic exploitation.

And like conspicuous consumption, nationalism is driven by the self's desire for the prestigious other's desire. Through identification with the predatory and thus honorable national establishment, the self comes to see itself as recognized, as respectable, as deserving honor. And "the common man [sic] still faithfully believes that the profits which these vested interests derive in this way from increasing the cost of his livelihood and decreasing the net productivity of his industry will benefit him in some mysterious way" ([1919] 1964, p. 133). While "the common man [sic] pays the cost" (p. 136) for imperialism, nationalism, and a predatory state that cloaks the naked interests of capital, that worker receives an "imponderable" "psychic income" in reflected honor. At least some workers willing forego material well-being in favor of a status wage paid through reflected national glory.

But Veblen's analysis of nationalism is not a functionalist reading that assumes the necessary consent of the dominated and exploited. He posits a fundamental "cleavage" of interests that divides the vested interests and the common lot, but because of the "American tradition," and the status wages provided by various symbolic forms of domination, the "common man [sic] does not know himself as such, at least not yet, and the sections of the population which go to make up the common lot as contrasted the vested interests have not yet learned to make common cause" ([1919] 1964, p. 174; Cassano 2009a; 2009b). Nonetheless, writing during the wave of post-war strikes, Veblen argues that, in addition to a long-standing cleavage of interests, a "vague and shifting...cleavage of sentiment is beginning to run between the vested interests and the variegated mass of the common lot" (Veblen [1919] 1964, p. 179). The effects of war, economic dislocation, inflation, and obvious inequality, produced a disruption of the status system, and at least some workers began to reject the status wages they were being offered in return for their consent.

> It is perhaps not unwarranted to count the I.W.W. as such a vanguard of dissent... [They] are likely not to be far out of touch with the undistinguished mass of the common sort who still continue to live within the law. It should seem likely that the peculiar moral and intellectual

bend which marks them as "undesirable citizens" will, all the while, be found to run closer to that of the common man than the corresponding bend of the law-abiding beneficiaries under the existing system. ([1919] 1964, p. 181)

Veblen's turn to the I.W.W. as a "vanguard of dissent" suggests that the status system did not function automatically, that extrinsic economic and ideological forces could interrupt and dislocate its operations. And, indeed, the Industrial Workers of the World rejected both nationalism and many leisure class normative ideals. But note, in Veblen's Manichean representation of class cleavage, only extrinsic forces disrupt normative processes of symbolic exchange. The Wobblies are the vanguard because they are outlaws rebelling against the conventional normative, as well as economic, systems. Precisely because they remain outside these systems, Veblen offers the possibility that their movement prefigures the common lot's radical rejection of the normative status wage. (And before the onset of the Red Scare, the 1919 strike wave and the Bolshevik Revolution gave force to Veblen's more hopeful speculations.) Veblen's use of the I.W.W. situates symbolic forces within economic and ideological contexts in such a way that these interacting fields can shape and disrupt one another's operations. The Wobblies offer at least some evidence that the power of conventional status systems is neither totalizing, nor complete. But while a status system may be overdetermined from without, its own internal workings don't produce necessary contradictions.

Much like Veblen, Du Bois will argue that economic forces and cultural crises can dislocate status systems and disrupt the conventional desire for status wages (in the form of white racial identity). But Du Bois also examines the perspective of those excluded from the status wage provided by normative whiteness. Arguing from the perspective of those colonized by the social hierarchy and yet excluded from its privileges, Du Bois finds that the status system potentially produces its own dynamic of resistance in the form of "double consciousness."

Double-Consciousness, Estrangement, and Conspicuous Whiteness

Like Charles Horton Cooley and Thorstein Veblen, Du Bois only rarely discussed the influence of his contemporaries upon his work.[2] And while I can find no reference in his writings to Veblen, nor to Cooley, Du Bois' Emersonian

---

2 I can find no reference to Cooley, nor Du Bois, in Veblen's work. Cooley, according to his biographer, makes a single, brief reference to Veblen in *Social Organization* (Jacobs, 2006,

pragmatism, absorbed from his Harvard mentor, William James, appears in his writing style, and his concern with the sociology of desire (Zamir, 1995). While Veblen provides a general theory of the active forms of internalized social discipline that define the dynamics of social desire, and thus, normative social domination, Du Bois examines this disciplinary desire within a social formation infected by normative white supremacy. And while Cooley's "looking glass self" describes the surveilling processes that condition social consciousness, Du Bois returns us to Durkheim's social fact, by way of the white other's *disapproving gaze*. Indeed, Du Bois begins *The Souls of Black Folk* (1907[1903]) with a description of his own discovery of his racial identity, which was also the recognition of his deviance within normatively white society. And it begins with the weight of the other's gaze, or, in Du Bois's words, her "glance."

> I remember well when the shadow swept across me. I was a little thing, away up in the hills of New England.... In a wee wooden schoolhouse, something put it into the boys' and girls' heads to buy gorgeous visiting-cards – ten cents a package – and exchange. The exchange was merry, till one girl, a tall newcomer, refused my card, – refused it peremptorily, with a glance. Then it dawned upon me with a certain suddenness that I was different from the others; or like, mayhap, in heart and life and longing, but shut out from their world by a vast veil.
>
> DU BOIS, 1907[1903], p. 2

Du Bois discovered his blackness in a disrupted social exchange, where his desire for the other's respect is refused "with a glance." At that moment he encountered a wall that was also a "veil" and a "shadow": normative whiteness. "It is a peculiar sensation, this double-consciousness, this sense of always looking at one's self through the eyes of others, of measuring one's soul by the tape of a world that looks on in amused contempt and pity" (Du Bois, 1907[1903], p. 3).

For Du Bois, as for Bonilla-Silva, race is a social fact. Whiteness becomes the norm; blackness represents deviance from that norm. But to say so is to imply a phenomenology of the self, and a dynamic theory of desire, as the processes underlying all normative structures. Race-making is driven by the desire

---

pp. 269–270). Further, Cooley's eugenic leanings made an exchange with W.E.B. Du Bois unlikely (on Cooley's white supremacy, see Jacobs, 2006, pp. 123–127).

for recognition and respect. Yet Du Bois does not suggest that the normative force of whiteness necessarily produces the acquiescence of the invidiously characterized "deviant" subject. In fact, this recognition of a normative whiteness that necessarily rejects the colonized subject's humanity produces, in turn, a dialectical "double consciousness" that simultaneously recognizes the force of the white norm, and recognizes that norm as the product of injustice and domination.

This "peculiar sensation" represents an emerging critical attitude directed toward Cooley's "looking glass self." When Du Bois argues that double consciousness is the sense of "always looking at one's self through the eyes of others, of measuring one's soul by the tape of a world that looks on in amused contempt and pity," he underscores not only recognition of the norm, but also the impact of that recognition upon the subject necessarily excluded from acceptance. One potential effect of normative whiteness upon the excluded subject is to bring to the surface this self-division, and so enable critical consciousness. In a personal vein, Du Bois writes: "One ever feels his two-ness, – an American, a Negro; two souls, two thoughts, two unreconciled strivings; two warring ideals in one dark body, whose dogged strength alone keeps it from being torn asunder" (1907[1903], p. 3). "Two unreconciled strivings" for recognition confront one another and the attempt to impose normative whiteness produces antithetical resistance.

Again perhaps from personal experience, Du Bois argues that the outcome of this struggle need not be the victory of either antithetical force. Rather, a synthetic, critical consciousness may result.

> In this merging [the American Negro] wishes neither of the older selves to be lost. He [sic] would not Africanize America, for America has too much to teach the world and Africa. He would not bleach his Negro soul in a flood of white Americanism, for he knows that Negro blood has a message for the world. He simply wishes to make it possible for a man to be both a Negro and an American, without being cursed and spit upon by his fellows, without having the doors of Opportunity closed roughly in his face.
>
> DU BOIS 1907 [1903], p. 4

"Double consciousness" does not necessarily produce the desire for whiteness, or for white approval; rather, it potentially creates the conditions for a critical sociological objectivity. Here Du Bois's characterization closely parallels Simmel's account of the stranger's objectivity. Simmel's model is the experience of

European Jews, rather than African Americans. But like Du Bois, Simmel finds that the outcast has a particular perspective on the normative social order. And, again like Du Bois, he argues that estrangement from normative patterns of desire result in a dynamic "unity of nearness and remoteness" (Simmel, 1950, p. 402). The "objectivity of the stranger" (1950, p. 404) comes from the fact that the stranger simultaneously participates in the group and experiences exclusion from full normative status. "As a group member... [the stranger] is near and far *at the same time...*" (1950, p. 407) The estrangement produced by double consciousness potentially enables a critical sociological imagination precisely because the Black American, like the European Jew, is both included within the social order and excluded from full normative status. By standing inside, and outside, at the same time, the excluded subject gains the capacity to conceive social norms objectively, critically, and, thus, to recognize the forces of domination that sustain these invidious norms.

Du Bois rejects easy determinism and functionalist explanations, and emphasizes that critical objectivity is not the necessary outcome of double consciousness, but only one possible result. "This waste of double aims, this seeking to satisfy two unreconciled ideals, has wrought sad havoc with the courage and faith and deeds of ten thousand thousand people, – has sent them often wooing false gods and invoking false means of salvation, and at times has even seemed about to make them ashamed of themselves" (Du Bois, 1907 [1903], p. 5). The experience of domination produces a variety of possible outcomes, from identification with the aggressor to Manichean rejection of the normative system. But one important variety of the experience of domination is an estrangement that enables critical objectivity.

While Du Bois suggests that for the excluded Black self, one possible consequence of normative whiteness is a critical objectivity toward normative systems of domination, he argues that white workers sustain white supremacy and receive an increment of prestige and recognition in return for their conspicuous participation. While there may be no direct influence, *Black Reconstruction*'s analysis of normative racism among white workers relies upon a Veblenian quest for the other's respect. Indeed, Du Bois describes a kind of *conspicuous whiteness* among southern workers.

> It must be remembered that the white group of laborers, while they received a low wage, were compensated in part by a sort of public and psychological wage. They were given public deference and tides of courtesy because they were white. They were admitted freely with all classes of white people to public functions, public parks, and the best schools. The police were drawn from their ranks, and the courts, dependent upon

their votes, treated them with such leniency as to encourage lawlessness. Their vote selected public officials, and while this had small effect upon the economic situation, it had great effect upon their personal treatment and the deference shown them. White schoolhouses were the best in the community, and conspicuously placed, and they cost anywhere from twice to ten times as much per capita as the colored schools. The newspapers specialized on news that flattered the poor whites and almost utterly ignored the Negro except in crime and ridicule.

    DU BOIS, 1935, pp. 700–701

An entire social and economic system was built in the South that paid "public and psychological wages" in the form of "public deference and tides of courtesy." While it "had small effect upon the economic situation" of the poor white worker, the investment of white identity with prestige and approbation paid dividends in community respect. Du Bois returns us to Veblen by way of the theory of social desire that posits social subjects driven more by the desire for respect and prestige than by the desire for material gain. Conspicuous whiteness and conspicuous consumption both represent the divided subject's search for recognition. And Du Bois might say, with Veblen (1994), "the usual basis of self-respect is the respect accorded by one's neighbor" (p. 20). Just as Veblen uses this proposition to analyze the symbolic exploitation that enables nationalism and conspicuous consumption, Du Bois finds that same exploitation at work in whiteness. Through their active participation white workers sustain white supremacy, and in return they receive conspicuous flattery and tides of courtesy, as an "increment of repute." As with the nationalist subject, the white subject emerges from an unequal exchange. Both nationalism and whiteness represent forms of symbolic exploitation in which workers generate symbolic surplus, symbolic profits are seized, and symbolic wages are paid. In turn, this symbolic exploitation interacts with and sustains economic exploitation and working class division.

    Through racial identification, white workers seek status, prestige, and recognition, sometimes without direct economic gain. But, here too, in his examination of the force white racial ideology, Du Bois rejects determinism and functionalism. While he argues that white worker complicity sustains normative whiteness, some ostensibly white workers turn against white supremacy. *Black Reconstruction's* chapter "The General Strike" recounts the general strike against plantation owners and slave self-emancipation during the Civil War (Du Bois, 1935, pp. 55–83; Roediger, 2014). While this strike was led by slaves and newly freed Blacks, nearly 500,000 workers, *Black and white*, took part. Although the plantation owning class increased its rhetorical appeal to the white identity of southern workers, some of those workers began to doubt the benefits of whiteness. In poverty and defeat "poor whites were losing faith. They saw that poverty was fighting the war, not wealth. ...The poor white not only began to desert and run away; but thousands followed the Negro into the Northern camps" (Du Bois, 1935, p. 81; Cassano, 2016). At least some white workers took their first steps toward interracial solidarity, and perhaps even toward the rejection of whiteness itself as a status ideal. In short, the social force of normative whiteness did not *necessarily* produce immediate compliance, even if white working class challenges to white supremacy remained rare throughout much of the 19th and 20th centuries. Like Veblen, Du Bois resists a functional determinism, and argues that the status system is overdetermined by economic, social, and political forces. And, like Veblen, Du Bois identifies moments of economic and cultural crisis that disrupt the desire for conventional status wages. For Veblen, the Wobblies, and for Du Bois, the general strike of the slaves, provide clear evidence that collective resistance can disrupt systems of symbolic exploitation and normative domination. In addition, both Veblen and Du Bois argue that economic forces interact with collective resistance and normative domination, an interaction that potentially creates the conditions for cultural crisis and revolution.

Conclusion and Limitations

Charles Horton Cooley, Thorstein Veblen and W.E.B. Du Bois each independently investigate the subjective search for recognition that sustains systems of domination. Cooley's account of the symbolic exchange between self and other suggests a rather smooth functionalism, and an uncritical attitude toward the symbolic and physical violence at the basis of social norms Both Veblen and Du Bois translate this same theory of dynamic subjectivity into a critique of dominant normative systems. Veblen uses this critique to deconstruct the forces that shape consumption patterns and nationalist fervor. He investigates the symbolic violence at the basis of taken-for-granted norms, but, in his analysis, transformation largely emerges from interactive tensions with other economic and ideological forces. Status systems do not necessarily produce their own internal contradictions. Du Bois, like Veblen, situates the search for status wages within economic and political contexts, documenting their interactions, for instance, in the waning days of the Civil War. And, like Veblen, Du Bois suggests that status systems are forms of symbolic exploitation, where status wages represent merely an increment of the symbolic surplus subjects

generate. But, writing from the perspective of the excluded, Du Bois also identifies the overdeterminations and contradictions within status systems themselves. Some colonized subjects remain in the system but outside its normative
boundaries. Or, more correctly, they are included within normative boundaries, but as strangers. Exclusion from normative systems of prestige produces
an estrangement that potentially allows for critical and objective observation
of the forces of domination that sustain status systems. Double consciousness,
"the [gift] of second sight in this American world," perceives the social world
from the critical perspective of the colonized. In short, Du Bois develops his
critical sociology based upon an implicit "standpoint theory" that anticipates
the standpoint theories developed by post-modern feminists and post-colonial
theorists (Harding 2004).

And this parallel with feminist research brings me to an important limita-
tion of the present study. A complete account of critical pragmatism's sociology
of desire in the early twentieth century must incorporate the critical theories
of desire developed by Jane Addams and Charlotte Perkins Gilman (Deegan,
1988). Accordingly, in a companion essay I intend to continue the present argument with close attention to Gilman (2002) and, especially, Addams (Cassano,
forthcoming). Gilman's analysis of gender, and Addams' intersectional investigations into class, gender, and ethnicity, compliment and enrich the critical
theories outlined by Du Bois and Veblen. Although in different volumes, these
two chapters are meant to be read together, each filling important gaps in the
other's argument. Together, Veblen, Du Bois, Gilman, and Addams represent
the critical edge of emerging sociological pragmatism in the early twentieth
century, and their (sometimes repressed) legacy continues to inform contemporary investigations into overdetermined and intersecting forms of domination, exploitation, and inequality.

When David Roediger introduced the idea of the "wages of whiteness," he
seemed to be combining the Marxism of E.P. Thompson with a broadly psychoanalytic perspective. But perhaps unrecognized within his theoretical synthesis is the ghost of American pragmatism. By examining the pragmatic roots of
this phrase, we begin to see that it contains within it the concentrated schema
for a critical phenomenology of the self and sociology of desire that systematically theorizes the perpetually renewed connections between micro practices
and macro patterns of action. Du Bois and Veblen situate this phenomenological process within dynamic social, economic, and political contexts. The result
is a critical pragmatism that challenges dominant social, economic and political relations by highlighting not only the socio-economic construction of normative life, but the symbolic violence that makes that construction possible.

References

Arendt, H. (1968). *The origins of totalitarianism.* New York: Harcourt.

Bonilla-Silva, E. (1999). The essential social fact of race. *American Sociological Review.* Dec. 64:6, 899–906.

Cassano, G. (2009). Choosing our ancestors: Thorstein Veblen, radical institutionalism and sociology, *Critical Sociology* 35:3, May, 367–377.

———— (2009). Symbolic exploitation and the social dialectic of desire, *Critical Sociology* 35:3, May, 379–393.

———— (2014). *A new kind of public: Community, solidarity, and political economy in New Deal cinema, 1935–1948.* Leiden and Boston: Brill Press.

———— (2016). Labor's 'strange blindness' and the end of Jubilee. *Ethnic and Racial Studies Review,* 39:3, Jan., 334–341.

———— (forthcoming). 'The senses become sodden and cannot be lifted from the ground': Jane Addams' critique of popular culture. In Cassano, Schultz, and Payette (forthcoming).

Cassano, G., Schultz, R.L., and Payette, J. (eds.) (forthcoming). *Eleanor Smith's Hull House Songs: The Music of Protest and Hope in Jane Addams' Chicago.* Leiden and Boston: Brill Press.

Cooley, C.H. (1902). *Human nature and the social order.* New York: Charles Scribner & Sons.

———— (1998). *On self and social organization.* Ed. Hans-Joachim Schubert. Chicago: University of Chicago Press.

Deegan, M.J. (1988). *Jane Addams and the men of the Chicago school, 1892–1918.* New Brunswick, NJ: Transaction Publishing.

———— (2008). *Self, war, & society: George Herbert Mead's macrosociology.* New Brunswick, NJ: Transaction Publishing.

Du Bois, W.E.B. (1907). *The souls of black folk: Essays and sketches.* Seventh Edition. Chicago: A.A. McClurg and Co.

———— (1935). *Black reconstruction.* New York: Harcourt, Brace and Company.

Dugger, W. & Sherman, H. (2000). *Reclaiming evolution: A dialogue between Marxism and institutionalism on social change.* London: Routledge.

Durkheim, E. (1982). *The rules of sociological method.* New York: The Free Press.

Emerson, R.W. (1866). *Essays: First and second series.* Boston: Ticknor and Fields.

Gilman, C.P. (2002). *The dress of women: A critical introduction to the symbolism and sociology of clothing.* Westport, CT: Greenwood Press

Harding, S., (ed.) (2004). *The feminist standpoint theory reader: Intellectual and political controversies.* New York and London: Routledge.

Jacobs, G. (2006). *Charles Horton Cooley: Imagining social reality.* Amherst and Boston: University of Massachusetts Press.

Jorgensen, E.W. & Jorgensen, H.I. (1999). *Thorstein Veblen, Victorian Firebrand*. Amonk, NY: M.E. Sharpe.

Kojeve A. (1969). *Introduction to the reading of Hegel: Lectures on the phenomenology of the spirit*. Ithaca: Cornell University Press.

Krier, D. & Swart, W. (2014). Trophies of surplus enjoyment. *Critical Sociology*. Sage On-line First edition. 1–22.

Marshall, D. (1988). *The surprising effects of sympathy: Marivaux, Diderot, Rousseau, and Mary Shelly*. Chicago: University of Chicago Press.

Mauss, M. (1979). Body techniques, in Mauss, Marcel, *Sociology and psychology: Essays*. London: Routledge.

Roediger, D. (1999). *The wages of whiteness: Race and the making of the American working class. Revised edition*. London and New York: Verso.

———— (2005). *Working toward whiteness: How America's immigrants became white*. New York: Basic Books.

———— (2014). *Seizing freedom: Slave emancipation and liberty for all*. New York: Verso Books.

Simmel, G. (1950). The stranger, In *The sociology of George Simmel*, edited by Kurt H. Wolff. Pp.402–408. New York: The Free Press.

———— (2011). *The philosophy of money*. London and New York: Routledge.

Smith, A. ([1759] 1976). *The theory of moral sentiments*. Minneapolis: Liberty Classics.

Veblen, T. ([1899] 1994). *The theory of the leisure class*. New York: Dover Publications.

———— ([1919] 1964). *The vested interests and the common man*. New York: Augustus M. Kelley.

———— (1997). *Absentee ownership: Business enterprise in recent times, the case of America*. New Brunswick, NJ: Transaction Press.

Watson, M. (2012). Desperately seeking social approval: Adam Smith, Thorstein Veblen and the moral limits of capitalist culture. *British Journal of Sociology*, 63:3: 491–512.

Zamir, S. (1995). *Dark voices: W.E.B. Du Bois and American thought, 1888–1903*. Chicago: University of Chicago Press.

CHAPTER 9

Dark Spectacle: Authoritarianism and the Economic Enclosure of American Motorcycling

William J. Swart and Daniel Krier

Introduction

The association of authoritarianism with automobility dates back at least as far as Hitler's emphasis on mass motorization and the dominance of the Nazi racing program in the 1930s Grand Prix (König, 2004, von Saldern, 1992). Other work on more contemporary American motorsports spectacles, especially Newman and Giardina's (2008; 2010; 2011) analysis of NASCAR *Nation* also emphasizes its affinity with authoritarianism, pointing to themes of patriarchy, militarism, neoliberalism, evangelical Christianity, white supremacy and government deregulation within these events as evidence of an overt, intentional strategy to produce and disseminate neoliberal and authoritarian attitudes amongst its spectators. Likewise, there is a developed literature that implies the rise of authoritarian rebellion in postWar American motorcycling. Although they do not reference authoritarianism generally or Adorno et al. (1950) specifically, Austin, Gagne and Orend (2010) point to outlaw and rebel themes in American motorcycle culture, drawn from American cinema and catalyzed by the post-war political climate, yet further appropriated, stylized, polished and amplified by the culture industry (Horkheimer & Adorno, [1944]1972; see also Barger, Zimmerman & Zimmerman, 2000; Klinger, 1997; Morton, 1999; Reynolds, 2000; Thompson, 1967; Wood, 2003).

This paper makes two contributions to this literature. First we align our analysis of American motorcycle culture closely with the authoritarianism literature, especially that of Adorno et al (1950) and Altemeyer (1981, 1988). This allows us to identify and explore the specific traits of two variations of authoritarianism in the history of American motorcycling. Early American or "heritage" motorcycling (1910–1950) exhibited a relatively orthodox authoritarianism that stressed submission and conventionality. These traits were overwritten with the anti-establishment, rebellious, and aggressive characteristics of "rebel" authoritarianism (Adorno et al., 1950, pp. 762–765) during the post-War era (1950–1980). Rebel authoritarianism became the leitmotif of contemporary American motorcycle rallying (1980-present), but has been increasingly coupled with anti-authoritarian themes as motorcycle companies and event organizers work to grow events into increasingly profitable megaspectacles (Best & Kellner, 1997; Kellner, 1995).

The focus on profitability foreshadows the second contribution of this paper. From its earliest years, the authoritarian structure and culture of American motorcycling were critical to its economic enclosure. The motorcycle industry, subsidiary merchandisers and event organizers used the authoritarian structure of heritage motorcycle clubs to transform groups of informal motorcycle enthusiasts into networks of loyal consumers. In addition, they relied upon rigid conventionality and in-group boundaries of heritage motorcycle culture to attract customers and solidify "consumer tribes" (Cova & Cova, 2002; Cova et al., 2012). When the orthodox authoritarianism of heritage motorcycling was challenged by post-War motorcycle "outlaws," the motorcycle industry enclosed rebel authoritarianism into an outlaw biker diegesis. This diegesis became the central narration of contemporary American motorcycling and served as a critical resource for marketing and promotion. We theorize the economic role of this diegesis as "dark spectacle." Dark spectacles transform authoritarianism into cultural commodities and market them to those who wish to see or be seen within an authoritarian themed diegesis.

Spectacular events and spectacular cultural products are the central commodities of mature capitalism; a leading growth industry amidst deindustrialized capitalism (Best & Kellner, 1997; Kellner, 1995). An economy of spectacle centers on three interrelated circuits: spectator markets, sponsorship markets, and trophy markets (Krier & Swart, 2014a). In general, economies of spectacle emerge when grassroots events are "enclosed" or privatized by an industry (Krier & Swart, 2015). Spectatorship markets emerge as industry organizes informal participants into networks of consumers and begins to commodify previously public events and activities. Over time, growing spectatorship yields a captive audience for sponsors, who pay to market their products within the growing field of spectatorship. Contemporary economies of spectacle are also enhanced by trophy markets, which allow spectators to gather tangible evidence of their spectatorship and display it to others outside the temporal and/ or geographic setting of the event (Krier & Swart, 2014b).

In what follows, we examine authoritarianism and its role in the spectator, sponsorship, and trophy markets of American motorcycling. In this sense, we focus on authoritarianism as a cultural commodity, not a personality. We have not taken "F" or "RWA" scale measurements of event participants, and while we would infer that authoritarian personality characteristics are present within many American motorcycle enthusiasts, we are not in a position to make claims about their personality structures. Instead, our goal is to analyze authoritarianism as a key element in the broad history of the American motorcycling subculture of consumption (Schouten & McAlexander, 1993, 1995) and an important catalyst to its economic enclosure. We analyze the cultural content of three distinct historical epochs of American motorcycle history – heritage motorcycling (1910–1950), outlaw motorcycling (1950–1980), and contemporary motorcycling (1980-present) – in order to delineate the characteristics of authoritarianism present within each and examine their role in the growing commodification of motorcycle culture in America.

Our research relies on a mixed methods approach undertaken during a multi-year case study of the economic structure of American motorsports spectacles. Case materials include field observations from motorsports events in five U.S. states (Virginia, South Dakota, Kansas, Iowa and Florida) interviews with city officials, rally organizers, motorsports customer experience professionals, local business leaders, motorsport event attendees and local residents, and the content analysis of images and text gathered from a variety of public sources. This research enabled us to conceptualize "dark spectacle" as an ideal type central to the history of economies of motorsports spectatorship. Though not emphasized in this article, comparative motorsports cases such as NASCAR, Grand Prix racing, dirt track racing and other motorsports events confirmed and delimited the generalizability of the ideal types we develop.

Authoritarianism in Early American Motorcycling

The image of American motorcycling in the contemporary public mind bears little resemblance to the reality of heritage motorcycle culture. Pre-War motorcycle culture, clubs, and activities were generally conventional, establishment, and civic minded – more akin to church socials than the Hell's Angels. Motorcycle enthusiasts of this era were middle and upper-middle class, and their clubs and activities were respectable and family friendly. Early heritage motorcycle events were local and spontaneous, often involving road tours, dirt track races, "tourist trophy" (TT) events or hill climbs that were modestly attended and relatively uncommodified. Cyclists gathered for evenings or weekends to ride and socialize, and events often included family picnics, dances, carnivals and field games with prizes for innocuous distinctions like the most neatly dressed lady and gentlemen riders or those who had come the furthest distance (Wooster, 2010). Even the "gypsy tour," whose name suggests an anti-social or at least vagabond quality, was consistent with establishment lifestyles. During such events, riders logged miles to and from events; "riding gypsy" meant riding self-contained, carrying one's necessities on their bike and camping in city parks or farm fields. Along the way, riders were expected to maintain decorum in an effort to "give the general public a convincing demonstration of the practical transportation and pleasurable possibilities of the motorcycle" (History of Laconia, nd.).

Despite this patina of wholesomeness there is clear evidence of authoritarianism in heritage motorcycle culture. Adorno et al. (1950) and Altemeyer's (1981, 1988) conceptualization of authoritarian attitudes provides a useful framework to explore these qualities. Both Adorno et al. (1950) and Altemeyer (1981, 1988) identify conventionalism, submission and aggression as three attitude clusters critical to the authoritarian personality.

Conventionalism involves high degree of adherence to the social conventions perceived to be endorsed by social authorities (1988 p. 2); the strong acceptance, commitment, and rigid adherence to traditional social norms (Altemeyer, 1981, p. 153) or middle class values (Adorno et al., 1950, p. 228). Authoritarians reject individualistic definitions of morality, believing instead that moral principles are obdurate, universal, and pre-defined by religious or political authorities. Importantly, adherence to conventional or traditional values may often be a standard not fully observed by the authoritarian himself; a "code" for how people *ought* to act but not necessarily *how* they act (1981, pp. 155–156). Authoritarian submission turns on the trust of and obedience toward established authorities, especially those perceived as legitimate. Authoritarians generally take the statements and actions of authority figures at face value and demonstrate a willingness to blindly comply with accepted authority figures (Altemeyer, 1981, p. 151). They hold strongly to the belief that those in an official capacity know what is best, that their authority should not be challenged, and that they are "owed" allegiance, obedience and respect (Altemeyer, 1988, p. 4). Finally, authoritarian aggression is the intent to harm or produce a negative state in an individual or group that they would usually avoid. Targets of authoritarian aggression are typically those outside the status quo – law breakers, minorities, or others who deviate from rigorously held group norms – thus authoritarian aggression is often coupled with the development and maintenance of rigid in- and out-group boundaries. Aggression typically becomes authoritarian when it is tied to the belief that an established authority approves of it or would be protected by it, and often centers on the drive to punish, isolate or demonize those who lie beyond in-group boundaries. On the other hand, aggression toward out-groups may be held in check under strong social prohibitions or the disapproval of authoritarian leaders (Altemeyer, 1988, p. 106).

We draw Adorno et al. (1950) and Altemeyer's (1981, 1988) conceptualization of authoritarianism in our study of American motorcycling. However, while they identify conventionalism, submission and aggression as "attitude clusters" or elements of a personality structure, we conceptualize these characteristics as social artifacts. In what follows, we read these characteristics in the culture and structure of American motorcycling and explore their role in the development of spectator, sponsor and trophy markets.

There was a strong conventional orientation in heritage motorcycle culture. Uniforms, for example, were *de rigueur* in heritage motorcycling and mirrored the conventional dress of the time. Matching shirts and breeches, bow or bolo ties, aviator hats and wing tipped shoes enforced respectability, mass conformity, and traditional values. Clubs mandated uniforms be laid out with specific attention to detail, noting acceptable color combinations and fabrics and identifying the specific location for embroidery, club insignia, and other pins and patches. Event organizers promoted this regimentation by awarding prizes the most neatly dressed and orderly uniformed clubs at tours or parades. They endorsed uniforms as a central element in the legitimation of American motorcycling, noting that "It's the uniformed clubs that get the admiring glances and the favorable comment as they swing down the street and highway" and that uniforms helped turn clubs into "civic institutions" (*The Enthusiast,* 1939, n.p.).

Conventionalism and submission were also promoted by the formal organization and rigid hierarchies of early twentieth century motorcycle clubs. Structured like branches of the military, clubs elected leaders, designated "ranks" (captain, first and second lieutenant, etc.), and evaluated applicants for membership. Membership typically involved a formal application; once approved, members were given visible club insignia (typically brass or bronze pins rather than patches) required to be worn on club uniforms. Local clubs brought structure to motorcycle events of the day by policing club tours and serving as the final authority for races. They elected "investigation committees" to provide social control during tours and events and to enforce rules for motorcycle competition. They published specific rank orders for riders during tours, and it was considered a violation of club rules for a rider to pass another member of higher rank who might be perceived to be driving too slowly. They employed graded point systems that "scored" members for acceptable participation. Members could earn (or lose) their good standing in a club based points earned for such activities as attending club meetings, participating in and assisting with club events, choosing to ride their motorcycles to club events during appropriate moths of the year, and following club rules and authority. Finally, clubs served as important sources of political organization; like the Harley Davidson Motorcycle Club of Lincoln Nebraska, most recognized their purpose was "to defend and protect the rights of motorcyclists" (Constitution and ByLaws, 1912).

Mass conformity and orderly conduct was solidified through the various national associations that evolved to provide structure, oversight, and political organization to early twentieth century American motorcycling. The earliest races, tours, hill-climbs and other events were subject to the rules of local motorcycle clubs, however, they lacked the standardization that was deemed necessary as participation and geographic representation expanded. In addition, the transition from motorcycles to cars as the primary form of automobility in America threatened the legitimacy of motorcycling and created the need for political mobilization for motorcycle rights. The patterns of authority first established by motorcycle clubs were standardized under the fledgling Federation of American Motorcyclists in 1903, who began to regulate motorcycle racing and other forms of motorcycle competition. Over time, the authority of the FAM was transferred to other organizations, including the Motorcycle and Allied Trades Association (1916–1924) and finally the American Motorcycling Association.

The AMA and its predecessors charged themselves with bringing structure and respectability to American motorcycling, consolidated the authority structures of local clubs into national bodies, and made themselves the final authority on motorcycle competition and recreation. Races and events had to be sanctioned by the AMA if their results were to be official. The AMA controlled the models and engine sizes of motorcycles allowed in competition, and speed and distance records could be challenged or disqualified if not made under the rigid guidelines and supervision of AMA sanctioning bodies. By the late 1920s, clubs were required to register with the AMA in order to be legitimate and recognized, and only clubs and members chartered with the AMA could participate in official AMA tours and events. Club members were expected to abide by the AMA code of conduct, and a club's charter could be threatened if its members did not demonstrate the middle class respectability and decorum required by the AMA (The History of the AMA, 2013).

Early motorcycle associations also saw themselves as political organizations charged with the responsibility to organize riders to fight for motorcycle rights. As early as 1903, the Federation of American Motorcyclists recognized that the novelty of the "motor bicycle" left its status open to various legal definitions and that political action was necessary to ensure the legal legitimacy of this new form of transportation. In 1924, one of the primary goals of the newly founded American Motorcycle Association was to build a member base that would turn the AMA into "a live and active fighting organization" that would make lawmakers "think long and seriously before they attempt to put over anything on the motorcycle riders" (*Western Motorcyclist and Bicyclists, 1924.*) Organizing under the slogan "An organized minority can always defeat an unorganized majority," the AMA mobilized riders to promote the motorcycle as a form of transportation equal to the automobile. Their "fight" took a two pronged approach: one centered on protecting and preserving the public image of motorcycling, the other emphasizing the rights of the motorcyclist amidst the growing centrality of the automobile in American transportation. On the former, the AMA and its predecessors saw respectability as central to the legitimacy of motorcycling in the public eye, and worked to regulate standards of behavior, demeanor, dress and decorum in heritage motorcycle clubs and activities. The AMA promoted uniforms, club authority, and rider respectability in heritage motorcycle publications while simultaneously demonizing deviants like the "open pipe goofs" who violated community noise standards by removing the baffles from motorcycle mufflers. In 1948, the AMA launched its "Muffler Mike" campaign, which encouraged members to pledge to quiet riding by not modifying exhaust systems. On the latter, the AMA organized motorcycle enthusiasts to fight against restrictive motorcycle legislation, including speed and traffic rights, city motorcycle bans, and later, state mandatory helmet laws. (*American Motorcyclist,* 1984, p. 50).

Heritage motorcycling culture valorized other authority figures beyond the AMA, especially the military and police as they became increasingly reliant on the motorcycle. Beginning in 1916, both Indian and Harley Davidson began providing motorcycles to the US military for use in patrolling the US border with Mexico, and over the next five years, some 20,000 Harley Davidson and 50,000 Indian motorcycles were sold to the US military to be used in the War effort (Nichol, 2007, p. 77). Motorcycle enthusiasts and manufacturers celebrated the military use of the motorcycle. One early Harley Davidson advertisement praised the role of Harley Davidson in providing motorcycles to US military service with an image showing a fleet of service members riding their Harley Davidsons out of the opening hands of Uncle Sam (*Uncle Sam's Choice* nd.) Motorcycle enthusiasts saw the military use of the motorcycle as a validation of their own identity, praising military sales as "another strong boost for the motorcycle" (Motorcycle Illustrated, 1917, p. 7) and celebrating the motorcycle as a symbol of national strength and versatility.

Motorcycle enthusiasts of this era also saw the legitimacy of the motorcycle bolstered by its use in policing. In 1928, the public safety division of Harley Davidson produced and distributed a series of posters to motorcycle clubs promoting the use of the motorcycle for traffic policing. In one, a bumpkin-looking cowboy cowers in his stopped car, arms raised in submission to a motorcycle traffic officer dressed as a member of the Canadian mounted police. Captions label the cowboy a "traffic outlaw run amuck" and the motorcycle as an "excellent steed" (The Only Force he Respects, nd). In another, drivers in gangster attire speed cars morphed onto the bodies of grimacing lions down city streets while a uniformed motorcycle officer directs kittens across a suburban street. The caption reads "Have you noticed now those roaring lions of traffic become meek little kittens when the "Lion Tamer" comes along?" (We need *more* Lion Tamers! N.d.). Still another reads "Day after day the Mounted Officer rides his best – a tireless warning to criminal and traffic law violators. Few are so foolhardy as to ignore his presence – his mere appearance on the street and highway compels obedience to the law" (Tireless Riders of the Law, 1928). The authoritarian optics of these posters is clear and suggests a coupling of aggression, submission, and rigid in and out-group boundaries. The officers always appear starched and stern, with chiseled bodies and facial features propped bolt upright on their motorcycles. Their military style haircuts and uniforms, coupled with references to "Mounties" or "Lion Tamers" give the image of authority and aggressiveness, and the message connotes strict in- and out- group boundaries: Automobile drivers are back country bumkins "run amok" or gangster "roaring lions;" their *"only cure"* is the "adequate and constant patrol of our streets" by making "every policeman a traffic policeman" (The *Only Cure* for our deplorable traffic conditions, n.d.).

While heritage motorcycle culture focused verbal and visual contempt on these "outsiders," there were seldom situations of outright punishment or aggressive control. Both Altemeyer (1981, 1988) and Adorno, et al. (1950) affirm that authoritarian aggression can be held in check by strong levels of conventionality and submission or strong social prohibitions (Altemeyer, 1988, p. 106). Thus we would expected to see less authoritarian aggression during periods of history where strong social conventions against outright aggression were in place. In the case of heritage motorcycling, the emphasis on conventionality outweighed potentially aggressive tendencies and channeled them into socially acceptable and organizationally sanctioned activities. The strong and vocal disapproval of anti-social behavior by policing bodies like the AFM, M&ATA or AMA limited the aggression displayed by motorcycle advocates in the pre-war era. As Adorno et al. suggest, it is not that aggressive tendencies have been outgrown but rather inhibited; the emphasis on conformity actually serving as a defense against an underlying hostility (1950, p. 162).

Adorno et al. (1950) and Altemeyer (1981, 1988) also note the role of ambivalence to conventional sexuality in expressions of authoritarianism, and this ambivalence is clearly notable within the culture of heritage motorcycling. In many ways, the concern over sexual mores mirrors that of society at large during this period, where the developing public life, greater independence, and new freedoms of expression for women increasingly challenged the Victorian gender sensibilities of the late-nineteenth century. This challenge was exacerbated by motorcycling in much the same way it was in equestrian culture of the Victorian era; focused quite literally on how a woman should "ride" and the sexual innuendo evident in that practice. In addition, concerns over the enhanced individualism and freedom that came with the motorcycle – like those of the bicycle that proceeded it – often questioned the greater potential for geographic independence the motorcycle allowed to women.

Heritage motorcycle culture, especially during the first decades of the twentieth century exhibits an almost obsessive concern the proper role of female motorcycle riders and their perceived challenge to conventional sexuality. The growing popularity of motorcycling during the early twentieth century drew increasing numbers of couples to this emerging leisure activity. This, in turn, fostered ongoing debate about the proper role of women in the sport. Did they belong? If so, what was their proper place? As a passenger or driver? Riding in a side-car, side saddle or astride the bike? And what should they wear? What stands out in this discussion is not a criticism of female riders *per se* but the criticism of women who choose to challenge conventional sexuality through their participation in motorcycling events. Magazines targeting motorcycle enthusiasts were filled with articles and editorials debating the respectability of female motorcyclists. A 1919 editorial about women riders at the Weirs Beach, NH rally is indicative of these gender politics. In an op-ed entitled "What's wrong with American Motorcycling," "Grandpa Grundy" complains about the attire and activities of female riders, arguing that women riding tandem in skirts and stockings, tight fitting jerseys or "clinging, form-fitting knitted sweaters" is "a crime against man's piece of mind" and, more importantly, gives the sport of motorcycling "another black eye" (Grundy, 1919, p. 23). Many readers agreed. Letters to the editor in the following issue, argued that "flappers in pants" left a blemish on the sport of motorcycling and should be prevented from participating either by city councils or an official ordinance of the Motorcycle and Allied Trades Association (The Viewpoint of the Reader, 1919).

The challenge of independent female drivers was also a source of concern among heritage motorcycle enthusiasts. "Are men necessary on a motorcycling trip?" asked an article in the July 5, 1917 issue of *Motorcycle and Bicycle Illustrated,* the debate centering on the propriety and safety of women touring unaccompanied by their husbands (The Manless Tour at Last!, 1917). Other articles explored women driver's ability to effectively handle a heavy motorcycle in tight turns or unpaved terrain or their aptitude for making adjustments or repairs in the field when unaccompanied by male riders. In 1940, Linda Dugeau formed the Motor Maids of America, the first female motorcycle club, dedicated to proving that women could ride motorcycles and maintain their femininity without being "mannish," "man-haters" or lesbians. While it took Dugeau three years to organize enough willing female participants to seek an AMA charter, the organization quickly expanded into a hierarchically organized and multi-state motorcycle club (About Motor Maids, 2013, Motor Maids, 2014, Yates, 1999).

Finally, the names of motorcycle field games popular at heritage events provides further evidence of the ambivalence toward conventional sexuality. While games such as "ride the plank" (which involved piloting a motorcycle in a straight line atop a series of wooden planks), "bite the weenie" (where drivers maneuvered in order to allow their passenger to bite a hot dog suspended from overhead) or "whack the murphy" (where drivers tried to knock a potato off a short post with a stick while driving one handed) were in many ways playful demonstrations of motorcycle skill, their names suggest a double entendre that clearly exposes ambivalent attitudes toward conventional sexuality of the day. These names, coupled with the silence or invisibility of sexuality in the events themselves, mirrors the dual expression and repression central to authoritarian attitudes toward conventional sexuality (Altemeyer, 1981, pp. 155–156).

In sum, the culture of heritage motorcycling, either as spontaneous and local or formally organized under national governing bodies reflect tendencies toward conventionality, submission, aggression and rigid in/out group dichotomies often associated with authoritarianism. Although focused on a specific microcosm of social life, the activities and ethos of heritage motorcycling were rigid, mass-identified, submissive to authority structures and condemning of those who didn't follow the general conventions of the time. Cyclists of this era clearly felt threatened by the possibility that their sport would meet with public disapproval. The threat was both internal and external; it emanated from those cyclists who might offend the general sensibilities of the public at large as well as the increasingly popular and dominant use of the automobile as the primary form of transportation in American society. Motorcycle enthusiasts, sanctioning bodies, and the motorcycle industry itself reacted to this threat by developing an authoritarian culture and organizational structure to promote and protect their legitimacy.

Authoritarianism and the Economic Enclosure of Heritage Motorcycling

The authoritarian culture of heritage motorcycling was an important resource to the burgeoning motorcycle industry of the early twentieth century. Although the use of the motorcycle had a spontaneous, grassroots and relatively uncommodified birth, it did not take long for private enterprise to begin enclosing this arena of public life. Between 1903 and the beginning of World War

II, nearly 300 motorcycle and scooter manufacturers went into business in the United States (Nichols, 2007, p. 104–115). Coupled with the development of a market for subsidiary products (accessories, parts, tools, apparel, etc.) their competition fueled the need to expand consumption and solidify a consumer base. The economic enclosure of heritage motorcycling turned on the development of spectator and sponsorship markets. The industry needed to create an organized body of people who wanted to be seen within the experience of heritage motorcycling (spectators) and then connect this audience to markets of advertising and promotion (sponsorship). Enclosure was the outcome of developing networks of spectators as markets for sponsorship, and the rigid structure, conventional habitus, and authoritarian ethos of heritage motorcycling facilitated this process in several important ways.

While the earliest national motorcycle organization (the Federation of American Motorcyclists) was a civic organization, the organizations that replaced it (the M&ATA and AMA) were trade associations. Arguing that "no sport has ever amounted to anything without a strong controlling body, loyally supported by its membership" (Clayton and Despain, 1984, p. 31), these organizations worked to develop the membership networks that would serve as the initial spectator markets in American motorcycling. They published recruiting guides, sponsored membership campaigns, and held membership contests, complete with prizes, banquets, and public recognition to members and clubs who recruited the most new members each month.

The authority of the M&ATA and AMA and their rigid control over motorcycle clubs and activities was critical to tying motorcycle enthusiasts directly into a consumer network (*History of the AMA*, nd.). As trade organizations, they served as middle men between motorcycle enthusiasts and the motorcycle industry. Their regulation of membership and club status, their rigid sanctioning of racing and tours, and their "members only" approach to events made membership a necessity for anyone who wanted access to the motorcycling events of the day. As the sport grew, the ranks of the M&ATA and AMA swelled, fostering a network of consumers who could be more easily targeted for marketing and promotion. In many cases, industry leaders served in ranking positions of M&ATA or the AMA, further solidifying the relationship between national organizations, industry, and motorcycle enthusiasts. For example, a January 25, 1917 article in *Motorcycle Illustrated* identifies Lacy Crolius as both the advertising manager for Harley Davidson and the chairman of the Educational Committee of the M&ATA. In this dual roles, Crolius was responsible for organizing M&ATA events, including the 1917 National Gypsy Tour (Date for National Gypsy Tours, 1917). Crolius' booklet, "Suggestions for Conducting National Gypsy Holiday Tours," outlines M&ATA standards for national motorcycle events and provides direction on event promotion (Gypsy Tour Promotion Plans, 1917). Thus by 1917, motorcycle events were not simply local or spontaneous, but aligned with a clear strategy to reach out and organize a spectatorship market into a subculture of consumption.

Membership networks also provided an important communication conduit that connected the motorcycling public with the industry. Magazines including *Bicycling World & Motorcycle Review, Motorcycle Illustrated, American Motorcyclists & Bicyclists, The Motorcyclist, American Motorcycling* (renamed *American Motorcyclist* in 1977), *Motorcycle Enthusiast,* and *The Indian News* were published by national organizations or the motorcycle industry and made available to motorcyclists, often as part of their membership in the M&ATA or AMA. These publications were important to the development of early spectator markets. The M&ATA and AMA used these publications as their primary means of cultural dissemination. The articles, editorials and images published in these magazines tied motorcycle enthusiasts to a shared set of principles and behavioral expectations. This not only solidified the ingroup boundaries of emerging spectator markets, it also reinforced the establishment ethos that was considered crucial to protecting the motorcycle market.

Finally, the spectator networks created by the M&ATA and AMA produced a body of obedient consumers sympathetic to pro-motorcycle political advocacy. One of earliest AMA slogans ("an organized minority can always defeat a disorganized majority") is an important indicator of their goal to mobilize riders into an organized political body. Industry leaders were aware that political restrictions on motorcycle use threatened the growth of their industry, and used the networks and publications of the M&ATA and AMA to create loyal interest group whose social and political capital could be mobilized to promote the legitimacy of motorcycle culture and thus protect the economic interests of the motorcycle industry.

The spectator markets developed in heritage motorcycling were also important to the development of early sponsorship markets. Although is well before the time of "official sponsorship," where events were named or corporations had exclusive rights to market themselves at or in association with an event, the early networks of motorcycle enthusiasts provided a captive audience for marketing and promotion. Industry publications, newsletters, and trade journals were filled with the advertisements of motorcycle and subsidiary manufacturers. Early tours and events were arranged in order to bring riders, dealers, and subsidiary merchandisers together. The M&ATA and AMA were considered mechanisms by which industry marketing could be standardized. In a 1917 editorial in *Motorcycle and Bicycle Illustrated*, J.H. Donehue argues that the M&ATA should produce and standardize window displays to be used by dealers in order for motorcycle dealers to represent the motorcycle in the best light possible (Donehue, 1917).

In sum, the economy of heritage motorcycling turned on the enclosure of a previously public and uncommodified social activity. This enclosure primarily involved the development of formalized spectatorship – networks of motorcycle enthusiasts organized into membership networks by the M&ATA and AMA. These organizations centralized spectatorship through a structure that exercised increasing control over motorcycle clubs and events and required membership for access. Membership networks facilitated the development of sponsorship markets by creating a captive audience for the motorcycle industry to target for advertising. The motorcycle industry used the membership structure and oversight of national motorcycle organizations to tap into a controlled and obedient consumer base – one that was submissive to national organizations, would cast the motorcycle in good light to the general public, and work together to promote the rights, respectability, and representation of the motorcycle as a legitimate form of transportation. The authoritarian habitus and structure of heritage motorcycling was thus a direct outcome of economic enclosure. In order to develop spectator and sponsorship markets, the M&ATA and AMA relied upon their rigid control of membership and access to activities, promoted submission to AMA rules and mandates, and advanced the conservative attitudes central to heritage motorcycle culture.

Outlaw Bikers and Rebel Authoritarianism

By the mid-1940s, the threat to conventionalism feared by heritage motorcycle enthusiasts was becoming a reality. Text from a speech given at the 1947 Harley Davidson dealers' conference is telling of the new in- and out- group boundaries being solidified in American motorcycling: "Well-dressed motorcycle riders on shiny, good-looking motorcycles are likely to stay out of trouble. Riders dressed in overalls, on motorcycles that are stripped down and generally dilapidated, are all dressed up for trouble and likely to find it." (Harley Davidson Dealers' Conference, 1947).

While an extant literature explores the post-war transformation of American motorcycle culture, a brief discussion is warranted here (for a full exploration see Austin, Gagne & Orend, 2010; Nichols, 2007; Reynolds, 2000; Thompson, 1967; Wood, 2003; Yates, 1999). In the immediate post-War era, increasing numbers of veterans were attracted to the libertarian possibilities of the motorcycle – especially its emphasis on freedom, adventure, risk and homosocial bonding. As Nichols notes, "this same strain of rebel had just returned, victorious, from

an epic struggle against a mighty enemy. He was ready to shake off the hor-
rors of war and get on with unbridled enjoyment of life in a vast, free country"
(2007, p. 80). The rebelliousness of many of these men was stirred by their disenfranchisement from an increasingly specialized labor market. Not expecting
to win, they had nothing to lose, and responded with a "full time social ven-
detta" organized under the structure of the motorcycle club (Thompson, 1967,
p. 54). Newly formed clubs remained outside the normative standards, rules,
sanctioning and membership structure of the AMA; they were "outlaw" in both
their rejection of the AMA as well as their reputation for disrupting sanctioned
AMA events and challenging civil authority.

The emerging habitus of post-war motorcycling challenged the "orthodox"
authoritarian emphases of heritage motorcycle culture, and marked a shift toward a type of authoritarianism best captured in Adorno et al. (1950) concept
of "the rebel." In language that bears a striking resemblance to outlaw motorcycle culture, Adorno et al. argue that a subspecies of the authoritarian personality has "emerged with the increased insecurity of the post-war existence;"
one that reflects nihilism and chance with a "penchant for tolerated excesses,"
anti-social destructiveness, the sadistic persecution of all things weak, and the
fortitude to tolerate risk and bodily injury (1950, p. 763). Unlike orthodox authoritarian, the rebel does not oppose the principles of rugged individualism
but rather carries them out *ad absurdum* (1950, p.171).

While the concept of rebel authoritarianism remains relatively undeveloped
in their work, their discussion of its characteristics bears a striking resemblance
to outlaw motorcycling. In what follows, we explore the evidence of rebel
authoritarianism in post-war motorcycle culture. Crucial to this analysis is
the tension between reality and rhetoric. While significant evidence of rebel
authoritarianism is present within the culture of outlaw motorcycling, virtually every analyst is quick to point out that rebellion among post-war motorcycle enthusiasts was exaggerated by sensationalist media attention and the
widespread public panic that ensued. This exaggeration was crucial to the
creation of dark spectacle and the enclosure of post-War motorcycling. The
rebel authoritarianism of post-war motorcycle culture became an important
cultural commodity exploited by the newspaper, magazine and film industries
and later capitalized on by the motorcycle industry itself. This new diegesis is
in large part responsible for the massive growth of the economy of motorcycle
spectacles after 1980.

Perhaps the clearest divergence from the orthodox authoritarianism of
heritage motorcycling was the strong anti-establishment sentiments of outlaw
motorcycle culture. While heritage motorcycling was organized under a structure that celebrated middle-class decorum, post-War motorcycling turned on

hostility and the flagrant violation of social conventions. Any behavior that raised the eyebrows of the establishment – commonly referred to as "showing class" in the outlaw vernacular – was considered appropriate. Stock bikes were "chopped" or "bobbed" with the addition of extended front forks, cut away fenders, and stripped down suspension and accessories. Muffler baffles were routinely "cut out" in order to make a motorcycle as socially disruptive as possible. Dress and deportment shifted from the clean and uniformed to the unkempt and disheveled; greasy hair, unshaven faces, dirty jeans and leather jackets or vests that were left purposely unwashed, all visible indicators of one's commitment to the post-War motorcycling lifestyle. Club names like the Pissed Off Bastards of Bloomington, The Boozefighters, Hell's Angels, Market Street Commandos, Vagos, Banditos, and the Warlocks, Sons of Silence, and Outlaws violated establishment values and public sensibly.

Anti-social behavior, most commonly excessive drinking and brawling, but also risky driving, crude humor, and brazen sexual practices (including open-mouthed kissing between club brothers), were all considered appropriate ways of "showing class" (Nichols, 2007). In his now classic work on the Hell's Angels, Hunter S. Thompson argues that outlaw motorcyclists had an almost instinctual anti-establishment orientation, their economic disenfranchisement producing a reaction formation against respectability (1967, p. 158). "Unlike the normal, middle-class, hard-working American, a motorcycle outlaw has no vested interest in the system... The values of that system are completely irrelevant to him...he doesn't give a damn" (Thompson 1967, p. 176).

Outlaw motorcycle clubs mirrored the strict regimentation and military style organization of heritage clubs, yet the level of their militarism challenged conventional limits. Many outlaw club members were veterans who were used to military order and had no problem accepting the rank and hierarchy of club structures. At the same time, their support for order, loyalty, and discipline often pushed the boundaries of traditional society. This can be seen in the predominant use of Nazi symbolism among the outlaw biker clubs of the 1960s and 70s. Nichols (2007) notes that the reason some outlaw bikers wore German WWII iron crosses, swastikas, SS medallions and helmets was because they respected the "organization, might, and spirit of the Third Reich" (2007, p. 146). While most took issue with the anti-Semitism of the Nazi agenda, they had respect and admiration for the discipline, loyalty and dedication of the party. Thompson quotes Sonny Barger, then President of the Oakland chapter of the Hell's Angels response to local tourist queries about the Angles being Nazis: "...there's a lot about [Germany] that we admire... They had discipline, There was nothin' chickenshit about 'em. They might not of had all the right ideas, but at least they respected their leaders and they could depend on each other" (1967, p. 148).

Strict in- and out-group boundaries were maintained by secrecy, suspicion and aggression. Club members used secret names that marked their in-group membership and frustrated local policing efforts. Outsiders were treated with the suspicion that they might be an informant, reporter or police investigator, and new club members were subject to intense initiation rights to prove their allegiance and value as club members. "Prospects" were treated as a long-term challenge of trust, often requiring years of menial and degrading service in order to prove themselves worthy of full club membership. Once proven, the prospect would be "patched," or given the official insignia of the club, to be sewn onto a denim or leather jacket or vest. Called "originals," a member's patch and cut were seldom if ever replaced; their accumulated grease and grime a visible challenge to conventional middle-class styles of dress and decorum (Nichols, 2007, p. 146). Originals were in many ways carryovers from the uniforms of heritage motorcycling – and were just as regimented. Patches, rockers and colors were strictly controlled by club leaders; they were to be displayed in specific locations and severe punishments were inflicted on those considered undeserving of their patch. Outlaw club insignia was also noticeably anti-establishment and, more importantly, anti-AMA. Early outlaw patches boasted "AOA" (American Outlaws Association) as a direct affront to the 1960 AMA "Put your best wheel forward" advertising campaign. These patches were the precursor to the diamond shaped "One Percenter" patches common in outlaw motorcycling today (Nichol, 2007, p. 161). When Harley Davidson began selling café style motorcycles in the 1970s some outlaw club members sewed the traditional winged Harley Davidson patch upside down in visible animosity to Harley Davidson for "selling out." Other patches were used to signify rebellion and anti-social behavior: having sex with a woman during her period, an interest in anal sex, sex with a black woman, or in some cases killing in defense of club honor (Nichol, 2007).

The strength of ingroup boundaries in outlaw motorcycling bound men together in a rigid homosocial bond. Club members regularly referred to each other as "brothers," a reference that wove them together as a unified force against outside influences. Thompson (1967) notes that despite their intense patriotism and high praise of capitalism, outlaw club members were strangely communistic, sharing food, money, lodging, beer and in some cases women with their brothers in need. They acted with strict discipline in following the dictates of club leadership, and their uniformity in thought and action fueled their narcissism and aggression. Outlaw biker literature is rife with references that denote club members as "wolves," "Vikings," or "Knights" and conventional middle-class society as "sheep." The imagery is clear; outlaw bikers are the free souls, acting with purpose and honor in a noble (yet often misunderstood) way. Outside their ranks are the sheep – stupid, senseless followers "who will inherit the earth in a bleating, vacant-minded void of dreamless, meaningless sleep" (Hays & Quattlebaum, 2010, p.13). Their group-think fueled extreme and un-predictable behavior, an "ethic of excess in all things" including drinking, vio-lence, sex, and retribution far beyond the boundaries of conventional society (Thompson, 1967, p 71–73; 165).

Post-war motorcycle culture demonstrates much greater ambivalence to authority than heritage motorcycle culture. On the one hand, the aggression and antisocial behavior of outlaw club members made then naturally antag-onistic toward authority figures. On the other, their military past and social regimentation gave them an odd affinity to the very sources of authority they despised. Thompson (1967) documents the remarkable similarities between the Hell's Angels and the California police, operating on "on the same emo-tional frequency" yet simultaneously vilified and valorized for their service to society (1967, p. 39). This ambivalence also explains the strong patriotism and pro-American sentiment in outlaw biker culture. Thompson considers the Hell's Angels' violent reaction to the anti-Vietnam protests – which were sup-ported by the same Berkeley hippies they had partied with a year before – as evidence of a "retrograde patriotism," that aligned the Angles with the same status quo and law enforcement that had persecuted them during the previ-ous years (Thompson, 1967, p. 248–249). In October 1965 Sonny Barger went so far as to write a letter to President Eisenhower indicating that members of the Hells Angels were available to train and serve as a branch of Special Forces behind enemy lines in Vietnam (Thompson, 1967, p. 257).

Finally, outlaw motorcycle culture demonstrates the sexual ambivalence of heritage motorcycle culture pushed to the extreme. Despite the unconvention-al sexual mores and behavior that are legend in outlaw biker culture, sexual activity wasn't chaotic or unstructured. In fact, a rigid structure lay beneath the anti-establishment sexuality of outlaw motorcycle enthusiasts that was firmly upheld and violently protected. Sexual partnerships were distinguished through a system of gender roles that applied predominantly to women. Though they weren't necessarily steady girlfriends or wives, "old ladies" were considered in a monogamous relationship and thus off limits to sexual advanc-es from other men. "Mammas" were women that were loosely affiliated with a motorcycle club but considered communal sexual property and open to all sexual advances. "Strange chicks" were women who were not previously asso-ciated with a motorcycle club but considered available for sexual exploitation. The boundaries between roles were transient; "old ladies" could risk becom-ing a "mamma" if they moved between committed partners too quickly or too often; men who made advances on another man's "old lady" were often subject to violent retribution for the offense (Thompson, 1967, p. 170–172).

Rebel Authoritarianism in Post-War Spectatorship and Sponsorship Markets

The post-War era was a crucial transition point in the culture of American motorcycling as the rebel authoritarianism of a new breed of motorcycle enthusiasts faced off against the conventional, submissive and establishment orientation of heritage motorcycling. The rise of rebel authoritarianism also had an important influence over the spectatorship and sponsorship markets of post-War American motorcycling. While initially limited, rebel authoritarianism captured the attention of police, newspapers, magazines, and the film industry, whose sensationalized accounts of outlaw activity were marketed widely to the public. In the process, media attention transformed the cultural narration, or *diegesis,* of American motorcycling from establishment to outlaw. Saturated with the characteristics of rebel authoritarianism, this new diegesis transformed post-War spectator markets. Although initially feared, the outlaw diegesis was eventually embraced by the motorcycle industry and tied to the sponsorship markets of the 1980s.

Outlaw motorcycling accounted for a relatively small proportion of all American motorcycle activity in the immediate post-War era. The number of outlaw clubs and club members was somewhat insignificant. Only a handful of clubs existed outside AMA sanctioning at that time, primarily located in southern California (Yates, 1999, p. 24). There were roughly 60 members of the Boozefighters in 1947, membership in the Hell's never exceeded 400 prior to 1965, when it reached an all-time low of 85 (Hays & Quattlebaum, 2010, pp 35–36; Thompson 1967, pp. 28–29). Evidence of rebel authoritarianism at this time was also limited. Hays and Quattlebaum (2010) argue that while members of the Boozefighters liked to drink to excess and had a hardened, tough exterior conditioned by combat, they had all the anti-social characteristics of "Spanky and Alfalfa with a pack of firecrackers" (Hays & Quattlebaum, 2010 p.53). Thompson (1967) refers to the Hell's Angels as "bush league hoods" involved in petty drinking and brawling prior to 1965; anti-social, but not posing the threat more commonly associated with their contemporary national reputation (1967, p. 37).

The transformation in both the reality and the representation of outlaw motorcycling was in large measure the result of sensationalistic media attention and the widespread moral panic (Cohen, 1980, DeYoung, 1988) that ensued. Gypsy tours and motorcycle races became the fodder of media spectacle as early as 1947, beginning with the Fourth of July Gypsy Tour in Hollister, California. While the majority of attendees camped peacefully on the outskirts of town, several "outlaw" clubs, including the Boozefighters and the Pissed Off Bastards of Bloomington partied in the bars and brawled on the main streets of

Hollister. Although several arrests were made (mostly on drunk and disorderly charges), the rally ended without fanfare the next morning when the California State Patrol escorted the more unruly participations out of town. Despite the limited impact, the event took on historic significance when Barney Peterson of the *San Francisco Chronicle* published a staged photograph of a drunk Boozefighter astride a parked Harley Davidson. The rider was recruited from the crowd (the motorcycle didn't actually belong to him), and Peterson littered the street and sidewalk with empty beer bottles for added effect (Nichol, 2007, p. 91; Yates, 1999, p. 17–18). The photo was picked up by the Associated Press and later reprinted full page in *Life* magazine. *Life* reproduced the image with the sensationalistic headline "Cyclist's Holiday: He and Friends Terrorize Town," and a 100 word description saturated with themes of rebel authoritarian. Similar reports were published throughout the 1950s and early 60. Gypsy tours and race events in Riverside, Porterville, and Monterey Beach, California, in Weirs Beach, North Carolina, and in other smaller communities across the United States were used as evidence of the growing threat of rebel authoritarianism in American motorcycling. Each time the media distorted facts, ignored countervailing information, sensationalized headlines and embellished stories in order to make good press (see Nichols, 2007; Reynolds, 2000; Shellow & Roemer, 1966; Thompson, 1967; Wood, 2003; Yates, 1999).

Media sensationalism of the 1950s fueled aggressive police attention that contributed to the further development of public panic over outlaw motorcycling. In 1965 Attorney General Thomas C. Lynch launched a six month investigation of outlaw motorcycle activities in the state of California. "Heavily biased and consistently alarming" (Thompson, 1967, p. 24), the Lynch report included "unsubstantiated absurdities" such as gang rape or the planned takeover of small townships by motorcycle rebels (Dulaney, 2005). Sensationalistic accounts of the Weir's Beach "riots" of 1965 led authorities in Prince George's County Maryland to engage in two months of riot preparations in advance of the Labor Day National Motorcycle Races in Upper Marlboro, Maryland (Shellow & Roemer, 1966). The fear of motorcycle rebels led to a self-fulfilling prophesy in police precincts across the country. Exaggerated reports led authorities to intensify their policing of motorcycle riders and activities (Reynolds, 2000) and fueled ongoing public concern over threat of outlaw motorcycling.

Most importantly, sensationalistic accounts of outlaw motorcycling became fodder for a genre of outlaw biker cinema during the 1960s and 70s. Film producers like Stanley Kramer, Samuel Z. Arkoff and Roger Corman quite literally capitalized on the moral panic sparked by sensationalistic accounts of Hollister, Riverside, Monterey, Laconia, and other notorious motorcycle events of the 1950s and 60s. *The Wild One* (1953), a cinematic interpretation of Frank

Rooney's 1951 *Harper's* magazine account of the Hollister "riots," became the first in a series of often low budget motorcycle films that targeted post-War youth culture (Nichol 2007). The films that followed, including *Motorpsychos* (1965), *The Wild Angels* (1966), *Hells Angels on Wheels* (1967), *Rebel Rousers* (1969), *Cycle Savages* (1969), *Satan's Sadists* (1969), and the iconic *Easy Rider* (1969) popularized the rebel authoritarianism of motorcycle culture. The plot lines and characters of this genre are remarkably similar – a destructive yet romanticized protagonist leads a group of motorcycle outlaws as they rampage some quiet community or terrorize law abiding citizens who run to the aid of rigid and unyielding police officers – yet are tied to every antisocial perversion of the day, including lesbianism and homosexuality, sadomasochism, devil worship, drug use, necrophilia, monsters, space aliens, Nazis, the mafia and virtually every aspect of the occult (Yates, 1999, p. 53)

Interestingly, the economic enclosure of post-War motorcycling turned more on the sale of newspapers, magazines and films than it did on the sale of motorcycles. The media found rebel authoritarianism a potent news theme and used it to enhance their sales. As a latent consequence, they transformed the diegesis of American motorcycling in popular culture. Rebel themes increasingly superseded the conventional, submissive, and middle-class optics of heritage motorcycling. As the atrocity tales of motorcycle mayhem spread, the public responded with fear and outrage. As Thompson (1966) notes, media attention situated the outlaw biker squarely in the public mind, firmly established as the all-American bogeyman (1966, p. 40). Relying upon rebel authoritarianism as a cultural commodity, the media produced and disseminated the outlaw biker diegesis as it worked to sell newspapers, magazines and films.

The moral panic generated by sensationalistic media accounts and the emerging outlaw diegesis was a critical catalyst to the emerging spectator and sponsorship markets of post-War motorcycling. The wide and exaggerated publicity turned outlaw clubs from unknown to well-known and inspired increasing numbers of young men to swell the ranks of outlaw clubs. New outlaw clubs like the Bandidos, Vagos and Warlocks sprung up to absorb the masses drawn to this new American counterculture (Nichol, 2007, Yates 1999). The outlaw biker diegesis also created a self-fulfilling prophecy among existing club members, who began living up to the reputation that had been seeded through the media orgy. The emerging outlaw diegesis gave members a legend to live up to. Thompson argues that the Hell's Angels as they exist today were quite literally "created" by *Time, Newsweek,* and the *New York Times* (1966, p. 36). Media attention gave them a "prima donna complex" that turned them from a "gang of bums" to a social menace with a national reputation to uphold (1966, p. 40–41).

The motorcycle industry initially shunned the outlaw biker diegesis of the post-War era and worked to disassociate itself from the newly emerging spectator markets. Clinging to the ethos of heritage motorcycling, industry leaders feared that the growing anti-establishment reputation of outlaw clubs would erode the marketplace. As early as 1947, Harley Davidson responded to events in Hollister, California with a public relations statement claiming that the vast majority of motorcycle riders were good, clean, God-fearing Americans with jobs and families, and that the "rough" element of motorcycling accounted for only "one percent" of all motorcycle riders. (Nichol, 2007, p. 135). Outlaw club members responded to this disparagement by popularizing the "one percenter" patch as an icon of outlaw motorcycling. By 1954, the collapse of the Indian Motorcycle Company had left Harley Davidson the only remaining motorcycle manufacturer in America. Even so, Harley Davidson continued to ignore the market potential of the emerging outlaw biker diegesis and see its market dominance championed by fighting outlaw motorcycling. The company refused to honor warranties and dealerships refused to service motorcycles that had been chopped or otherwise modified from stock standards (Yates, 1999, p. 33). Harley Davidson retooled its marketing and manufacturing strategies to reflect those of Japanese motorcycle manufacturers that flooded the American marketplace in the 1950s and 1960s. They hoped the establishment advertising themes ("You meet the nicest people on a Honda") would rub off on their own brand, and began producing café style road bikes that emulated the styling of strong selling Asian motorcycles (Nichols, 2007).

Although Harley Davidson toyed with the outlaw diegesis in 1971 when it began production of the "Super Glide" – a stock motorcycle that roughly emulated a chopper – it was not until the early 1980s that it began to exploit the sponsorship potential of the outlaw diegesis. In the interim, the company was acquired by American Machine and Foundry (AMF), whose "cash cow" approach to ownership boosted production while eroding quality. AMF executives had little working knowledge of the motorcycle market and little desire to associate their brand with the outlaw biker diegesis (Yates, 1999). As a result, Harley Davidson's market share dwindled in comparison to their British and Japanese competition and the company approached bankruptcy (Austin, et.al., 2010; Reynolds, 2000, Shembri, 2009).

Harley Davidson stockholders staged a leveraged buyout from AMF in the early 1980s. The company's resurgence during the 1980s was a result a number of variables, including increased federal tariffs on imported motorcycles, the relaxation of admissions standards set during Clinton administration (Yates, 1999), and the development of their more reliable and powerful Porsche designed Evolution engine (Nichol, 2007). Crucial to the rebirth of Harley

Davidson, however, was a marketing strategy that situated the company directly within the outlaw motorcycle diegesis. In 1980, Harley Davidson began production of the FXDB Sturgis model, which associated the company with the Sturgis Motorcycle Rally, the quintessential outlaw motorcycle gathering in the United States. In 1983, they launched the first Harley Owners Group (HOG). HOGs were critical to Harley Davidson's enclosure of outlaw motorcycling. They exploited the intense loyalty and pro-American outlook that outlaw clubs had demonstrated since the 1940s. Akin to earlier AMA membership networks, HOGs allowed Harley Davidson to stay in touch with their base, promote communication, and market itself as the sole remaining motorcycle manufacturer in the United States. As such, HOGs provided a crucial link between spectators, sponsors and the outlaw biker diegesis itself.

The success of Harley Davidson's enclosure of the outlaw motorcycling is remarkable. Though its market share had crashed from 60% to 23% by 1983, Harley boasted nearly 90,000 HOG members and its market share rebounded to 40% by the end of 1987 (Nichol, 2007; Yates, 1999, p. 157; 165). That same year, Harley Davidson led a successful campaign to eliminate the same import tariffs that had lifted it back on its feet in 1981. The publicity stunt mirrored the aggressive, scrappy, against all odds qualities of rebel authoritarianism. As the final coup, Harley Davidson make its first public stock offering in July 1987. Harley executives and loyal HOG members paraded down Wall Street on bikes reflecting the legend of the outlaw biker, escorted by the New York Police Department, who also rode Harleys. The underdog resurgence of Harley Davidson – knocked down by Japanese and British motorcycle manufacturers, further offended by AMF mismanagement, yet struggling back on its feet – mirrored the rugged individualism of rebel authoritarianism and is good evidence that Harley Davidson had situated itself squarely within the outlaw biker diegesis.

In sum, the post-War era was an important point of transition in the authoritarian characteristics and economic circuitry of spectatorship and sponsorship in American motorcycling. Exaggerated media and police attention to clubs outside the sanctioning of the AMA produced a moral panic that was crucial to the development of spectator markets of this period. As the media exploited the rebel authoritarianism of outlaw motorcycle clubs and used it to sell newspapers, magazines and films, they developed a new diegesis in American motorcycling, one that substituted the characteristics of rebel authoritarianism for the orthodox authoritarian characteristics of the heritage era. Although initially feared by industry, this new diegesis became central to the sponsorship markets of the 1980s – especially that of Harley Davidson – as it sought to align its brand with a diegesis that had taken over American motorcycling culture.

Rebel Authoritarianism and the Outlaw Biker Diegesis in Contemporary Motorcycle Culture

Harley Davidson's pioneering work to enclose motorcycle spectatorship and develop its sponsorship markets had a significant impact on the expansion of the outlaw biker diegesis in American motorcycling. Their marketing strategies popularized outlaw biker culture at the same time they commodified it. Less feared than fabled, the outlaw biker diegesis became a legend resonating deeply with a growing proportion of the motorcycle community. Infused with the characteristics of rebel authoritarianism, this diegesis grew to become the leitmotif of contemporary American motorcycle culture, firmly established in the cultural narration of American motorcycling

The ubiquity of the outlaw biker diegesis is perhaps most clearly apparent in contemporary large displacement motorcycle rallying. These events are filled with images and activities that celebrate hostility, aggression, in-group loyalty, and anti-intraception. Virtually all rally merchandize – from t-shirts to shot glasses to body art – is themed with images that connote aggression or destructiveness. Screaming eagles, growling wolves, charging bison, coiled rattlesnakes, skulls, stylized flames, iron crosses, Nazi helmets, barbed wire, and blazing firearms associate a kind of hard, aggressive attitude with motorcycle rallies. Place names like the Knuckle, Full Throttle, Broken Spoke, One-Eyed Jacks or Dirty Harry's suggest an atmosphere of rebellion, danger and riskiness. Activities that celebrate displays of aggression are commonplace, from public cage fighting and bare knuckle boxing matches to roller derby to the "Guns of Freedom" weapons ranges, where spectators "pull the trigger and feel the power" as they shoot military grade weapons at effigies of Saddam Hussein, Osama bin Laden, or other caricatured terrorist figures (Guns of Freedom, 2014). Posted placards openly display widespread NRA sloganeering that vilifies firearm regulations and the Obama administration. "One-percenter" motorcycle clubs typically make their presence public during motorcycle rallies by occupying official club houses in the public areas of rally sites and displaying their insignia and patches on leather jackets and cuts throughout town. Public accounts of past gang fights are common, and local and national news agencies contribute to their legend by highlighting the gang presence and reminding spectators to take care around gang members visible in public.

Large displacement motorcycle rallying also exudes elements of rebel authoritarian submission. Rally organizers regularly stage events that promote an uncritical attitude toward idealized moral authorities. One clear example is the staunch pro-Americanism and the passionate and uncritical celebration of the U.S. military at motorcycle rallies. Aircraft flyovers and military appreciation days are common at the larger rallies in Sturgis, Daytona Beach, and Laconia, and veteran's rides are annual events at most of the smaller rallies. The "American Veterans Traveling Tribute," a scale model replica of the Vietnam Memorial Wall makes an annual stop at the rallies in Sturgis and Daytona Beach. Sturgis' Buffalo Chip Campground proudly earmarks one day of the Rally for its annual "Freedom Celebration," during which past and present members of the military are honored with concerts, public speeches, book signings, and meet and greet opportunities with veterans, pro-military journalists and activists, and government experts on global terror. The event is co-sponsored with the Patriot Guard Riders Motorcycle Club, who travel the country to veteran's funerals in order to "shield the mourning [families] from protest or groups of protestors" (American Veterans Traveling Tribute Memorial Wall, 2013). America flags are sacralized at the Rally and appear within virtually every sightline; on t-shirts, leathers, bandanas and other wearable merchandise, motorcycle saddle bags and gas tanks. A massive American flag flies at the entrance of the Buffalo Chip Campground, beneath which a battlefield cross marks the entrance to their veteran's memorial. Hyper-nationalist slogans including "these colors don't run," "try burn'in this one, asshole," and "America! Love it or leave it" appear throughout the rally. Fanatically conservative musical groups including Ted Nugent, Toby Keith, Lynyrd Skynyrd, Madison Rising (who opened the Buffalo Chip's 2014 "Stand Behind our Heroes" concert with their heavily advertised performance of the Star Spangled Banner) and other lesser known bands are regular performers at rallies across the country.

Many of the activities at contemporary motorcycle rallies reinforce binary group boundaries – especially political boundaries – by celebrating insiders and vilifying outsiders. This is perhaps most obvious in the acclaim given to conservative politicians and policies and the blatant denigration their "liberal" counterparts. To date, no Democratic politician or candidate has made an appearance at a motorcycle rally, though Republican and Tea Party politicians make regular stops. Most famously, John McCain gave a stump speech at the Sturgis Rally prior to the 2008 Presidential election during which he paused for a veterans salute before criticizing Barack Obama for his plans to withdraw US troops from Iraq and his refusal to exploit US oil reserves. To the roar of the crowd, he also implied his wife could serve as both First Lady and Miss Buffalo Chip (the featured winner of the campground's notorious wet t-shirt contest). In 2010, the Tea Party hosted its first annual Freedom Rally in conjunction with Daytona Bike Week. The event celebrated the anniversary of the first Tea Party protests in Washington DC, and was organized in an effort to "recharge the movement" against President Obama's bailout plan and other "massive spending measures" (Schilling, 2010). In 2011, Ted Nugent vilified

"Japs," "Canadians," and the "French" for being "weak" and got a near sold-out audience at the Full Throttle Saloon to give President Obama the finger. The pop band "Liquid Blue" decided to remove the "Obama 2012" decals from its tour bus after receiving verbal insults and physical threats prior to their 2012 Sturgis debut (Sanford, 2012). The Young Obama Haters regularly set up vendor stands at motorcycle rallies and other motorsports venues, where they draw crowds by shouting "Obama Sucks!" through megaphones and hock "Deport Barack *Hussein* Obama" and "My country, my future" t-shirts that proudly display the United States superimposed by two crossed flintlock rifles. Members of numerous conservative and evangelical Christian motorcycle clubs work the rally circuit converting lost souls and encouraging appropriate behavior.

Finally, the diegesis of contemporary motorcycle rallies exhibit evidence of authoritarian anti-intraception. First defined by Henry Alexander Murray as the avoidance of "an imaginative, subjective human outlook or Romantic action" (Murray, [1938]2008, p. 148), anti-intraception involves inability or unwillingness to be intersubjective or empathetic. The outlaw biker diegesis includes an egocentric tenor that celebrates individualism and limits responsiveness to others. T-shirts that read "I can't hear you over the roar of my freedom," "my other toy has tits," "I'd rather see my sister in a whorehouse than my brother on a Honda," or "if you can read this, the bitch fell off" suggest a distaste or at least skewed perspective on intersubjectivity and empathy. Motorsports spectacles condense the sensations of noise and vibration into a diegesis that blocks opportunities for shared experience. Multiple city block lines of tandem V-twin motorcycles roar their way through town, a visual and auditory mass-ornament (Kracauer, 1975) that reduces all to a coagulated mass. Concert spectators roar their engines in "throttle applause" as a sign of approval and appreciation. Spectators find themselves amidst amorphous sexualized pulsations: greased midget bowling, jello-wrestling, pickle-licking contests, burnout pits, automatic-weapons trials, mechanical bull-riding and the ceaseless, disoriented milling of carnivalesque bodies as an indistinct conglomerate of oppressive, grotesque yet enticing sensations.

The Outlaw Biker Diegesis and the Economy of Dark Spectacle

The rapid evolution of the outlaw biker diegesis has been critical to the growth of spectator, sponsorship and trophy markets in American motorcycling. By the 1990s, motorcycle event coordinators and many American motorcycle manufacturers had come to rely on the outlaw diegesis for marketing and promotion. Unlike heritage or even early rebel cyclists, the spectators of the 1980s and 90s were less bonded by cross-cutting social ties or a deeply-shared sense of community. Increasingly, they shared little more than a desire to purchase access to a spectacular diegesis replete with industry and media-disseminated images of outlaw biker counter-culture. Event coordinators monetized their desire through the production and expansion of the outlaw diegesis to ever more diverse settings, experiences, and products (Krier & Swart, 2014a).

We conceptualize events organized around this kind of authoritarian diegesis as "dark spectacle;" a hybrid form of "dark tourism" (Lennon & Foley, 2000) in which spectators immerse themselves in a commodified environment themed with authoritarian and destructive motifs. Much of the literature on dark tourism lacks a specific authoritarian framing. For example, all of the conceptualizations of dark tourism in Seaton's (1996) typology focus on travel to specific sites or memorials/museums that allow for "actual or symbolic encounters with death" (1996, p.15) rather than the actual immersion in a dark diegesis. While Stone's (2006) "dark tourism spectrum" theorizes that "lighter" forms of dark tourism may have a contrived, commercialized quality (see also Seaton, 1999), and the emphasis on suffering, death rituals, morbid products, and thanatotic imagery (Stone, 2006) closely aligns with Erich Fromm's (1973) theorization of malignant aggression, the dark tourism literature is generally devoid of references to the more general authoritarian characteristics discussed above or the diegetic and mimetic qualities of motorsports spectacles and spectators.

Dark spectacle, especially as evidenced within contemporary large displacement motorcycle events, serve as a form of form of perfomative tourism (McCannell, 1976; Edensor, 2001), where spectators come to play, perform, see and be seen within an authoritarian themed environment. As they load authoritarian images onto products and infuse authoritarian themes into experiences, dark spectacles turn authoritarianism into a cultural commodity to be bought and sold within the spectator markets of the economy of spectacle. The diegesis of dark spectacles and mimesis through which spectators organize their activities at these events are thus the result of an economic circuit that provides an opportunity for participation without the necessity of real authoritarian personality characteristics.

The work of Erving Goffman (1967) helps explain the centrality of dark spectacle to the growth of spectator markets in contemporary American motorcycling. Goffman argues that "action" occurs when a person voluntarily assumes risk in a chancy situation, especially one that is critical to an individual's social reputation. Often this occurs through *"ephemeral ennoblement"* – temporarily occupying settings above our normal boundaries of prestige and status. Yet our study of dark spectacle demonstrates the opposite – that action may also be found in occupying settings below one's station. Thus, while ephemeral ennoblement produces action by improving social character through "*fancy milling*" (Goffman, 1967, p. 197), we argue that *ephemeral debasement* produces action through *"degraded milling"* as people temporarily abandon middle-class norms and simulate potentially disreputable identity characteristics (Krier & Swart, 2014a). Ephemeral debasement attracts new markets of spectators as performative tourists who find action in the diegesis of dark spectacle. As Goffman (1967) notes, action requires social recognition. Ephemeral ennoblement or debasement done in secret does nothing to prove character beyond the individual ego, thus the value of action resides in its display. As sites of dark spectacle, contemporary motorcycle rallies provide popular locations for such display to occur. They serve as stages where riders risk character by performing in scenes steeped in rebel authoritarianism.

Motorcycle industry and event coordinators have successfully exploited the outlaw biker diegesis and the dark spectacle of motorcycle rallies to expand contemporary spectator markets. Rally attendance across the country grew dramatically with the exploitation of the outlaw biker diegesis. For example, between 1965 and 1985 attendance at the Sturgis Motorcycle Rally grew at an annualized rate of 295%, and by 2000 boasted an attendance of 633,000 spectators. During this time the Rally was officially lengthened from two to seven days, although the residual crowds at Rallys since 2000 arguably make it a 10 day event (Krier & Swart, 2014a). Recognizing the profit potential of growing spectatorship, the Daytona Beach Convention and Visitors Bureau created a second motorcycle rally in 1991. Since then, "Biketoberfest" has served as an off-season supplement the spectatorship markets realized during the long standing Daytona Bike Week.

Spectator markets have seen an especially dramatic growth in upper-middle class riders and event participants, who increasingly turn to dark spectacle for leisure. Since 1983, the annual income of the average Harley Davidson owner has increased from $37,000 to $67,000 (Yates 1999; see also Thompson, 2009, 2012; Austin, Gagne, & Orend, 2010). Upper-middle class suburban outlaws have also become the primary demographic at large displacement motorcycle rallies across the country (Galahan, 2010). Thus, while the habitus of the lower and working classes may best fit the outlaw biker diegesis, it is the well-off, white collar professional who now figures most prominently in the spectator markets of American motorcycling. RUB's ("Rich Urban Bikers") – whose desk jobs, airbag equipped minivans, and banal family activities generally lack opportunities for "action" yet whose incomes afford opportunities for high cost equipment, apparel, and leisure time – have turned to the dark spectacles of motorcycle riding and rallying as a way to consume prepackaged action that simultaneously tests and displays character. As Freud (1955) argued, the purpose of festivals is to recapture that which has been given up in pursuit of the ego ideal. In this sense, upper-middle class spectators use dark spectacle and their mimesis of the outlaw within it to replace their first life prohibitions. Freed from the constraints and impositions of everyday life, consumers of dark spectacle experience a "magnificent festival of the ego" (Freud, [1921]2010, p. 8401; see also Bakhtin, 1968, Krier & Swart, 2012, and Langman & Ryan, 2009).

Sponsorship markets exploded as the motorcycle industry and event coordinators capitalized on increasing levels of spectatorship. The Sturgis Motorcycle Rally, which had relatively small scale economy through the 1970s, experienced massive economic growth as city officials and Rally organizers capitalized on the growing crowds of Rally participants. In 1979 the City of Sturgis began granting temporary vendor licenses. Although initial growth was small (less than 120 vendor licenses were requested in 1985), sponsorship markets swelled to nearly 1000 over the next fifteen years. Paying to "be seen," temporary vendors, official sponsors, and motorcycle manufacturers themselves associated their products with the outlaw diegesis of American motorcycle rallying. A host of cross marketing licensing agreements among companies such as Ford, Jack Daniels, Sony, Budweiser, Coca-Cola link their brands to the outlaw biker diegesis, and in some cases one another. In an attempt to commodify anti-intraception, Harley Davidson has worked since the early 1990s to trademark its exclusive exhaust sound, and in 2013, Harley-Davidson cross-marketed country-rock artist Kid Rock's famous lyric "I can't hear you over the rumble of my freedom" and used it to market the company's 110th anniversary. The integration of vendors and corporate sponsorship with the outlaw biker diegesis has had a significant impact on the profitability of the Sturgis Rally. Taxable revenues grew from $150,000 in 1965 to over $3,000,000 in 1985, and in the fifteen years that followed, Rally annual profits exceeded $14,000,000, increasing at an annualized rate of over 26% (Krier & Swart, 2014a).

In recent years, the drive to expand spectator and sponsor markets has also stretched the boundaries or in some cases directly negated the outlaw biker diegesis of motorcycle rallies. Much outlaw club activity has become legal and commercial rather than rebellious and violent. Clubs like the Hells Angels make millions of dollars selling trademarked apparel, and violence is intentionally avoided in settings like Sturgis and Daytona in order to protect profit streams (Kovaleski, 2013). Soft and adult rock bands like Boston, Loverboy, and Journey play alongside groups that express more fanatical right-wing lyrics; Train, a band whose lyrics can hardly be interpreted as fascist or authoritarian, headlined the 2014 Buffalo Chip concert series. Local church and community pancake breakfasts, chili suppers, and other folksy "pop odom" events gather the same groups annually for camping or reunions and mirror the "rotary club" ethos of heritage motorcycling. An increasing diversity of "off brand" products (Bayer Aspirin, Geico Insurance, Lakota Foods, South Dakota Pork) co-mingle with those that play upon themes more central to the outlaw/rebel diegesis (Jack Daniels, Harley Davidson, Old Smokey Moonshine, Sons of Anarchy). Angieland Exotic Dancers (a regular feature at the Full Throttle Saloon) donates a portion of their annual Sturgis proceeds to an animal rescue aimed at reducing the number of rescue kill facilities in the US. Charity rides that raise money for organizations including Toys for Tots, Muscular Dystrophy, or the Boys and Girls Clubs have become important events for local motorcycle clubs. While these sponsors, products and promotions expand spectatorship to more conventional people, their "progressive decontextualization" (Krier & Swart, 2014a) of spectator markets threatens dark spectacle and its rebel diegesis. Hell's Angels food stands, Gieco insurance stalls, and twelve foot high inflatable Bayer aspirin advertisements stretch thin or in some cases openly negate outlaw themes. They appear absurd and contradictory as they circulate within the diegesis of dark spectacle, and threaten the profit potential that has to this point been realized by the sponsorship markets of American motorcycling.

Finally, while there is evidence of very limited trophy markets in heritage motorcycling (motorcycle manufacturers and the AMA often provided souvenir items such as pins, watch fobs or belt buckles to gypsy tour participants), trophy markets have become one of the most profitable circuits in contemporary economies of spectacle. Trophies are crucial to the social recognition of action and ephemeral debasement. Echoing Veblen ([1899] 1934; see also Cassano, 2009; 2013), the psychic life of consumers of dark spectacle is energized by the imagined or realized envy of others. This invidiousness takes three forms. "Status trophies" generate envy by signaling superior status and prestige to others. "Action trophies" generate envy by revealing one's willingness to risk character or immerse oneself in ephemeral debasement. "Trophies of *jouissance*" generate envy by displaying one's participation in scenes of enjoyment or debauchery not available to others (see Krier & Swart, 2014b for a thorough discussion of the envy dynamics of motorsports trophies). The trophy markets of American motorcycling provide opportunities for spectators to gather evidence of their participation in dark spectacle and display it to others for the purpose of status, action, and *jouissance*. Apparel emblazoned with the trademarked logos of motorcycle companies or events imply superior levels of wealth and leisure time. T-shirts suggesting the dark diegetic themes of large displacement motorcycle culture prove action and ephemeral debasement to those outside the immediate temporal or geographic setting. Digital photography – enhanced in the past decade by the personalization of mobile technologies and their connection to social media outlets – allow evidence of status, action and *jouis-sance* to be instantaneously transferred to those not *in situ*.

Although relatively limited in heritage motorcycling and virtually non-existent during the post-War era, trophy markets have exploded in contemporary motorcycling as one of the more important sources of industry revenue. Rally cities have optimized their built environments to support the trophy industry. Parking lots are cordoned off to accommodate vendor stalls, pushing parking to city streets and local access roads. City sidewalks have been built with wide setbacks in order to make space for temporary vendor stalls and still leave room for pedestrian traffic. Leases for commercial property in downtown Sturgis require that they be vacated for the month of August so that they can be converted into more valuable retail space. Major clubs, restaurants and bars sublease merchandising stalls in front of and inside of their buildings, stacking vendor upon vendor in order to maximize retail space. As a result, trophy markets appear to upstage the rally itself; the vast sea of vendor stalls and crowds of milling shoppers suggest that hunt for trophies has become the primary activity at motorcycle rallies (Krier & Swart, 2014b).

The active and rather obvious "stage-managing" of opportunities for photographic trophy collection has also become critical to the trophy markets of contemporary motorcycling. Event coordinators cover over the all-too-apparent lack of rebel authoritarianism "in the wild" with staged events that maintain the fantasy of dark spectacle. Scantily-dressed, tattooed, or body painted waitresses and barmaids double as subjects for trophy-photography. Cage-fighting matches, motorcycle "burn outs," and pickle-licking contests are meticulously scheduled and publicized so as not to interfere with other events and draw the largest crowds of spectators possible. Manufacturer exhibits encourage attendees to photograph themselves astride heavily modified and outrageously expensive designer motorcycles. In one instance, bodyguards escorted women to and from an open-air bar, where they rode a mechanical bull modified into a penis as a contrived photo-op for gathering crowds. When questioned, attendees we interviewed regularly displaced "authentic" scenes of dark spectacle – it was never here and now, but always someplace else at some other time. Often they willingly shared photographic evidence from their smart phones. We do not believe that this resulted from our consistent inability to be in the right place at the right time, but rather evidence of participant's desire to maintain the fantasy of dark spectacle and preserve the value of the trophies they had collected. The fact that many of these events were staged demonstrates the importance of maintaining of the outlaw biker diegesis to the profitability of dark spectacle. Trophies not only preserve the outlaw diegesis, but in doing so, fuel the growth of spectatorship markets.

When missing in reality, contrived opportunities to display action and ephemeral debasement and extract the envy of others are crucial to spectator's desire for immersion in dark spectacle.

In sum, the outlaw biker diegesis has become central to the cultural narration of American motorcycling since the 1980s; its' dark spectacle a crucial resource to the development of modern spectator, sponsor, and trophy markets. The diegesis and its profitability expanded as sponsors tied increasingly diverse events, products and services to the rebellious and authoritarian themes of outlaw motorcycling. Spectators flocked to engage in performative tourism centered in action and ephemeral debasement, as well as collect trophies that could be consumed for invidious social recognition. Authoritarian images and narratives thus remain central to the economic circuitry of American motorcycling and its ongoing enclosure by the motorcycle industry.

Conclusion

This paper has explored the role of authoritarianism in the economic enclosure of American motorcycling. Our first order reading provided evidence of the orthodox authoritarian ethos and structure of heritage motorcycling and the transition to rebel authoritarianism in post-War motorcycle culture. Our second order analysis examined the role of this authoritarian culture and structure in the economic enclosure of American motorcycling. Authoritarian structures of submission and control allowed the AMA to build networks of riders during the early and mid-twentieth century. These networks fueled early spectator and sponsorship markets by tying motorcycle enthusiasts, clubs, and their spontaneous events to the motorcycle industry. Although the rise of rebel authoritarianism in post-War motorcycling was initially feared, the motorcycle industry, especially Harley Davidson, eventually embraced rebel themes and coopted them into a marketing strategy centered on an outlaw biker diegesis. This diegesis provides the framework for dark spectacle – economic markets and performative tourism centered in the tropes of rebel authoritarianism of outlaw motorcycling. By 1990, the spectator, sponsorship, and trophy markets built upon this diegesis became the dominant circuits of the American motorcycle economy.

Debordian (1988) readings of spectacle suggest that they serve a dangerous ideological function – one that ingests all opportunities for democratic participation while reinforcing conservative and authoritarian mindsets. Similarly, much of the literature on authoritarianism would imply that those who would be drawn to situations of dark spectacle possess "real" authoritarian character structures. Our research shows that the authoritarian diegesis of dark spectacle serves an equally important economic function. This diegesis certainly *may* play a role in bringing out nascent authoritarianism or attracting spectators with already developed authoritarian personalities, but that argument lies beyond the scope of this paper. What our data suggest is that the authoritarian ethos and organizational structures of American motorcycling were crucial to its economic enclosure and the continued profitability of its spectator, sponsorship and trophy markets.

Our study also suggests that while any megaspectacle has the potential for massing and the development of authoritarianism, economic circuits of spectatorship and sponsorship may serve to diffuse this potential. In late capitalism – a period of the near-total commodification of spectacle – this negating quality is even more pronounced. Markets erode *real* authoritarian tendencies by focusing psychic energy on the consumption of products rather than a conscious connection to a leader or ego-ideal. Like the Freudian father, economic structures (taxes, fees, licenses, permits, trade-marking, charging for bathrooms, channeling bodies through or between vendor stalls, restaurants, bars, concerts or other attractions) impose an order that disrupts pure massing and thus the potential for fascism to emerge. This is particularly evident at contemporary motorcycle events. Sponsorship circuits have expanded to include a diversity of products and services that are antithetical to authoritarianism. As motorcycle spectatorship circuits erupted, myriad regulations and structures were put in place that eroded the potential for massing (see Hall, 2002 for similar evidence in the history of NASCAR). City regulations for traffic control, camping, alcohol consumption, and parking; the regulations against public nudity; the permitting and licensing of temporary vendors, increased policing and even admission fees (which limit spectatorship to those who can afford to pay) reduce the potential for the mass psychology of fascism to emerge.

As a result, dark spectacle becomes a "rally without rallying;" an event whose purpose is not to assemble people to reconstitute and realign them with an overarching authoritarian identity but to consume a diegesis that is themed in ways that support the ongoing revenue generated from spectators, sponsors and trophy markets. In fact, much of the real authoritarianism at motorcycle events has been pushed to the fringes; marginalized from the commodified event and pushed out to locations exempt from the economic circuits of dark spectacle. For those who remain, dark spectacle serves as deep play that allows them a temporary escape from the Protestant ethic and the extraction of envy from those without the resources to attend. In this sense, authoritarianism is central to the economy of American motorsports.

Acknowledgements

The authors are grateful for the insightful comments, criticisms, and suggestions of Kevin Amidon, Graham Cassano, Tony Feldman, Christian Lotz, Patrick Murray, Susan Schrader, David Smith, Tony Smith, Harry Thompson, and Mark P. Worrell. In addition, they wish to thank the College of Liberal Arts & Sciences, Iowa State University for its sponsorship of the 3rd Biennial Symposium on New Directions in Critical Theory and Augustana College for the support of the Augustana College Artist and Research Fund (ARAF).

References

About Motor Maids. (2013). Motor Maids Incorporated. Available at http://www .motormaids.org/AboutUs/AboutMotorMaids.aspx.

Adorno, T.W., Frenkel-Brunswik, E., Levinson, D., & Sanford, R. (1950) *The authoritarian personality.* New York, NY: Harper & Brothers.

Altemeyer, B. (1981). *Right wing authoritarianism.* Winnipeg, MB, Canada: The University of Manitoba Press.

———, (1988). *Enemies of freedom: Understanding right wing authoritarianism.* San Francisco, CA: Jossey-Bass Publishers

American Veterans Traveling Tribute Memorial Wall at the Buffalo Chip was erected with the help of active duty service men and the Patriot Guard Riders. (2013). Available at http://www.buffalochip.com/EVENTS/Military-Tributes/Veterans-Memorial-Wall

Austin, D.M., Gagne, P. and Orend, A. (2010). Commodification and popular imagery of the biker in American culture. *Journal of Popular Culture,* 45(5): 942–963.

Bakhtin, M.M. (1968). *Rabelais and his world.* Bloomington, IN: Indiana University Press.

Barger, R., Zimmerman, K., & Zimmerman, K. (2000). *Hell's angel: The life and times of Sonny Barger and the Hell's Angels Motorcycle Club.* New York: HarperCollins.

Best, S. & Kellner, D. (1997). *The postmodern turn.* New York, NY: The Guilford Press.

Cassano, G. (2009). Symbolic exploitation and the social dialectic of desire. *Critical Sociology,* 35 (3) 379–393.

———, (2013). Working class self fashioning in 'Swing Time.' *Critical Sociology* sagepub. co.uk/journalsPermissions.nav. DOI: 10.1177/0896920512444636.

Cohen, S. (1980). *Folk devils and moral panics: The creation of the mods and the rockers. 2nd edition.* New York, NY: St. Martin's Press.

Cova, B. & Cova, V. (2002). Tribal marketing: the tribalisation of society and its impact on the conduct of marketing. *European Journal of Marketing* 36(5/6): 595–620.

Cova, B., Kozinets, R., & Shankar, A. (2012). *Consumer tribes.* New York, NY: Routledge.

Date for National Gipsy Tours. (1917). *Motorcycle Illustrated.* 25 January. Available at https://books.google.com/books?id=46kAAAAAMAAJ&printsec=frontcover&auth user=0&source=gbs_ge_summary_r&cad=0#v=onepage&q=Gipsy&f=false.

Debord, G. (1988). *Comments on the society of the spectacle.* London: Verso.

DeYoug, M. (1988). Another look at moral panics: the case of satanic day care centers. *Deviant Behavior* 19(3): 257–278.

Donehue, J. (1917). M&ATA Bureau of window displays needed. *Motorcycle and Bicycle Illustrated* June 7.

Dulaney, W.L. (2005). A brief history of "outlaw" motorcycle clubs. *International Journal of Motorcycle Studies.* Available at http://ijms.nova.edu/November2005/IJMS _Artcl.Dulaney.html

Edensor, T. (2001). Performing tourism, staging tourism: (Re)producing tourist space and practice. *Tourist Studies* 1(1): 59–81.

Freud, S. ([1921]2010). Group psychology and the analysis of the ego. pp. 8280–8427 in Smith, I. (ed.). *Freud – Complete Works.* Available at http://www.valas.fr/IMG/pdf/ Freud_Complete_Works.pdf

Fromm, E. (1973). *The Anatomy of Human Destructiveness.* New York, Holt, Rinehart and Winston.

Galahan, K. (2010). 00s: a new century. *Rapid City Journal*, August 10. Available at: http://rapidcityjournal.com/news/local/state-andregional/article_91958fcc-9d3f-11df-ab9d-001cc4c03286.html.

Goffman, E. (1967). *Interaction ritual: Essays on face-to-face behavior.* New York, NY: Anchor Books.

Grundy, Grandpa (1919) "What's wrong with American Motorcycling." *Motorcycling and Bicycling* July 2. Available at https://books.google.com/books?id=4gI9AAAA YAAJ&pg=RA1-PA25&lpg=RA1-PA25&dq=grandpa+grundy&source=bl&ots=v_qou-NNJX&sig=JkZhaMNAiIs8xymtU2r301PJhSk&hl=en&sa=X&ei=8xz5VLvmO4Hsgw SyioC4AQ&ved=0CDwQ6AEwBw#v=onepage&q=grandpa%20grundy&f=false

Guns of Freedom: The ultimate 2nd amendment experience. (2014). Available at http://gunsoffreedom.com/.

Gypsy Tour promotion plans. (1917). *Motorcycle Illustrated.* 15 March. Available at https://books.google.com/books?id=46kAAAAAMAAJ&printsec=frontcover&auth user=0&source=gbs_ge_summary_r&cad=0#v=onepage&q=Gipsy&f=false.

Hall, R.L. (2002). Before NASCAR: The corporate and civic promotion of automobile racing in the American South, 1903–1927. *The Journal of Southern History* 68(3): 629–668.

Harley Davidson Dealers Conference. (1947). Available at the Harley Davidson Museum, Milwaukee, WI.

Hayes, B. & Quattlebaum, J. (2010). *The original wild ones: Tales of the Boozefighters Motorcycle Club.* Minneapolis, MN: Motorbooks.

History of Laconia. (n.d.) Available at (http://www.weirsbeach.com/Largejpgs/bikeweekguidecovers.html).

Horkheimer, M. & Adorno, T.W. ([1944]1972). *Dialectic of enlightenment.* Trans. Cumming J. New York: Herder and Herder.

Kellner, D. (1995). *Media culture: Cultural studies, identity and politics between the modern and the postmodern.* London: Routledge.

Klinger, B. (1997). The road to dystopia: Landscaping the nation in Easy Rider. pp. 170–203 in Cohan, S. & Hark, I.R. (eds). *The road movie book.* New York: Routledge.

Kovaleski, S.F. (2013). Despite outlaw heritage, Hells Angel's sue often. *New York Times.* Available at http://www.cnbc.com/id/101235239.

König, W. (2004). Adolf Hitler vs. Henry Ford: The Volkswagen, the role of America as a model, and the failure of a Nazi consumer society. *German Studies Review, 27*(2), 249–268.

Kracauer, S. (1975). The Mass Ornament. *New German Critique* (5), 67–76.

Krier, D. & Swart, W.J. (2012). The dialectics of carnival: From Bakhtin to Baudrillard. In: Braun, J. & Langman, L. (eds.). *Alienation and the Carnivalization of Society.* New York, NY: Routledge, 133–165.

———, (2014a). The commodification of spectacle: spectators, sponsors and the outlaw biker diegesis at Sturgis. *Critical Sociology* 0896920514524605.

———, (2014b). Trophies of Surplus Enjoyment. *Critical Sociology,* 0896920514528819.

———, (2015). How legends become brands: The Culture Industry in the Second Enclosure Movement. *Current Perspectives in Social Theory,* Vol. 33.

Langmann, L. & Ryan, M. (2009). Capitalism and the carnival character: The escape from reality. *Critical Sociology 35*(4): 471–492.

Lennon, J. & Foley, M. (2000). *Dark tourism: The attraction of death and disaster.* London: Continuum.

MacCannell, D. (1976). *The tourist: A new theory of the leisure class.* New York: Schocken Books.

Morton, J. (1999). Biker Movies. pp. 55–66 in Sargeant, J. & Watson, S. (eds.). *Lost highways: An illustrated history of road movies.* New York: Creation Books.

MotorMaids.(2014).Wikipedia.Availableathttp://en.wikipedia.org/wiki/Motor_Maids.

Murray, H.A. ([1938]2008). *Explorations in personality.* New York, NY: Oxford University Press.

Newman, J.I. & Giardina, M.D. (2008). NASCAR and the "Southernization" of America: Spectatorship, subjectivity, and the confederation of identity. *Cultural Studies↔ Critical Methodologies, 8*(4), 479–506.

———, (2010). Neoliberalism's last lap? NASCAR nation and the cultural politics of sport. *American Behavioral Scientist, 53*(10), 1511–1529.

———, (2011). *Sport, spectacle, and NASCAR Nation: Consumption and the cultural politics of neoliberalism.* New York, NY: Palgrave Macmillan.

Nichols, D. (2007). *One percenter: The legend of the outlaw biker.* Minneapolis, MN: Motor Books International.

Reynolds, T. (2000). *Wild ride: How outlaw motorcycle myth conquered America.* New York, NY: TV Books, Inc.

Sanford, J.A. (2012). Liquid Blue battles bikers at Sturgis, Playing Democratic Nat'l Convention. *San Diego Reader.* Available at http://www.sandiegoreader.com/weblogs/jam-session/2012/aug/15/liquid-blue-battles-bikers-at-sturgis-playing-demo/#.

Schembri, S. (2009). Reframing brand experience: The experiential meaning of Harley–Davidson. *Journal of Business Research,* 62(12), 1299–1310.

Schilling, C. (2010). Tea Party weekend: Daytona Bike Week Freedom Rally ready to rock. *The other McCain.* Available at http://theothermccain.com/2010/02/26/tea-party-daytona-bike-week-freedom-rally/.

Schouten, J.W. & McAlexander, J.H. (1993). Market impact of a consumption subculture: the Harley-Davidson mystique. *European Advances in Consumer Research,* 1(1): 389–393.

———, (1995). Subcultures of consumption: an ethnography of the new bikers. *Journal of Consumer Research* 1(1): 43–61.

Seaton, A.V. (1996). Guided by the dark: From thanatopsis to thanatourism. *International Journal of Heritage Studies,* 2(4), 234–244.

———, (1999). War and thantourism: Waterloo 1815–1914. *Annals of Tourism Research,* 26, 130–158.

Shellow, R. & Roemer, D.V. (1966). The riot that didn't happen. *Social Problems,* 14(2), 221–233.

Stone, P. (2006). A dark tourism spectrum: Towards a typology of death and macabre related tourist sites, attractions and exhibitions. *Tourism: An Interdisciplinary International Journal, 54*(2), 145–160.

The Enthusiast. (1939). Milwaukee, WI: Harley-Davidson Corporation.

The History of the AMA. (2013). American Motorcycle Association. Available at: http://www.americanmotorcyclist.com/about/history.

The Manless Tour at Last! (1917). *Motorcycle and Bicycle Illustrated.* New York: Trade Journal Corporation.

The Viewpoint of the Reader. (1919). *Motorcycling and Bicycling.* July 16. Available at https://books.google.com/books?id=4gI9AAAAYAAJ&pg=RA1-PA25&lpg=RA1-PA25&dq=grandpa+grundy&source=bl&ots=v_qou-NNJX&sig=JkZhaMNAiIs8xymtU2r301PJhSk&hl=en&sa=X&ei=8xz5VLvmO4HsgwSyioC4AQ&ved=0CDwQ6AEwBw#v=onepage&q=grandpa%20grundy&f=false

Thompson, H.S. (1967). *Hell's Angels: A strange and terrible saga.* New York: Ballentine.

Thompson, W.E. (2009). Pseudo-deviance and the "new biker" subculture: Hogs, blogs, leathers, and lattes. *Deviant Behavior, 30*(1), 89–114.

————, (2012). *Hogs, blogs, leathers and lattes: The sociology of modern American motorcycling.* Jefferson, NC: McFarland.

Veblen, T.B. (1934 [1899]). *The theory of the leisure class: An economic study of institutions.* New York, NY: Modern Library Press.

Von Saldern, A. (1992). Cultural conflicts, popular mass culture, and the question of Nazi success: The Eilenrieder Motorcycle Races, 1924–1939. *German Studies Review,* 15(2), 317–228.

Wood, J. (2003). Hell's Angels and the illusion of the counterculture. *The Journal of Popular Culture,* 37, 336– 51.

Wooster, K. (2010). '40s: Heck of a good time. *Rapid City Journal,* August 10. Available at: http://rapidcityjournal.com/news/local/state-andregional/article_91958fcc-9d3f-11df-ab9d-001cc4c03286.html.

Yates, B. (1999). *Outlaw machine: Harley-Davidson and the search for the American soul.* New York: Little, Brown and Company.

Index

absence   160, 181, 193, 195, 197

abstraction   3, 48, 104, 107, 114, 115, 121, 127, 138, 169
   applicable   126
   bad   121

abstract labor   34, 46, 48, 123
   congealed   129, 130

academia   18, 19

account
   sensationalistic   260
   structural   222, 223
   systematic Marxian   94
   systematic Marxist   115

Ackerman   72, 74, 87, 92

actuality   106, 133, 169

Adam Smith's theory   225

Addams, Jane   239, 240

Adorno   16, 20, 26, 58, 64, 99, 104–5, 112, 113, 160, 175, 215, 242, 245, 249, 255

agents   67, 70, 73, 75, 79, 82, 83, 86, 96, 98, 99, 105, 106, 190, 193
   social   71, 81, 103, 105, 112

aggression   187, 203, 245, 249, 251, 257, 258, 264

alienation   1, 3, 5, 6, 23–24, 84, 122, 139, 140, 153, 162, 177, 213, 214, 276

Alstott   72, 92

Altemeyer   20, 21, 45, 58, 64, 242, 245, 249, 251, 274

altruism   164, 172, 177

AMA   247–49, 252, 253, 254, 255, 257, 263, 270, 272, 277

ambivalence   21, 37, 207, 249, 251, 258

America   64, 146, 148, 159, 164, 217, 235, 241, 244, 247, 250, 262, 276

American
   capitalism   230
   Journal of Sociology   216, 217
   motorcycle culture   242, 254
   motorcycling   242, 244, 245–47, 250, 252, 253, 254, 259, 260, 261, 263, 264, 266, 272, 273
   contemporary   243, 267
   economic enclosure of   6, 242, 272
   trophy markets of   243, 270

   Motorcyclists   247, 248, 252
   Philosophical Society   215
   society   152, 221, 251
   society and sociology   175
   sociology   223–24

Americans   17, 57, 62, 235, 243

Amidon   45, 150, 154, 155

Amidon and Krier   3, 140, 144, 146, 148, 150, 152, 154, 156

amused contempt   234, 235

analysis
   economic   102, 219
   foregoing   172
   overlook Marx's   102

anamorphosis   165

anguish   199, 200, 212

animalization   99

animus   192

antagonisms   103, 107

Antek   187, 195, 196, 197, 199, 201, 204, 206, 207, 208, 211, 213

anti-bank politics   12, 37, 38, 40

anti-capital   149

anti-capitalism   42

anti-Masonry   40

anti-Semitism   12, 16, 17, 18, 38–40, 42, 59, 60, 63, 156, 256

apparatus
   coercive   70
   theoretical   219

apparatuses   142, 145

appearance forms   129, 130, 131

approbation   223, 226, 227, 231, 237

appropriation   74, 86, 87, 119, 149

Arendt   27, 28, 29, 57, 59, 64, 221, 239–40

Aristotle   120, 135, 138, 171

ascetic Protestantism   148

Asch   18–19, 59, 64

Asia   50, 62, 64

assets   124, 144
   financial   78, 91, 128

assumptions   15, 44, 74, 95, 105, 106, 107, 108

asymmetry, extreme   73, 81, 83

Atlantic Highlands   94, 114, 136, 137

attitudes   13, 20, 245

attractions   273, 276, 277
Auerbach   182, 215
austerity   44, 45, 52, 94
authoritarian
    aggression   245, 249
    character   179, 272
    culture   251, 272
    families   178
    personality   12, 16, 17, 18, 19, 21, 26, 27,
        58–59, 179, 188, 215, 245, 255, 274
    structures   243
authoritarianism   1–2, 11, 12, 13, 17, 18, 20, 26,
        27, 44, 242, 243, 245, 251, 273
    right wing   274
    right-wing   20, 58
    study of   18, 19
authoritarians   2, 5, 19, 21, 27, 29, 45, 58, 181,
        214, 243, 245, 267, 269
Authorities/Authority fetishism
        Commodities/Commodity   12
authority   21, 22, 23, 24, 25, 26, 27, 30, 31–32,
        46, 63, 245, 247, 258, 260
    fetishism   1, 12, 13, 14, 17, 20, 22, 24, 25, 28,
        30, 63
    figures   198, 245, 248, 258
    final   246, 247
    political   76, 245
    structures   247, 251
    symbolic   198
    traditional   12, 22, 23, 24, 27, 197
automobile   247–48, 251
autonomy   71, 76, 99, 101, 102, 142, 145, 169
Autumn   184, 195, 196, 202, 203, 204, 207,
        208, 209
Aydelotte   182–83, 215

background conditions   74, 78, 80, 83, 85, 86
    proper   68, 72, 73
Backhaus   114, 123, 136, 137
Backhaus's criticism of Marx's dialectical
    development   130
Badiou   95, 96, 97, 98, 99, 100, 101, 103, 108,
        112, 113, 114, 139, 142
Badiou's reduction of capital   98
Balzac   215
bankers   36, 37, 38, 39, 40, 42, 52, 76
banks   39, 43, 52
barbarism   2, 26, 44
bargaining power   73, 81, 82, 83

basic income   81, 83, 84
Basic Psychotic Features of Peasant Social
    Character   202
Basingstoke   136, 137
behavior
    anti-social   249, 256, 257
    normative   223, 228, 229
Beiser   165, 167, 171, 175
belief   30, 31, 33, 37, 47, 202, 207, 217, 227, 245
Bentham   129
Bidet/Kouvelakis   100, 103, 112
bifurcation   80, 81, 83, 84, 86, 88, 135
bikers   274, 277
Binet   32, 59, 64
Bismarck   150, 151, 153
Bismarckian Welfare State   150, 151, 153
blackness   222, 234
blame   8, 37, 38, 196
blame finance capital   37
Blessed Virgin   202
Blum   180, 183, 184, 187, 188, 215
bodies   30, 60, 99, 102, 133, 199, 212, 213, 224,
        248, 251, 252, 253, 271
    people's   188
Bonilla-Silva   220, 222, 234, 240
Boozefighters   256, 259, 276
Boryna   186, 197–98, 204, 205, 207
Boryna family   187
boundaries   28, 118, 208, 212, 256, 258, 269
    normative   239
bourgeois
    horizon   135
    society   124, 130, 175
        modern   134
    subjectivity   184
    subjects   153, 214
branches   98, 146, 147, 246, 258
brands   262, 263, 269, 276
breathe   199, 200, 205
brothers   189, 190, 257, 266
bubbles   91, 93, 130, 144, 165
Buch   61
bureaucracy   153, 154
business   41, 43, 54, 230, 231, 252
buyers   34, 35, 128, 129

Calvinism   3, 147, 148
Campbell   62, 123, 126, 135, 136, 137
capacity   71, 75, 76, 77, 82, 89, 126, 163, 192, 236

capital   1–5, 35, 52–53, 61, 70, 76–77, 83, 87,
        88, 90, 92, 106, 118–37, 139, 140
    accumulation   37, 42, 76, 77, 83, 87, 89, 91,
        92, 124, 126
    accumulation process   77
    assets   74
    beast   92
    fetishism idealize   37
    cheap   62
    circuit   78
    circulation of   133–34
    constant   57
    critiqued   139
    culmination of   62, 137
    cultural   229
    damn   52
    dark   144, 149
    delineating   124
    development   3, 144
    discursive effects of   133, 135, 136
    fact   30
    fetish   46
    fetishists   37
    fictitious   93
    financial   144
    first volume of   76, 137
    flight   90
    form   80, 85
    GE   43, 53
    the good of   68, 75
    goods   52
    hardens   125
    holders of   75, 86
    human   120, 145
    intellectual   120
    logic of   85, 105
    long term interest of   70–71, 76, 80
    meta-productive   52
    natural   121
    parent companies transfer   45
    particular factions of   70, 75
    personified   53
    personifies   52
    political   120, 253
    pooled   153
    positions   99
    productive   52
    raffende   39
    rapacious   39
    relation   106
    representatives of   75, 80, 81, 83, 84
    social theory proclaiming   75
    taxing   45
    their   85
    theorize   7
    theory of   8, 122
    units of   81, 85
    universal   139
    values   90
    variable   57, 58, 131
    volumes of   125, 126
    vulture   40
capital fetishism   12, 35, 37, 39, 40, 41, 42, 58
    fusing   38
capital fetishism and anti-bank politics   12
capital fetishism and anti-Semitism   12, 38,
        39, 40
Capital for descriptions of commodities   166
capital-form   108
Capital in Marx's *Capital*   136
capital investments, previous   90
capital market mechanisms, recent   144
capital ownership   74
    dispersing   74, 87
Capital Shapes   3, 116, 124, 126, 134
capital shapes climate   125
Capital shapes space and time   124
capitalism   1–2, 7, 25–27, 36–37, 40–45, 48–51,
        68, 75, 94, 98, 108–11, 139, 140–41, 143, 149
    21st-century   63
    analysis of   110, 141
    contemporary   2, 143, 155
    corporate   68
    criticizing   37
    deindustrialized   243
    development of   111, 140
    emergence of   141, 149
    existing   102
    global   64, 93, 139
    history of   3, 41
    incorporating   71
    late   166, 273
    lock   36
    managerial   159
    mature   243
    modern   118, 184
    naturalization of   139
    origin of   94, 111

capitalism (cont.)
   pecuniary   230
   placed   3
   political defining   86, 88
   positivist accounts of   108
   predate   134
   preserving   2
   probe   58
   productive   51
   prospers   11
   push   77
   speculative   3
   spirit of   3, 63, 64, 140, 146, 148, 149, 152,
     153, 156
   story of   57, 103
   stumbles   42, 58
   treating   142
   welfare   154
   welfare-state   150
   capitalism wobbles   11, 25
Capitalism and Critical Social Theory   6
capitalism with a human face   89
capitalism's astounding flexibility   77
Capitalism's destiny   33
Capitalism's diversity   154
capitalist
   agriculture   131
   basis   117, 118, 123, 134
   class   69, 70
   countries   89
   crisis and anti-Semitism   12
   culture   241
   development   77, 87, 140, 146, 185
     stimulate   76
   development tend   76
   dynamics   141
   economy   39, 73, 80, 85, 93, 152
   Enlightenment boomerangs   128
   entrepreneurs   130
   expansion   91
   firms   84
   history   76
   homo oeconomicus   139
   logic   103
   market societies   68, 69, 71, 72, 77, 80, 89
     push   81
   market societies matters   78
   modernity   118, 134, 178
   modernization   177

   nature   81
   order   126
   practice   146, 149, 150
   production process   35, 36
   rationality   91
   regimes   68
   relations   102
   schema   114
   schematization   114
   sociality   111
   society   3, 6, 79, 80, 81, 82, 105, 110, 111, 116,
     117, 118, 129, 134, 135
     modern   118
   society shadow forms   133
   spirit   14, 26, 147
   subjectivity   3, 139, 140, 142
   totality   112
   valorization interests   105
   welfare state   68
   workplaces   86
   world market   69
Capitalist Accumulation   140
capitalistic   153
capitalists   35, 36, 37, 41, 42, 52, 53, 54, 55, 79,
   80, 81, 122, 123, 132
   large   132
   particular   70
   unproductive   37
Capital's apologists   92
capital/wage labor relation   2, 67, 68, 71, 72,
   75, 81, 82, 88
capital/wage labor relationship   2, 74, 79, 81,
   82, 84, 88, 92
captive audience   243, 253, 254
Carnivalization of Society   276
carnivals   211, 212, 244, 276
Cassano   56, 220, 222, 224, 226, 228, 229, 230,
   232, 234, 236, 238, 239–40, 270, 274
Cassirer   162, 163, 175
catastrophe   3, 116
categories   4, 23, 73, 74, 89, 91, 98, 106, 110, 111,
   125, 126, 127, 163, 171
   internal   103
   social   102, 108, 186
character armor   178
characters   178, 180, 183, 184, 186, 188, 194,
   200, 203, 207, 209, 210, 217, 221, 226
   double   120
   fetish   46, 124, 127

charisma   1, 25, 26, 27, 63, 155, 161
charismatic   2, 23, 25, 26, 27
    authority   12, 24, 25, 26, 27, 28
    dictators   28
Chayanov   181, 215
Chestohova   183, 185, 200, 201, 202
China   26, 41, 42, 51, 52, 53, 56, 64, 90
Chinese   13
Chinese state   52, 53
Christian soul   208, 209
church   186, 198, 199, 205
citizens   67, 70, 84, 222
city   56, 150
Civil War   40, 61, 237, 238
Clarke   62, 117, 118, 136
class consciousness   14
classes   69, 70, 78, 79, 96, 97, 99, 103, 105, 106,
    163, 228, 231, 232, 236
    showing   256
    working   14, 15, 16, 17, 55, 62, 100, 148, 153,
    268
classical Ricardian theory   46, 122
classical social theory   177, 180, 189
class relationships   78–79
Clemens   113
club members   247, 257, 259
clubs   210, 244, 246, 247, 252, 257, 259, 263,
    269, 271, 272
    local   246, 247
    outlaw   259, 261, 262, 263
coalitions   70
coat   31, 33–35, 47, 48
codetermination   73
coercion   71, 72, 73, 74, 81, 86, 87, 222
Cohen   62, 119, 136, 259, 275
Collected Works   93, 137
colonialism   57, 61
colors   221, 257
column   13
command   25, 30, 127, 181
command people   25
commodification   132, 274, 276
commodities   13, 29, 30–35, 46, 47, 48, 49, 78,
    82, 117, 118, 122, 123, 127–31, 165–66
    cultural   243, 255, 261, 267
    world of   13, 29, 33, 47, 127, 128
commodities column   13, 32
commodity
    capital   123

complex form   129
chains   41
circulation, simple   127, 128, 133–34
exchange   124, 127, 128, 129
    sphere of   129
fetishism   2, 12, 29, 32, 33, 35, 37, 46, 49,
    63, 102, 177
form   6, 118, 123, 127, 128, 129, 131, 132
producers   30
production   7, 37, 51, 126
    generalized   82, 88, 134
relations   13, 46, 47
society   48
world   1, 13, 30
Commune, Paris   38, 39, 54, 61
communication, primary   225
communism   98, 99, 113
communities   73, 83, 84, 145, 147, 215, 216,
    227, 230, 237, 240, 260, 267
company   55, 204, 240, 262, 263, 269, 278
    joint-stock   224
compensation   130, 150, 214
complicity   28
comprehension   109, 110, 173
concept   15, 16, 23, 27, 96, 101, 103, 104, 106,
    109, 110, 111, 121, 142, 174
    capital   121
    central   97, 106
conception   108, 120, 121, 160, 163
    historical materialist   118
conceptualism   163
conceptualization   150, 245, 267
conceptualize   101, 244, 246
concerts   145, 151, 265, 273
conditions   112, 113, 120, 143, 145, 149, 211, 215,
    221, 223, 228, 230, 234, 235, 238
conflicts   96, 102, 105, 194, 231
    normative   105
    social   105, 106, 231
congruent   144, 145, 214
connection   11, 14, 26, 32, 36, 44, 125, 127, 160,
    168, 221, 271
consciousness   1, 16, 36, 162, 221, 224
    collective   161, 165, 177, 182, 206
    critical   235
    double   220, 233, 235, 236, 239
    false   36
    working-class   15
consent   5, 22, 82, 219, 232

consequences   39, 40, 50, 67, 87, 106, 119, 121,
        123, 135, 141, 147
    economic   221
    real   132
conspicuous consumption   227, 230, 232, 237
conspiracy theory   38, 39, 40
Constitution of Capital   137
constraints, given   77, 78
construction   28, 52, 126, 189, 190, 239
    social   47, 63, 165, 220, 221
constructionism   163, 165, 166
consultation   84, 85
consumer demand   56
Consumer Research   277
consumption   12, 52, 89, 181, 227, 244, 252,
        253, 273, 277
context   5, 26, 72, 73, 85, 89, 148, 219, 220,
        221, 224
continents   40, 41, 202
contingency   13, 70
Continuum   21, 60, 113, 175, 276
contradictions   98, 109, 111, 119, 168, 173, 233,
        239
control   54, 70, 80, 83, 86, 100, 103, 127, 182,
        194, 272
    capital   52, 75, 83, 86
    money capital   78
conventicle   147, 148
conventionalism   245, 246, 254
conventionality   6, 242, 249, 251
Cooley   5, 219, 223, 224–27, 233, 234, 235, 240
corporations   43, 45, 53, 54, 78, 141, 253
cost   4, 85, 87, 232, 237
country   18, 40, 41, 42, 50, 53, 55, 144, 223,
        260, 265, 268
    capitalistically-backward   181
courtesy   236, 237
Cova   243, 275
credit cards   51
crisis   2, 11, 12, 41, 42, 50, 63, 93, 124, 145,
        149, 155
    climate   49
    cultural   233, 238
    fetishism Capitalist   12
    overaccumulation   89, 90, 91
Critical Interpretations   114, 136, 137
Critical Pragmatism's Status Wage   5, 219,
        221, 223, 225, 227, 229, 231, 233, 235, 237,
        239, 241

critical
    social theory   1, 6, 11, 160, 176, 213, 215
    theorists   67, 95, 139, 180
    theory   1–3, 5, 7, 8, 9, 11, 12, 15, 58, 60, 63,
        109, 111, 155, 239
        classical   5, 105
    theory of society   99, 106, 109
critics   4, 63, 79, 140, 155, 165
critique   7, 8, 12, 13, 24, 25, 49, 63, 92, 109, 110,
        112, 139, 140, 238
    authentic Marxist   15
    critique capitalist   2
    fundamental Marxist   2
critique of political economy   2, 7, 12, 13, 32,
        36, 48, 61, 65, 95, 110, 111, 125, 136, 176
critique of political psychology   4, 12, 13, 14,
        58, 157
crowds   205, 225, 260, 265, 266, 271
Cultural values   7, 74
culture   114, 209, 224, 246, 255
curses   188, 198, 205, 206, 209, 213, 214
custodian   52
cyclists   244, 251

Daniels, Jack   269, 270
dark spectacle   242, 243, 244, 245, 247, 249,
        251, 253, 255, 257, 259, 265, 266, 267,
        268–73
    fantasy of   271
dark tourism   267, 276
daughter   192, 210
Davidson, Harley   248, 252, 254, 257, 262,
        263–64, 269, 270, 272, 276
Daytona Beach   265
death   48, 120, 170, 183, 198, 200, 205, 211, 213,
        267, 276, 277
debasement, ephemeral   268, 270, 272
debt   90, 219, 223, 226
Deegan   239, 240
deficit   56
Deleuzian poetry of capital   102
delusions   83, 86, 189, 192, 206, 207
democracy   15, 17, 20, 62, 94, 100, 101, 113, 115,
        178, 230
democratic   19, 20, 24, 71, 74
    accountability   69, 84
    societies   74
Desai   89, 90, 93
destruction   50, 90, 91, 94, 196, 200

deutsche Genossenschaftsrecht 60
devaluation 90, 91, 124
development 6, 7, 111, 125, 126, 145, 159, 160, 252, 253, 254, 262, 263, 272, 273
    economic 80, 111
    free 67
deviance 234
devotion 170, 193, 201
DeYoung 259
dialogue 12, 117, 119, 134, 240
Dicks 17–18, 59, 64
dictatorships 25, 27
diegesis 243, 255, 259, 261, 263, 264, 266, 267, 272, 273
diegesis of dark spectacle 267, 268, 270
difference 21, 31, 78, 79, 103, 105, 110, 118, 164, 221
dimensions 31, 57, 75, 90, 163, 167
direction 64, 112, 132, 215, 253
direction Marx 14
Directors 73
discipline 7, 117, 141, 142, 150, 164, 189, 219, 256
discourses 96, 107, 135, 141, 143, 209, 210
discursive effects, capital's 131, 134
display 166, 189, 203, 243, 264, 266, 268, 270
distance, social 223
distribution 20, 72, 85, 102, 117
division 14, 130, 198, 231, 235
dogs 195, 202, 205, 209, 210
dollars 33, 35, 42, 51, 54, 57, 92, 269
domination 5, 22, 23–24, 71–74, 77, 78, 84, 85, 86, 87, 88, 219, 220, 235, 236
    experience of 236
doubt 207, 208, 209, 214, 221, 238
Dover 175, 176
downturn 44, 90
dress 223, 225, 240, 248, 256, 257
drivers 148, 248, 250, 251
Du Bois 5, 6, 219, 220, 221, 223, 226, 228, 230, 233, 234, 235, 236, 237, 238–40
Dugger 229, 240
Durkheim, Emile 4, 6, 26, 63, 64, 159, 160, 161, 162, 163, 164–77, 181, 182, 215, 222–24
Durkheimian 165, 212
    Sociology 161, 164, 172
Durkheim's
    characterizations of social facts 166
    conception 159

critique of idealism 4, 159, 166
critique of social self-destructiveness 161
sociology 4, 160, 161, 162
Suicide 166, 176
theory 222
work 159, 175
dynamic process 220
dynamics 18, 27, 59, 93, 125, 141, 142, 143, 145, 223, 226, 229, 234
dynamism, technological 91, 92

economic
    circuits 267, 273
    situation 237
the economic, illusion of 135
economics 3, 11, 43, 93, 98, 117, 118, 119, 123, 124, 126, 134, 136, 138, 141
    mainstream 118, 135
    neoclassical 117, 121
economism 69, 70, 71, 74, 76, 77, 79
economy 44, 69, 71, 76, 77, 79, 80, 136, 174, 243, 244, 254, 255, 266, 267
    global 52, 62, 89, 91
Economy and society 64, 152, 156, 218
economy-in-general 135, 136
egalitarian capitalism 92
egalitarian society 128
egalitarianism 98, 133, 134
ego 168, 169, 170, 212, 216, 269, 275
egoism 164, 166, 167, 168, 169, 172
    unity of 166, 167
egoism-altruism 164
Eleanor Smith's Hull House Songs 240
Elliott 113
emancipation 180, 215
embodiment 149, 187, 193, 204
emergence 11, 18, 37, 91, 103, 140, 142, 143, 145, 159
    capitalism's 149
    historical 76, 142
Emerson 224, 226, 240
empire 93, 94, 113
empirical data 98
empiricism 4, 161, 163, 166, 174
employment 72, 73, 81, 82, 83, 84, 86, 90, 92, 93, 144
emulation 229
enclosure 187, 252, 254, 255, 272
    economic 6, 243, 244, 252, 254, 261, 273

Encumbered Subject   3, 139, 141, 143, 145, 147, 149, 151, 153, 155
Engels   2, 14, 26, 40, 44, 54, 60, 61, 64, 93, 114, 119, 134, 137
English-speaking world   184, 186
enjoyment   102, 189, 190, 212, 270
Enquête Ouvrière   12, 13, 14, 62
enterprise   14, 36, 86, 121, 144, 167
entrance   265
envy   187, 188, 196, 202, 203–4, 270, 272, 273
ephemeral ennoblement   267–68
Epicureanism   166, 167
equality   17, 20, 21, 58, 72, 93, 97, 128, 129, 134
    social   128
equilibrium   160
equivalence   31, 33, 34, 48, 104
    relationship of   33, 34
Erster Band   61
essence   17, 36, 37, 108, 110, 111–12, 129, 229
essentialism   49, 57, 58
estrangement   220, 233, 236, 239
ethics   93, 96, 102, 104, 105, 106, 107, 108, 176, 217
    economic   147, 148, 150, 152
ethnicity   16, 58, 239
Eurocrisis   85
Europe   40, 51, 52, 56, 67, 148, 180, 181, 182, 217
European
    capitals   89
    Jews   236
    peasantry   183, 215
events   97, 100, 242–44, 246, 247, 251, 252, 253, 254, 264, 265, 267, 268, 270, 271
    club   246
    motorsports   244
evidence   19, 24, 223, 233, 242, 243, 251, 255, 258, 260, 266, 270, 271, 272, 273
evil eye   203, 204
excess   89, 90, 145, 259
exchange   30, 31, 32, 33, 34, 35, 43, 47–48, 104, 129, 140, 143, 222, 223, 234
exchange-value   107, 118, 126, 130
exchangers   127, 128
experiment   18, 19, 217
exploit   74, 262, 265
exploitation   68, 71–74, 86–88, 142, 186, 229, 237, 239, 268
    process Marx calls   36
    rate of   85, 90, 91

exports   52
expropriation   44, 45, 79

factions
    dominant   69
    particular   70, 75
factories   37, 43, 53, 76, 178, 179
factors, complicating   78
family   60, 124, 178, 184, 186, 194, 197, 202, 217, 244, 262, 265
fantasies   144, 192, 207, 213
    people's   229
farmers   44, 205, 222
farms   44, 51, 198, 211
fascism   1, 11, 15, 17, 18, 57, 177, 178, 188, 217, 273
Fast Capitalism   176
fatalism   166, 167, 168, 172, 177
fathers   185, 188, 189, 190, 193–99, 201, 211
    dead   190
    primal   189, 190
    real   190, 191
fear   2, 26, 173, 179, 193, 195, 196, 197, 202, 204, 209, 213, 260, 261
Feldmann   178, 180, 182, 184, 186, 188, 190, 192, 194, 196, 198, 200, 202, 204, 206
Feltham   113
fetishes   30, 31, 46, 124, 127
fetishism   13, 28, 29, 30, 31, 32, 33, 35, 36, 47, 48, 49, 50, 57, 58
fetishist, ardent capital   37
fetishistic ways   46, 47
fetishized people   2
fiction   6, 182–83, 215
films   6, 261, 263
finance   29, 39, 41, 56, 143, 150, 230
finance capital   39, 148, 149, 152
    speculative   8, 93, 153
financial markets   149, 150, 152
financialization   40, 41, 51, 91
finitude   96, 108, 109, 110
Fink   189, 191, 194, 209, 212, 215
firms   89, 91, 92, 141
    foreign   45
First World War   154, 230
floating   56
focus   11, 17, 42, 70, 103, 123, 139, 141, 143–47, 179, 180, 188, 243
folk   198, 203, 204, 206, 209, 210

folk sayings   210
followers   1, 25, 26
food   44, 50, 87, 208, 211
forces   53, 103, 139, 159, 160, 164, 207, 238
    active   161
forecasting   144
foreign trade   124, 125
formation   80, 83, 131, 178
forms
    capitalist   131, 154
    constitutive   125, 126, 134
    definite   119
    national   141
    revenue   130
forthcoming   63–64, 89, 92, 94, 238, 239, 240
Foucault   142, 143, 155
foundations   4, 22, 95, 107, 116
Fowkes   61, 137, 176
France   4, 38, 39, 40, 54, 61, 155
Frankfurt   16, 62, 63
Frankfurt School   1–2, 7, 15, 16, 17, 64, 95, 106
freedom   58, 60, 129, 142, 145, 149, 152, 155,
        175, 249, 250, 264, 266, 274, 275
    individual   152
freemasons   39
Freud   32, 58, 60, 64, 178, 179, 182, 189, 190,
        193, 194, 214, 215–16, 269, 275
Fromm   15, 16, 17, 20, 49, 58, 60, 64, 176, 178,
        179, 201, 203, 215, 216
function   25, 68, 97, 105, 193, 196–97, 214,
        231, 233
funds   50, 83, 87

gaze   5, 165, 212, 213, 223, 224, 226, 227, 234
GDP, global   49
Geertz   180, 216
Geist   156, 160, 164, 165
gender   49, 57, 58, 60, 239
    relations   49
General Economic History   147, 149, 153,
        156, 218
General Law of Capitalist Accumulation   140
generalization   13, 123, 128, 129
generations   14, 23, 24, 28, 96, 173
genesis   106, 108, 109, 110
genre   186, 260, 261
German
    Lutherans   186, 187, 205
    social policy   151

Society for Race Hygiene   149
Germans   19, 62, 205
Germany   14, 17, 37, 38, 52, 58, 62, 89, 151, 155,
        175, 256
Gerth   64, 141, 148, 156
Geschichte   113, 114
gesellschaftlichen Seins   114
Ghosh   146, 147, 148, 149, 155
Gierke   12, 23, 24, 60, 64
Gilman   239, 240
Glencoe   59, 64, 215
global crisis of capitalism   50
globalization   41, 62, 90, 93, 115, 140, 142
globe   41, 43, 90, 91
God   195, 209, 211
Goffman   177, 196, 216, 267, 268
Golden Dawn   11, 44
goods   55, 71, 73, 87, 119, 121, 123, 127, 179, 203
gossip   179, 202, 203, 204, 210
government bonds   45, 50
governments   45, 54, 55, 59, 73, 100, 231
Graham   56, 57
Gramsci   51, 76, 181, 216
grants   83, 86, 87
gravity   123–24
Great Depression   41, 50, 55
Great Recession   12, 40, 41, 44, 51, 85, 144
Greece   11, 41, 44
ground   153, 203, 205, 240
groups   13, 16, 17, 37, 149, 151, 178, 181, 203, 204,
        205, 220, 261, 265, 269–70
growth   51, 89, 91, 126, 253, 266, 267, 268, 271
Grundrisse   107, 114, 124, 125, 126, 136, 137
gypsies   187, 205
Gypsy tours   244, 259, 260

Habermas   95, 105, 109, 180
Halbband   114
Halle   150
Halls   114, 155, 175–76, 273, 275
hallucinations   185, 188, 192, 206, 207, 208
Hamburg   61
Hampshire   137
Hamsun   183
Hanka   187, 200, 201, 208, 213
Harcourt   59, 62, 240
Hardt   113, 114
Harley   262, 263
Harmon   89, 90, 93

Harmondsworth   137

hate   195, 203, 206, 207, 208

heart   4, 77, 166, 199, 201, 212, 234

heavens   199, 200, 201

Hegel   31, 32, 109, 124, 135, 136, 137, 159, 160,
        169, 170, 173, 174, 176, 223

Hegelian   4, 105, 160, 165

Heidelberg   14, 146

Hell's Angels   244, 256, 258, 259, 261, 270, 278

Herder   276

heritage motorcycling   242, 244, 246, 249,
        251, 252, 253, 254, 255, 257, 259, 261, 270,
        271, 272

    culture of   248, 249, 251

    economic enclosure of   251, 252

    orthodox authoritarianism of   243, 255

Herrnhut community   147, 148

high RWA scorers   21

Historical levels   41, 97

history   15, 46, 47, 111, 112, 113, 136, 139, 140, 141,
        142, 176, 242, 243, 244

Hitler   15, 25, 26, 242

Hocart   23, 60, 64

Hogarth   216

hogs   263, 278

hole   192, 195, 197, 199, 207

Hollister   259–62

Holt   155, 216, 275

homes   55, 56, 128, 173, 211

Honneth   68, 93, 95, 104, 105, 106, 107, 108,
        109, 114

Honneth's claim   107

honor   153, 186, 188, 231, 232, 257

horizons   120, 135

Horkheimer   15, 60, 63, 64, 154, 180, 276

households   50, 184

Hudson   87, 93

human self-understanding   119

huts   204, 209

hypocrisies   193, 196, 197

idealism   4, 102, 159, 161, 162, 165, 166, 167,
        169, 170, 171–72, 176

    speculative   160, 170

    transcendental   161, 167, 168, 169

idealism of Kant   168, 170

idealists   163, 172, 174, 193

ideation   48, 170

identification   5, 193, 219, 222, 229, 232,
        236

identity   28, 32, 34, 48, 96, 161, 169, 192, 209,
        220, 221, 248, 276

    national   230, 231

    white   221, 237, 238

ideology   28–29, 59, 113, 155, 165, 178, 228

idling workers   41

illusion   30, 79, 129, 131, 135, 137, 166, 173, 197,
        222, 231, 278

images   30, 100, 202, 244, 248, 249, 253, 260,
        264

imaginary   68, 84, 191, 195, 197, 198, 200

    capitalist utopian   68, 69

imagination   23, 42, 159, 166, 170, 224, 226,
        228, 229

inability   78, 202, 209, 266

incomes

    disposable   87

    psychic   230, 231, 232

incongruity, quantitative   130

inconsistencies   139, 193, 195, 196

increment of repute   229, 237

individual

    capitalists act   149

    surplus-values   131

individualism, normative   67, 68

individuality   164, 166, 176, 224

individuals   46, 47, 74, 75, 119, 120, 141, 142,
        143, 151, 152, 159, 162, 164, 171

    capital-holding   144

industrial capitalism   189

    modern   141

industrial investment, rate of   54, 55

industrialists   36, 37

industry   36, 41, 42, 50, 53, 54, 55, 91, 230, 232,
        243, 252, 253, 263, 267

    leaders   252, 253, 262

inequality   55, 58, 72, 90, 107, 232, 239

Infinite thought   113

inquiry   16, 18, 28, 178, 214, 216

    drive Marx's   135

instances   21, 32, 42, 80, 207, 208

Institute for Social Research   15, 60, 64

institutions   103, 144, 145, 149, 150, 152, 278

instruments   69, 87, 143, 144, 160, 173, 174

intelligence   173

interaction   111, 164, 208, 222, 223, 227, 238

interests   36, 52, 69, 70, 76, 83, 85, 86, 99, 100,
        227, 228, 230, 231, 232
    undivided   231
    vested   231, 232, 241, 256
International Publishers   93, 136, 137, 155, 176
interviews   17, 101, 114, 244
investment   35, 37, 41, 42, 43, 53, 57, 72, 87,
        90, 153, 237
    rate of   89, 90
    capital   53, 86
    capital grants   80
Investment Firm   43
investments, expanded   83
investors   37, 41, 51, 53, 55, 73, 86
irony   7, 24, 170, 174
Italians   56–57
    southern   56–57

Jacobs   225, 233, 234, 240
Jameson   155, 182, 215, 216
Jesus   199, 208
Jews   17, 29, 38, 39–40, 42, 62, 63, 205
jobs   42, 43, 44, 45, 50, 51, 54, 56, 93, 144, 185,
        262
Jorgensen   230, 241
jouissance   191, 211–12, 214, 270, 271
    flooding of   212
Joyce   191, 215, 217
Jubilee   240
judgments   59, 110, 170, 173, 195
justice   2, 73, 94, 105, 203

Kalecki   87, 93
Kant   4, 110, 142, 167, 168, 169, 170, 224
Kantianism   168, 169
Kapital   61, 113, 114
Karl Marx's theory   136
Kegan Paul   216, 217
Kellner   243, 274, 276
king   12, 23, 30, 31, 46, 60, 162
knowledge   14, 70, 142, 143, 172, 173, 179, 181, 207
Kouvelakis   95, 113, 114
Krier, Daniel   1–6, 8, 91, 93, 139–40, 142, 144,
        146, 148–50, 154–56, 177, 229, 242, 276
Krier & Swart   243, 267, 268, 269, 270, 271
Krier & Feldmann   178, 180, 182, 184, 186, 188,
        190, 192, 194, 196, 198, 200, 202, 204, 206
Kritik   61, 114, 115

Krzyzanowski   185, 216
Kuba   187, 198, 207, 208

labor   14, 46, 83, 102, 115, 117, 122, 123, 127, 128,
        130, 132, 140, 149, 181
    commodity-producing   123
    concrete   34, 48, 118
    free   149
    markets   71, 73, 81, 82, 83, 86, 87, 88, 90
    organizations   89
    power   37, 55, 57, 71, 78, 81, 82, 86, 127, 140
    power capitalism   82
    producing   127
    productive   139
    processes   1, 37, 44, 71, 73–74, 84, 86, 87,
        88, 89, 90, 118, 126, 131
    products   1, 30–31, 33, 34, 46, 47, 48, 58,
        108, 127, 128, 130
    theory
        classical   131
        classical Ricardian   122
    unproductive   131
    valorized   95, 108, 110
    wage   71, 82, 122, 186
labor-power   35, 130
laborers, non-productive   131
Lacan   8, 180, 189–94, 200, 207, 213–17
Lacanianism   165, 166, 197
    model of Western peasant
    subjectivity   213
Laclau   95, 96, 97, 100, 103, 108, 109, 112, 114
Lady of Chestohova   183, 200, 201
land   35, 44, 50, 56, 121, 142, 164, 195, 197, 201,
        202, 204
landed property   125
landlords   36, 37, 52
language   27, 64, 153, 162, 176, 189, 190, 192,
        196, 197, 209, 213, 214, 217, 221
law   24, 25, 93, 99, 124, 129, 189, 190, 193, 194,
        196, 197, 213, 214, 249
    international   124
    social insurance   151
leaders   1, 25, 27, 28, 29, 38, 53, 197, 256, 273
leather jackets   256, 257, 264
Left Liberalism   2, 67, 69, 71, 73, 74, 75, 77, 79,
        81, 83, 85, 87, 89, 91
Left Thatcherism   3, 95, 96, 97, 99, 101, 103,
        105, 107, 109, 111, 113, 115

legal-rational authority   23, 24
legend   258, 261, 263, 264, 276, 277
legitimacy   248, 251, 253
leisure class   226, 227, 228, 229, 233, 241,
     276, 278
lenders   36, 37, 45, 130
Lenin   25, 61, 64, 115
Levenstein   14, 61, 64
Leviné   15, 61, 64
liberal-capitalist thought   142
liberal egalitarian theorists   68–69, 83, 86, 87
liberal egalitarianism   67, 68, 69, 88, 92, 94
     core thesis of   71, 81, 84, 86, 87, 88
liberal egalitarians   68, 71, 72, 73, 74, 88, 89
liberals, left   72, 73, 75, 86, 90
liberties, civil   20
life   38, 40, 99, 101–2, 118, 119–22, 134, 135, 170,
     187, 188, 207, 228, 229, 230
     psychic   207, 270
     religious   4, 26, 56, 59, 175, 182, 215
limitations   2, 174, 238, 239
linen   31, 33, 34, 47, 48
     yards of   31, 33, 34, 47
Lipka   181, 186, 187, 199, 200, 201, 202, 203,
     205, 209, 211, 212
     peasants in   198, 205, 206
loans   45, 56
Lódź   183, 185, 186
logic   23, 97, 111, 115, 152, 166, 175
     inner   110
looking glass self   5, 219, 225, 226, 227, 234,
     235
lords   77, 127, 197, 204, 210, 215
Lotz   96, 97, 98, 100, 102, 104, 106, 108, 110,
     112, 114
love   32, 60, 97, 100, 102, 192, 195, 207, 208,
     210, 212, 265
loyalty   231, 256
Luchterhand   114
Lukács   7, 61, 64, 97, 111, 114, 155, 183, 184, 217

Maccoby   179, 194, 201, 203, 210, 216
machinofacture   77
MacIntyre   116, 136
Madonna   201, 202
magazines   250, 253, 255, 259, 261, 263
magnitudes   127
mana   26, 161–62
managers   53, 56, 73, 84, 85, 86

Marchart   97, 114
marketing   6, 243, 252, 253, 262, 266, 275
marketing strategies   263, 264, 272
markets   41, 43, 73, 74, 138, 140, 144, 145, 243,
     252, 253, 262, 263, 274, 277
market share   263
Marx   119, 120, 125, 127, 128, 129, 133, 134
     idea   168
Marx, Karl   60, 62, 95, 113, 116, 139, 224
Marx, mature   161, 162, 165
Marx & Engels   64, 67
Marxheimian Sociology   160, 175
Marxianism   98, 109, 111
     basis for analyzing society   106
     conception of capital   122
     concept of critique   109
     Critique   88, 105, 110
     framework   111
     par-lance   71
     Social Ontology   3, 95
     theory   55, 75, 95, 134, 137
     renewed   119
     theory of capitalist society   118
     value theory   119
Marxism   4, 7, 94, 97, 98, 101, 115, 155, 176, 221,
     239, 240
     contemporary   113
Marxism and ecological economics   136
Marxschen Ökonomiekritik   114
mask   193, 197
masons   39, 40
mass conformity   246
masses   28, 96, 99, 178, 214, 261
massing   273
master signifier   166, 197, 209
masters   77, 180, 191, 194, 195, 197
materialism   4, 161, 166, 167, 170, 171, 172
     historical   4, 7, 118, 119, 137, 163, 166
materialist   161, 174
materiality   161, 187–88
matrix   12, 13, 15, 32, 103
Matthias   187
Mauss   176, 239, 241
McDonaldization of society   138
McNally   89, 91, 93
mechanics, quantum   168, 169
media   6, 260, 261, 263
media attention   259, 261
Meissner   61

members   69, 70, 71, 72, 73, 84, 85, 107, 224,
    227, 228, 246, 247, 252, 259
membership   221, 246, 252, 253, 254, 259
membership networks   252, 253, 254
membership structure   254, 255
memories   25, 186, 202
mercy   34, 200, 201, 212, 213
metaphors   162, 209, 220, 224
Mexican Village   179, 203, 216
middle   20, 21, 28, 102, 150, 244, 252
middle managers   53
Milgram   18, 19, 59, 62, 64
military   153, 246, 248, 264, 265
Mills   29, 62, 64, 148, 156, 174, 182, 215
Mills & Schneider   64
mimesis   186, 215, 267, 269
mind   126, 135, 163, 164, 165, 168, 169, 170, 200,
    206, 212, 213, 224, 225, 226
    idolatry of   4, 159, 161, 163, 165, 167, 169,
       171, 173, 175
misery   167, 168, 178
mistook Marx   117
misunderstood   18, 119, 123, 257
model   8, 94, 105, 141, 160, 189, 213, 214, 247,
    276
modernity   6, 93, 145, 177, 180, 189, 191,
    197, 209
moments   25, 42, 76, 150, 154, 166, 169, 208,
    212, 238
money   32, 33, 34–37, 39, 43, 45, 47, 50, 104,
    114, 121, 123, 124, 130, 136
money capital   78, 79, 86
    initial   78
money fetishism   12, 33
    appearance Marx calls   35
money/price/profit   131
money surplus   36
monstrosities   160
moral discourse, modern   116
moral panics   259, 260, 261, 263, 275
Moral Sentiments   223, 224, 226, 241
Moseley   62, 64, 114, 136, 137
mother   60, 187, 188, 191, 192–93, 195, 200,
    201, 225
motives   27, 179
motorcycle   89, 245, 246, 247, 248, 249, 250,
    251–54, 256, 260, 261, 268, 271, 275
    clubs   247, 248, 252, 254, 255, 258, 276
    competition   246, 247

culture
    heritage   243, 244, 245, 246, 249, 250,
       254, 255, 258
    post-War   6, 255, 258, 272
    enthusiasts   244, 248, 250, 251, 252, 253,
       254, 259
    events   246, 253, 273
       contemporary   267, 273
    industry   6, 243, 251, 252, 253, 254, 255,
       259, 262, 269, 272
    industry and event coordinators   268,
       269
    manufacturers   262, 263, 269, 270
    rallies   264, 265, 266, 268, 269, 271
       contemporary   265, 266, 268
    rebels   260
    riders   247, 260, 262
    rights   247
motorcycling   6, 248, 249, 250, 253, 262, 275,
    277, 278
    contemporary   244, 271
    events   250, 252
    legitimacy of   247, 248
    post-War   255, 261, 272
    sport of   250
motorcyclists   246, 248, 253
Motor Maids   250, 251, 274, 276
mountains   1, 29
movement   7, 28, 96, 98, 99, 100, 127, 170, 208
multitude   100, 102, 113
München   114
murder   189, 190
Murray   114, 118, 120, 121–22, 124, 126, 128, 130,
    131–32, 134, 136, 137, 138, 266, 276

Nachgelassene Schriften   113
Name-of-the-Father   190, 191, 192, 193, 194, 209
nascar   244, 273, 275, 276
nationalism   230, 231, 232, 233, 237
national reputation   261
nations   54, 57, 91, 140, 150, 227, 230, 231, 276
    the wealth of   117, 118
Nazi consumer society   276
Nazism   19, 28
negativity   27, 112, 202
Negri   96, 97, 99, 100, 102, 113, 114
Negro   235, 237, 238
neoliberal capitalism   2
    globalized   143

neoliberalism   67, 90, 91–93, 145, 242, 277
Netherlands   136
networks   143, 243, 253, 254, 272
    consumer   252
neurotics   188, 189, 190, 191, 192, 195, 198, 200,
        207, 208, 209, 211, 212
neurotic structure   189, 190, 214
New Park   61, 64
New York politician Thurlow Weed   40
newspapers   237, 255, 259, 261, 263
Nichols   248, 252, 254, 256, 257, 260, 261, 262,
        263, 277
nineteenth century   40, 80, 150, 152, 215
Nobel Prize   184, 185, 186, 217
non-capitalist   131
non-capitalist group interests   75
normative
    domination   5–6, 220, 238
    systems   232, 236, 239
    whiteness   222, 229, 230, 233, 234, 235,
        236, 237, 238
normativity   105, 106, 227
norms   105, 228, 234, 235
Norton   215, 216–17
novel   180, 183, 184, 186, 187, 196, 198, 201, 204,
        205, 208, 213, 216
Nugent, Ted   265

obedience   19, 59, 62, 195, 245, 249
object   7, 24, 30, 31, 104, 109–11, 128, 135, 144,
        165, 171, 180, 208, 227
    individual   163
    physical   133
Objective Idealism   167
objectivity   166, 173, 220
    critical   236
    social   127
obligations   198
occupying settings   267–68
oceans   41, 43, 208
odyssey   7, 160, 162
Oedipus   190, 214
officials   15, 186
ombre   133
ontologies   3, 96, 114, 170, 171
opinion   18, 19, 20, 22, 24, 25, 40, 45, 47,
        58, 160
order   99, 100, 128, 165, 193, 194, 228, 229, 230,
        251, 253–54, 256, 257, 269, 271

capitalist world   125, 126
organizations   62, 79, 100, 108, 223, 247, 250,
        252, 254, 256, 270
    national   6, 252, 253, 254
    social   84, 88, 97, 98, 99, 100, 112, 160,
        233, 240
originals   257
origins of totalitarianism   27, 59, 240
Orthodox Marxism   14, 173
Osborne   92, 93
Ostrogorski   24, 62, 64
outlaw
    biker culture   258
    biker diegesis   6, 243, 261, 262, 263, 264,
        266, 268, 269, 271–72, 276
    club members   256, 257, 258, 262
    diegesis   259, 262, 266, 267, 269, 271
        emerging   261
    motorcycle culture   255, 258
    motorcycling   244, 255, 257, 259, 260, 262,
        263, 272
outlaws   6, 242, 243, 255, 256, 259, 269
own/control money capital supply   79
owners   53, 70, 83, 84
ownership   24, 80, 94, 262
ownership/control   79

pains   195, 199, 210
Pan, Peter   133
paradigms, existing   98
parallel Marx   32
Parsons   64, 149, 156, 179, 194, 201, 215, 217
participation   84, 85, 116, 232, 247, 250, 267,
        270
particles   168
party   11, 15, 24, 25, 28, 52, 53, 100, 104, 256
party fetishism   24
passage   75, 153, 222, 223
passenger   250, 251
past century   2, 25, 26
patches   246, 257, 264
paternal function   188, 189, 190, 191, 192, 193,
        194, 195, 197, 198, 213
Paternal Function in Peasant Society   194
paternal signifier   193
paths   25, 71, 80, 81, 86, 87, 90, 175, 223
Patnaik   83, 94
patriarch   194
Payette   240

peasant
 character 188, 189, 202
 communities 196, 213
 cultures 201, 210, 211
 experience 183, 211
 fathers 194, 196
 life 181, 185, 186, 188, 203, 216
 novels 184, 193
 producers 181
 realist 183, 184
 realist novels 183, 184
 society 181, 194, 196, 209–10
 subjectivity 5, 189
 subjects 197, 213, 214
 villages 177, 181, 183, 184, 185
 world 184
  pre-capitalist 180
performative tourism 272
perspectives 1, 63, 67, 166, 174, 216, 220, 233, 239
philosophers 1, 26, 96, 104, 105, 109, 170, 171
philosophy 97, 98, 113, 124, 136, 138, 161, 169, 172, 175, 176
 social 3, 4, 116
philosophy of money 217, 241
phrase 21, 22, 31, 35, 36, 39, 48, 79, 124, 160, 165, 219, 220, 239
phrase fetishism 30
Pietism 146, 147, 148, 155
pietist thought 147, 151
Piketty's Capital 155
pilgrimage 183, 185, 200
pirates, capitalists resemble 37
pity 168, 200, 205, 234, 235
plan Marx 124
Poland 183, 185, 186
Polanyi 136, 137, 138
polarity 123
policies 28, 67, 70, 72, 74, 76–77, 79, 80, 87, 88, 151, 265
 social 148, 151, 152, 153
Polish peasants 180
the Political, bifurcation of 79–80, 83, 88
political agent 96, 101
political contexts 238, 239
political economists 7, 111, 116, 135
political economy 1–4, 7, 8, 12, 13, 14, 61, 105, 106, 110, 111, 116, 135, 141, 176
political movement 100

political organization 98, 181, 246, 247
political parties 24, 62
political psychology 1, 4, 12, 13, 14, 20, 58, 59, 157, 179
political reactionaries 181
political sphere 69, 77, 78, 87
political subjects 96, 99, 100, 154
politics 23, 59, 64, 95, 97, 98, 99–102, 108, 112, 113, 150, 151, 174, 276
 cultural 277
Politischen Ökonomie 61
Pollock 58, 62, 64
Pope 159, 176
populations 142, 143, 151, 155, 180, 199, 232
position 78, 79, 95, 96, 101, 103, 104, 144, 145, 192, 193, 194, 197, 198, 200
positivism 160, 162
positivist 161, 163, 165
possessions 182, 202, 203
post-capitalist 41, 134
Post-Marxist philosophers 96, 106, 113
post-Marxists 96–97, 100, 113
post-Marxist thought 104, 108, 109, 112
post-structuralist 95
posters 248, 249
Postone 62, 64, 115, 123, 125, 138
Poulantzas 101, 102, 114, 115
poverty 50, 89, 91, 136, 227, 238
poverty line 50
power 15, 23–26, 30, 46, 47, 70, 71, 83, 100, 127, 142, 181, 194, 195, 227
 capital's 81, 124, 134
 conceptual 139, 144
 constituent 101–2, 114
 new men of 29, 62
 political 86, 151
 stock market 155, 216
 symbolic 194, 196, 197
practices, social 143, 148, 221
praxis 98, 114, 115
prayer 202
preconditions 149, 190
predecessors 166, 247, 248
prejudice 18, 21, 38, 42, 57, 59
presentation 2, 12, 112, 183, 216
President Obama 265–66
prestige 6, 164, 188, 227, 228–29, 231, 236, 237, 239, 267, 270
 normative 226, 227

presupposition   119, 125, 168
price   31, 34, 82, 87, 114, 130, 131, 218
priest   188, 195, 198, 199, 201, 208, 211, 213
primacy   96, 97, 101, 103
principle   24, 68, 70, 74, 84, 87, 95, 96, 101,
        103, 104, 108, 169, 253, 255
    normative   88, 89
a priori categories   170
prison   17, 201, 208, 224
private matter   79
prizes   244, 246, 252
problem   1, 5, 6, 41, 45, 50, 54, 56, 63, 68, 101,
        102, 141, 152, 153
processes   4, 7, 78, 99, 105, 140, 142, 143, 174,
        178, 222, 223, 232, 234, 252
    capital's   92
Produced resources   120, 121
producers   33, 128, 186
    fellow   34, 35
production   35, 36, 37, 40–43, 46, 51, 85, 108,
        113, 116, 117, 119, 120, 121–23, 230
    alienated wage-labor   177
    capitalist   36, 41, 54, 60, 61, 116, 132, 140
    capitalist mode of   117, 118, 123, 124, 125,
        126, 129, 130, 131, 136
    forces of   101, 119
    mode of   82, 119, 120, 121, 122, 123, 131,
        132, 135
    particular modes of   121, 122, 135
    particular social form of   116, 117
    peasant   181
    peasant mode of   181, 183, 184
    relations of   96, 98, 101, 103, 119, 126
    social   108, 126
    social relations of   113, 116
    stimulate   43, 56
production-in-general   121, 122, 135
production paradigm   105, 109
production process   36, 47, 61, 137
productive capacity   89, 90
productive investments   37, 55
productive resources   78, 83
productivity   36, 58
    collective   106, 107
    human   106, 107
products   30, 31–34, 46, 47, 48, 49, 127, 128,
        171, 172, 267, 269, 270, 272, 273
products of labour   127
Produktionzprozess   61

profit   36, 42, 50, 52, 53, 89, 90, 118, 120, 130,
        131, 143, 144, 230, 231–32
profit rate   52, 53, 54–55, 90, 130
profitability   175, 269, 271, 272, 273
programs   72, 73, 222
projective outhating   205
Promised Land   185, 217
promotion   6, 194, 243, 252, 253, 266, 270
property   94, 129, 198, 204, 227
proponents   108–9, 165
proposals   2, 67, 71, 72, 81, 82, 83, 84, 86,
        87, 88
    liberal egalitarian   75, 81, 88
protestant ethic   3, 64, 140, 155, 156, 273
    the   145, 146, 147, 148, 149, 153
Protestantism   146, 147
Prussian state   150
psychosis   188, 189, 191, 192, 193, 195, 206, 212,
        213, 214, 216
psychotic
    breaks   167, 189, 192, 197, 198, 199, 200, 214
    structures   189, 190, 191, 193, 214
    subjects lack   208, 212
psychotics   188, 189, 191, 192, 193, 194, 195–96,
        200, 207, 208, 209, 211–14
psychotics lack   195, 198, 200, 207, 209
public conscience, the   222
purely social   3, 123, 129
Puritan-Calvinist capitalist traditions   146
Puritan-Calvinist trajectory   146

Quakers   147, 148
qualitative sociological side   122
quantities   33, 46, 130
quasi-revolution   38
queens   23
questionnaire   13, 59

race   49, 56, 57, 58, 62, 142, 154, 220, 234, 240,
        241, 246, 247
race thinking   221
racialization   56, 57
rallies   260, 265, 268, 269, 271
Ranciere   95, 97, 100, 101, 103, 112, 115
ranks   203, 226, 228, 236, 246, 252, 256, 257,
        261
rate   42, 43, 55, 89, 91, 120
rationalism   4, 163, 166, 172
Rawls   68, 72, 73, 94

real expulsion   43, 44
real people   33
real subsumption   131, 132–34, 137
Real Subsumption in Capital   137
real wages   81, 82, 91
realism   4, 161, 165, 166, 170, 172, 183, 216
　　naive   2, 67, 131, 134, 274
　　social   4, 163, 165, 166
　　speculative   4, 170
realist   161, 163, 165, 176, 184, 185
realist novels   180, 182, 183, 187, 189, 215
realist philosophy, see futility
reality   30, 31, 36, 97, 98, 99, 100, 106, 107, 165,
　　169, 191, 192, 195, 207
rebel   21, 254, 255
rebel authoritarianism   6, 242, 254, 255, 259,
　　260, 261, 263, 264, 268, 271, 272
　　characteristics of   259, 263, 264
rebel authoritarianism of post-War motor-
　　cycle culture   6, 255
recapitulate   143, 153
Recent Critical Theory   3, 95, 141
recognition   5, 96, 107, 145, 191, 197, 219, 226,
　　227, 228, 231, 234–38
　　social   105, 227, 268, 270, 272
reductionism   3, 4
reexamination   136, 137
reference list   64, 67, 72, 85, 96, 100, 104, 109,
　　126, 135, 170, 175, 268, 274, 275
reflective understanding   135
reforms   2, 52, 67, 71, 74, 75, 80, 81, 82, 83, 86,
　　87, 88
regard labor products   47
regions   76, 85, 89, 90, 91, 140, 150, 183
regulations   70, 84, 88, 155, 252, 273
Reich   7, 177–78, 189, 212, 214, 217
reification   33, 102, 162, 163, 219
rejection   95, 100, 106, 167, 238, 255
relations   31, 34, 97, 98, 100, 101, 103, 105, 107,
　　108, 128, 129, 134, 147, 150
　　capitalist market   106
　　capital/wage   83, 86
　　recognitional   105
　　wage labor   88, 92
relationship   57, 79, 82, 88, 104, 117, 152, 153,
　　192, 197, 200, 226, 252
religion   6, 26, 56, 58, 64, 128, 137, 149, 169,
　　170, 171, 175, 188, 191
rent   36, 37, 52, 121, 126, 130

reorganizes   98, 99
representation   4, 63, 139, 143, 146, 162, 172,
　　183, 184, 215, 254, 259
representatives   54, 83, 86
Representing Capital   140
repression   190, 191, 195–96, 198, 207–8, 211,
　　213, 214, 217, 251
reproducing   126, 214
reproduction   96, 101, 102, 108, 116, 119
　　social   82, 83, 86, 88, 96, 102, 112
　　standpoint of   96, 101
　　systematic   82
research   13, 16, 17, 18, 20, 21, 45, 51, 54, 63,
　　244, 273
resemblance   212, 244, 255
resignation   166, 167, 168
resistance   3, 70, 80, 81, 83, 86, 167, 188, 233
　　collective   238
resources   8, 49, 72, 73, 80, 83, 93, 120, 121, 122,
　　251, 272, 273
respectability   147, 247, 248, 250, 254, 256
responsibility   28, 53, 247
return   3, 4, 97, 100, 101, 102, 105, 112, 113, 126,
　　127, 228, 229, 236, 237
　　rate of   52
revenues   45, 273
revolution   92, 103, 115, 119, 238
　　anticapitalist   6
　　scientific   3, 116, 117, 126
revolutionaries   181
Reymont   182, 183, 184, 185, 186, 187–89, 195,
　　198, 199, 200, 201, 202, 203, 204, 205, 206,
　　207, 208, 2012
Reymont's novel   5, 180, 184, 195, 196, 203,
　　206, 213
Reymont's Peasants   180, 184, 186, 207
Reynolds   242, 254, 260, 262, 277
Ricardian theory of value   122
Riccardo Bellofiore   137
riders   244, 246, 247, 253, 254, 260, 272
　　female   250
rights   73, 84, 85, 246, 248, 254
riots   187, 260, 261, 277
risk   45, 91, 143, 144, 147, 152, 153, 173, 254, 255,
　　258, 267
　　pooled   150, 151, 152, 153
risk pooling   3, 152, 153
risk society   156
rituals   182, 211, 214

rivals   23, 100, 193, 197
Riverside   260
Roach   51–52, 62, 64
robots, cheerful   29, 36
Roediger   57, 62, 64, 219, 221–22, 237, 241
role   80, 102, 122, 126, 159, 196, 243, 244, 246,
        248, 249, 258, 272, 273, 276
    determinant   101
    proper   250
Rubin   115, 122, 138
rubric   29, 134
rulers   22, 23
rules   22, 23, 24, 25, 69, 70, 72, 163, 164, 182,
        203, 246, 247, 255
    club   246
ruling blocs   75
rupture   68, 112, 189
Russian   186, 187
RWA   20–22, 27, 28, 243
    research   20
RWAs, high   21

sabotages   230
sale   30, 47, 123, 185, 186, 261
salvation   28, 146, 147, 236
Sandel   132, 138
sandwich   32
Sartre   160, 176
savage society   217
saviors   27, 28
schema   100, 219, 226, 227
    theoretical   229, 230
scheme   228, 229
scheme of life   228
scholars   7, 23, 26, 29, 151, 219
Schultz   240
SDO   20, 21, 22, 27, 28
    scales   20, 22
Seaton   267, 277
sectors   15, 53, 87, 89, 90–92
secures   231, 232
securitization   3, 141, 143, 144, 145, 146, 149,
        150, 151, 152, 153, 154
securitization and speculation   143, 145, 150,
        152
security   3, 20, 139, 142, 143, 144, 145, 155
seeds   131, 161
self   5, 178, 179, 212, 223, 224, 225, 226, 227–29,
        232, 234, 235, 238, 239, 240

self-exploitation   85, 86
selfhood   224, 225
self-interests   77, 105
self-reliance   224
sellers   82, 127, 128, 129
sensation, peculiar   234, 235
sentence   76, 79, 103, 137, 185, 188, 199, 201,
        202, 204, 206, 208, 210, 256, 258
sentiments, anti-bank   40
serfdom   180
serfs   77, 78, 180, 186
services   5, 14, 24, 71, 73, 78, 87, 119, 121, 180,
        231, 258, 272, 273
sex   49, 183, 217, 257, 258
Sex and repression in savage society   217
sexual advances   258
sexual affairs   196
Sexuality   60, 142
sexuality, conventional   249, 250, 251
shadow forms   133, 134
    capital's   133, 134
    contrast capital's   134
shadows   23, 133, 134, 199, 208, 234
    capital's   134
shame   182, 198, 202, 225
shareholders   53
sheep   210, 257
shift   104, 106, 107, 255
ship of fools, see philosophers
signification   172, 191
signifiers   190, 191, 192, 193, 209
Simmel   164, 167, 176, 177, 194, 215, 217, 220,
        222, 236, 241
Simmel's stranger   220
sins   39, 201, 210, 211
sinthomes   192, 200
skin   221
slaves   77, 78, 194, 197, 221, 237, 238
Smith   2, 28, 29, 43–44, 46, 47–52, 54, 56, 64,
        89–92, 94, 224, 225, 226, 228
Smith, Adam   223, 224, 225, 241
Smith, David Norman   11, 161
Smith, Tony   2, 67, 131, 134, 274
Social Character in Western
    Pre-Modernity   177, 179, 181, 183, 185, 187,
        189, 191, 193, 195, 197, 199, 201, 203, 205
Social Ontology of Capital   1
Social Research   15, 16, 60, 64
socialism   2, 15, 26, 42, 44, 114, 135, 151, 153

socialists 14, 15, 38, 185
sociality 107, 110, 111, 119, 120, 124, 150
sociology 3, 4, 63, 117, 118, 119, 135, 136, 161, 174–76, 215, 216, 217, 240, 241
  critical 1, 4, 8, 93, 155, 239, 240, 241, 274, 276
  modern 116, 117, 118, 136
  speculative 7
solidarity 16, 63, 64, 107, 153, 160, 166, 215, 231, 240
souls 31, 199, 208, 210, 212, 214, 234, 235, 240
South Africa 41
Sozialforschung 60, 62
space 69, 71, 74, 124, 154, 171, 200, 220, 271
  empty 191, 199, 200
  negative 124
species 49, 163
spectacle 15, 243, 267, 272, 273, 275, 276, 277
spectator markets 243, 253, 263, 267, 268, 270
spectators 242, 243, 252, 254, 263, 264, 266, 267, 268, 269, 270, 271, 272, 273, 276
spectatorship 243, 259, 263, 269, 270, 273, 276
spectrum 17, 20, 21
speculation 3, 41, 42, 51, 56, 96, 139, 141, 143–46, 149, 150, 151–54, 233
speech 41, 192, 194, 203, 209, 210, 254
spektive neuerer Marx-Lektüren 113
spending 43, 51, 87
sphere 23, 42, 71, 79, 124, 129, 133, 144, 145
  domestic 124
  economic 78, 79, 87
spirit 7, 14, 19, 64, 141, 147, 149, 153, 160, 161, 165, 169, 201, 202, 241
spiritualism 164
sponsors 243, 246, 263, 270, 272, 273, 276
sponsorship 243, 252, 262, 263, 266, 272, 273, 274
  markets 243, 252, 254, 259, 261, 263–64, 269, 270, 272
sport 250, 251, 252, 277
Spring 184, 201, 202, 205, 208, 209, 212
stakeholder grant 72, 74, 87, 92
stakes 146, 150, 152
standpoint 3, 5, 6, 7, 101, 102, 173, 174, 219, 221, 223, 225, 227, 229, 231
  theories 239

state 27, 28, 45, 52, 53, 54, 69–71, 75, 76, 77, 79–81, 87, 124, 153, 228
  capitalist 77, 79, 80, 86, 88
state apparatus 69, 79
state form 80, 88
state officials 69, 70, 74, 76, 78, 79
state policies 69, 76, 77, 79, 80
  content of 70, 76, 80, 87
  welfare 152, 153
statement 95, 100
status 46, 47, 48, 51, 143, 145, 169, 173, 219, 226, 237, 238, 267, 270, 271
  normative 236
status systems 232, 233, 238–39
status wages 228, 229–30, 232, 233, 238
statuses 31, 49
Steinert 140, 146, 147, 149, 156
Stone 267, 277
stranger 5, 6, 219, 220, 236, 239, 241
structuralism, post 3
structures 77, 78, 174, 178, 207, 219, 220, 222, 223, 246, 247, 254, 255, 272, 273
  capital shapes class 124
  psychic 5, 189, 190, 211
Sturgis 265, 269, 276, 277
Sturgis Motorcycle Rally 263, 268, 269
subjectivity 5, 141, 143, 152, 154, 219, 229, 276
subjects 19, 30, 141, 142, 143, 145, 146, 147, 159, 167, 168, 169, 189, 190–92, 231
  individual 141, 145
  nationalist 231, 237
  neurotic 190, 191, 206, 207, 214
  psychotic 192, 207
submission 178, 181, 245, 246, 248, 249, 251, 272
subsistence 78, 79, 82
substance 4, 82, 101, 129, 133, 159, 163, 171
subsumption 123, 131, 132
  formal 132, 133
  ideal 131, 132, 133
subsumption concepts 131, 132
Suhrkamp 113, 114, 115
suicide 4, 159, 160, 164, 166, 168, 169, 170, 175, 215
Summer 184, 198, 200, 201, 203, 205, 211, 213
surface 28, 33, 34, 36, 130, 209, 235
surplus 7, 36, 74, 77, 78, 79, 83, 88, 172
  symbolic 229, 232, 237
surplus labor 130, 131

surplus production   79, 83
surplus products   36, 82
surplus regions   91
surplus value   3, 36, 37, 62, 71, 78, 79, 83, 86, 87, 90, 117, 139, 165, 175
surplus-value   118, 120, 123, 126, 130, 131
surplus value
   accumulation of   6, 116
   production of   86, 177
surveillance   222
suspicion   112, 188, 202, 204, 257
Swart   229, 244, 246, 248, 250, 252, 254, 256, 258, 260, 262, 264, 266, 268, 276
symbol   6, 72, 133, 191, 248
symbolic castration   190, 191, 200, 211, 212, 214
symbolic exchange   219, 222, 228, 229, 233, 238
   unequal   229
symbolic exploitation   229, 230, 232, 237, 238, 240, 274
symbolic order   190, 191, 194, 207, 209, 211, 214
sympathy   223, 224–27, 241
Sympathy in Smith and Cooley   223
symptoms   4, 5, 41, 166, 192, 207, 214, 215, 217
system   6, 8, 13, 28–30, 42, 47, 99, 112, 125, 127, 172, 228–29, 233, 256, 258
   organic   125

taxes   17, 45, 90, 131, 273
Tea Party   265, 277
technologies   73, 77, 84, 85, 86
tension   53, 70, 147, 148, 149, 150, 152, 167, 255
territory   142, 155, 187
terror   38, 59, 169, 199, 200, 208
test subjects   19
theory   7, 8, 98–99, 105, 107–8, 113, 117, 122, 169, 215, 219, 223, 226, 228, 241
   political   60, 103
   realist   94
   sociological   63, 224
theory of society   60, 96, 103
third thing   129
third way   4
Thomas   136, 187, 215, 217
Thompson   239, 242, 254, 255, 256, 257, 258, 259, 260, 261, 268, 278
threats   11, 194, 206, 251, 254, 259, 260
tides   159, 236, 237
topic   35, 87, 117, 121, 123
top managers   53

Toscano   99, 103, 112
totalitarianism   12, 27, 28, 59, 240
totality   97, 104, 109, 111, 112, 118, 125, 140, 155, 174, 176
   social   96, 98, 107, 108, 112, 174
totems   162, 182, 189, 216
tours   246, 247, 252
town   197, 259, 260, 264, 266
trade   23, 34, 43, 47, 49, 91, 135, 149, 277
Traditional Marxism   15, 123
traditions   23, 25, 28, 109, 147
   parallel capitalist   146
traits   188, 242
transformation   67, 81, 88, 130, 137, 238, 259
transportation   245, 247, 251
treatment   85, 128, 149, 212, 214
Trinity Formula   121, 130, 137
trophies   6, 229, 270, 271, 272
trophy markets   243, 246, 266, 270, 271, 272, 273
truth   2, 25, 30, 42, 54, 75, 97, 113, 123, 160, 169, 207
Tsiganes   205
twentieth century, early   219, 239, 247, 250, 251

UK   63, 155
unemployment   41, 89, 90
uniforms   246, 249, 257
United States   14, 16, 24, 38, 40, 44, 51, 52, 55, 146, 152, 252, 260, 263, 266
unity   36, 61, 106, 111–12, 169
use-values   117, 119, 121, 123, 124, 126, 127, 129, 130, 132
   produced   181
utility   31, 134
utopias   49

valorization   85
value   6–8, 31, 32, 33, 34, 35, 46, 47, 61, 106, 118, 122–24, 130, 131, 144
   bearers of   32, 46, 47
   individual   131
   magnitude of   127, 130
   middle class   245
   political   7
   products have   33
   qualitative sociological side of Marx's theory of   122
   substance of   130
   traditional   245, 246

value character 127
value-form 94, 108, 120, 123, 130, 131, 132, 136
value status 47
value system 228
    shared 107
value forms 3, 95, 118, 122, 123, 126, 132, 134
vanguard 232, 233
vanity 227
variables 174, 262
variant 67, 68, 69, 142, 179
varieties 94, 143, 146, 150, 155, 156, 163
Veblen, Thorstein 5, 219–20, 223, 224, 226,
    227, 228, 229, 230–34, 237–39, 240–41,
    270, 278
Veblenian analysis of normative
    domination 6, 220
Veblen's nationalist self 235
vendor stalls 271, 273
vendors 266, 269, 271
vengeance 201, 202
village 179, 181, 186, 187, 195, 198, 203, 204,
    205, 208, 209, 216
villagers 181, 187, 188, 198, 202, 205, 207, 208,
    209
violence 111, 138, 189, 258, 269
    symbolic 220, 226, 238, 239
Virgin 201, 214
Vitek 198, 208
vocation 64, 147, 148, 154
voices 19, 164, 199, 200, 206, 207, 208, 213
volume 1, 30, 35, 93, 137, 140, 142, 155, 161, 184,
    185, 186, 217, 239
Vorlesungen 113
votes 11, 44, 237

Waarenwelt 13, 30, 41, 47
wage contracts 72, 73
wage-form 130
wage-labor 122, 125, 181
wage laborers 78, 83, 85, 222
wage-labour 125, 126
wages 36, 45, 51, 52, 57, 58, 73, 82, 83, 89, 90,
    118, 130, 221, 222
    symbolic 222, 230, 231, 237
war 17, 59, 113, 230, 232, 238, 240, 255, 277
Watson 226, 227, 229, 241, 276
wealth 29, 100, 107, 117, 118, 120, 121, 123, 131,
    134, 135, 147, 227, 228, 238
    commodity form of 127, 129
    production of 120, 121, 135
    social form of 117, 120, 121, 122, 127
Weber
    calls 22, 27
    calls capitalism 141
Weber's
    categories 22, 140
    claims 146
    essay 140, 148
    interest 147, 148
    list of preconditions 149
    text 140, 147, 149
    theses 146
    treatment 148, 149
    writings 141, 147
Weber, Max 3, 14, 22, 23–24, 26–28, 32, 48,
    63–64, 116, 117, 140, 141, 146–56, 161,
    182–83, 217, 224
Welch, Jack 53
Western capitalism 50
Western Pre-Modernity 177, 179, 181, 183,
    185, 187, 189, 191, 193, 195, 197, 199, 201,
    203, 205
whiteness 57, 58, 62, 221, 222, 228, 234, 235,
    237, 238, 241
    wage in 221
    wages of 5, 57, 62, 219, 220, 239, 241
Wladyslaw Reymont 5, 177, 184
Wobblies 233, 238
wolves 210, 257
women 57, 74, 91, 203, 205, 240, 249, 250,
    258
words 23, 26, 27, 30, 32, 34, 35, 36, 53, 78, 163,
    194, 207, 209, 213
workers 13, 14, 15, 16, 35–38, 45, 55, 73, 74, 83,
    84, 85, 231, 232, 237–38
    southern 236, 238
    white 236, 237, 238
workforce 73, 85, 86
Workingman's Party 13, 14
workplace 73, 84, 85, 86
world 11, 12, 30, 31, 41, 42, 46, 49, 133, 154, 173,
    195, 202, 234, 235
    capitalist 95
    economy 51, 89, 90, 92
    history 124
    market 83, 89, 124, 125
    market credit money 91
World War 14, 15, 17, 84, 89, 251

Worrell   1–2, 4, 6, 8, 64, 159, 160, 161–62, 164,
          166, 168, 170, 172, 174, 176

Yagna   187, 195, 200, 204, 205, 206, 207, 208,
        212, 213
Yagustynka   187, 196, 203, 204
Yates   251, 254, 259, 260, 261, 262, 263,
        268, 278

York   59, 62, 93, 94, 113, 175, 216–17, 277

Zeitschrift   62, 114
Zimmerman   274
Zinzendorf   148, 150
Zizek   8, 49, 64, 96, 102, 103, 113, 115, 140, 142,
       156, 165, 166
Zombie capitalism   93